CULTURE UNDER CROSS-EXAMINATION

The international community created The Special Court for Sierra Leone to prosecute those who bore the greatest responsibility for crimes committed during the country's devastating civil war. Tim Kelsall examines some of the challanges posed by the fact that the Court operated in a largely unfamiliar culture, in which the way local people thought about rights, agency and truth-telling sometimes differed radically from the way international lawyers think about these things. By applying an anthropolitical perspective to the trials, he unveils a variety of ethical, epistemological, jurisprudential and procedural problems, arguing that although touted as a promising hybrid, the Court failed in crucial ways to adapt to the local culture concerned. Culture matters, and international justice requires a more dialogical, multicultural approach.

TIM KELSALL works as an Associate of the Africa, Politics and Power Programme and as a Visiting Fellow at the Berkeley War Crimes Studies Center based in Phnom Penh. In the past he has taught Politics at the universities of Oxford and Newcastle and has been an editor of the journal *African Affairs*.

CAMBRIDGE STUDIES IN LAW AND SOCIETY

Cambridge Studies in Law and Society aims to publish the best scholarly work on legal discourse and practice in its social and institutional contexts, combining theoretical insights and empirical research.

The fields that it covers are: studies of law in action; the sociology of law; the anthropology of law; cultural studies of law, including the role of legal discourses in social formations; law and economics; law and politics; and studies of governance. The books consider all forms of legal discourse across societies, rather than being limited to lawyers' discourses alone.

The series editors come from a range of disciplines: academic law; socio-legal studies; sociology; and anthropology. All have been actively involved in teaching and writing about law in context.

Books in the Series

Diseases of the Will
Mariana Valverde

The Politics of Truth and Reconciliation in South Africa: Legitimizing the Post-Apartheid State
Richard A. Wilson

Modernism and the Grounds of Law
Peter Fitzpatrick

Unemployment and Government: Genealogies of the Social
William Walters

Autonomy and Ethnicity: Negotiating Competing Claims in Multi-Ethnic States
Yash Ghai

Constituting Democracy: Law, Globalism and South Africa's Political Reconstruction
Heinz Klug

The Ritual of Rights in Japan: Law, Society, and Health Policy
Eric A. Feldman

The Invention of the Passport: Surveillance, Citizenship and the State
John Torpey

Governing Morals: A Social History of Moral Regulation
Alan Hunt

The Colonies of Law: Colonialism, Zionism and Law in Early Mandate Palestine
Ronen Shamir

Law and Nature
David Delaney

Social Citizenship and Workfare in the United States and Western Europe: The Paradox of Inclusion
Joel F. Handler

Law, Anthropology and the Constitution of the Social: Making Persons and Things
Edited by Alain Pottage and Martha Mundy

Judicial Review and Bureaucratic Impact: International and Interdisciplinary Perspectives
Edited by Marc Hertogh and Simon Halliday

Immigrants at the Margins: Law, Race, and Exclusion in Southern Europe
Kitty Calavita

Lawyers and Regulation: The Politics of the Administrative Process
Patrick Schmidt

Law and Globalization from Below: Toward a Cosmopolitan Legality
Edited by Boaventura de Sousa Santos and Cesar A. Rodriguez-Garavito

Public Accountability: Designs, Dilemmas and Experiences
Edited by Michael W. Dowdle

Law, Violence and Sovereignty among West Bank Palestinians
Tobias Kelly

Legal Reform and Administrative Detention Powers in China
Sarah Biddulph

The Practice of Human Rights: Tracking Law Between the Global and the Local
Edited by Mark Goodale and Sally Engle Merry

Judges Beyond Politics in Democracy and Dictatorship: Lessons from Chile
Lisa Hilbink

Paths to International Justice: Social and Legal Perspectives
Edited by Marie-Bénédicte Dembour and Tobias Kelly

Law and Society in Vietnam: The Transition from Socialism in Comparative Perspective
Mark Sidel

Constitutionalizing Economic Globalization: Investment Rules and Democracy's Promise
David Schneiderman

The World Trade Organization Knowledge Agreements, 2nd edition
Christopher Arup

Justice and Reconciliation in Post-Apartheid South Africa
Edited by François du Bois, Antje du Bois-Pedain

Militarization and Violence against Women in Conflict Zones in the Middle East: A Palestinian Case-Study
Nadera Shalhoub-Kevorkian

Child Pornography and Sexual Grooming: Legal and Societal Responses
Suzanne Ost

Darfur and the Crime of Genocide
John Hagan and Wenona Rymond-Richmond

Planted Flags: Trees, Land, and Law in Israel/Palestine
Irus Braverman

Fictions of Justice: The International Criminal Court and the Challenge of Legal Pluralism in Sub-Saharan Africa
Kamari Maxine Clarke

Conducting Law and Society Research: Reflections on Methods and Practices
Simon Halliday and Patrick Schmidt

The Practice of Human Rights: Tracking Law Between the Global and the Local
Edited by Mark Goodale and Sally Engle Merry

CULTURE UNDER CROSS-EXAMINATION

International Justice and the Special Court for Sierra Leone

Tim Kelsall

CAMBRIDGE
UNIVERSITY PRESS

CAMBRIDGE UNIVERSITY PRESS
Cambridge, New York, Melbourne, Madrid, Cape Town, Singapore,
São Paulo, Delhi, Dubai, Tokyo

Cambridge University Press
The Edinburgh Building, Cambridge CB2 8RU, UK

Published in the United States of America by Cambridge University Press, New York

www.cambridge.org
Information on this title: www.cambridge.org/9780521767781

First published 2009

Printed in the United Kingdom at the University Press, Cambridge

A catalogue record for this publication is available from the British Library

Library of Congress Cataloguing in Publication data
Kelsall, Tim, 1970–
Culture under cross-examination : international justice and the special court for Sierra Leone / Tim Kelsall.
p. cm. – (Cambridge studies in law and society)
ISBN 978-0-521-76778-1
1. Special Court for Sierra Leone. 2. International criminal courts–Netherlands. 3. International criminal courts–Sierra Leone. 4. War crime trials–Social aspects–Sierra Leone. 5. War crime trials–Social aspects–Netherlands. I. Title. II. Series.
KZ1208.S53A154 2009
345.664′01–dc22 2009025731

ISBN 978-0-521-76778-1 hardback

In memory of Ed Sawyer

CONTENTS

ILLUSTRATIONS

PREFACE

Every weekend in post-war Freetown, members of the international community head out to the fine sandy beaches on the former colony's peninsula at Lakkah, Tokeh and River Number Two. On the way they often stop off to eat fish and lobster at Franco's, an excellent Italian restaurant by the sea. Dotted along the rutted, pot-holed road to these destinations are muscle-bound men, many of them ex-combatants, breaking boulders into piles of gravel with pick-axes, newly built houses clinging to denuded hillsides, decomposing car-wrecks, and small children demanding money at roadblocks made from pieces of string. One often also sees Mercedes Benz vehicles, some antique, some the latest European model, weaving slowly down the road, painstakingly trying to not scrape the red dirt with their low-slung chassis. These prestigious cars are rapidly overtaken, meanwhile, by shiny four-wheel-drive Land Cruisers and Pajeros, and also by podapodas – local minibuses crammed with passengers, that, in spite of their decrepit appearance, bounce past with insouciant speed. I will argue in this book that the Special Court for Sierra Leone was a bit like one of these Mercedes: in many respects a fine vehicle, but not well adapted to the local terrain. Its laws, legal doctrines and truth-finding procedures all lacked traction with local cultural realities, leading to difficult trials and, in some cases, serious questions over the quality of the convictions of the accused. I will argue that the experience of the Special Court holds important lessons for the way international courts should proceed when trying complex crimes in unfamiliar cultures, and that the international justice community needs genuinely hybrid solutions, somewhere between the all-terrain vehicle and the local minibus, if it is to achieve its intended aims.

Many people have assisted in my journey to complete this book. Newcastle University's Arts and Humanities Research Fund provided funding for a pilot project in Sierra Leone in 2003. This was followed by a Larger Grant from the British Academy in 2005. Barbara Oomen, Phil Powrie and Tony Zito all helped in the process of applying for a

Research Leave Grant from the Arts and Humanities Research Council of the United Kingdom, which allowed me to write a draft of the manuscript in 2007 – I am grateful to them all, and also to my former colleagues in Politics at Newcastle, most especially Derek Bell and Andy Gillespie, for facilitating research leave. I am also indebted to a group of West Africa experts who were exceptionally generous in sharing their contacts, insights and advice with me when I first embarked on this project. Deserving of special mention are Thierry Cruvellier, Ron Fennel, Stephen Ellis, Paul Richards and Richard Fanthorpe. Other individuals provided invaluable help and advice on the ground, including Comfort Ero, Allison Cooper, Alice Jay, Vanessa Wruble, David Hecht, Sara Kendall, Vivek Maru, Umarr Kargbo, Paul Allen, Ed Sawyer, Alfred Carew, Taziff Koroma, Wayne Jordash, Andrew Bernard, Saleem Vahidy, Peter Andersen, Tejanie Bah, Esther Kortu, Michael Lansana, Rupert Skilbeck, Rebekka Ehret, Tom Perriello, Eric Witte, Harpinder Athwal, Nancy Sesay, Simeon Koroma and Ahmadu Mannah. Rosalind Shaw gave both help and advice in the field, and included me in a stimulating workshop in Bellagio in 2006; similarly, Martha Carey was a fieldwork confidante and facilitator for an excellent conference on humanitarian intervention in Atlanta in 2007. Returning from the field, Krijn Peters, Bill Murphy, Lans Gberie, Tunde Zack-Williams and Danny Hoffman were kind enough to comment on draft chapters; Harvey Weinstein commented on a book proposal, and on two occasions I stayed with Mariane Ferme in Berkeley, where a little of her deep knowledge of the Mende rubbed off on me, I hope. I thank all these people for their help with this work, and apologise in advance for its limitations, which are entirely my own. Much of the book was written while a visiting scholar at the East West Center in Honolulu. I am grateful to Phil Estermann, Nancy Lewis, and Carolyn Eguchi for making me welcome there, and in particular to David Cohen, who also introduced me to surfing, which proved welcome relief from a daily diet of war crimes transcripts; Peter Maguire, another Hawai'i-based war-crimes expert, was also an inspiration. At Cambridge University Press I am grateful to Finola O'Sullivan and Martin Chanock for supporting this project, and to three anonymous referees, one of whom I later discovered to be Kieran McEvoy, for helpful, critical advice. Philip Stickler of Cambridge University made me a map and Danny Hoffman generously supplied a cover photo.

Most of all I thank Michelle Staggs, whom I was lucky enough to meet in Freetown in June 2005, and even more fortunate to marry in Hawai'i in January 2007. Not only has she been the most loving, caring and fun companion imaginable during the writing of this book, rarely protesting about my self-absorption and bad moods, but she has also commented on my drafts, tried to keep me the right side of the law and immeasurably improved my thoughts.

CHAPTER 1

WHITE MAN'S JUSTICE? SIERRA LEONE AND THE EXPANDING PROJECT OF INTERNATIONAL LAW

The Special Court for Sierra Leone stands on a sprawling site in central Freetown, shielded from the rest of the country by imposing grey walls. An outer wall, ranging between five and eight feet in height, displays signs warning people that to park or even stand in the court's vicinity is forbidden; an inner one, about fifteen feet tall, is crowned by coils of razor wire. A policeman brandishing an AK-47, accompanied by other security personnel, guards the entrance from a sentry post; above it, a sand-bagged gun turret takes aim at the main road. Visitors who pass through the court's steel gate are obliged to acquire a security pass from a razor-wired concrete reception area in the shape of a pill box, then walk through a car park area and into the court's inner compound through two sliding, steel doors; vehicles, meanwhile, are subjected to bomb checks. Inside, to the left, stand the prefabricated huts of the Office of the Prosecutor, reminiscent of a military barracks or prisoner of war camp, ringed by razor wire and a six-feet high fence carrying signs that read 'ID Cards Must be Shown at All Times', 'Restricted Access', 'Authorised Personnel Only', 'Visitors Must Be Escorted'. At various junctures gun-toting Nigerian soldiers stand guard, wearing dark sunglasses, blue helmets and military fatigues; sometimes they conduct drills and simulate combat situations. Past the Office of the Prosecutor and up a path stands the gleaming structure of the courthouse itself, architecturally designed, apparently, to evoke an impression of the scales of justice. It is protected not only by the Nigerian troops, but by blue-uniformed security personnel, the public gaining entrance through a metal detector. Down the hill to the left are the Defence offices and opposite them another set of steel doors, walls, and razor wire, which guard the entrance to the detention centre where defendants indicted for war crimes are held. Between the prison and the courthouse resides a tank, a UN logo emblazoned on its side.[1]

Inside this enclave the Special Court is implementing a global project to bring accountability under the rule of law to a region formerly destabilised by conflict and war. In this book I discuss some of the challenges posed to that project by the fact that the Court is surrounded by an unfamiliar social and legal culture, in which the way people think about human rights, human agency and appropriate social conduct often differs radically from the way international lawyers think about these things. I do so by focusing on the trial of the alleged leaders of the Kamajors, a popular militia that fought on the side of the democratic government in the country's eleven-year civil war. The Kamajors, several thousand strong, were widely believed to be able to make themselves immune to bullets through magic, a technique which allowed them to defend their communities from rebel attack, won them widespread applause, and even helped them to restore civilian rule.[2] The Kamajor Society, however, was far from being universally benign. Some of its members reputedly looted and burned Sierra Leonean towns, indulged in acts of cannibalism, and committed violent acts of a grotesque and terrifying nature, such as decapitating victims and dancing around with their heads on poles.

The Civil Defence Forces (CDF) trial, as it was called, is a case with tremendous significance for the expanding global project of international criminal law, as well as for other post-conflict justice modalities. For reasons explained below, we are unlikely in the near future to witness international prosecutions in developed Western nations: international trials will focus mainly on countries that are part of the 'Third World', a trend already indicated by the first arrest warrants of the International

[1] Adapted from fieldnote, September 2004. By 2006 Mongolians had replaced the Nigerians. Vivek Maru, an astute observer of justice in Sierra Leone, once remarked to me that looking down on the Court from the Freetown hills, its saucer shaped roof glowing in the darkness, one could be forgiven for thinking that an alien spacecraft had landed in Sierra Leone. Prosecutor David Crane appears to have picked up on this imagery in a speech he gave in 2007 entitled, 'The spaceship has landed' (Crane 2007).

[2] Precise figures for Kamajor and CDF membership are hard to come by. After the war some 37,216 CDF were officially demobilised, the majority among whom would have been Kamajors (Humphreys and Weinstein 2004, 13). However, the real figures are likely to be much larger, since in some areas fewer than one in five CDF fighters possessed a modern weapon that would qualify them for demobilisation.

Criminal Court, all of which target African individuals.[3] As in the CDF case, witnesses and defendants in these trials will come from societies with very different cultures or cultural mixes to those that predominate in the West, with varying ideas about morality, responsibility, evidence and truth. International justice, because of this, needs to learn the lessons of working with unfamiliar cultures fast.

Although the Special Court is regarded in some circles as 'a promising hybrid' (Dougherty 2004; Stromseth, Wippman and Brooks 2006), suggesting that it successfully blends elements of international and indigenous law and expertise,[4] I will argue in this book that it failed in crucial ways to adjust to the local culture in which it worked. In its prosecution of the crime of enlisting child soldiers, for example, it levelled an inappropriate and ethnocentric charge at the CDF defendants. In its handling of the phenomenon of bullet-proofing, it proved deaf to an enormously important system of local magical belief. In its ruling on superior responsibility, it drew on an unrealistic Western norm. And in its assessment of evidence, it failed to find convincing means for assessing the credibility of witnesses, some of whom deployed, I argue, culturally grounded strategies of concealment in court. These failures had profound implications: they contributed to a laborious trial-process that dragged on for more than two years – one of the defendants dying before a verdict could be returned – and they raised serious questions about the quality of the convictions of the two surviving accused. Meanwhile, at a societal level, these failures threatened the Court's legacy in Sierra Leone.

In light of these depressing results, critics of the international justice project will doubtless find in my study more evidence that the aspiration to globalise law's rule is not only malign but misconceived. Supporters of the project will hopefully find stimuli to rethinking and reform.

AN EXPANDING PROJECT

Today, international criminal justice (ICJ) casts a wider net and has a longer reach than at any time in previous history. Inaugurated at Nuremburg and Tokyo with the International Military Tribunals to try the top leaders of the defeated Axis powers, ICJ was re-animated in the 1990s with the creation of the International Criminal Tribunal for the

[3] The countries concerned are Uganda, Democratic Republic of Congo, Central African Republic and Sudan.

[4] For a less sanguine view, see Sriram (2006).

Figure 1. The Court compound and environs.

former Yugoslavia (ICTY) (to try alleged perpetrators of war crimes and violations of international humanitarian law that occurred during the internecine conflict that convulsed the Balkans in the early 1990s) and the International Criminal Tribunal for Rwanda (ICTR) (to prosecute the masterminds of genocide that decimated the population of that tiny central African republic in April and May of 1994), following a forty-five year, Cold War freeze (Maguire 2000; Minear 1972; Minow 1998; Sands 2003).

These two landmark courts, known as the *ad hoc* tribunals, shaped the emergence of a new breed of *hybrid* tribunal in the next decade. Novel experiments in international and national law, situated in the countries where conflict occurred, hybrid tribunals have been opened in Bosnia (mopping up some of the lower level leaders not tried at the ICTY); Kosovo (targeting alleged perpetrators of violations that occurred during the conflict in Serbia-governed Kosovo in 1999); Timor Leste (where pro-Indonesia militias terrorised the population in the wake of the UN-sponsored referendum on independence in 1999); Sierra Leone (where a ghastly civil war raged from 1991 to 2002); and now Cambodia (targeting surviving leaders of Pol Pot's murderous Khmer Rouge regime (1975–1979)). The most recent addition is a hybrid tribunal in The Hague to try those suspected of the car bomb killing of Lebanese Prime Minister Rafik Hariri in February 2005.

Contemporaneously, in 1998, over a hundred states signed the Rome Statute of the International Criminal Court, a new, permanent tribunal located in The Hague, with the power to try suspected war criminals and human rights violators in cases where national states are unable or unwilling to pursue prosecutions themselves. It has subsequently issued arrest warrants for individuals in Northern Uganda (where for years the Lord's Resistance Army has been forcing women and girls into sexual slavery, abducting children, and mutilating and murdering the civilian population), the Central African Republic (where sexual violence was widely used as a weapon when the country slid into civil war in the wake of its failed democratic transition), the Sudan (where as many as 400,000 people may have died in conflict driven by government-backed *janjaweed* militias) and the Democratic Republic of Congo (where domestic and foreign armies and ethnic militia devastated the civilian population in the course of Africa's 'first world war'). Its first indictee, Congolese militia leader Thomas Lubanga, was transferred to The Hague in March 2006.

This ICJ expansion is nested in broader processes of 'transitional justice' and projects to build the rule of law. Transitional justice is a term used to describe the diverse mechanisms by which a society recently emerged from repressive rule or violent conflict attempts to hold wrongdoers accountable for their actions (Elster 2004; Roht-Arriaza 2006; Teitel 2000, 2003; ICTJ 2007). These mechanisms may include prosecutions, purges, publicly shaming offenders, opening police files, truth commissions, memorials and reparations, to name but a few (Minow 1998, 23; ICTJ 2007). In recent years transitional justice initiatives have multiplied with transitions to democracy in former dictatorships in Latin America, East and Central Europe and Africa, and by a spate of so-called 'new wars' in the more fragile of these transitional states (Kaldor 2006). Meanwhile, rule of law projects attempt to institutionalise accountability under the law for present and future events. According to Jessica Matthews, 'the rule of law is often held out these days as the solution to almost every international policy problem, from consolidating shaky democratic transitions, establishing sustainable economic development, and stabilizing post-conflict societies, to fostering new global norms' (foreword to Carothers 2006, vii).

These developments are supported by a billion-dollar international industry (Oomen 2005, 890) of lawyers, scholars, journalists, transitional justice experts and consultants, departments or sections in First World governments, and the lobbying, intervention and participation of a host of influential legal and human rights NGOs, including Human Rights Watch, Amnesty International, the Open Society Justice Initiative, Lawyers without Borders, No Peace Without Justice, The International Center for Transitional Justice, and the Coalition for an International Criminal Court (which is itself a network of over 2,000 NGOs); they are the legal arm of what Alex de Waal has called the 'humanitarian international' (De Waal 1997), a global social movement that drives UN peace-keeping interventions and post-conflict accountability projects in crisis states around the world. Today, the conventional UN response to political transitions and post-conflict situations is to dispatch teams of legal technocrats who, with the support of the UN Office of the High Commissioner for Human Rights and the Office for Legal Affairs, support and assist local actors to implement transitional justice mechanisms, believing that accountability for past atrocities is required for rehabilitation to begin (Lutz 2006, 332).

The expansion of international justice has often been written about in triumphalist tones. In the field of criminal prosecutions, much of the early commentary has been by avid supporters, 'the generation of the founders', who are often practitioners themselves (Drumbl 2005, 546–7). Human rights lawyer Geoffrey Robertson, for example, has gone so far as to claim a 'millennial shift, from appeasement to justice, as the dominant factor in world affairs' (Robertson 2002, xiii), stating confidently that 'International criminal justice is here to stay' (Robertson 2007, 1). Early apparent successes have led some to make exuberant claims, presenting ICJ as a panacea for post-conflict societies. Take for instance Antonio Cassese, first President of the ICTY, who has written that:

> Trials establish individual responsibility over collective assignation of guilt … justice dissipates the call for revenge, because when the Court metes out to the perpetrator his just deserts, then the victims' calls for retribution are met … victims are prepared to be reconciled with their erstwhile tormentors, because they know that the latter have now paid for their crimes; a fully reliable record is established of the atrocities so that future generations can remember and be made fully cognizant of what happened.
>
> (Cited in Stover and Weinstein 2004b, 3–4.)

Others argue that prosecutions provide an end to impunity: 'drawing a clear line for all to see' (Stromseth, Wippman and Brooks 2006, 251), a foundation for peace, and a deterrent to future violations (Rudolph 2001).

All these claims have been contested, of course. The impunity claim has been criticised on the grounds that international prosecutions tend only to target ordinary perpetrators or weak leaders in weak states (Minear 1972; Moghalu 2005, 125–52; Rudolph 2001; Allen 2006, 22; Maguire 2000; Sriram and Ross 2007). The deterrent effect of international trials has been thrown into doubt by the fact that some leaders have continued to order atrocities even after being indicted – for example in Bosnia – while in Congo, East Timor, Liberia and Sudan, the presence or threat of tribunals appears to have done little to abate war crimes (Rudolph 2001; Hazan 2006; Snyder and Vinjamuri 2003/4). The idea that retributive justice heals the wounds of victims and society has been dismissed on grounds that testifying may represent an 'injudicious catharsis' for victims (Stover and Weinstein 2004, 13), while for many survivors, tribunal justice fails to palliate their sense of injustice (Stover and Weinstein 2004a, 333). There is some evidence that criminal trials drive communities further apart 'by causing further suspicion and fear' (Stover and Weinstein 2004a, 323). When it comes to establishing a reliable record, it is clear that while some trials, for example Nuremburg, can produce a strong documentary record, courts more often tell implausible or impoverished histories (Minear 1972; Osiel 1997, 61; Minow 1998, 47). Meanwhile, the lessons of these histories are often lost on the populations at which they are aimed (Maguire 2000, 131; Stover 2004, 116; Fletcher and Weinstein 2004, 33; Stover and Weinstein 2004a, 324, 334; Osiel 1997, 160). The quality of justice dispensed by international trials has also come under fire, with problems of lawlessness, retroactivity, prosecutorial bias, over-protection of witnesses, undue delay, unqualified judges, corruption of court officials and frequent changes to procedures and rules being just some of the problems identified (Minow 1998, 30; Elster 2004, 84; Minear 1972, 169; Forges and Longman 2004; Weinstein *et al.* 2006; Robertson 2007; Laughland 2007). And all this has come at vast expense, 'a scandalous waste of money' in the view of some commentators (Allen 2006, 12), with the *ad hoc* tribunals alone consuming around 15 per cent of the UN's entire budget (UNSC 2004), and convictions at the ICTR costing around $25 million a piece (Drumbl 2005).

INTERNATIONAL JUSTICE AND THE POLITICS OF CULTURE

There is also disquiet about the global role of international criminal justice, with some commentators using terms like 'new' or 'liberal' imperialism (Stromseth, Wippman, and Brooks 2006; Weinstein and van de Merwe 2007), 'liberal peace' (Duffield 2001), 'international judicial intervention' (Laughland 2007), 'international law fundamentalism' (Branch 2004) and 'lawfare' (Comaroff and Comaroff 2006). Behind this terminology is the idea that leaders in the West are seeking to pacify and civilise the Third World using peacekeeping missions, high-level prosecutions, and then programmes to strengthen the rule of law. Inevitably, this has led to concerns about culture. Is the new judicial intervention also a form of cultural imperialism? Can international criminal trials function satisfactorily in unfamiliar cultures? What are the prospects for the rule of law earning legitimacy if international interventions are imposed on local cultural beliefs and practices?[5] Legal scholar Mark Drumbl, for one, has argued that the transplantation of domestic criminal law into the international context is based on the pernicious fiction

[5] '[T]he law may be categorized as "imposed" in the sense that it does not reflect the values and norms of the majority of the population or of that segment which will be subject to it' (Burman and Harrell-Bond 1979, xiii).

that Western justice modalities are value-neutral and universal, when '[t]hey are in fact deeply culturally contingent' (Drumbl 2005, 551). Even the UN Secretary General noted recently that 'the international community has, at times, imposed external transitional justice solutions' (UNSC 2004, 7) and official documents increasingly include nods to respecting indigenous justice beliefs, though the practical implications are sketchy at best.[6]

Cultural anxieties such as these stem from the fact that international criminal law is Western in origin: its ethical tenets flow from a Judaeo-Christian tradition (Kahn 1999, 46), while its standards of evidence are rooted in a scientific worldview and enlightenment philosophy. The 'rationalist' tradition of evidence in Anglo-American courts, for example, rests on a foundationalist epistemology, a correspondence theory of truth, and a scientific rationality. That is to say, courts function according to the principle that there exists an objective reality independent of what anyone thinks about the world, that knowledge corresponding to this value-free reality has the status of truth, and that the truth can be discovered by drawing inferences inductively from relevant evidence. In this tradition, judicial decision-making consists essentially in applying substantive law to the objective 'facts', as scientifically ascertained (Nicolson 1994, 727).

To be precise, Michael S. Moore has argued that the Western conception of criminal law requires a particular structure of moral and metaphysical belief. Morally, criminal answerability applies to an individual when (1) it can be shown that s/he acted, (2) that s/he did so intentionally, recklessly, or negligently (in other words that they had the requisite guilty mind, or *mens rea*) and (3) that in so acting, s/he caused some morally bad result (Moore 1985, 13). At a metaphysical level, this theory of moral culpability depends on the idea that persons are rational and autonomous. By rational, Moore means simply that individuals act for reasons, or on the basis of what he calls 'valid practical syllogisms', no matter how bizarre the premises. By autonomous is meant that individuals are in control of the actions of their own bodies; that is, that they have a will, even if it is not completely free (Moore 1985, 20, 23). Moore appears to think that these criteria are widely applicable cross-culturally; but this contention is the subject of some debate. The very stripped

[6] A policy paper for the International Criminal Court also states that the prosecutor 'will take into consideration the need to respect the diversity of legal systems, traditions and cultures' cited in Allen (2006, 129).

down nature of the criteria for criminal responsibility, rather than guaranteeing the idea's universality, just as easily reveals its cultural particularity.[7] Lawrence Rosen, for example, has argued that while, on a trivial level, Moroccan individuals share the inner states, frames of mind and intentional structures identified by Moore, in practice Moroccan courts always inquire into the total social context of an individual's acts, since intentionality is regarded as a *socially embedded* phenomenon (Rosen 1985). In addition, the category term 'morally-bad result' would appear to be contingent on culture.[8]

A growing number of voices echo these and similar concerns. The critical legal studies movement, legal anthropology, feminist legal scholarship and post-modern legal scholars, among others, have in recent years criticised the patriarchy and ethnocentricity of Anglo-American law. For example, legal discourse theorists Joseph Conley and John O'Barr have pointed to the way in which male biases are built into the micro-linguistics of the disputing process itself (Conley and O'Barr 1998, 60–77). Donald Nicolson has criticised the politics of 'fact-positivism', arguing that, contrary to the law's ideology, fact and law are mutually constituted with potentially discriminatory effects; what counts as a punishable crime or a valid defence (a question of law) is inextricably bound up with perception-shaping assumptions one holds about the world (matters of fact) (Nicolson 1994; see also Geertz 1983, 173). People of colour, women and the poor, for example, often bring background assumptions at variance with those of the legal establishment to their interpretation of legal cases: 'Those whose stories are believed have the power to create fact; those whose stories are not believed live in a legally sanctioned "reality" that does not match their perceptions' (Scheppele 1989, 2079). In cases involving different social groups in which different versions of the facts are offered, 'Whole worldviews may have come into collision' (Scheppele 1989, 2098).

Certainly, the perceptual faultlines that separate the Western legal tradition from non-Western cultures have already been remarked upon in international trials. According to Harvard lawyer Judith Shklar:

> When … the American prosecutor at the Tokyo trials appealed to the law of nature as a basis for condemning the accused, he was only applying a foreign ideology, serving his nation's interests, to a group of people who

[7] There is a similarity here to criticisms of John Rawls' *Theory of Justice*. See, for example, Sandel (1992).

[8] For a critique, see Shapiro (1985).

> neither knew nor cared about this doctrine. The assumption of universal agreement served here merely to impose dogmatically an ethnocentric vision of international order. It was the claim that these universal rules were 'there' – the assumption of general agreement, which was so contrary to the cultural realties of the situation.
>
> (Shklar 1964 and 1986, 128.)

Apparently, the Tokyo defendants themselves appeared to struggle with the trial, rejecting legal advice and pursuing their own legally irrelevant patterns of thought. One Asian judge castigated the tribunal for its cultural narrowness, ethical dogmatism and historical emptiness (Shklar 1964 and 1986, 156–7). The prosecution justified its mission by reference to the Christian-Judaic ethic, but '[w]hat on earth', asks Shklar, 'could the Christian-Judaic ethic mean to the Japanese?' (Shklar 1964 and 1986, 183). The result was that the Tokyo trial was 'a complete dud' (Shklar 1964 and 1986, 124), its impact on the popular memory of the Japanese has been 'virtually nil', and the bodies of the executed are today housed in official shrines (Osiel 1997, 181, 182).

The problem of culture has not been lost on some of the new generation of international criminal justice advocates. In a brave and remarkable – if ultimately perplexing – speech, David Crane, formerly prosecutor at the Special Court for Sierra Leone, asks rhetorically whether the justice 'we seek to impose' is not merely '[w]hite man's justice'. He proceeds to confess that:

> Our perspectives are off-kilter. We simply don't think about or factor in the justice victims seek ... We approach the insertion of international justice paternalistically. I would even say with a self-righteous attitude that borders on the ethnocentric ... We consider our justice as the only justice ... We don't contemplate why the tribunal is being set up, and for whom it was established ... After set up, we don't create mechanisms by which we can consider the cultural and customary approaches to justice within the region.
>
> (Crane 2006, 1685–6.)[9]

Cultural epiphanies such as Crane's echo canonical anthropological studies that highlight important differences between Western and non-Western legal systems. As Merry notes, legal systems, 'are often embedded in very different ways of thinking about the fact/law

[9] After making these startling admissions Crane proceeds to imply that 'White Man's Justice' is the best justice, and that the Special Court for Sierra Leone enforced it in a culturally appropriate way. The evidence to be presented in this book suggests otherwise.

dichotomy, the nature of evidence, and the meaning of judging' (Merry 1988, 871). Studies of the law in Africa have suggested that African legal processes are more participatory, conciliatory, consensual, restorative and open to a wider notion of evidence than the typical Western court. For example, in his influential study of the Liberian Kpelle moot, Gibbs describes the way in which the moot is structured to produce a social outcome of consensus. He observes that the airing of grievances is more complete than in a courtroom, allowing the moot to consider the total social situation of the litigants: there is little delay between an offence and its airing; the setting is more informal, '[t]he robes, writs, messengers, and other symbols of power which subtly intimidate and inhibit the parties in the courtroom, by reminding them of the physical force which underlies the procedures, are absent'; cross examination is in the hands of all the parties, and, further, 'the range of relevance applied to matters which are brought out is extremely broad. Hardly anything mentioned is held to be irrelevant' (Gibbs 1963, 282–3). Gibbs claims that the moot produces a consensual outcome, in contrast to the imposed justice of formal adjudicators (Gibbs 1963, 283).

Similarly, Gluckman's famous study of Barotseland courts revealed a judicial process which, while closer to Western practice than the Kpelle moot, nevertheless displayed similar features. According to Gluckman, a Lozi litigant comes to court, 'not as a right-and-duty bearing *persona*, but in terms of his total social personality' (Gluckman 1964, 65). Lozi judges tried at all costs to reconcile litigants, since they disapproved of irremediable ruptures in social relationships, dispensing justice that made it possible 'for the parties to live together amicably in the future'. Consequently, judges 'constantly have to broaden the field of their enquiries, [to] consider the total history of relations between the litigants, not only the narrow legal issue' (Gluckman 1964, 63–4).[10] Similar findings have been made for other non-Western societies. Pospisil describes a situation among the Kapauku of Papua-New Guinea in which disputes were adjudicated by the local *tonowi*, or headman, noting, as in the African cases, that litigants' 'total personalities, and not only some arbitrarily selected or "logically related" facts, were relevant'

[10] Sounding a sceptical note, Van Velzen has criticised the presumed dichotomy between Western and African law, arguing that illegitimate comparisons have been drawn from different levels of the justice system. Discussed in Moore (1969, 272). Conley and O'Barr have also queried the competence of classical anthropologists in the languages of the systems they were studying (Conley and O'Barr 1998, 98–115).

(Pospisil 1981, 107). The system described by Pospisil was later disrupted by colonial rule, with the effect that:

> to the Kapauku the state's legalistic procedure appears ridiculously over-formalized, relying only on partial evidence, making the judge into a mechanical mouthpiece of the written rules, destroying his creativity, and turning the formerly dynamic, ever (although slowly) changing law into a rigid set of rules. In their view, all this amounts to, in most cases, is hopeless injustice.
>
> (Pospisil 1981, 108.)

In another study, Sally Falk Moore found that the politics of witnessing in Tanzanian colonial courts differed significantly from Western assumptions about what the role of witnesses should be. Colonial officers frequently complained about difficulties in finding the facts and the truth in their cases, adducing that local elders lacked Western fact-finding techniques, since they either already 'knew' the facts, or divined them by supernatural means. Added to this was the realisation that witnesses typically came to give partisan evidence, their testimony representing the current social standing of the plaintiff in the community, rather than the actualities of the case. African communities, Moore explains, are 'social settings where obligatory partisanship is a general rule of public behaviour'. For her, 'witnesses often testify (or fail to appear) with the idea of helping to construct a story favourable to the person to whom they owe a partisan account, either because of kin relationship, or for favours done in the past, for favours anticipated, for fear of displeasing, or the like' (Moore 1992, 37–8). Later in this book we will need to remember the importance of inter-group politics when we consider the testimony of witnesses at the Special Court.

Cultural difference is beginning to be taken seriously in the wider transitional justice community. While in 2002 a review of the truth commission literature decried the fact that 'the notion of culture hardly arises at all' (Avruch and Vejerano 2002, 42, 43), by 2005 astute observers such as Priscilla Hayner were beginning to ask whether truth commissions were always culturally appropriate: 'indigenous national characteristics may make truth-seeking unnecessary or undesirable, such as unofficial community-based mechanisms that respond to the recent violence or a culture that eschews confronting reality directly' (Hayner 2001, 186). Scholars of Cambodia have argued against raking over the truth in a Buddhist culture characterised by high social ideals of forgiveness (Hayner 2001; for a more exasperated view, see Maguire

2005). Rosalind Shaw is another author to have criticised the methodology of truth commissions. She argues that truth commissions stem from a distinct Western tradition of confession and cathartic healing that is alien to local people in Sierra Leone, where the attainment of a 'cool heart' is more important to reconciliation than factually truthful accounts of past atrocities (Shaw 2005, 2006). Studies of the richness of Shaw's alert us to the *sui generis* impact of culture on accountability, an issue to which we shall have cause to return.[11]

In the field of international criminal justice, the question of cultural difference has been most vigorously debated in the case of Northern Uganda (Allen 2006; Baines 2007; Branch 2004). In December 2003 Uganda's President Museveni invited the International Criminal Court to investigate the situation in the north of the country, and in particular the question of atrocities committed by the Lord's Resistance Army (LRA), a millenarian movement led by spirit-medium Joseph Kony, which has been terrorising the region in a conflict lasting more than a decade. The invitation immediately met with uproar. A vociferous constituency of local activists and their foreign supporters argued, among other things, that retributive justice was foreign to local traditions of forgiveness and reconciliation. According to James Otto, head of Human Rights Watch in Gulu: 'The ICC timing is bad. It has no protection mechanism. We have our own traditional justice system. The international system despises it, but it works. There is a balance in the community that cannot be found in the briefcase of the white man' (cited in Allen 2006, 87). For Paramount Chief David Acana II: 'The best way to resolve the 18 year old war in our region is through *Poro lok ki mato oput* (peace talks and reconciliation) as it's in the Acholi culture … I wonder who will help [the ICC] in giving evidence to prosecute Kony since the Acholi do not buy their idea of taking him to court because the Acholi have forgiven all the LRA' (cited in Allen 2006, 134). *Mato oput* (literally bitter root or juice) refers here to a traditional reconciliation ceremony in which the perpetrator of an offence and a representative of the victim's clan participate in a joint ritual in which the offender admits his wrongdoing and promises to compensate the offended party; both parties then drink the blood of a slaughtered sheep mixed with bitter herbs and roots, binding them in reconciliation. If the conflict is between entire clans, it ends with *gomo tong*, the bending of spears (Allen 2006, 132–3). In recent years, elements of this ceremony and others (such as dipping the

[11] See also the chapters in Huyse and Salter (2007).

toe in a broken egg), have been directed toward re-integrating ex-LRA combatants by urban based peace-building NGOs – often of Christian inspiration – who claim great success for these rituals, as have some foreign journalists and transitional justice proponents.

Through interviews with the inhabitants of IDP camps, ex-combatants, and traditional authorities, including spirit mediums, Tim Allen, an anthropologist with extensive experience in the area, uncovers a rather different story. Away from the staged consensus of official meetings, Allen says, internees in IDP camps are quite willing to countenance prosecution for the top leaders of the LRA, and admit to living together with ex-LRA combatants only with difficulty. In the words of one local councillor: 'According to me the people are very open to the ICC because Kony has committed atrocities. He has refused to come back home when people have tried to talk to him. Some people say they should kill such people. Some want to forgive them. Most people think they should go to court' (Allen 2006, 142). Further, authentic *mato oput*, though enjoying something of a revival in clan disputes, is not being used to re-integrate ex-combatants, while peace-making ceremonies such as 'the bending of the spears', much lauded by advocates of traditional justice, have not taken place in twenty years. The ersatz rituals concocted in town by peace-NGOs are, by comparison, not given much credence by Allen's informants. Extracted from their rural setting, and presided over by a generation of modern leaders with a controversial genealogy, they lose some of their traditional efficacy. Instead, the popularity of the new rituals is driven, at least in part, by the political-economic interests of the professional peace-makers. Allen concludes that: 'People in northern Uganda require the same kinds of conventional legal mechanisms as everyone else living in modern states. Far from there being widespread antipathy for the ICC, those that know about it are generally positive' (Allen 2006, 168).

Allen's book provides a convincing antidote to romanticised notions of indigenous accountability and misinformed ideas about the fundamental incompatibility of retributive justice and African culture.[12] But it leaves several questions unanswered. For instance, Allen reports that for some local people, Kony's actions are to be explained by the fact that he is possessed by an evil spirit (see also Behrand 1999 for the antecedents of the LRA). How would such claims fare in a Western-style

[12] Richard Wilson, finding a virulent strain of popular, retributive justice in South African townships, makes a similar critical observation in respect of that country's TRC (Wilson 2001).

criminal court? As suggested by Moore's criteria of culpable action, and as we shall see in Chapter 4, which discusses the role of the supernatural, the Western jurisprudential tradition would tend either to dismiss such claims out of hand, or else treat them as indicia of insanity, leading in all probability to acquittal. Would acquitting Kony satisfy local desires for retribution? According to one of Allen's informants: 'If they arrest him, will they arrest the spirit? It will jump elsewhere … If they arrest Kony, the spirit will just continue. It is the spirit that has forced Kony to do things' (Allen 2006, 156). Would incarcerating Kony solve the problem of his evil spirit? What resonance can Western judicial mechanisms have when Western and local views of human responsibility are incommensurate?

Further, Allen has little to say about whether the procedural form of a Western criminal court would be adequate or suitable to trying Kony. As some commentators have observed, getting the type of evidence a Western court demands from out of a non-Western culture, is no mean feat. On the basis of some of the judgements at the ICTR Robert Cryer, for example, has observed that: 'It is no novelty to say that inter-cultural understanding of demeanour, conduct and character can be difficult.' Problems are created when cultures encourage evasiveness, exaggeration, euphemism or understatement, and by the wide variations that govern norms of eye-contact and facial expression: 'These factors are highly relevant in determining the credibility of a witness and the possibility of inter-cultural misunderstanding is very real' (Cryer 2007, 4). In these circumstances, '[i]t would be all too easy for judges to apply social and cultural standards of trustworthiness and openness to witnesses who do not share them' (Cryer 2007, 1). These observations are consistent with a literature on inter-ethnic communication that points to the large potential for miscommunication even between ethnic groups who speak the same first language (Gee 1996; Gumperz 1982). They resonate also with the argument of Stromseth *et al.* that 'interveners need to be *better educated about the language and culture* of the societies in which they are working' (Stromseth, Wippman, and Brooks 2006, 326). Holding a meaningful trial in a context such as Northern Uganda may be extremely problematic, then. It is a huge leap from the finding that there is some indigenous desire for retribution and some scepticism about the invented traditions of peace-keeping NGOs, to the conclusion that an international criminal trial, doubtless costing millions of dollars, located thousands of miles from Uganda, is the solution.

In this book I will argue that, rather like Uganda and Rwanda, Sierra Leone is a society with a number of cultural features that contributed to making the application of international justice a fraught affair. Anthropologists and historians have long argued that, for some of Sierra Leone's peoples, the visible world is believed to be activated by an invisible reality beneath the surface of everyday events; local conceptions of time and space differ significantly from those in the West; fighting factions in the country's civil war made frequent recourse to supernatural help; some individuals were thought to be able to 'shape-shift' (indeed Allieu Kondewa, alleged 'High Priest' of the Kamajor militia and a defendant at the Special Court, is widely thought to have been able to turn himself into a snake, and to make himself invisible); and, in addition, everyday culture is said to be characterised by an 'aesthetics of ambiguity' and the valorisation of secrecy, founded in the region's long tradition of 'secret societies'. In short, and as I will discuss at greater length in the following chapters, many Sierra Leoneans have different ideas of social space and time, of causation, agency, responsibility, evidence, truth and truth-telling from those employed by international criminal courts.

STUDYING CULTURE IN INTERNATIONAL TRIALS

If culture is important to international trials, how should we study it? The existing literature on international justice provides few positive clues. To date, the vast majority of scholarship on international trials falls into two main categories: legalistic and politico-historical. Regarding the first, several books have concentrated on the rules, procedures, and decisions of international tribunals (Boas 2007; Cryer *et al.* 2007; Jones and Powles 2003; Schabas 2006). Written by lawyers or legal scholars, this literature tends to focus on the tribunals' foundation in law, the form and scope of indictments, the procedures for hearing and admitting evidence, and the legal arguments used to secure convictions or acquittals. The burden of analysis falls on tribunal rules, legal doctrines, procedural submissions and judicial decisions. The question of culture rarely arises, and this is for two reasons. First, international jurisprudence is, or at least claims to be, a self-enclosed and self-referential system of knowledge that justifies its decisions largely by reference to legal precedents. Logically speaking, anything that stands outside this system – radically different systems of knowledge and belief, for instance – is regarded as irrelevant: international lawyers do not generally have to justify their decisions by reference to the beliefs of the Tutsi, the Serbs, the Mende or the Acholi, since, in the world of international law, sub-national ethnic communities have no role.[13] Second, focusing on rules and decisions, jurisprudential analysis pays little attention to the status of the trial as a social encounter, where different modes of being and different world-views might conceivably collide. Unless such collisions are expressly referenced in judicial decisions – and there are good reasons why they are not – they do not figure prominently on the radar of most legal scholars.

To a great extent, this oversight is shared by historical and political analyses of trials. Take for instance Kenneth Minear's account of victor's justice at the Tokyo tribunal (Minear 1972). It consists mainly of an analysis of the political debates surrounding the form of the tribunal and its indictments, the shortcomings of the Bench and its legal decisions, and the inherent prosecutorial bias. Except by reference to a few pivotal remarks by legal counsel, and vivid description of the courtroom, the encounter of the trial itself is barely discussed. Thus the cultural collisions remarked upon by Shklar (Shklar 1964 and 1986) hardly figure at all, except obliquely in a section on translation. Peter Maguire's excellent book on the International Military Tribunal and the American trials at Nuremburg takes a similar form (Maguire 2000). The analysis ranges across a large number of trials, scrutinising the indictees, the arguments of the prosecution, the reasoning – both onstage and offstage – of the judges, and the post-trial aftermath. But, save for a few dramatic exchanges that are used to enliven the story, what really went on in court goes largely unaddressed. John Laughland, likewise, has produced a blistering attack on the trial of Slobodan Milosovic, in which he criticises the legality of the trial, the scope and nature of the indictment, judicial bias in the proceedings, the fact that the court was a law unto itself, the numerous changes to the indictment and the rules, the provisions for protecting witnesses, and the conditions of Milosevic's detention and his trial in absentia, drawing on numerous court documents to make his case (Laughland 2007). Nevertheless, the number of courtroom exchanges described is rather few, and when they do appear, it is usually to illustrate an egregious example of prosecutorial bias, or because Milosevic is making Laughland's argument in his own words.

[13] In my experience, international lawyers are often quite interested in these issues, though the professional demands of the courtroom encourage them to focus on the black letter aspects of the case. The recent UN and ICC guidelines on this matter provide some grounds for optimism that sensitivity to cultural difference is now on the agenda.

I do not mean to criticise these books, which are highly successful in illustrating the arguments they wish to make. But those arguments are not, to any great extent, about culture, perhaps because culture – at least in the European context of the Nuremburg and Yugoslav tribunals – was not a pressing issue at trial.[14]

The same cannot be said for the ICTR. Reports suggest that the tribunal experienced some of the same cultural difficulties as the Sierra Leone court (Cryer 2007), but these have not been extensively written about. Kingsley Moghalu, in one of only two book-length accounts of the tribunal, focuses instead on the high politics of the trial (Moghalu 2005). Chapters are devoted to, among other things, the task of capturing indictees, to the challenges of holding the tribunal in Arusha, to the substantive content of some of its most celebrated cases, to the political controversy surrounding the release of media defendant Jean-Bosco Barayagwiza, and to the political obstacles put in the place of Carla del Ponte's pursuit of the Rwandan Patriotic Front. The courtroom, however, remains pretty much a closed set, with Moghalu content to assert blithely that, while the tribunal itself has been surrounded by politics, the judicial process was largely politics free (Moghalu 2005, 4). Although the story Moghalu tells is itself fascinating, it misses the opportunity to unpack the cultural politics of the trials.

In order to illuminate the role of culture in an international tribunal, my study takes a different approach, which I refer to as *anthropolitical*. I provide a case study, of a single trial, informed by a combination of anthropological and political methods.

Of all the social sciences, anthropology – and in particular cultural anthropology – has been most closely connected to the study of culture.[15] Culture itself is a controversial concept, and has generally been understood by anthropologists to mean one of four things. Put simply, 'culture' can refer to: (1) the ontology, cosmology, or worldview of a people, community or society; (2) their systems of signification, encompassing obviously language (verbal and non-verbal), but also art, monuments, music,

[14] The same can be said for Hannah Arendt's famous account of the Eichmann trial, which, though dedicated to a critique of the show-like nature of the trial refers to rather few actual courtroom exchanges, while spinning off into reflections about the nature of evil, humanity, and totalitarian regimes, and a detailed account of Nazi atrocities only part of which is drawn from the trial (Arendt 1963). See also Simpson (2007); Bass (2000).

[15] There is a long history in anthropology of studying courts, and an emerging literature that targets transnational legal processes (Collier 1975; Merry 1988, 1992; Moore 1969); but there has been very little ethnographic work to date on international trials.

and dance; (3) their traditions, by which I mean patterns of valued behaviour carried into the present from the not-too-recent past; and (4) their total way of material and symbolic life. The first three of these definitions, upon which most of my analysis focuses, are nicely captured by Clifford Geertz's famous premise that 'man is an animal suspended in webs of significance he himself has spun', culture being those webs (Geertz 1973, 5). The fourth definition, associated most obviously with Edmund Tylor, I invoke when I discuss some characteristic forms of Sierra Leonean social organisation.[16]

Clearly, there is overlap between these different definitions or dimensions of culture. Clearly also, most communities are to some extent culturally heterogeneous, meaning that when we talk about culture, we often mean 'cultures'. Critics of 'culturalist' arguments often attack them on the grounds that they 'reify' culture, or 'essentialise' it, or make it 'determining', or 'unthinking' or 'homogenous', or assume that it is 'timeless'.[17] I hope that no-one will be able sensibly to level those accusations against my argument. In this work, I argue that culture is the key to understanding certain features of the CDF case, and certain forms of behaviour in court, without arguing that 'people do things simply because that's their culture, or because they've been conditioned by society to do those things, or that they merely enact whatever script the sociocultural order places in their hands' (Paul 1990, 431). The un-nuanced idea that culture is a kind of blueprint that programmes behaviour is a misconception that I associate more with the judges at the Special Court for Sierra Leone (see Chapter 6) than with my own argument.

Culture, in my understanding, is diverse, changing and, rather than determining, a fund of resources on which individuals draw, as well as a structure of constraints they face. To provide a hypothetical example: If I, a UK citizen, wish to forcibly overthrow a British government I regard as illegitimate, the mainstream of my culture presents certain resources, such as ideas about political legitimacy, models of military or paramilitary organisation, traditions of struggle against undemocratic regimes,

[16] 'Culture, or civilization, taken in its broad, ethnographic sense, is that complex whole which includes knowledge, belief, art, morals, law, custom, and any other capabilities and habits acquired by man as a member of society' (Tylor 1958 [1871], 1).

[17] Some critics prefer the term 'ideology' to 'culture': 'The term ideology reminds analysts that cultural frames have social histories and it signals a commitment to address the relevance of power relations to the nature of cultural forms and ask how essential meanings about language are socially produced as effective and powerful' (Woolard and Schieffelin 1994). I agree with this take on culture, but I am not so sure we need the term 'ideology' to remind us of it. For a similar critique, see Mitchell (1995).

modes of communication and rhetorical techniques stretching back at least to the overthrow of King Charles I, all of which have evolved over time. But it also presents certain constraints. Unlike the defendants in Sierra Leone's CDF trial, I could not, for example, mobilise my supporters on grounds that I was able to make them invisible or immune to bullets by means of special immunising medicines. To begin with, I do not know how to make such medicines, and there are no analogues in the culture on which I could improvise. Next, even if I possessed the medicines and understood the rituals to activate them, very few people would follow me, since the cultural mainstream in Britain is generally sceptical of magical belief.

With these caveats in mind, I can now state that this work is anthropological in two main senses. First, my reading of the trial has been informed by a reading of the anthropological literature on Sierra Leone and its culture area, drawing in particular on the work of contemporary anthropologists such as Mariane Ferme, William Murphy, Danny Hoffman and Rosalind Shaw.[18] To a large extent, I have viewed the transcript through an anthropological frame. This has meant that certain cultural features of the conflict, the case and the courtroom have been more obvious, and hopefully more transparent to me, than they would be to someone who lacked this background, for example a lawyer or a historian. Second, the study has relied for part of its insight on ethnographic methods. I began studying the Special Court for Sierra Leone in 2003, making repeat field trips in 2004, 2005, 2006 and 2008, amounting to a little over seven months in all. I was present at the Court when the first indictees were still held in a detention centre on Bonthe Island, and when the controversial indictment against Charles Taylor was unsealed. I was there in 2004 for an extended period during the opening of the trials, and I returned to consolidate my findings on three subsequent occasions, including at the very close of the CDF trial. During these trips I was able easily to integrate into the Court's social scene: attending its parties, sharing its gossip, discussing with international lawyers their views about international justice and their experience of the trials, as well as on occasion conducting formal interviews. During the days I spent most of my time observing and taking notes on trial proceedings, where one of the things that struck me most was the laboured, tortuous, inconclusive nature of many of the encounters between counsel

[18] Hoffman actually appeared as an expert witness in the CDF trial, and his insights have been extremely helpful to me.

and witnesses, a feature that I was later to discover characterised the entire trial.[19] Witnesses struck me, and many of the lawyers, as evasive. However, I knew from my knowledge of the anthropological literature that this was not necessarily because witnesses were telling lies. It was clear that much would hinge on how the judges would interpret evasive speech genres. I also knew from the anthropological literature that magical beliefs were deeply held in Sierra Leone, and testimony about magical beliefs rapidly began to emerge in the trial.[20] Again, an enormous amount hung on what weight the judges would give to magical belief, both as a source of military power, and, as we shall see, as a form of military discipline. I also spent some of 2005 studying local courts in an upcountry town, an experience that taught me about the legal culture in which the trial operated, and provided a useful point of comparison to the proceedings in Freetown.

In addition to being anthropological, I also describe my approach as 'political'. Teaching and researching African politics for more than a decade has sensitised me to certain aspects of the trial that non-Africanists might not have noticed, or might not have interpreted in the same way. One was the importance of religion and the occult to local questions of power; another was the dominance of patron-client and patrimonial relations, both of which will be discussed in due course. In addition, and like the works by Minear, Maguire and Moghalu referred to above, this study is alive to the international and institutional politics that informed the trial, though these are not its main focus. Instead, this study is political primarily in the sense of being concerned with the *micro-politics of meaning production*. Truth, in this optic, is not simply 'out there' waiting to be discovered. As Michel Foucault observed in a now famous interview:

> Each society has its regime of truth, its "general politics" of truth: that is, the types of discourse which it accepts and makes function as true; the mechanisms and instances which enable one to distinguish true and false statements, the means by which each is sanctioned; the techniques and procedures accorded value in the acquisition of truth; the status of those who are charged with saying what counts as true.

[19] Sitting in the public gallery as a member of the court audience provided me an invaluable exposure to the character of courtroom encounters; but the structure of the British academic year meant that I could only be present for a fraction of the trial. To fill in the gaps, I have been reliant on trial transcripts. I should also note that requests to interview the defendants and the judges fell on deaf ears, except in the case of Judge King.

[20] Indeed, they are even referred to in the indictment.

Meaning that power, knowledge, and truth are inextricably intertwined (Foucault 1980, 131). As I hope to show, the truth, or verdict, that emerged from the trial would be intimately connected to questions of power and resistance within the courtroom.

My approach to these questions has been influenced by discourse analysis and social linguistic techniques (Gee 1996, 2005; Gumperz 1982; Locke 2004; Phillips and Hardy 2002). Like much ethnography, most discourse analysis is concerned with the way in which language (broadly conceived) is used to produce, negotiate, mediate and reproduce social power. As Gee notes: 'language in use is everywhere and always "political"' (Gee 2005, 1). Language inevitably involves us taking perspectives on 'what is "normal" or not; what is "acceptable" or not; what is "right" or not; what is "real" or not' (Gee 2005, 2). A popular sub-field of discourse analysis has been cross-cultural encounters, focusing on how representatives of different cultural groups manage their relationships with one another through language (Gee 1996, 2005; Gumperz 1982). Much of the resulting work highlights instances of intercultural misunderstanding, which has been instructive for my analysis of trial sessions at the Special Court.

Particularly influential has been the work of legal discourse analysts John Conley and William O'Barr. A key theme in their research has been to demonstrate how language has been used to exert power in the courtroom:

> For most people the law's power manifests itself … in the details of legal practice, in the thousands of mini-dramas re-enacted every day in lawyers' offices, police stations, and courthouses around the country. The dominant element in almost every one of these mini-dramas is language. To the extent that power is realized, exercised, abused or challenged in such events, the means are primarily linguistic.
>
> (Conley and O'Barr 1998, 2.)

Conley and O'Barr's close analysis of courtroom interactions has provided me with inspiration for the broader analysis of trial transcripts that follows here. It is by analysing actual interactions in court that I have been able to reveal the ways in which, as Umphrey has noted, 'trials literally stage clashes of meaning' (Umphrey 1999, 412).

If Conley and O'Barr have focused in particular on the overwhelming power that the structure of the courtroom provides to lawyers, Marco Jacquemet's *Credibility in Court* has helped me to see that witnesses are not always passive objects of manipulation (Jacquemet 1996). Jacquemet discusses the Camorra trials in Southern Italy, a period of Southern Italian history in which hundreds of individuals were convicted on the basis of insider-witness testimony during an offensive against organised crime. Just a couple of years later, almost all this insider witness testimony was thrown out by appeals judges. Jacquemet's point is that credibility, and thus truth, is a communicative construct framed by wider structures of power. His work demonstrates brilliantly the ways in which insider witnesses (the *pentiti*) brought the elliptical genres of Neapolitan gang talk into the courtroom, a mode of discourse that either by accident or, more likely design, avoids reference to deictic markers such as specific dates, places, times and even names – facts that could be cross-checked and therefore refuted by the defence. Jacquemet shows how in the original trial the judges connived with the *pentiti* in their creation of a vague and sketchy evidential record that was nonetheless dignified with the status of a 'truth' used to convict defendants, while in the appeal hearings, a more exacting bench dismissed evidence that suffered from these imprecisions (Jacquemet 1996). I have used Jacquemet's analysis of courtroom encounters in the Camorra trials to light up problems in evidence at the Special Court for Sierra Leone.

Discourse analysts such as Gumperz, Jacquemet and Conley and O'Barr have developed a range of techniques for analysing language, some more detailed than others. 'Narrow' techniques, which can be incredibly detailed, utilise an extensive notational grammar for coding in minute detail prosodic variations: 'The ways in which words and sentences of a text are said: their pitch, loudness, stress, and the length assigned to various syllables, as well as the way in which the speaker hesitates and pauses' (Gee 1996, 94; see also Locke 2004). Even narrower techniques record variations in facial expression or bodily comportment. 'Broad' techniques, by contrast, limit themselves to recording precisely the content of speech. For reasons of choice and necessity, I have mostly used the latter (for an overview of different approaches, see Brenneis 1988). Narrow techniques are extremely time consuming, and, with thousands of pages of trial transcript to analyse, it was clear to me that my time would be more productively spent using a broad approach that attempted to capture the importance to the entire trial of the cultural encounters I was studying. Added to this, the trial at the Special Court for Sierra Leone is conducted in simultaneous translation, with transcripts transcribing the English translation, which is what the judges and lawyers generally listen to. Though translators are instructed to mimic the style of original speech, they inevitably do this imperfectly, so a minute analysis of translators' changes in pitch and stress would seem not to advance our knowledge very far. Neither are audio recordings of native language testimony currently available and, even if they were, I do not speak a native language, and would thus be completely dependent on research assistance for my insights. Of course, the slippage between original testimony and its translation is a fascinating question, and would be well served by these techniques; but it is not the principal object of my study here.

Following an initial period of ethnographic observation, then, my method was to read the entire public transcript of the trial, coding it according to features that my knowledge of the anthropological literature and my ethnographic experience of the trial had led me to think were important, such as testimony about the supernatural or about the wider political context of the war, or occasions where communication ran into difficulties, either because of problems with translation, misunderstanding, or evasion. I then focused on what appeared to be the most consistently occurring, or most critical of these features to the case, reviewing each occurrence, and constructing an illustrative and analytical narrative that draws on specific excerpts from trial testimony. The end product is an interpretive analysis of the role of cultural difference in the CDF trial.

A HISTORY OF THE CONFLICT AND OVERVIEW OF THIS BOOK

The territory known today as Sierra Leone was given its name (*Serra Lyoa*) by the Portuguese explorer Pedro da Sintra in 1462. For the next three centuries the territory experienced more or less constant warfare, as it was repeatedly invaded by peoples fleeing the expansion of Islamic empires in the Mande world of the Western Sahel (Kup 1962; Shaw 2002). Europeans profited from and encouraged the trade in slaves that went with these struggles, further exacerbating violence, population displacements, and ethnic realignments (Kup 1962; Shaw 2002). In 1787, the British established a settlement for freed slaves at Freetown on the western peninsula, which in 1808 became a crown colony; in the hinterland, however, insecurity continued to reign, as warrior chiefs and war-mongering merchants fought over the spoils of long-distance trade (Abraham 1974, 1978; Clapham 1976; Gberie 2005; Kup 1962;

McGowan 1990; Migdal 1988; Shaw 2002). In 1896, Britain extended its authority inland, creating a Protectorate over Sierra Leone's modern borders. It governed the colony under a dual system of law: the English law for the Western Area, where the Anglophile Krio – descendants of the freed slaves – predominated, and customary law, administered by native chiefs, for the hinterland. After an early rebellion and one or two subsequent revolts, a modicum of peace was secured, and some economic development in agriculture and minerals – especially diamonds – ensued (Kilson 1966; Gberie 2005).

In 1961, Sierra Leone was granted independence, its first President being Milton Margai of the Sierra Leonean People's Party (SLPP), which had its base in the ethnically Mende districts of southern Sierra Leone. In 1967, the SLPP was defeated at elections by the All People's Congress of Siaka Stevens, which was stronger among the Temne and Limba people of the North, and among ethnically mixed populations of diamond diggers in the east of the country. Immediately there was a pro-SLPP coup, before a second coup restored Stevens to power. Stevens proceeded to create a *de facto* and then *de jure* one-party state, staying in power by using a mixture of coercion and bribery. By the time he handed the reins to his successor, Joseph Momoh, in 1985, the state was perilously weak (Reno 1995; Kpundeh 2004; Richards 1996; Gberie 2005; Abdullah 2004; TRC 2004). Then, in 1991, a group of around 100 men, comprised largely of high school drop-outs, mercenaries from Burkina Faso, and fighters from Charles Taylor's National Patriotic Front of Liberia, invaded Sierra Leone from neighbouring Liberia, calling themselves the Revolutionary United Front (RUF). They were led by one Foday Sankoh, a cashiered army corporal imprisoned in the 1970s for his part in an alleged coup plot, who had subsequently worked as an itinerant photographer. In the 1980s, Sankoh had fallen in with a group of student radicals and disaffected urban youth influenced by Pan-African ideology and the Green Book radicalism of Libyan leader Muammar Ghadaffi. Towards the end of the decade he and a handful of these radicals found their way to Ghana, and thence to Libya, where they received training in guerrilla warfare. It was in Libya, allegedly, that Sankoh met Charles Taylor and a deal was struck whereby each would assist the other in overthrowing their respective country's regimes (Abdullah 2004a; Gberie 2005).

Thus began Sierra Leone's most recent war. In addition to the Revolutionary United Front (RUF), the most prominent factions in the conflict were the National Provisional Ruling Council (NPRC), a faction of the army that overthrew the government of Joseph Momoh in 1992; the Civil Defence Forces (CDF), a collection of militias based on local hunting societies, including the Tamaboros, the Gbethis, the Donsos, the Kapras, and most importantly the Kamajors, that arose to protect local communities from rebel attack, frequently using magical methods; Executive Outcomes, a South African mercenary organisation employed by the NPRC to fight the RUF; the Economic Community of West African States Monitoring Group (ECOMOG), a largely Nigerian peace-keeping force; the Armed Forces Revolutionary Council (AFRC), a military faction that took power in 1997, forming an alliance with the RUF; the West Side Boys, a splinter group of the AFRC; and the United Nations Mission in Sierra Leone (UNAMSIL), a multinational peace-keeping force.

To provide a basic timeline: after the RUF invaded Sierra Leone in 1991 they were engaged unsuccessfully by the army, a faction of which returned to Freetown and overthrew the government in 1992, forming the NPRC. The NPRC enjoyed some initial success, but its efforts soon foundered, evidence emerging that some army soldiers – dubbed 'sobels' – were colluding with the rebels to strip the civilian population of their assets. In May 1995, Executive Outcomes arrived, providing government forces a shot in the arm. Working in tandem with the neo-traditional hunting societies, they scored significant victories against the rebels, paving the way for civilian elections in February 1996, which were won by Ahmad Tejan Kabbah's SLPP. In November, the rebels signed a peace agreement at Abidjan. However, the terms of that agreement were soon violated and hostilities resumed; Sankoh travelled to Nigeria, where he was detained, while Sam Bockarie – a former hairdresser and disco-dancing champion – assumed charge of the RUF. Then, in May 1997, the government was overthrown in a military coup led by junior officers: Kabbah and his cabinet went into exile in Guinea; Major Johnny Paul Koroma – a poorly educated, corrupt, and over-promoted soldier – became head of the AFRC, teaming up with the RUF to form 'the junta', or 'People's Army'. In February 1998, the junta was driven from Freetown and major towns in the south and east of the country by a combination of the hunting societies, now organised as the CDF, and ECOMOG, who restored the Kabbah regime. As we shall see, events during this period – May 1997 to February 1998 – were the focus for most of the CDF trial. After losing power, the AFRC and RUF regrouped in the north and east of the country, launching a devastating assault on Freetown in January 1999. After a few weeks they were pushed back up north by ECOMOG, and signed a peace agreement with the government at Lomé in July 1999 (Gberie 2005; Hirsch 2000; Keen 2005; TRC 2004).

The Lomé Accord granted the rebels a blanket amnesty, provided for UN peacekeepers and a Truth and Reconciliation Commission, and made Foday Sankoh (who had previously been captured, tried, and condemned to death) chairman of a new Commission on Strategic Minerals, effectively granting him control over the diamond industry plus vice-presidential protocol status. In spite of these blandishments, it was clear that some RUF cadres wanted to keep fighting (Gberie 2005, 162). UN peacekeepers were harassed, and in May 2000, 500 UN troops were kidnapped, including an entire Zambian battalion (Keen 2005, 262). With RUF troops moving towards Freetown, only to be halted by soldiers and CDF, Sankoh appeared to be plotting a government takeover (Gberie 2005, 166). On 8 May 2000, his house was surrounded by a mob wanting to arrest him. Shots were fired, civilians killed, and Sankoh escaped dressed as a woman, only to be apprehended some days later and charged by a Freetown court (Gberie 2005; Keen 2005, 265; TRC 2004, vol. 3A, 412–18). The British government sent additional troops to shore up the faltering UN mission the same day.

These events spelled the beginning of the end for the RUF, who were overawed by British military strength. In April 2000, a small British contingent successfully defended Lungi airport from attack, inflicting heavy casualties on a much larger RUF force. Then, on 10 September, they more or less annihilated AFRC splinter group the West Side Boys, which had taken a group of British soldiers hostage. In September 2000, the RUF began incursions into Guinea, but were pounded by Guinean helicopter gunships, operating with South African and British logistical support (Gberie 2005, 171–4). In 2001, the RUF positions in the diamond fields were overrun by the Donsos, a hunter group also receiving support from Guinea. At the same time, a ban on diamond exports from Sierra Leone was squeezing the RUF's economic receipts, and with support from Liberia drying up, a new, more moderate leadership under the control of Issa Sesay began to cooperate more enthusiastically with demobilisation (Gberie 2005; Keen 2005, 267–76). By January 2002, 72,490 combatants had been demobilised and Kabbah declared the war officially over, a collection of ministers, peacekeepers, journalists and aid workers gathering to burn a mound of weapons at Hastings just outside Freetown (Hoffman 2004, 47). In May 2002, Kabbah's party was re-elected in countrywide elections with a large majority (Kandeh 2003).

The conflict had several defining characteristics. The RUF and the Sierra Leonean Army shunned pitched battles for the most part, preferring to avoid each other and prey upon the civilian population instead (Keen 2005). All the armed factions, the RUF in particular, used child soldiers, many of whom were forcibly abducted from their communities and then inducted into the movement by committing atrocities, sometimes against their own relatives (Keen 2005; TRC 2004; Zack-Williams 1999). Indeed, the war became notorious for the encyclopaedia of spectacularly violent acts perpetrated mainly on civilians, which included mutilations, decapitations, immolations, physical and sexual humiliation, sexual slavery, and the RUF signature atrocity of limb amputation, an outrage adopted with even more enthusiasm by the AFRC. Many young fighters reported being given drugs to make them fearless (Peters and Richards 1998), and the violence sometimes appears to have taken a saturnalian form. The RUF had a definite cultish, sect-like aspect, and Foday Sankoh on various occasions claimed that his rebellion was inspired by visions from God (Gberie 2005, 60, 136; Richards 2004). Early on in the war, certain RUF commanders claimed magical powers – Rambo, for instance, being believed in some circles to be bullet-proof (Opala 1994) – and, as we shall see, bullet-proofing and other uses of magic were employed to great effect by hunting societies such as the Kamajors. Various commentators have noticed the chameleonic nature of the conflict, armed factions frequently disguising their identity, soldiers sometimes dressing as rebels and vice versa (Keen 2005; TRC 2004, 550–2), while rebels sometimes donned the traditional garb of Kamajors. The conflict did not have a strong ethnic character. However, there is some evidence that the Kamajors, who were mostly Mende, tended to associate the RUF and the army with northern groups, especially the Temne and the Limba, and that they targeted the lives and property of Temne and Limba individuals, as well as members of other northern tribes, during sweeps of Bo town, at roadblocks, and when the diamond fields were invaded in 1998 (TRC 2004, vol. 3A, 518–23). Finally, the violence often fed on or ignited complex local political feuds (Bangura 2004, 31; TRC 2004, vol. 3A, 514–15).

There have been several debates in the literature about the motivating factors behind the war. One of the first analyses, by journalist Robert Kaplan, blamed the conflict on state corruption, population pressure, and environmental catastrophe, a nexus that was driving unemployed youth into forms of atavistic violence and criminality, a thesis that became known as 'new barbarism' (Kaplan 1994). This was responded to by Paul Richards, who rebutted the environmental catastrophe thesis, and portrayed the rebels instead as excluded if misguided intellectuals wedded to a radical egalitarian vision, who, quite rationally, resorted to spectacular forms of violence in order to get their voices heard (Richards 1996). Richards' position was fiercely challenged by a group of Sierra Leonean academics, among them Yusuf Bangura and Ibrahim Abdullah, who played down the intellectual roots of the movement, arguing that the individuals who eventually invaded Sierra Leone, and the cohort they attracted, were from a lumpen class socially predisposed to wanton, criminal violence (Abdullah 2004a; Bangura 2004; Rashid 2004). Another group of scholars found the root cause of the war in diamonds. Diamond wealth provided the incentive for Charles Taylor to finance and support the war, diamond proceeds paid for many of the RUF's guns, and the armed factions, peacekeepers included, spent much of their time mining (Gberie 2005, esp 180–96; Hirsch 2000; Keen 2005). David Keen has shown how in a context of economic collapse, the perpetuation of war sustained multifarious economic agendas (Keen 2005, esp 36–50, 107–31). In addition, he explains the extravagant violence and cruelty of the armed factions by reference, among other things, to the feelings of anger and humiliation young men experienced under a social system that failed to grant them respect (Keen 2005, esp 56–81). The TRC, meanwhile, prefers to explain the savagery by reference to 'traumatic initiations' and to the administration of drugs (TRC 2004, vol. 3A, 531, 556, 562–4). Recent work has shown that most RUF recruits came from rural areas, heavily qualifying the 'urban lumpen' thesis, though many do seem to have come from an excluded social class (Fanthorpe 2001; Peters and Richards 1998; Humphreys and Weinstein 2004). Richards has pointed to the way in which many recruits had earlier been victims of rough justice at the hands of chiefs, accused of offences such as adultery, and forced either into conditions of debt-bondage, or out of the community and into the diamond mines (Richards 2005). Krijn Peters has revived the idea that fighters were engaged in an intergenerational struggle for a fairer society, and that at least some elements of the RUF did have a transformative social vision, which, he says, had some affinities with that of Cambodia under Pol Pot (Peters and Richards 1998; Peters 2006).

The story of the Special Court, meanwhile, begins on 12 June 2000, when President Kabbah wrote to UN Secretary General Kofi Annan, requesting that he create a court 'powerful enough to bring justice to his country' which would try the leaders of the RUF, 'for crimes against the people of Sierra Leone and for the taking of United Nations peacekeepers as hostages' (Dougherty 2004, 316). At the time when he wrote, the Lomé Peace Accord – which provided for a general amnesty and TRC[21] – had been breached by the rebels, four UN peacekeepers had been killed and around 500 taken hostage, and the RUF clearly posed a threat to the government (Dougherty 2004). The request for a court appears to have been an idea to lock the UN into a long-term solution to Sierra Leone's conflict.

The UN proved receptive and, five days later, in Resolution 1315, the Security Council declared that, 'a credible system of justice and accountability for the very serious crimes committed [in Sierra Leone] would end impunity and would contribute to the process of national reconciliation and to the restoration and maintenance of peace' (SCSL 2003a, 2) – talks between the government of Sierra Leone, the Secretariat, and the Security Council began. After a series of discussions, it was agreed to establish a court that would fulfil some of the same functions as the pre-existing *ad hoc* tribunals for Rwanda and the former Yugoslavia, but at a much reduced cost. The court would be established by a treaty between the government of Sierra Leone and the UN, created simultaneously in international and Sierra Leonean law, it would be situated in-country, with a mixed staff, be funded by voluntary contributions, and have a three-year mandate (Dougherty 2004). It would be tasked with prosecuting a small number of perpetrators, expressed in the statute as:

> persons who bear the greatest responsibility for serious violations of international humanitarian law and Sierra Leonean law committed in the territory of Sierra Leone since 30 November 1996, including those leaders who, in committing such crimes, have threatened the establishment and implementation of the peace process in Sierra Leone.
>
> (SCSL 2002, Article 1, para. 1.)

The statute, which was finalised in February 2001, was a medley of international and national law. Many of the international clauses were lifted from the ICTY and the ICTR while national laws, for example the 1926 Prevention of Cruelty to Children Act and the 1861 Malicious Damage Act, were included because their provisions were thought better

[21] The TRC began collecting statements and holding public hearings in 2003, issuing its multi-volume report in 2004 (TRC 2004). For accounts, see Kelsall (2005); Shaw (2005); Stovel (2005).

able to capture some of the conflict's most prevalent violations, such as abusing girl children or abducting girls for immoral purposes, and setting fire to dwellings, public buildings or other buildings (Dougherty 2004, 317–18). In the event, these national crimes were not charged in the indictments.

The Court was also intended to leave a powerful legacy in Sierra Leone. This included its state-of-the-art, twin-chamber courthouse, office blocks for the defence and prosecution, and high-security detention centre – what Prosecutor David Crane described as 'a wonder multi-acre justice site' (ICG 2003, 19–20). It was hoped also that indictments of former leaders would go some way to changing the legal culture in Sierra Leone, proving that even 'big men' were not above the law; it was believed that working at the Court would help build the capacity of Sierra Leonean staff, creating competencies that would later diffuse throughout the domestic justice sector; and finally, it was thought that the Court would be a spur to some harmonisation of domestic law (ICG 2003; Kerr and Lincoln 2008; Sriram 2006).

Because of funding bottlenecks, the Court was not finally established until 16 January 2002. The first court staff arrived six months later. The Prosecutor, David Crane, was an American, Pentagon lawyer, nominated by the UN. His deputy, Desmond de Silva, a British QC (who had earlier defended one of the CDF defendants for his part in the 1967 coup), had been chosen by the government of Sierra Leone (Dougherty 2004). Joining the Court later was Head of Investigations Alan White, a friend and colleague of Crane's, who was deputised by Tamba Gbeki, a Sierra Leonean detective. The Court's main funders were the United States, Britain, the Netherlands and Nigeria.

A little over a year later, the Court indicted thirteen persons for crimes that included murder, rape, enslavement, looting and burning, sexual slavery, extermination, acts of terror, conscription of children into an armed force, forced marriage and attacks on UNAMSIL peacekeepers (SCSL n.d.). Of those indicted, RUF leader Foday Sankoh was subsequently turned over to the Special Court but died in custody before his trial could begin. His right-hand man, Sam Bockarie, was murdered in Liberia before he could be captured by the Court. AFRC leader Johnny Paul Koroma disappeared, and it is not clear at time of writing whether he is alive or dead. Liberian president Charles Taylor found exile in Nigeria, though he was later handed over to the Court, which is trying him in The Hague. That left Issa Sesay, acting RUF leader at the time the RUF finally complied with the Lomé peace deal, Morris Kallon,

Figure 2. The Bench, Trial Chamber 1. From left to right: David Crane (foreground), Justice Thompson, Justice Itoe, Justice Boutet.

a high-ranking commander and one of the initial RUF contingent to invade Sierra Leone in 1991, and Augustine Gbao, connected in most people's minds with the kidnap of UN peacekeepers. On the AFRC side were the little-known Alex Tamba Brima, Santigie Borboh Kanu and Ibrahim 'Bazzy' Kamara, tried and convicted in 2007. Finally, to most people's surprise, were the alleged leaders of the CDF: the widely popular Chief Samuel Hinga Norman (by then Minister for the Interior), a former businessman called Moinina Fofana, and the notorious but mysterious Allieu Kondewa.

The Prosecutor charged Samuel Hinga Norman (National Coordinator), Moinina Fofana (Director of War) and Allieu Kondewa (High Priest) with eight counts of war crimes, crimes against humanity and other serious violations of international humanitarian law. The trial was remarkable for a number of reasons: it prosecuted an individual – Hinga Norman – and an amalgamation of local militia groups – the CDF – that were hugely popular in some Sierra Leonean circles; it was punctuated by political drama at various points; it was built on an investigation that in many respects was incompetent; it relied mostly on witnesses who were illiterate, and who testified in ways that revealed their unfamiliarity with the culture of a Western courtroom; and it elicited large amounts of evidence of supernatural phenomena that came to form a plank in the defence of the accused. In Chapter 2 I provide an overview of the CDF trial.

In addition to charging Norman, Fofana and Kondewa with committing, ordering, planning, instigating or aiding and abetting war crimes and crimes against humanity, the prosecution alleged that they were responsible *as superiors* for crimes committed by their subordinates. Two expert witnesses in the CDF trial testified about the CDF's military character. The prosecution argued that it was an unconventional yet recognisable military organisation, with clear lines of command and control. The defence argued that it was more in the nature of a militarised social network, in which command and control were fluid and decentralised. Each interpretation had very different implications for the fate of the accused, and for the broader question of prosecuting international crimes in conflicts of this kind. In Chapter 3 I outline the arguments and discuss the evidence in the light of broader historical and political knowledge about the nature of non-Western societies.

Superior responsibility is the subject for Chapter 4 also. For the first time in an international court, the proseuction alleged that a defendant (Allieu Kondewa) was responsible for the crimes of his subordinates by virtue of the *mystical powers* he possessed, the trial chamber eliciting a considerable body of evidence centred on ritual ceremonies in which CDF initiates were reportedly rendered immune to bullets via the consumption or application of esoteric medicines. Bullet-proofing was central, for reasons to be explained, to the charges against the three accused, two of whom used its obverse side as a plank in their own defence. In Chapter 4 I show how, through this testimony, the worldview of the court and that of the accused and witnesses threatened to collide.

The Court also made jurisprudential history when it became the first international tribunal to try defendants for the crime of enlisting children in hostilities. By doing so it had to perform two tricky operations: first, it had to prove that even though the Rome Statute was not in effect for most of the period covered by the indictment, enlisting child soldiers was nevertheless a crime under customary international law; and, second, it had to show that an international benchmark of childhood was relevant to a country where children are often feared for their close relations with the spirit world, and where becoming an adult is intimately connected to rituals of initiation, such as were practised by the Kamajors. In Chapter 5 I deploy a critical analysis of the trial testimony and motions surrounding the child soldiers charge to show how the international community imposed its norms on Sierra Leone.

I have already referred in passing to the importance of secret societies. Although secrecy and strategies of concealment are not unique to Sierra Leone, they are particularly prevalent there. In Chapter 6 I discuss how techniques of secrecy and dissimulation affected the trial. I hypothesise that witnesses viewed court staff with circumspection. In some cases this led them to not tell the full truth in their pre-trial statements; in others it led to them not telling the full truth in court, problems that became particularly acute under questioning by hostile lawyers from the opposite team. During these moments, I suggest, witnesses fell back on a repertoire of culturally prized linguistic strategies designed to protect them from the possibly malefic intentions of potential adversaries. They hedged, they qualified, they equivocated, they evaded, and in many cases they ran rings around the lawyers, problems compounded by a slipshod investigation and a witness protection regime that provided witnesses incentives to lie.

In Chapter 7 I look at cultural issues in the Special Court's other trials: the RUF, AFRC and Charles Taylor. Although the issue of mystical powers was much less pronounced in these trials, superior responsibility, child soldiers and witness credibility caused similar problems, as did the issue of forced marriage, another new charge under international law.

I conclude the book by suggesting some practical reforms that could help mitigate some of the difficulties encountered when trying to hold a Western-style trial in a non-Western culture. I discuss some ethical issues, some epistemological problems, and I end by advocating a more pluralistic, dialogical, polyphonic approach.

CHAPTER 2

THE STORY OF THE CDF TRIAL

On this solemn occasion mankind is once again assembled before an international tribunal to begin the sober and steady climb upwards towards the towering summit of justice. The path will be strewn with the bones of the dead, the mourns of the mutilated, the cries of agony of the tortured echoing down into the valley of death below. Horrors beyond the imagination will slide into this hallowed hall as this trek upward comes to a most certain and just conclusion. The long dark shadows of war are retreated. Pain, agony, the destruction and the uncertainty are fading; the light of truth, the fresh breeze of justice moves freely about this broken and beaten land. The rule of law marches out of the camps of the downtrodden onward under the banners of never again and no more.

(David Crane, 3 June 2004.)

With these dramatic words delivered to a Freetown courtroom packed with local and international press, international observers, the cream of Sierra Leonean civil society NGOs and relatives and supporters of the accused, the prosecution opened its case in the CDF trial. In a speech which figured, on the one hand, the tropes of ascent, progress, light, brightness, truth, justice, the law, civilisation and humanity; and, on the other, darkness, bestiality, barbarism, impunity, evil, death and hell, Prosecutor David Crane set a Manichean scene. He scripted the trial as a contest between justice, anthropomorphised as a Christian soldier, and impunity, depicted by a beast or hound of hell. He claimed that Sierra Leoneans now stood 'shoulder to shoulder', staring down 'the beast of impunity', that '[t]he jackals of death, destruction and inhumanity are caged behind bars of hope and reconciliation', and that the trial marked 'a beginning of the end to the life of that beast of impunity which howls in frustration and shrinks from the bright and shiny spectre of the law' (2004e, 3 June 2004, 6).[1] Sierra Leone, claimed Crane, had witnessed 'events that will make men of reason and civility recoil' (2004e, 3 June 2004, 11).

[1] The full reference to the transcript is in the References at SCSL 2004e.

The trial was to span another 162 days over the next twenty months, hear from 119 witnesses and scrutinise 230 documentary exhibits. Its spectators peered through a thick shield of bullet-proof glass into a semi-circular, spot-lighted chamber whose walls soared to a rarefied ceiling painted in refulgent white. At the bar were mixed-nationality legal teams robed in black gowns and seated at curving desks. Presiding over them were Justices Benjamin Mutanga Itoe from Cameroon, Pierre G. Boutet from Canada and Rosolu John Bankole Thompson from Sierra Leone.[2] Resplendent in scarlet and black robes, they towered over the Court from a high hardwood Bench, beneath which sat court officers behind a phalanx of computers. Facing them was the witness box, which for much of the trial was obscured from the public gallery by a screen.[3] In the dock, figuratively speaking, were Chief Samuel Hinga Norman, Moinina Fofana and Allieu Kondewa. Hinga Norman, then 64 years old, had been a British-trained army officer imprisoned for his role in the 1967 coup, who sought exile in Liberia in the 1970s, before returning to Sierra Leone in the 1990s. There, he became a Regent Chief in Bo District and participated in training traditional Kamajor hunters and other civilians to defend the chiefdom from rebel attack. By 1996 Norman's reputation had grown to the point at which he had been made Deputy Minister of Defence and, by 1997, National Coordinator of the CDF. It was in the latter role that he stood charged as the first accused in a criminal conspiracy to defeat the rebel forces and take control of Sierra Leone by any necessary means. Second accused in this plan was Moinina Fofana. The son of a fisherman believed to have been born in 1950 in Nongoba Bullom chiefdom, where he was later to become Chiefdom Speaker, Fofana was an illiterate trader and businessman who rose to prominence funding Kamajor activities, eventually becoming its National Director of War around 1997, and Director of Peace from around 1999, in which role he was decorated with a medal by President Kabbah. Doctor (aka 'King') Allieu Kondewa, the trial's third accused, was a farmer and herbalist thought to have been born in Bo. He enjoyed a meteoric rise to fame as an initiator who bestowed bullet-proofing powers on the Kamajors, ultimately in 1997 becoming the movement's High Priest. Having already spent around a year in pre-trial detention, all three now stood charged with horrendous crimes for which, if found guilty, they could expect to spend the rest of their lives in jail.

2 The judges' biographies can be found at the Special Court website: www.sc-sl.org/chambers.html.

3 An official of the Court confided in me that, despite the impressive appearance of the courtroom, hundreds of gallons of water were accumulating on the roof and threatening to trickle down onto the electric circuitry below, thereby imperilling the opening date of the trial.

Figure 3. The CDF defendants. Second row, from right: Norman (in white cap), Fofana, Kondewa.

Subsequent chapters will pick up the importance of patron–client relations and command responsibility, the extraordinary contribution of the supernatural, the novelty of the child soldiers charge, and troubles with trial testimony in a foreign culture. The current chapter, as a prelude, provides the trial's overview. It is impossible to provide an exhaustive summary of trial testimony in a book of this length;[4] instead, my aim is to map the main lines of attack and defence, and the decisions of the judges, laying the foundation for the more interpretive chapters to follow.

THE PROSECUTION CASE

The blueprint for the prosecution's case was provided in its consolidated, eight-count indictment.[5] There, it charged the accused with unlawful killings, in particular murder (Counts 1 and 2); inhumane acts and cruel treatment (3 and 4); pillage (5); terrorising the civilian population (6); collective punishments (7); and, finally, enlisting children in an armed force

[4] The best source in this respect are the prosecution and defence final trial briefs (SCSL 2006d, 2006h, 2006e, 2006g).

[5] The timing of the serving of the consolidated indictment on Chief Norman, and its alleged vagueness, was a recurring source of controversy at trial. See SCSL (2007d, Annex F).

or using them in hostilities (8). Counts 1 and 3 were treated as crimes against humanity; Counts 2, 4, 5, 6, and 7 as war crimes – namely, violations of Common Article 3 of the Geneva Conventions and Additional Protocol II; Count 8, a novel charge, was treated as an 'other serious violation of International Humanitarian Law' (SCSL 2004c, 7 ff).

The charges were brought on the theory that the CDF was 'an organized armed force comprising various tribally based traditional hunters', among whom the Kamajors were the most prominent (SCSL 2004c, 2). Samuel Hinga Norman was the National Coordinator and the principal force in 'establishing, organizing, supporting, providing logistical support, and promoting' that movement. Moinina Fofana, the second accused, was the CDF's Director of War and had 'direct responsibility for implementing policy and strategy and prosecuting the war'. Third accused, Allieu Kondewa, was the movement's High Priest, supervising or controlling all initiators in the CDF as well as frequently leading or directing operations, with direct command over certain CDF units (SCSL 2004c, 4). The prosecution claimed that together the accused planned to use 'any means necessary' to defeat the RUF/AFRC rebel forces and gain control over the territory of Sierra Leone (SCSL 2004c, 5).

In furtherance of that plan, Kamajors committed war crimes and crimes against humanity between 1 November 1997 and 1 April 1998 in Tongo Field and surrounding areas; on or around 15 February 1998 in Kenema; in or about January and February 1998 in the towns of Bo and Koribundo; between October 1997 and December 1999 in Moyamba District; between October 1997 and December 1999 in Bonthe District including Bonthe town and the village of Talia; and in an operation called 'Black December' in which the CDF blocked major roads and highways. Pursuant to Article 6(i) of the Special Court's statute, the prosecution alleged that Norman, Fofana and Kondewa were criminally responsible for the aforementioned crimes which they planned, instigated, ordered, committed, or else aided and abetted, or which were part of a common purpose, plan or design in which they participated, or else a foreseeable consequence of such a plan. In addition, pursuant to Article 6(iii), the prosecution alleged that the accused were responsible as superiors for all the criminal acts of their subordinates that they knew or had reason to know about, and which they failed to punish or take reasonable steps to prevent (SCSL 2004c, 6).

Prosecuting attorney Joseph Kamara, a Sierra Leonean national, expanded on these allegations in his opening statement to court. Following the AFRC coup in 1997, Sam Hinga Norman was tasked with organising the southern and eastern wings of the CDF, he alleged. Subsequently, he took over the CDF leadership, Fofana became the National Director of War, and Kondewa the High Priest. These three held several meetings where they coordinated, directed and commanded military operations from the stronghold of 'Base Zero' in the village of Talia in the Bonthe District (SCSL 2004e, 3 June 2004, 15). A War Council comprising ten senior members of the movement was established to ensure effective control over the Kamajors, but the accused soon usurped its powers (SCSL 2004e, 3 June 2004, 17). Later, when the accused were frustrated in their efforts to dislodge the rebel factions they, 'turned on their own people, their fellow citizens and the Mende people' (SCSL 2004e, 3 June 2004, 12). They issued instructions to Kamajors to 'kill all persons deemed collaborators or members of the AFRC and RUF'. Further, despite the 'clear and repeated notice that they had of the type and scale of crimes' they, 'failed woefully to take any adequate, necessary and reasonable measures to prevent or punish the perpetrators of these horrific crimes' (SCSL 2004e, 3 June 2004, 26). The evidence, claimed Kamara, would show a 'systematic and widespread pattern of physical violence, murder and looting' (SCSL 2004e, 3 June 2004, 27). He proceeded to give lurid details from a catalogue of horrors: severed heads displayed on sticks in Koribundo; summary execution of suspected collaborators in Kenema; consumption of a civilian's intestines, garnished with cooked cassava in Talia; brutal machete murders of civilians in Bo; torture and burning of a civilian in Moyamba; and slaughter of civilian after civilian in the diamond-rich area of Tongo – descriptions that left some members of the public gallery in tears.

Close to the end of his address, Kamara reminded the Court that the accused were collectively and individually responsible for the indicted offences, '[a]nd as prosecutors, we are determined that such grave offences against the people of Sierra Leone and the conscience of humanity do not go unpunished'. Expanding the trial's horizons, Kamara hoped that: 'This is the time that people in leadership positions all over the world realise that they can be held accountable for human rights violations and breaches of international humanitarian law' (SCSL 2004e, 3 June 2004, 30).

In the trial proper, the prosecution planned its attack by crime base. It began by presenting evidence from Koribundo, a town in Norman's own chiefdom, where it sought to show a pattern of atrocious crimes for which Norman himself would claim responsibility. Next it presented testimony from Kenema, a town in the CDF heartland where it alleged

Figure 4. Freetown and crime bases.

that Kamajors systematically killed police officers and suspected civilian collaborators. Bonthe and Talia Yawbecko, the site for Base Zero, allegedly the nerve centre of CDF operations, were the next stops on this depressing tour. Here, the prosecution provided further testimony to support the counts of the indictment and provided increased evidence of the three accused acting in leadership roles. From Base Zero, the prosecution moved to Bo, Sierra Leone's second largest town located in the heart of Mende country. There, it unveiled a policy of systematically targeting members of ethnic groups Kamajors associated with rebels and junta. Tongo, situated in Sierra Leone's diamond fields was the next stop. Here, the pattern of ethnic and civilian killings continued in the wake of Kamajors' occupation of the area. Finally, the prosecution moved its case to Moyamba District, where it attempted to demonstrate a widespread and systematic pattern of legal violations in Bradford and its surrounds. To make good its offensive, the prosecution called victim-witnesses who primarily narrated the occurrence of the crimes charged in the indictment, 'insider witnesses', primarily used to place the accused in the frame of responsibility and 'expert witnesses', who attempted to connect the dots of the case by bridging the gaps left between the two. In the rest of this section, I will focus on a few highlights of testimony which were to prove particularly important to the judgment, and hence to my own analysis.

On 4 June 2004, the prosecution began with the Koribundo crime base, leading eight witnesses.[6] Between them, they described how up until the 1997 coup, the Kamajors had been living in Koribundo relatively peaceably with Sierra Leonean Army soldiers (the 'SLA' or 'soldiers'). After the coup, the Kamajors evacuated the town, and later launched a number of assaults to try to dislodge the soldiers, who were now loyal to the AFRC junta. All of these were repelled, but after a CDF attack on Friday 13 February 1998, soldiers abandoned Koribundo. One or two days later, the Kamajors marched into town and went on a looting, killing and burning spree. To give just one example, witness TF2-159 testified to the killing of five Limba palm-wine tappers, two of whom – Sarrah and Momoh – were decapitated, their heads placed at a junction. In another episode, he described the murder of eight captives, two of whom, the wives of soldiers, were killed by having sticks forced into their genitals until they exited their mouths; they were then disembowelled and parts of their intestines were eaten. In another incident, he returned one day to find his own house burned, with his grandparents inside it. The same witness counted twenty-five houses burned along the Blama Road, having earlier seen Kamajors torch houses, joking that they were 'burning their farm'. Crucially, some weeks after these events, Sam Hinga Norman apparently arrived in town and took responsibility for the Kamajor's actions in a public meeting. He claimed that he had instructed the Kamajors to leave only three houses standing in Koribundo, and admonished them for not destroying more. He also told the town's inhabitants not to blame Kamajors for the destruction wrought on Koribundo, but to blame him instead (SCSL 2004e, 9 September 2004).

[6] Together, witnesses TF2-198, TF2-157, TF2-176, TF2-012, TF2-162, TF2-159, TF2-032 and TF2-140. Note that the Prosecutor had determined that his investigative and prosecutorial teams, much like that of a military operation, should be divided into task forces. Hence, as the CDF trial began, witnesses were labelled with a 'TF2-' tag-line, signifying that they belonged to the investigations undertaken by 'Task Force Two'. Nearly all the witnesses that testified in the trial did so using a 'TF2-' pseudonym and from behind a screen, in order to preserve their anonymity.

I turn next to Bonthe District, home to the village of Talia, the site for 'Base Zero'. The prosecution called six witnesses.[7] They variously described an attack on Bonthe Town which saw the by now familiar pattern of looting, burning, unlawful killing and inhumane treatment of civilians. One of the prosecution's most lucid witnesses here was John Garrick (TF2-147), a Bonthe parish priest. In a lengthy testimony he described a delegation to meet with Kondewa at Base Zero. They found him sitting on his veranda while a small boy sang praise songs on a locally made guitar. After imprisoning them, 'King' Kondewa explained to them his uncompromising philosophy of war: 'according to him, war means to know that you will die; to know that you have no control over your life; to know that you have no dignity; to know that your property is not yours. According to him, that is what all war is about, and that is war' (SCSL 2004e, 10 November 2004, 21). Later, he testified about the occupation of Bonthe by Kamajors on 15 February 1998, having witnessed looting, extortion, and the corpses of civilians killed by Kamajors, which partly corroborated other testimonies. He narrated how Kamajor Commander Morie Jusu Kamara claimed that he could not control the Kamajors, since they were under the authority of Kondewa, who apparently received field reports of their actions. To release prisoners, Garrick paid bribes, and in one case he enlisted the help of Kondewa to secure safe passage of a chiefdom speaker. Several other witnesses described crimes that took place at Base Zero itself, crimes for which Kondewa was implicated to a greater or lesser degree. Most significantly, TF2-096, a 37-year-old woman, described an incident in which Kondewa personally shot a man.[8]

After hearing from the crime bases of Koribundo, Kenema and Bonthe, the case moved to the town of Bo, Sierra Leone's second town. Ten witnesses testified to events surrounding the Kamajor occupation.[9] In a pattern that supported multiple counts of the indictment, they narrated tales of looting, burning, unlawful killing, cruel and inhumane

[7] Witnesses TF2-096, TF2-086, TF2-116, TF2-004 (who testified to events mainly in the Pujehun District), TF2-147, TF2-071.

[8] Talia was returned to in Trial Session Five, when six women testified to their experiences there. Their testimony was constrained by a previous ruling which controversially prohibited the admission into evidence of any testimony relating to sexual violence; nevertheless their accounts contained direct evidence of crimes committed at Base Zero, and indirect evidence of Kondewa's responsibility for them; indeed, one of the witnesses emotionally confronted Kondewa in court. See Kelsall and Stepakoff (2007).

[9] Witnesses TF2-119, TF2-030, TF2-156, TF2-088, TF2-057, TF2-067, TF2-007, TF2-058, TF2-056, TF2-006.

treatment, and terrorising the civilian population. To give one example, TF2-119 was a Bo police officer who in a long, clear, gripping and linear narrative, described how he was robbed and mutilated by Kamajors, and how he then cheated death on several more occasions before being rescued by ECOMOG (SCSL 2004e, 23 November 2004). To give another, TF2-001 was a police officer who described being tortured by Kamajors, witnessing them killing unarmed police officers at the police barracks, and seeing them beating three of his colleagues. He also spoke about a meeting in Bo at which Hinga Norman said he was disappointed to see so many police officers alive and to find the police barracks still standing (SCSL 2004e, 14 February 2005).

The next crime base, testified to in the Fourth Session of the trial, was Tongo, to which the Prosecution dedicated nine witnesses.[10] The testimony related to three attacks on Tongo town. TF2-047 narrated how some time before the attack, Kamajors had been sending letters to Tongo advising civilians to leave. When Kamajors finally arrived, they ordered civilians to the 'security HQ', where the witness saw the corpses of AFRC soldiers. Commander BJK Sei addressed the Kamajors, telling them not to kill the people. However, after Sei had left, a Kamajor named Kamabote[11] decapitated a man who had been identified as a soldier. Later, the witness buried over 150 bodies, among which some had been chopped, decapitated and disembowelled (SCSL 2004e, 22 February 2005). There were more atrocities in the Tongo environs. For example, in one of the trial's most spectacular testimonies, TF2-015 narrated how he fled Tongo but was stopped at Kambona with a group of other civilians; they were put into lines and his line, containing 65 people, was taken behind a house where one by one its members were shot or hacked to death, before being rolled into a swamp; he himself was hacked on the back of the neck and left for dead, and he had the scars to show for it (SCSL 2004e, 11 February 2005).

The final crime base was Moyamba District, where the counts of the indictment related to incidents in Bradford Town and surrounding villages. Seven witnesses testified to several terrifying crimes.[12] In one of the milder of these testimonies, TF2-073 narrated various episodes of Kamajors harassing civilians from November 1997 onwards, beating

[10] Witnesses TF2-015, TF2-022, TF2-035, TF2-027, TF2-048, TF2-144, TF2-047, TF2-016, TF2-053.

[11] Variant spelling 'Kamagboty', 'Kamabootie'.

[12] TF2-073, TF2-168, TF2-173, TF2-165, TF2-170, TF2-167, TF2-166.

them up and looting their property, including his own car, which was allegedly commandeered for the use of Allieu Kondewa (SCSL 2004e, 2 March 2005).

In addition to this crime-base testimony, the prosecution called three former child soldiers as witnesses, who testified to their experiences in the Kamajor movement. I will examine this testimony in greater detail in Chapter 5.

Insider witnesses

Ordinary witnesses, then, provided voluminous testimony of atrocities that covered all the indictment's counts. To connect that evidence more convincingly to the three accused, the prosecution relied on the testimony of ten ex-Kamajors or 'insider-witnesses'. Some of these were members of the War Council at Base Zero and some were Kamajor commanders.[13] Although rather sketchy when it came to details, especially in the case of Fofana, they tended to give testimony that supported the prosecution's characterisations of the accused as the 'top leaders' or 'executive' of the Kamajor Society: Norman as the 'National Coordinator' and overall commander, Fofana as the 'Director' or 'Director of War', supplying logistics, planning and executing strategies for war operations, and Kondewa as a man who held authority on account of his mystical powers: 'They have the executive power of the Kamajor society. These people – nobody can take decision in the absence of this group. Whatever happen, they come together because they are the leaders and the Kamajor look up to them', said one (SCSL 2004e, 16 November 2004, 51). I will focus here on three insiders: Borbor Tucker, Albert Nallo, and TF2-222.

Borbor Tucker, alias *Jengbema*, commander of the CDF 'Death Squad', was an important witness because he painted a picture of authority relations at Base Zero which was detrimental to all three accused and particularly to Allieu Kondewa. For example, he described a period when Kondewa appeared to be in effective control at Base Zero, instructing and supplying a variety of Death Squad operations in the Bonthe District. Later, he described a meeting at Talia in 1997 from which Norman emerged as the National Coordinator, Fofana as the Director of War, and Kondewa as the High Priest. He described the planning and execution of the attack on Koribundo, in which he participated in some looting, moving from there to occupy Bo, where he saw burned houses

[13] They were: Albert Nallo, Borbor Tucker, TF2-017, TF2-201, TF2-005, TF2-008, TF2-011, TF2-079, TF2-082 and TF2-223.

and looting. In another incident he described recovering looted vehicles for Norman which were distributed to Fofana, Kondewa, and a journalist (SCSL 2004e, 10 February 2005).

TF2-222, another insider, was a War Council member who provided crucial testimony about the planning of the attack on Tongo, which we will return to in Chapter 6. Specifically, he testified to an address Norman made to Kamajors assembled at the Talia parade ground. Norman allegedly told the Kamajors that the battle for Tongo would determine the outcome of the war; that they had no place to keep captured junta and collaborators; and that while the international community was taking care of human rights abuses, they should take care of the 'human left', viz. they should cut off the left hands of juntas or collaborators (SCSL 2004e, 17 February 2005, 104). Norman also told the fighters to spare the houses of those who had burned their own houses, which the witness understood in ironic terms. Moinina Fofana told any fighter who did not accomplish his mission that he should 'kill himself', and Allieu Kondewa said that 'a rebel is a rebel', and the time for surrendering had past.

Most important of all the insiders, however, was Albert Nallo (TF2-014). Nallo was a former mission worker and Kamajor initiate who claimed to have risen to the rank of National Deputy Director of Operations and Regional Director of Operations for the Southern Region. Unusually, Nallo chose to testify in open session. Recorded highlights[14] show him to be a plump, middle-aged, moustachioed man with sloping shoulders and hooded eyes. Sometimes he hunched over the microphone as he spoke; at other times he leaned back in his chair. Occasionally, small smiles or smirks flickered across his lips; at others his eyebrows rose and his brow creased. To me, the small smiles suggesed a barely concealed glee at testifying, while the raised eyebrows said: 'I know this is an incredible sounding story, yet I'm telling you it's true.'[15] Much of the time he seemed to look down towards the floor, though at others he appeared to make eye contact with his audience. Often he answered without hesitation, though there were sometimes long pauses, such as when Ibrahim Yillah, Counsel for Norman, discussing the subject of inconsistencies in his prior statements, asked when and why it was that he finally chose to tell the prosecution the full truth (an exchange discussed at greater length in Chapter 6).

[14] These can be viewed at www.sc-sl.org/Videos/Video-SCSL15.wmv.

[15] Of course, this is an ethnocentric reading from within the context of my own culture.

Nallo described the three accused as 'the Holy Trinity' of the CDF. He testified to three macabre ritual murders in which he participated in the presence of the accused (for a fuller discussion, see Chapter 4). He also described helping Moinina Fofana plan operations for the southern region and gave critical testimony relating to the planning and execution of the Koribundo and Bo attacks. He also described his participation in or knowledge of a series of crimes, many of which could be linked to the accused, especially Norman. For example, he described how he was instructed by Norman to kill 'infiltrators' in nearby villages, and how he subsequently killed around fifteen civilians, burned down nearby Dodo Village, cut the ear off Joseph Lansana, a suspected rebel, threw Lansana's mother into a fire, and killed a man on a motorbike who had some cigarettes. In a later episode, he reported to Norman that Kamajors had killed the Ribbi chiefdom speaker and Norman said he deserved it. On a number of occasions, Norman had intervened to prevent the punishment of Kamajors who had been killing or abusing civilians, he claimed (SCSL 2004e, 10, 11, 14 March 2005). We will return to Nallo in Chapters 3, 4, and 6.

To complete its case, the prosecution also called three expert witnesses. TF2-EW1, Richard Mortimer Iron, was a British military analyst, currently working for NATO. Based on interviews with prosecution witnesses and visits to the field, he charted the evolution of the CDF from a more or less spontaneous movement under the decentralised authority of chiefs, aimed at defending local communities against rebel attacks in the early period of the war, to a more centralised, organised force at Base Zero, geared to a strategic counter-attack on junta positions post-1997. I will discuss Col Iron's testimony at greater length in Chapter 3. TF2-EW2 was an expert witness on the subject of child soldiers, who in closed session testified to initiation being a stepping stone *en route* to military service. William D. Haglund (TF2-EW3), meanwhile, was a forensic anthropologist from Seattle. He testified to having visited and photographed some twenty possible grave-sites, of which he had excavated two, describing injuries to four victims who died by a combination of sharp and blunt force blows. The findings on manner of death tended to corroborate previously heard eye-witness testimony that described murders committed by Kamajors,[16] and the photographs of slashed limbs

[16] We can infer that the bodies belonged to the brothers of witness TF2-156, a witness who on 25 November 2004 testified to events in Bo, and who spoke – rather confusingly it has to be said – about identifying the bodies to the Special Court, which exhumed them.

and shattered skulls were certainly compelling. But the fact that only these two small graves had been investigated, rather than the alleged mass graves in Tongo, spoke volumes about the poverty of the forensic evidence in this case.

To sum up, ordinary prosecution witnesses delivered a great deal of evidence, covering a wide area, of unlawful killings, physical violence, collective punishments, cruel and inhumane treatment, looting and burning, and some use of child soldiers in the various crime bases. The defendants were linked to these events by a smaller volume of evidence that appeared to show them acting in positions of responsibility: for example, Norman's speeches in Koribundo and Bo, the testimony of John Garrick and the Talia women about Kondewa's role at Base Zero. This was reinforced by the testimony of insider witnesses, who, as well as directly implicating the accused in individual crimes, painted a picture of Base Zero as a hub for Kamajor operations where the accused held positions of command responsibility, planning attacks on locations such as Koribundo, Bo and Tongo that would systematically violate the laws of war, and failing to take action against subordinates whom they knew to have violated such laws. There was also the testimony of various closed session witnesses to consider, which presumably made the case still stronger. To complete things, expert witness Col. Richard Iron testified to the CDF having a recognisable hierarchical military command structure post-1997, at the apex of which were the accused.[17]

THE DEFENCE CASE

This then was the scale of the offensive against which the accused had to muster a defence. According to my reading of the trial, it ranged its case along five main lines. The first was an attempt to impeach the credibility of prosecution witnesses, by pointing to ambiguities or impossibilities in their testimonies, or to inconsistencies between their pre-trial statements and courtroom testimony, often confronting them with the charge that the events they described were 'a figment of your imagination'. We will examine the credibility of witnesses in more detail in Chapter 6. The second was led by Fofana and consisted in a challenge to the prosecution's theory of command responsibility,

[17] At the close of the prosecution case, the defence teams submitted motions of acquittal for their respective clients. The Chamber dismissed these, though it did throw out a handful of the prosecution's allegations, most of which related to the 'Black December' operation (SCSL 2005c).

drawing heavily on the testimony of Daniel Hoffman, an American anthropologist. We will scrutinise this defence in Chapter 3. The third came from Kondewa and constituted a challenge to the prosecution's theory that initiation was a form of military recruitment, together with additional exculpatory evidence of supernatural beliefs. We will look at this more closely in Chapter 4. The fourth, to be discussed in a moment, was led by the Norman team and took the form of a challenge to the court's mandate, its constitutionality, and its politics. This strategy dovetailed with cross-examinations that sought to widen the context of discussion, pointing to the general ethics or politics of the war. The final line was led by all the teams and consisted in an assortment of counter-theories for the different crime bases, which I will consider at the end of this section.

Politics

Politics played a pivotal role in the CDF defence. Many people in the country were former Kamajors, many regarded Kamajors as saviours of the nation, and many in the public regarded Hinga Norman as a national hero. Perhaps it was these facts that inspired the Prosecutor to attempt to make a distinction between political and criminal acts in his opening statement: 'Despite the obvious political dimensions of this conflict', Crane said, 'these trials – this trial is about crimes ... war crimes and crimes against humanity' (2004e, 3 June 2004, 7).[18] Going on to say,

> The issues before you are not – cannot be political. We have not charged political crimes. The court of law – this Chamber must focus on the alleged acts of these jointly charged indictees; politics must remain barred from these proceedings.
>
> (2004e, 3 June 2004 12.)

And yet, from the trial's very beginning, Norman tried hard to make the proceedings a political affair. For example, the trial began with a number of dramatic episodes in which he first dismissed his entire legal team, then asked to be tried in absentia, and then accepted court-appointed counsel.[19] When the trial resumed on 15 June, he made a brief opening statement in which he refused to recognise the legitimacy of the

[18] Elsewhere, I have argued that court conventions and procedures put limits on what was sayable in the courtroom, producing an 'anti-political' regime of truth (Kelsall 2006b).

[19] Obviously this echoed to some extent events in the Milosevic trial (Boas 2007).

court, claiming, *inter alia*, that it lacked constitutional authority: 'there is or are no charges legally placed before this Chamber against me' (SCSL 2004e, 15 June 2004, 3). Since these arguments had already been dismissed at pre-trial stage, they were unlikely to cut much ice with the judges. However, it was clear that Norman was at least as interested in being tried in the court of public opinion as he was in a court of law, and at the close of his speech Norman's supporters, who took up more than half of the public gallery, cheered and jubilantly waved their arms, provoking the following judicial response:

> Please, this is not – I'm sorry, let me warn the gallery, please. This is not a political forum, it's not a political arena, and if anybody is caught behaving as if he were in a political arena, he will be called upon to withdraw from this courtroom … Please, you are here to follow the proceedings which are judicial proceedings. We are not here in politics.
>
> (SCSL 2004e, 15 June 2004, 5.)

Later on, Norman boycotted most of the proceedings – another political gesture.[20]

When he did attend, Norman frequently used his cross-examinations to try and widen the field of debate: to go beyond a narrow description of events to the broader context of war, and, by implication, to shift moral responsibility away from him and onto larger social forces: 'What I'm trying to achieve is in fact to assist the Prosecutors that the investigation in this country, based on this case, is of significance and is relevant to issues that occurred in this country. And it all emanated from this conflict in Sierra Leone that went to international bodies, started in fact from these incidents' (SCSL 2004e, 17 June 2004, 26–7). This was a tactic also used by his counsel: 'Did you ever hear that Chief Norman saved the people of Jaiama Bongor chiefdom?', 'Did you hear or did you see the Kamajors repel RUF attacks?', 'Can you tell the court why you gave the prosecution no record of Chief Norman protecting lives and property in Koribundo?', 'And would you agree that they were therefore – the Kamajors, they were therefore defending both the local people and the government of the country?', a tactic also employed by counsel for the third accused, Charles Margai, 'the people of Bonthe were yearning for the Kamajors to come to their rescue'.[21] These attempts to elicit exculpatory evidence, however, often ran aground on the rules of cross-examination and the

[20] The initial pretext was that Norman objected to the witnesses being screened from the public.
[21] Video summary, 1–12 November 2004: www.sc-sl.org/video.html.

conventions of courtroom discourse, together with the judge's preconceptions of the kind of evidence 'material' to the case. Even though later on the Bench relaxed these strictures a little, the defence by then had become self-disciplining, knowing that there were lines it could not cross. This perhaps explained, when it came to the defence case, Norman's determination to deny every charge the prosecution laid against him, rather than to admit some of the charges but claim mitigating circumstances on political grounds.

Politics was also evident in the defence's attempts to implicate President Kabbah. Kabbah, as well as being President, was the Minister for Defence when Norman was Deputy Defence Minister and National Coordinator of the CDF. The obvious implication, only insinuated at trial, was that Norman was merely following orders. Indeed, he challenged the prosecution's characterisation of him as the CDF supreme military commander with the idea that he was merely a civilian administrator and go-between for ECOMOG, the Kamajors, and the exiled government in Guinea. To shed more light on this, Norman gave notice of his intention to call Kabbah as the first witness in his defence, and submitted a request to *subpoena* him on grounds that his evidence would be necessary to the purpose of conducting the trial. Kabbah, however, declined the request, while the Sierra Leone Attorney General appeared in court to argue against the need to issue a *subpoena*, issuing veiled threats: 'assuming that your Lordships grant the *subpoena*, we submit and we request that this Honourable Court should not act in vain. No court in any part of the world has ever made orders that will make them look – that will diminish their authority because it's difficult to enforce' (SCSL 2004e, 14 February 2006, 74). Asked by Justice Boutet to clarify these remarks, he replied that even were the Court to issue a *subpoena*, he could not imagine himself issuing a warrant for the President's arrest. On 15 June 2006, with Norman's case almost complete, the majority judges rejected the defence motion, and with it the contention that Kabbah's testimony would be necessary to the trial. In a separate concurring opinion, Justice Itoe opined that Kabbah, as Head of State, had immunity from the Court, and that to *subpoena* one of the 'Princes who govern us' would be to act in vain, and may even threaten, 'the interests of peace, law and order and the stability of the Country'! (SCSL 2006a) Needless to say, this was not the rule of law's finest hour.[22]

[22] Judge Thompson, to his credit, dissented from the majority opinion.

Counter-theories

As the trial wore on it became increasingly apparent that defence counsels Bu-Buakei Jabbi, John Wesley Hall, Quincy Whitaker, Ibrahim Yillah (Norman); Michiel Pestman, Victor Koppe, Arrow Bockarie, Steven Powles (Fofana); and Charles Margai and Yada Williams (Kondewa), had a number of working counter-theories which bore differently on the evidence. I will discuss these by crime base. In respect of Koribundo, the defence's theory was that Jaiama-Bongor, the amalgamated chiefdom in which Koribundo was situated, and of which Hinga Norman was Regent Chief, was riven by factional rivalry. Norman had located his chiefdom seat in Telu in the Bongor section of Jaiama-Bongor, and was allegedly thought by Jaiama residents to favour this part. Thus Koribundo residents – Koribundo being located in Jaiama – bore him a grudge. Added to this, there was a split in Koribundo between those citizens, mostly elders, who profited from and favoured collaboration with the AFRC junta, and those, mostly youths, whose loyalties lay with the Kamajors. Insofar as any illegal events took place in the attack on Koribundo, then, they could be laid at the door of these youths, or else with the departing soldiers. Meanwhile, all the witnesses who testified against Norman could be regarded as pursuing a local political vendetta.

For Bo, the defence relied heavily on the idea that the authors of atrocities were 'Kamabels', that is, soldiers or rebels who disguised themselves as Kamajors. The idea that looting, burning and killing was conducted by township vigilantes also figured. For Bonthe, defence counsel tried to suggest that the junta had used civilians as human shields, hence the civilian corpses in the town, and it tried to chip away at the credibility of individual witnesses, but there was little in the way of a counter-theory. For Tongo, the thrust of the defence seemed to be that civilians killed at the NDMC were caught in a stampede, or a cross-fire. For Moyamba, the defence tried to insinuate that the crimes in evidence were the expression of numerous local personal vendettas, not the result of some centrally organised plan.

Counsel did succeed in eliciting some scraps of evidence to support these counter-theories. Michiel Pestman, for example, got TF2-159 to admit that civilians joined Kamajors in looting and burning Koribundo, and that it was Kamajor commander Joe Tamidey who put a stop to the burning (SCSL 2004e, 9 September 2004). TF2-032 eventually agreed with Norman that he had referred to a split between groups in his Koribundo speech. The same witness admitted to Charles Margai that his people had been unhappy about the amalgamation of Jaiama and Bongor chiefdoms, that the relations between soldiers and civilians in 1998 were lukewarm and confusing, that there was a group of 'vigilantes' in the town, and that Jo Tamidey disciplined errant Kamajors (SCSL 2004e, 13 September 2004). For Bonthe, Arrow Bockarie got John Garrick to admit that no particular group of Kamajors was in control (SCSL 2004e, 10 November 2004). Margai had TF2-071 say that the actions of the Kamajors had the endorsement of the President and Attorney General (SCSL 2004e, 11 November 2004). Insider witness TF2-008 seemed to admit that Kamajors were organised locally, rather than centrally, and that communication between Base Zero and areas such as the Eastern Front was poor (SCSL 2004e, 16 November 2004). The same witness gave evidence of some of the good deeds of the Peace Office, of which Moinina Fofana was in charge. Counsel for Kondewa Yada Williams showed him some minutes which appeared to show the War Council directing CDF restructuring and appointments, though their significance remained ambiguous (SCSL 2004e, 16 November 2004). Victor Koppe established from Bob Tucker that Moinina Fofana told Kamajors neither to loot, burn, kill civilians or kill enemy soldiers. Margai got him to admit that there were taboos against harming civilians, and that Kamajor commanders had a large amount of discretion on the battlefield (SCSL 2004e, 10 February 2005). At Tongo, TF2-022 agreed with Counsel that no-one was really in charge at the NDMC (SCSL 2004e, 11 February 2005). Victor Koppe confronted TF2-005, a member of the War Council, with a letter to show that the War Council had appointed Fofana and Kondewa. In addition, the witness admitted that although the CDF had central command, its area of operation was so wide that sometimes fighters acted on their own. Back at the NDMC, TF2-027 agreed with Yada Williams that some of the casualties died in a stampede (SCSL 2004e, 22 February 2005), as did TF2-048, who also admitted that the Kamajors appeared to be without clear control (SCSL 2004e, 23 February 2005). In Moyamba, it was clear that the killing of TF2-166's father was partly motivated by the fact that he was a creditor to his killers (SCSL 2004e, 8 March 2005). Albert Nallo confirmed that when the AFRC retook Bo, they were disguised as Kamajors (SCSL 2004e, 14 March 2005). Ibrahim Yillah's cross of TF2-079 provided some evidence of imperfect communication between Base Zero and the field (SCSL 2004e, 26 May 2005). Koppe confirmed that Moinina Fofana was illiterate, so any frontline reports were for onward transmission to Chief Norman.

These fragments and others like them gave some support to the defence's attempts to re-appraise the prosecution's characterisations of their clients. Norman, as we have already seen, was a mere go-between. Fofana, rather than a military strategist, was simply an aide-de-camp to Norman, or the guy who held the keys to the ammunition store. Kondewa, rather than a man capable of recruiting and directing fighters on account of his presumed supernatural powers, was merely the equivalent of a conventional army priest. All of them were subordinate to the War Council, or to ECOMOG, or to the government in Guinea. Individual Kamajors, meanwhile, were subordinate to chiefdom authorities.

Witnesses for the defence

The counter-theories were given mixed support by the defence's own witnesses. First up was Norman himself. Norman's evidence, which took several days to recount, told a melancholy story of how he, a loyal and humble servant, had risen through the ranks of public service only to be unfortunately and unjustly accused and imprisoned on three separate occasions, the final and most altitudinous fall culminating in his present predicament. The precise details of his role as CDF National Coordinator, however, remained unclear. Norman claimed that instructions to fighters at the front flowed through ECOMOG, 'When they were not under ECOMOG control, they would be under their own commanders on the spot in the field' (SCSL 2004e, 27 January 2004, 100); that he was never a member of the War Council, but that he was grateful for their advice; that it was the War Council that gave orders to Joe Tamidey in the Koribundo operation; that Koribundo was divided into factions, and that at the meetings he held there he told the audience that it was *not only* the Kamajors who were to blame for the town's destruction, but the soldiers, civilians and in particular the elders also; he told the Court that he had heard of a Death Squad, a local defence unit, but he had never seen it; that Tongo Field was an operation organised by ECOMOG and he had no knowledge of the crimes committed there, nor in Bonthe, nor Moyamba; that only towards the end of the war did he become aware of the participation of children in Kamajor hostilities, and then he made strenuous efforts to stamp out the practice, even rehabilitating some ex-combatants himself. Albert Nallo, he said, was a man of 'mild inconsistency' and one of the ritual murders he attributed to Norman was 'a wicked lie'. Moinina Fofana, meanwhile, was simply one of the elders at Talia, becoming Director of War in 1999. He did not spend a lot of time with either Fofana or Kondewa. He summarised his role as: 'to receive whatever was a support, whether in the form of arms, ammunition, food, medicine, transport, from ECOMOG and then have it delivered to the men on the ground through their commanders and this was done between myself and the one appointment that had been made in the person of MS Kallon as administrator' (SCSL 2004e, 6 February 2006, 93–4). Kevin Tavener for the prosecution summarised Norman's approach well:

Q. So, to put it simply, your defence is to deny each and every criminal allegation made against you by witnesses that have been called by the Prosecution.

A. I deny them, My Lord.

Q. Isn't it the truth, Chief Norman, that you find yourself wholly unable to answer these allegations and have simply resorted to blanket denial of everything to escape the consequences of your action.' (SCSL 2004e, 7 February 2006, 81.)[23]

In addition, the defence put up a series of witnesses who offered their versions of the conflict's events, sometimes adding weight to the defence's counter-theories, sometimes serving as a direct counterpoint to prosecution evidence. For example, Albert Joe Demby, Vice-President at the time of the interregnum, explained how, after the restoration of the legitimate government, he was part of a committee that investigated alleged abuses by Kamajors, but in most cases they found nothing. When asked by the prosecution 'who was in charge of the Kamajors during the junta period?', Demby said it was the 'chiefs in their chiefdoms'; he knew Hinga Norman was not in charge, nor Moinina Fofana (SCSL 2004e, 15 February 2006, 32–3). In addition, the defence presented witnesses who, like Norman, offered blanket denials of all the charges laid at the Kamajors' door, sometimes to the point of implausibility, which gave strong grounds for thinking that they were partisan witnesses of the sort referred to by Sally Falk Moore (see Chapter 1). To give just one example, MT Collier testified to the growth of the Kamajors via mass initiations around Talia. He told how the people of Talia requested Norman to come from Liberia and assist them in defending the community against the soldiers. Regarding Norman's role: 'He was just there. Whatever the Kamajors wanted, he would go and tell the President. Whatever the President said, he would bring the answer, the reply' (SCSL 2004e, 16 February 2006, 91–2). He claimed it was not the job of the accused to direct operations: 'That was not their job at all. They didn't send anybody to go and fight'

[23] Note that Fofana and Kondewa chose not to testify in their own defence.

(SCSL 2004e, 17 February 2006, 17). But under cross-examination, he was evasive on the subject of the Death Squad, the *Poro* Bush, child soldiers, and prisoners at Base Zero. Exasperated, the prosecution asked: 'Mr Collier, can you tell us anything about what the Kamajors were doing in 1997 through to 1998 in Talia', to which the reply was, 'Just that I saw them being supplied with rice, they would cook that rice and eat and they would depart' (SCSL 2004e, 17 February 2006, 67). Several Defence witnesses even scored own-goals. For example, Billoh Conteh, who was an in-law of Fofana, said that when he visited Base Zero he was too timid to approach Fofana, since he was the kind of man you would only speak to when summoned, and all the Kamajors feared him (SCSL 2004e, 28 September 2006, 49). Baimba Jobai said of Kondewa that: 'if someone initiates you, you would have to fear that person … he's your Kamoh, and you have to respect and fear him, (SCSL 2004e, 12 October 2006, 87–8). Chief Joseph Ali-Kavura Kongomoh II, paramount chief of Fakunya District, claimed that one had to be eighteen years old to be initiated as a Kamajor, but was forced by the prosecution to admit that upon initiation his own grandson was under eighteen (SCSL 2004e, 4 June 2006, 87).

To sum up, the defence succeeded through cross-examination to raise question marks over the credibility of many of the prosecution's witnesses, and to secure a slender amount of evidence to support its own counter-theories. Some of its own witnesses bolstered those counter-theories, but many of them proved unreliable on the stand, actually contradicting each other, themselves, or the testimony of the first accused. Add to this the fact that many witnesses were evasive or uncooperative and seemed determined merely to deny, to the point of implausibility, all the evidence unflattering to the Kamajors and the accused, and one could be forgiven for thinking that the defence was in a stronger position *before* it called its own witnesses than after it had rested its case.

CLOSING ARGUMENTS

In his closing statement on 28 November 2006, Christopher Staker summarised the prosecution's case:

> The case is that the three accused, Norman, Fofana and Kondewa established unchallenged control and authority over the CDF, and that they used their unrivalled positions to create an ordered framework under which the CDF operated throughout the war against the so-called rebels. The three accused had a number of options as to how that war would

> be conducted and the option chosen by the three accused was to implement a strategy of winning the war at all costs. And, in order to do this, of adopting a policy of attacking, neutralising and/or punishing anyone they considered to be a rebel or a collaborator of the rebels.
>
> (SCSL 2004e, 28 November 2006, 24.)

The CDF was not an inherently criminal organisation he said; however: 'those who formulated and caused the implementation of a policy that included attacks on civilians and captured combatants, and the use of child soldiers, crossed the line into the realm of criminality' (SCSL 2004e, 28 November 2006, 25).

Staker then moved to questions of evidence. In the prosecution's view, and perhaps reflecting the weakness of some of the individual testimonies, each item of evidence, he said, 'had to be looked at in light of all of the evidence as a whole' (SCSL 2004e, 28 November 2006, 25). The idea that the crimes of which the Court had heard resulted from the uncoordinated actions of individual Kamajors was not credible, he argued, once the evidence was taken *in toto* (SCSL 2004e, 28 November 2006, 28). And even though much of the evidence was uncorroborated, the fact that it fitted within a general pattern must, he said, go to its weight (SCSL 2004e, 28 November 2006, 29). Further, he claimed, to establish guilt beyond reasonable doubt, it was not necessary to prove every single fact beyond reasonable doubt (SCSL 2004e, 28 November 2006, 29).

Driving home the prosecution's attack, Kevin Tavener argued that the only reasonable explanation for the near simultaneity of the CDF attacks around the country, was that there was a central command unit (SCSL 2004e, 28 November 2006, 79). The Norman defence would argue, he said, that the Kamajors were under the control of ECOMOG and chieftain leaders, but ECOMOG were not even in the country between May 1997 and February 1998 (SCSL 2004e, 28 November 2006, 89). Rounding up, he claimed that: 'all the evidence points to one inescapable conclusion. The three accused exercised absolute control over the CDF, and the CDF concomitantly followed the orders of the three accused ... Each of the three men, finally, the Prosecution submits, are criminally responsible for the offences now before you on the indictment' (SCSL 2004e, 28 November 2006, 100).

Next it was the defence's turn. Speaking on behalf of Hinga Norman, Dr Bu Buakei Jabbi complained that, owing to the vagueness of the indictment, there had been a prejudice against Norman all along (SCSL 2004e, 28 November 2006, 108) and consequently the weight of the evidence against him should be considerably reduced (SCSL 2004e, 28 November 2006, 119). As Staker had anticipated, he proceeded to argue that the prosecution had failed to reach a burden of proof sufficient to convict Norman beyond reasonable doubt, and pointed to the fact that several of what he called 'very significant' pieces of evidence were either hearsay, or lacked corroboration (SCSL 2004e, 28 November 2006, 122–7). Taking another tack, he pointed to exhibits which purported to show that ECOMOG and the government of Sierra Leone were clearly in control of the Kamajors (SCSL 2004e, 29 November 2006, 4), including supplying them arms and ammunition (Transcript, 29 November 2006, 5). He argued that the concept of 'greatest responsibility' destroyed the presumption of innocence (SCSL 2004e, 29 November 2006, 12), and finally, he argued that the court was unlawful, not having been correctly incorporated into Sierra Leonean law (SCSL 2004e, 29 November 2006 14–16).[24]

After Jabbi had spoken, Steven Powles tore into the Prosecution's case against Fofana. Not only did Fofana not bear the greatest responsibility for the crimes of the Kamajors, he said, Fofana bears 'absolutely no responsibility' (SCSL 2004e, 29 November 2006, 28). Powles rebutted prosecution allegations one by one, occasionally making them appear ridiculous, as when he pointed out that the prosecution's claim that 'Fofana was perceived by the majority of witnesses as being an important person, someone from whom orders originated and were enforced', was based on a CDF wall calendar. More importantly, when it came to TF2-222's evidence about the attack on Tongo, in which Fofana allegedly gave support to Norman's alleged instructions to kill enemy collaborators and burn their houses, Powles pointed out that Fofana's actual words were 'Just hold your ground', which most probably indicated support for a perfectly legitimate previous strategic instruction, words he followed with, 'any commander failing to perform accordingly and losing your ground, just decide to kill yourself there and don't come and report to us'. 'Suicide', observed Powles, was not a crime under the statute of the Special Court (SCSL 2004e, 29 November 2006, 51–2). Albert Nallo, the prosecution's star witness, was, claimed Powles 'a reprehensible, cold-blooded, murderous liar', naming other members of the CDF in court in a frenzied and frantic attempt to save his own skin (SCSL 2004e, 29 November 2006,

[24] This was a claim for which the judges had little patience, since it had already been ruled upon by the Appeals Chamber and the Supreme Court of Sierra Leone (SCSL 2004e, 29 November 2006, 22).

61–2). On the question of supplying the Kamajors with arms, ECOMOG, President Kabbah, Mustapha Lumeh and others supplied arms as well as Fofana, who only did so on the instruction of Norman. 'For this reason we say Fofana can, in many ways, be said to be a glorified storekeeper, shopkeeper, keymaster, door opener; call him what you will. The man was a relative nobody' (SCSL 2004e, 29 November 2006, 63).

Finally, it was the turn of Allieu Kondewa. Speaking on his behalf, Yada Williams opined that: 'our client, Mr Kondewa, sitting over there looking rather relaxed in his usual smiling face, did not commit any of the crimes alleged in the indictment' (SCSL 2004e, 30 November 2006, 27). The prosecution, he claimed, had 'left the reality at Talia Yawbecko and … brought fiction to Freetown' (SCSL 2004e, 30 November 2006, 29). On the question of command responsibility, Williams submitted that Kondewa lacked the power or authority to discipline troops. The prosecution had presented no evidence to show that he could do so; no evidence to show that following initiation, the Kamajors were under his spell (SCSL 2004e, 30 November 2006, 51). That Kamajors were scattered all over Sierra Leone further weakened the credibility of the prosecution's claim (SCSL 2004e, 30 November 2006 54). There was also an important distinction to be made, he said, between initiation and immunisation – processes that were close to tribal custom – as well as between those practices and enlistment and recruitment, a distinction the prosecution had failed to draw. In particular, Williams, as we shall see in Chapter 4, drew attention to the oaths Kamajors swore against harming civilians, which were tantamount, he implied, to an education in the laws of war (SCSL 2004e, 30 November 2006, 32, 38). Further, there was a huge difference, he thought, 'between going to war with somebody's blessing and going to war after being blessed by someone'. The latter did not connote approval, he thought, but 'can be compared with wishing someone a safe journey' (SCSL 2004e, 30 November 2006, 38). In that light: 'We would submit that what Kondewa did was to bestow a blessing on [the Kamajors], just as a pastor or vicar would on a British or American soldier going to war' (SCSL 2004e, 30 November 2006, 38).

THE DEATH OF THE FIRST ACCUSED

On several occasions during the course of the trial, Norman complained about his health. Indeed, on the day of the closing statements, he sent a Delphic message to Court saying that he would not attend for reasons that he would tell only to the judges. Later on that day he did appear in chamber, and expressed his concerns about his health: 'the condition is deteriorating every day right up to today. And it is my fear that after the Court retires to consider its decision, my condition will be neglected even further and worse' (SCSL 2004e, 28 November 2006, 78–9). In January 2007 the Court sent Norman for an operation in Senegal to replace the hip injured at the time of his arrest,[25] and on 22 February, while in post-operative care, he collapsed and died. His death sparked controversy in Sierra Leone, with some media voices doubting the authenticity of the Court-appointed autopsy and inquiry, and with speculation that he had been murdered, either by the Court itself, or by the SLPP, against which he had begun to speak out.[26] Trial Chamber One decreed immediately that it would not issue a verdict in his case. The Sierra Leonean people, then, would be denied an answer to the question of whether or not one of their most cherished, if most controversial sons was guilty of war crimes.

JUDGMENT AND APPEAL

Approximately six months later, the Chamber handed down its judgment. It presented its factual findings in the form of a narrative charting the rise and decline of the Kamajor Society within the Civil Defence Forces, constructed out of the evidence it found relevant and credible, drawing from both defence and prosecution, but tending to place more weight on the side of the latter. Thus it found that the Kamajor Society was formed in 1991 and 1992 as an initiative of Dr Alpha Lavalie and Dr Albert Joe Demby. In 1996, the paramount chiefs appointed Sam Hinga Norman as Chairman for the Southern Region (SCSL 2007d, 16–17). Following the coup on 25 May 1997, the Kamajors took to the bush, reassembling some time later in the Pujehun District. There followed a meeting between Norman, Kabbah, representatives of foreign missions and ECOMOG in Guinea-Conakry. It was decided that Norman should use 'the hunters' to help restore the legitimate government. On 15 June 1997, Kabbah established the CDF, and appointed Norman as the National Coordinator. His mandate was to coordinate CDF activities with ECOMOG, and to obtain assistance and logistics

[25] Apparently, Norman had had a problem with this hip that pre-dated his arrest. Peter Andersen, personal communication, June 2008.

[26] For an example, see *Awareness Times*, Sierra Leone News and Information, 1 August 2007: http://news.sl/drwebsite/publish/article_20056151.shtml, accessed on 29 September 2007.

from ECOMOG in Liberia. Norman subsequently went to Liberia, from where he returned to Gendema in Pujehun District with munitions (SCSL 2007d, 18–20).

Contemporaneously, some of the residents of Talia in the Bonthe District, including Moinina Fofana and Borbor Tucker, vowed to resist the military government, forming a militia of twenty men under the command of Tucker which they called The Death Squad. Subsequently, they held a meeting with Allieu Kondewa, 'who was chief initiator at that time' (SCSL 2007d, 91–92). The group decided to send a delegation to Norman expressing their solidarity with him. Kondewa, meanwhile, continued to initiate fighters and to give orders to the Death Squad, setting himself up as a minor king (SCSL 2007d, 93). In late August 1997, Kondewa was visited by a delegation from the town of Bonthe, complaining about Kamajors mistreating civilians in the surrounding area. In spite of this the violations continued (SCSL 2007d, 93–4).

Norman arrived in Talia by helicopter on around the 15 September 1997, naming the village 'Base Zero'. Over the next six months, thousands of civilians travelled to Base Zero for military training and to be initiated into the Kamajors; in addition, it became the main base for distributing logistics. Norman took charge, but was unable or unwilling to prevent Kamajor atrocities, which led the Talia elders to propose setting up a War Council to advise him. The War Council worked well at first, but it soon became clear that Norman did not want an organ to check his power and he began to take decisions without it. Meanwhile, some members of the War Council were intimidated by Kamajors, with the connivance of Allieu Kondewa, which rendered it and its disciplinary recommendations ineffective (SCSL 2007d, 90–102).

There followed crucial findings on the planning of CDF operations at Base Zero, drawn mainly from prosecution witnesses. For example, the Chamber found that between 10 and 12 December 1997, the three accused held a mass meeting at the Talia parade ground, where they gave instructions to Kamajors for the operations in Tongo Field and Black December. The account of this meeting (based largely on the testimony of TF2-222), which was to prove pivotal to the judgment, will be discussed at length in Chapter 6. Following it, Norman held a meeting with Kamajor commanders in a secret location, where he advised them not to spare anyone working for the juntas or mining for them, saying that all collaborators should have their property taken and be killed. Fofana and Kondewa contributed to the discussion, though the Chamber did not know in what way, and Fofana was placed in charge of supplying the operation (SCSL 2007d, 102–4).

In early January 1998, Norman called another mass meeting at the training grounds. Here, he gave instructions for 'an all-out offensive' in all of the junta areas including in Koribundo and Bo. He said: 'whoever knows that he is used to fighting with the cutlass, it is time for him to take up the cutlass[; w]hoever knows that he's used to fighting with a gun, it is time for him to take up the gun[; w]hoever knows that he's used to fight with a stick, it is time for him to take up his stick' (SCSL 2007d, 105). Fofana also spoke, and advised commanders who failed to accomplish their missions not to return to Base Zero. He also told them to 'destroy the soldiers' and to 'go and capture Koribundo'. Kondewa then promised to bestow his blessings and medicines on the fighters. Subsequently, a commanders' meeting was held, at which Norman told commander Joe Tamidey that Koribundo should be taken 'at all costs', that only three buildings should be allowed to stand, and that he should kill the remaining inhabitants as rebels (SCSL 2007d, 105–6). In a second meeting that day, at which Fofana and Kondewa were also present, Norman discussed with commanders the forthcoming attack on Bo Town. He told them to kill enemy combatants and people with connections to the rebels, to burn houses and loot big shops and pharmacies. He instructed James Kailie and Joseph Lappia to go and attack Kebi, a town near Bo. Fofana provided the supplies. In another meeting in early February 1998, Norman met with Albert Nallo to discuss the Koribundo and Bo attacks; Fofana was also present. He placed Nallo in overall charge of the Koribundo operation, and reiterated that not a farm or a fowl should be left alive. He gave Nallo a list of places to loot and people to kill in Bo (SCSL 2007d, 106–8).

When it came to command structure, and again drawing mainly on prosecution evidence, the Chamber found that Norman, Fofana and Kondewa, were the high command or the 'Holy Trinity' of the CDF:

> The three of them were the key and essential components of the leadership structure of the organisation and were the executive of the Kamajor society. They were the ones actually making the decisions and nobody could make a decision in their absence. Whatever happened, they would come together because they were the leaders and the Kamajors looked up to them.
>
> (SCSL 2007d, 108–9).

Fofana, the Chamber found, was the Director of War, appointed by Norman to plan and execute the strategies for war operations, even though he was 'never seen on the battlefield or even with a gun and was only considered to have fought because the man who feeds you is a fighter too' (SCSL 2007d, 110). According to the Chamber, he was the overall boss of the commanders at Base Zero (giving orders to a commander on at least one occasion), he provided logistics for the frontline, he received reports from the field, and he planned the Black December operation. Fofana was 'seen as having power and authority at Base Zero and he was frequently quoted on the BBC, and because people did not approach him unless he summoned them' (SCSL 2007d, 110). However, it also found that he could not distribute ammunition without Norman's say-so, that the final authority on troop deployment was Norman, that Nallo helped Fofana with the reports, and that Nallo also planned Black December with him (SCSL 2007d, 109–10).

Kondewa, meanwhile, was known as the High Priest and was head of all the CDF initiators. Whenever a Kamajor was going to war, he would go to Kondewa for advice and blessing. Kondewa decided who would go into combat, much as a fortune-teller would do. The Chamber found that: 'Because of the mystical powers Kondewa possessed, he had command over the Kamajors from every part of the country' (SCSL 2007d, 110–11).

Having discussed the origins and command structure of the CDF, and the planning of the Tongo, Bo and Koribundo operations, the Chamber then discussed in some detail its factual findings for the various crime bases, detailing numerous instances of killing, cruel treatment, collective punishment and pillage, before discussing the crime of initiating or enlisting child soldiers (SCSL 2007d, 120–209). In its legal findings, it meticulously sorted out the evidence that could be convincingly linked to the accused, under the counts and during the timeframe of the indictment, from that on which the link was in reasonable doubt, providing conclusions on the responsibility of the accused for each crime base.

Reading the verdict in court on 2 August 2007, Benjamin Itoe pronounced that the Chamber found Fofana and Kondewa unanimously *not guilty* on indictment Counts 1 (murder) and 3 (inhumane acts) which were charged as crimes against humanity. Recalling the Prosecutor's admission that the CDF 'fought for the restoration of democracy', it reasoned that that the civilian population was not 'the primary object of the attack'. It also acquitted on Count 6 (acts of terrorism) on grounds that there was reasonable doubt that spreading terror was the accused persons' express intent (SCSL 2007d, 220 ff). For similar reasons, the Chamber rejected the prosecution's allegation that the three acted in furtherance of a common criminal plan, or joint criminal enterprise (SCSL 2007d, 220 ff). Finally, it also summarised the evidence pointing to the responsibility of President Kabbah, though it did not pass comment on its implications (SCSL 2007d, 212–15).[27]

By contrast, on indictment Counts 2 (murder), 4 (cruel treatment), 5 (pillage) and 7 (collective punishments), which were charged as war crimes, it proceeded by majority opinion to find Fofana *guilty* while Kondewa was also *guilty*, by majority opinion, of these counts *plus* another serious violation of international humanitarian law, namely the crime of enlisting child soldiers (Count 8).

In terms of modes of liability, it found that Fofana was responsible for *aiding or abetting* crimes committed by Kamajors in the Tongo Field area by virtue of his speech at the Talia parade ground. It also found that he had *responsibility as a superior* for crimes committed in Koribundo and Bo, by virtue of a chain of command that ran from him through Albert Nallo to the commanders on the ground. Kondewa, meanwhile, was responsible for *commission* of murder in Talia when he shot a local town commander, and responsible for *aiding or abetting* crimes committed by Kamajors in Tongo Field, also on account of his words at the parade ground. It also found that he had *superior responsibility* for numerous crimes committed in Bonthe, since it was shown that he issued verbal and written instructions to inferiors, threatened them with punishment, and could release prisoners. In Moyamba, it found he had superior responsibility for pillage on account of having taken possession of a looted car. It had reason to doubt his responsibility for all the other crimes charged, except for that of enlisting child soldiers.

Given these factual findings, there appears little doubt that Norman, had he been alive, could, and probably would, have also have been convicted of war crimes. Under Article 6(i) of the Special Court Statute, he could have been found guilty of committing, ordering, planning, instigating, or aiding and abetting crimes in Tongo, Koribundo, and Bo. Under Article 6(iii) he could have been found guilty on account of his superior responsibility over the perpetrators for crimes in Kenema and Bonthe, and in particular for his failure to prevent and punish those crimes. The same reasoning could have applied to Moyamba District, had the judges not thrown out most of the Moyamba evidence on grounds that it did not fall within the scope or timeframe of the indictment. Superior

[27] In a separate opinion, Judge Boutet opined that he found the issue of Kabbah's responsibility to be largely irrelevant (SCSL 2007d, Annex B).

responsibility was probably also the mode under which Norman could have been found guilty of enlisting child soldiers.

Prior to sentencing, Fofana pointed to the circumstances in which he had been propelled into the conflict without military training, and to his subsequent role in restoring peace. Both Fofana and Kondewa, while not admitting responsibility, expressed regret for the terrible events that occurred in Sierra Leone and claimed empathy with the victims. In addition, both stressed that they were fighting to restore democracy and reinstate President Kabbah, and asked that this be considered as a mitigating factor. Counsel for Kondewa, Charles Margai, had this to say:

> We thank God, My Lords, that the war is over, but this war was described and has been described as the most brutal known to mankind. We should not lose sight of that. If it were not for the sacrifice of the CDF, God knows whether some of us, including my learned friend [Prosecuting Attorney] Kamara, would be here today. That I submit, My Lords, is a factor to be considered, because otherwise, if a sentence is severe and there occurs a rebel war, whether in Sierra Leone or elsewhere, Government militias are going to ask themselves the question: Is it advisable for us to intervene? If we do, might we not be treated in the same manner as Allieu Kondewa and the others?
>
> (SCSL 2004e, 19 September 2007, 83–84.)

The Chamber proved sympathetic to these arguments, and handed down relatively light sentences as a result. Fofana was sentenced to six years' imprisonment on Counts 2 and 4 of the indictment, to three years on Count 5, and four years on Count 7, the sentences to run concurrently. Kondewa was sentenced to eight years on Counts 2 and 4, five years on Count 5, six years on Count 7, and seven years on Count 8, the sentences again to run concurrently (SCSL 2007e).[28]

After the judgment came appeals. Kondewa filed six grounds of appeal, and the prosecution filed ten. Fofana, in a decision that was accompanied by strong rumours of fee splitting, chose not to appeal. The Appeals Chamber subsequently granted four of Kondewa's grounds, acquitting him of murder in Talia (to be discussed in Chapter 6), of pillage in Moyamba, of collective punishments in general, and of enlisting child soldiers (discussed in Chapter 5). It also granted four of the prosecution's grounds, reversing, most importantly, the Trial Chamber's acquittals for crimes against humanity, reasoning that the Trial Chamber had erred

[28] Insiders told me that this was a compromise between Judges Itoe and Boutet, with Itoe preferring an even more lenient sentence.

in claiming civilians were not the primary target of the attacks, confusing the purpose of the attack (to restore democracy) with the target of the attack (civilian 'collaborators') (SCSL 2008b, 104–5). In addition, it reasoned that the Trial Chamber had erred in finding that fighting for a just cause could be a mitigating factor. It raised Fofana and Kondewa's sentences to fifteen and twenty years accordingly.[29]

Dissenting opinions

Neither judgment nor appeal were unanimous, however. Of particular note was the fact that in dissenting opinions to the judgment and appeal respectively, Bankole Thompson, and Gelaga King, both Sierra Leonean judges, acquitted the defendants of all charges. In addition, Jon Kamanda, the third Sierra Leonean judge, while concurring with the appeals judgment in most respects, dissented from the sentence hike. I will discuss the substance and significance of these objections in this section.

Appended to the main judgment was a separate concurring and partially dissenting opinion from Justice Bankole Thompson. Thompson disagreed with the majority opinion on two scores. On the first, he disagreed with some of the findings of fact on ritual killings and initiation, though he did not say why. On the second, he agreed with the majority that the accused were factually guilty. However, he dissented from the judgment because he found their actions excusable. He went on to argue on behalf of the accused the defences of necessity and *salus civis suprema lex est* (SCSL 2007d, C-24). He cited Aristotle, Hobbes, Kant and the Canadian Law Reform Commission, among others, in support of the necessity doctrine, opining that the proper test to apply was: 'Was what the accused did actually necessary to avoid the evil in question?' (SCSL 2007d, C-29). Entering the realm of political ideology, he proceeded to postulate that:

> The preservation of democratic rule in the contemporary world setting with its emphasis on a global culture that espouses freedom and human dignity as key values of modern civilisation is a vital interest of individual states and the international community in general worthy to be defended at all costs in the face of rebellion and anarchy.
>
> (SCSL 2007d, C-32.)

[29] The sentence for Fofana was raised to fifteen years on Counts 2 and 4, and five years on Count 5. For Kondewa it was raised to twenty years on Counts and 2 and 4, and seven years on Count 5. Additionally, Fofana and Kondewa were sentenced to fifteen and twenty years on Counts 1 and 3, all sentences to run concurrently (SCSL 2008b, 187–8).

Further, in the context of wartime Sierra Leone: 'fighting for the restoration of democracy and constitutional legitimacy could be rightly perceived as an act both of patriotism and altruism, overwhelmingly compelling disobedience to a supranational regime of prescriptive norms' (SCSL 2007d, C-33). Reasoning along similar lines, he also argued that the accused could be acquitted on grounds that 'the safety of the state is the supreme law' (SCSL 2007d, C-34). Notwithstanding their legal transgressions, he could not hold the accused liable for taking up arms in defence of democracy, and he found them 'not guilty' of the offences charged.

This was a strange decision for two main reasons. First, in the early stages of the trial, Thompson had been one of the most restrictive judges, dissuading the defence from making an explicit political defence (see above). This restriction probably altered the entire course of the trial, with Norman subsequently choosing to deny, quite unrealistically, all the prosecution's charges, instead of explicitly arguing the necessity of his acts. It seemed strange then that, at the trial's close, Thompson should make this defence for the accused. Second, it was a barely reasoned opinion, failing to examine in any detail which of the accused's actions were justifiable and which were not, effectively granting any supporter of a democratic regime *carte blanche* to oversee acts that included hacking unarmed members of opposing ethnic groups to death, murdering civilian women by inserting sticks through their genitals, and decapitating and dismembering traditional leaders who were alleged to side with the rebels.

Justice King's dissent took a different tack. On the question of crimes against humanity, he argued that ECOMOG, representatives of the British and Nigerian governments, and President Kabbah's government in exile had all enlisted the Kamamjors to help restore the civilian government. In addition, the rebel-held areas of Tongo, Koribundo, Bo and Bonthe were all legitimate military targets, and Kamajors frequently spared or took action to protect civilians. The Trial Chamber, he argued, had all the evidence before it, had carefully considered the facts and concluded, he thought correctly, that the civilian population was not the primary object of the attack. The prosecution, he thought, had failed to show that no reasonable trier of fact could have acquitted the defendants.

On the matter of war crimes, King scrutinised the Trial Chamber's finding that Kondewa had responsibility as a superior for crimes committed in Bonthe District. In an opinion whose subject matter we will examine in more detail in Chapter 4, he argued that the Chamber had attributed too much weight to Kondewa's *de jure* status as High Priest: 'It boggles the imagination to think that on the basis of purporting to have occult powers ... Kondewa could be said to qualify as a 'commander' in a superior/subordinate relationship'. For the first time in the history of international law, he sputtered, 'a civilian Sierra Leonean juju man or witch doctor, who practised fetish, had never been a soldier, had never before been engaged in combat, but was a farmer and so-called herbalist ... can be held to be a commander ... "by virtue" of his reputed superstitious, mystical, supernatural, and suchlike fictional and fantasy powers!' (SCSL 2008b, Judge King's dissenting opinion, 23).[30] In addition, in an opinion which concerns the subject matter of Chapter 3, he criticised the Chamber's reasoning with respect to the elements of Kondewa's *de facto* control. For King, the findings did not stand up in light of the fact that 'the CDF was a militia guerrilla fighting force or an "irregular" army, which although it had a hierarchical command structure, was comparatively less trained, organised, resourced, and staffed than a regular army' (SCSL 2008b, Judge King's dissenting opinion, 24–5).

When it came to Kondewa's responsibility for aiding and abetting war crimes in Tongo Field, King argued that the Trial Chamber had misinterpreted the import of Kondewa's words at the parade ground, and also pointed to the fact that there was no proven nexus between the Kamajors at the parade ground and those committing crimes in Tongo. Finally, he argued that the Appeals Chamber had erred in raising the sentences of the accused, since the Trial Chamber had rightly regarded the restoration of democracy as a mitigating factor. In the course of doing so, he queried whether Britain, Nigeria, the US and the international community could not be regarded as having superior responsibility over Allieu

[30] Partially dissenting opinion of Justice Gelaga King, Appeals Chamber Decision, p. 23. King disagreed with both Chambers' attribution of superior responsibility to Kondewa for crimes in Bonthe, claiming that it placed too much weight on Kondewa's *de jure* status as High Priest. However, if my reading of the Trial Chamber's judgment is correct (see Chapter 4), this was not the principal reason for convicting Kondewa on this count under Article 6(iii). I got a greater insight into Justice King's dissent when I interviewed him in his Chambers a few days after the decision. In this interview he accepted that, on account of the beliefs people held, characters like Kondewa could wield influence at village level. He reasoned, nevertheless, that because crimes often took place miles from Kondewa's location, and because Kondewa acted with the backing of international powers, then holding him responsible was both unrealistic and unjust. Interview, Justice Gelaga King, Freetown, 3 June 2008.

Kondewa and the Kamajors, while alluding to the lack of prosecutions after NATO bombed Serbia in 1999 (SCSL 2008b, 30).

Justice Jon Kamanda, arguing that the sentences should be fixed at six and eight years respectively, adopted Justice King's reasoning on mitigating circumstances as his own opinion, and also entered a passionate dissent of his own:

> … the accused were not charged as persons who committed these acts directly. Criminal responsibility was thrust upon these two men by the operation of the Statute. I have mentioned the import of these [*sic*] assumed criminality because it is my considered view that this factor must be viewed from the perspective that these lowly placed men could be clothed with the garment of major players in a very confused warfare where fighters more often than not were on a frolic of their own. Since the law holds them culpable in any case, it is my strong view that that same law should in an even-handed manner operate also as a mitigating factor on the accused men's behalf.
>
> (SCSL 2008b, partially dissenting opinion of Justice Jon Kamanda, 2.)[31]

CONCLUSIONS

In this chapter, I have tried to sketch the main lines of the prosecution and defence cases, as well as summarising the findings of the judges. Although a huge amount of detail has been left out, I hope to have shown something of the timeline and geography of the conflict as it was represented at trial. I also hope to have demonstrated some of the controversy of the case, since the arguments in court and indeed the judgments and dissenting opinions revealed deep fault lines between Sierra Leonean and international judges on the question of whether or not it was legitimate to inflict violent acts on civilians in a context of war. Instead of a well-integrated hybrid, then, the Special Court appeared to be more of a *pushmi-pullyu*, the Sierra Leonean and international

[31] Justice Winter also dissented from the majority in the Appeals Chamber judgment on several grounds. She opined that Kondewa was guilty of enlisting children and of using them in hostilities, and she also argued that Fofana must have known about this too. In addition, she argued that Kamajors did inflict collective punishments on civilians, that the Trial Chamber erred in not allowing the prosecution to amend the indictment so as to include sexual violence charges, and that although reconciliation could be a mitigating factor in certain circumstances, these circumstances did not apply to the case of Allieu Kondewa (SCSL 2008b, partially dissenting opinion of Justice Renate Winter, 1–35). The arguments surrounding child soldiers will be discussed in more detail in Chapter 5.

heads determined to go their separate ways. I have also introduced, very briefly, some of the key issues that will preoccupy us in the forthcoming chapters. Specifically, I have referred to a number of issues at trial – the nature of superior responsibility in a Third World militia, Kondewa and his mystical powers, the legitimacy of recruiting child soldiers and the credibility of witnesses, all of which require cultural as well as legal scrutiny. In the remaining chapters I hope to show that by training an anthropological lens on them, we arrive at legal conclusions at variance with those of the Court.

CHAPTER 3

AN UNCONVENTIONAL ARMY: CHAINS OF COMMAND IN A PATRIMONIAL SOCIETY

The Special Court charged the CDF defendants not only with individual responsibility for committing, ordering, planning, instigating, aiding and abetting criminal acts, but also with superior responsibility for crimes committed by their subordinates.[1] In doing so, it drew on an identifiable stream of jurisprudence that ran from the Middle Ages in Europe, through the military tribunals at Nuremburg and the Far East, to the *ad hoc* tribunals for Rwanda and the former Yugoslavia. But despite being quite well established in international law, the doctrine of superior responsibility had yet to be applied to a society or a conflict that was quite like Sierra Leone's. In particular, the historical fragility of formal authority relations and the pervasive nature of informal, patrimonial arrangements, while placing Sierra Leone together with many other Third World countries, differentiated it from other states previously the target of international trials, including even Rwanda.[2] These facts notwithstanding, Fofana and Kondewa had, by the end of the trial, been found guilty as superiors for crimes in Bo, Koribundo and Bonthe. I begin the chapter by outlining some of the most important jurisprudence on command responsibility.

[1] Article 6(i) of the Statute stipulated: 'A person who planned, instigated, ordered, committed or otherwise aided and abetted in the planning, preparation or execution of a crime referred to in articles 2 to 4 of the present Statute shall be individually responsible for the crime', while Article 6(iii) stipulated that: 'The fact that any of the crimes referred to in articles 2 to 4 of the present Statute was committed by a subordinate does not relieve his or her superior of criminal responsibility if he or she knew or had reason to know that the subordinate was about to commit such acts or had done so and the superior had failed to take the necessary and reasonable measures to prevent such acts or punish the perpetrators thereof' (SCSL 2002).

[2] Widely regarded as having one of the strongest states in Africa (Prunier 1995).

Then I provide an overview of informal authority relations in peace and wartime Sierra Leone. Next, I summarise the testimony of two expert witnesses to the Special Court, one a British military expert, the other an American anthropologist, who debated the nature of command authority in the CDF. Finally, I examine some of the trial's more pertinent evidence, focusing on the case against Fofana, and arguing that his conviction for war crimes and crimes against humanity under this mode needs to be rethought, as does the entire doctrine of superior responsibility in countries like Sierra Leone.

SUPERIOR RESPONSIBILITY IN INTERNATIONAL LAW

The doctrine of superior military responsibility that was ultimately used to convict the defendants can be traced to a handful of laws rooted in European and American legal history. In 1439 Charles VII of France issued the Ordinance of Orleans that rendered army captains responsible for the crimes of their subordinates, as though they had committed them themselves. In 1479, a tribunal of the Holy Roman Empire found Hagenbach, Archduke of Austria, guilty for his failure to prevent a reign of terror in the Upper Rhine. In 1621, a Swedish military code empowered courts to punish officers who ordered their subordinates to undertake illegal acts, while in the nineteenth century, a variant upon this theme, the Lieber Code, governed soldiers in the American civil war. In 1907, The Hague Conventions imposed duties on commanders for the acts of their subordinates (Langston 2004, 149–50; Maguire 2000, 36–42).

In the post World War II era, the International Military Tribunal at Nuremburg found Interior Minister Frick culpable for crimes committed by his subordinates against their patients, crimes of which he was fully aware. Shortly thereafter, the US military trials at Nuremburg found, in particular in the *Hostages* case, that superiors were liable for the criminal acts of their subordinates about which they knew, *or should have known*. In the *High Command* case, a commander was held to have responsibility to maintain security and safety in areas under the scope of his territorial command. Shifting to Asia, the 1945 trial of General Yamashita by the American Military Commission in the Philippines found the Japanese General liable for crimes committed by his subordinates, one of the first expressions of the doctrine of 'negative responsibility', and a negative responsibility provision anchored prosecutions at the International Military Tribunal for the Far East in Tokyo, where it was claimed that the accused, 'deliberately and recklessly disregarded their legal duty to take adequate steps to secure the observance and prevent the breaches of the laws and customs of war' (Langston 2004, 154). The tribunal found that superiors could be found liable for negligence in their supervision of subordinates, as in the case of Foreign Minister Hirota, convicted of crimes committed during the rape of Nanking (Langston 2004, 150–3).

In the 1970s, the international law on superior responsibility was given further definition in Additional Protocol II of the Geneva Convention, which held that superiors were responsible for the crimes of individuals under their command *in a practical sense*, emphasising the extension of liability from *de jure* to *de facto* forms of authority. *De facto* responsibility was extended even further by the ICTY, and in particular by the *Celebici* judgment, in which four defendants had been charged with killing, torturing and sexually assaulting inmates at the Celebici prison camp in central Bosnia. The Appeals Chamber in *Celebici* argued that in a contemporary conflict characterised by the disintegration of formal power structures, it was essential to look at who actually wielded control, regardless of their formal appointment: 'A commander or a superior is thus one who possesses the power or authority in either a *de jure* or a *de facto* form to prevent a subordinate's crime or to punish the perpetrators' (cited in Knoops (2007, 515). In a cognate example, the ICTR's Musema case, the defendant, the director of a tea factory, was found to have both *de jure* and *de facto* authority over his factory workers (Langston 2004, 168–9).[3]

In superior responsibility cases, the critical idea is 'effective control' in the sense of having 'the material ability to prevent or punish' the crimes of subordinates (Langston 2004, 169). Individuals in authority positions, are required to take 'necessary and reasonable' measures to prevent criminal acts – about which they know or have reason to know – committed by those under their 'effective control', that is, those whom they have the 'material ability' to prevent and punish (Langston 2004, 178–9).

In practice, assigning superior responsibility may be very difficult, especially considering the nature of many contemporary and especially

[3] The doctrine of superior responsibility evolved at the ICTY to allow it to engage with changes in the nature of conflict, in particular, the disintegration of formal authority structures in the context of so-called 'new wars'. But in Sierra Leone, it is more accurate to say that formal authority structures have not disintegrated, since they were never really effective in the first place. Rather, this is a society founded on informal power *par excellence*.

Third World conflicts. Geert-Jan Alexander Knoops, for example, a defence lawyer in the AFRC case at the Special Court for Sierra Leone, has pointed to the problems of the doctrine in cases of guerrilla warfare. Discussing the nature of *de facto* control, he argues that:

> *De facto* control requires the existence of a goal-directed hierarchy, coupled with a general awareness of a chain of command. Also, there must be a widely accepted exercise of issuing and receiving orders, as well as an expectation that insubordination will trigger disciplinary reaction. This entails a mutual expectation that orders will be obeyed. Moreover, the superior must possess effective means enabling him to suppress an illegal act and punish the perpetrators.
>
> (Knoops 2007, 516.)

These conditions are unlikely to be fulfilled in circumstances of guerrilla warfare, he argues, and especially not in a war with the degree of factional fluidity that was witnessed in Sierra Leone (Knoops 2007, 516–17). He continues:

a. The mere use of terms such as 'boss' or 'commander' is in itself insufficient to infer subordination without evidence of the overall behaviour and duties of an alleged superior, for 'it is the cumulative effect of evidence showing *both* subjugation to orders and respect for the authority of the accused that is necessary to convince a tribunal of the existence of a superior-subordinate relationship' (Knoops 2007, 518 citing Bantekas), and
b. In military structures, a commander can normally rely on an effective chain of command and therefore be held responsible for the deficient information, education and supervision of the 'forces.' In the event such system is lacking it is questionable whether effective control is a reasonable proposition (Knoops 2007, 518).[4]

AUTHORITY AND SOCIETY IN SIERRA LEONE

The doctrine of command responsibility emerged from a European historical context in which an increasing proportion of social institutions, including the military, came to be governed by what Max Weber

[4] The problem is doubtless a difficult one. As Osiel has noticed: 'If we make it very hard to find that 'effective control' exists, we risk acquitting many whose role in the ultimate result, whose contribution to it, was quite considerable – even if they didn't completely dominate the behaviour of other participants …[but if] we make it very easy to find sufficient control, we risk classifying too many people as 'commanders,' when their contribution was actually little different from that of many around them, including those of inferior rank' cited in Langston (2004, 174).

termed 'legal-rational' authority. Among the characteristics of this type of authority were formal hierarchies with codified rules to govern the activities of office holders, and clear chains of command linking superiors with subordinates. In this system, individuals follow the chain of command, rather than the personalities that occupy it, or their personal or familial interests. Consequently, there is a high degree of fit between *de jure* and *de facto* authority (Weber 1968, 956–1070).

It is important to recognise that, throughout history, only a minority of peoples have been governed by this authority type – its emergence in the West should be regarded as a historical and cultural aberration. One explanation is the high levels of education and technical expertise it presumes. Another is its expectation that office holders should divorce their professional duties from their personal or social interest, which appears to contravene basic human instinct (Clapham 1985, 44–50). Even in the West, legal-rational authority systems face a constant struggle to uphold obedience to the rules, a struggle that has more success in some countries than in others (Chabal and Daloz 2006). In addition, attempts to export the model to non-Western countries have encountered a great deal of resistance, as a long history of failed capacity building and public sector reform programmes in developing countries shows (see for example Leonard and Straus 2002).

In Third World countries, authority is more likely to correspond to one of the various 'pre-modern' types identified by Weber, namely charismatic, traditional or patrimonial. Put simply, charismatic authority takes the form of obedience to a leader on account of his presumed superhuman qualities. Traditional authority often stems from a 'routinisation of charisma', under which a particular group has convinced its followers that it has a prerogative to rule. Patriarchal authority, in which a male head enjoys authority over his household members, is the simplest version of this type. Patrimonialism, explained Weber, is a version of patriarchal authority in which a leader – usually a big chief, big man, warlord or king – exerts authority over his followers by means of his personal relations with an intermediate administrative staff – usually chiefs, warriors or even slaves (Weber 1947, 297–354). That staff meanwhile tends to exert authority over smaller segmented populations through a combination of coercion and personal favours. Patrimonialism, then, is a triadic system that incorporates a collection of dyadic patron-client arrangements. For example, patrons (who may be elders, chiefs, or 'big men') provide resources, opportunities and services (for example, land, employment, protection) to their clients (who may be descendants, followers or slaves), who provide tribute, services and allegiance (for example, gifts, labour, political support), in return, while helping to buy off or coerce potential opponents and dissenters (Lemarchand 1972; Médard 1982; Murphy 2007).

For our purposes there are two important points to note about patrimonial systems. One is that the link between a patrimonial ruler and his subjects is indirect, mediated by an exchange of favours and coercion with an intermediate staff whose own authority is also founded on a favour-coercion exchange. This tends to mean that getting things done is rarely so simple a matter as passing orders down the line. It usually involves a political process of bargaining, mediation and exchange of favours with intermediaries whose own allegiance and authority cannot necessarily be relied upon. The other is that authority is personalised rather than rule based, informal rather than formal. This means that even if the system has a formal system of rule-bound offices with specified roles and functions, this is probably not a good guide to the realities of power and authority on the ground. In legal terms, there can be a large gap between *de jure* and *de facto* responsibility.

Third World states, generally speaking, are best described as having 'neo-patrimonial' systems in which real power is exercised to a greater or lesser degree patrimonially, behind a bureaucratic facade (Berman 1998; Bratton and Van de Walle 1997, 61–96; Chabal and Daloz 1999; Médard 1982; Schatzberg 2002). The concept of the neo-patrimonial state fits Sierra Leone well, since it has always been at the extreme end of a continental tendency towards personal rule. To understand why, we need to turn briefly to history. English traders arrived in upcountry Sierra Leone in the mid-sixteenth century, whereupon they witnessed a massive invasion by a people calling themselves the Mani, who entered the country from the south-east. A Mande speaking people, the Mani had probably been driven into the forest region by a ruler in present-day Senegal (Kup 1962, 128). Around a century and a half later, in what experts have speculated was the rear-end of the original Mani invasion, the Mende, who are today Sierra Leone's largest ethnic group, entered from the south, while the Mandingo and the Fulani descended on the country from the north (Kup 1962). The people overrun in these invasions were displaced into other regions of the country, where they frequently came into conflict with existing settlers, triggering a myriad of new small wars and a kaleidoscope of ethnic realignments. The invasions laid the foundation for two different variants of patrimonialism and patron-clientelism. First, the conquering invaders appear to have governed by parcelling out pieces of land and population to trusted warriors with the latter being permitted to extract rents and profit from these possessions, provided they paid tribute to their superiors. Secondly, groups of refugees were sometimes permitted to settle in new communities, and to govern themselves fairly autonomously, provided their leaders paid tribute to the existing rulers (see Murphy 2007, 5).

In a context where bureaucratic technology is not well developed, patrimonialism is an efficient means of broadcasting power over an extended area. But it is also inherently unstable, creating 'a social physics of centrifugal forces' (Murphy 2007, 9). This is because the authority of the patrimonial ruler is constantly under threat from that of his subordinate staff, since the latter's direct links to clients and to economic resources, for example agricultural products, captives, or precious minerals, provide them with opportunities to empower themselves and break away from or challenge the ruler. In pre-colonial Mende country, for example, big chiefs or leaders would often bestow settlement sites on prominent warriors in return for their services, adding fresh settlements or sections to existing towns. However, in some of these settlements warriors were strong enough to build up a kind of sub-chiefdom which ultimately came to challenge the authority of the existing chief, leading to conflicts between putative ruling houses (Murphy 2007, 14).[5] In the nineteenth century, these centrifugal forces appear to have been magnified as war chiefs competed with one another for the spoils of trade (Abraham 1978).

Patrimonialism then has deep roots in pre-colonial Sierra Leonean history, and things did not change much under colonial rule. When, in 1896, the British created a Protectorate over Sierra Leone, they tended to utilise rather than transform these patrimonial arrangements, entering into treaties and agreements with local rulers in about 400 land units, which they designated as chiefdoms (TRC 2004, vol. 3A, 7). Britain did not intend to build a strong, modern state in Sierra Leone: it was more interested in ensuring social order, a modicum of economic exploitation and 'civilisation' of the natives (McGowan 1990, 27). To this end it governed the protectorate via the system of Indirect Rule, a form of 'hegemony on a shoestring' (Berry 1993), under which a handful of colonial administrators ruled through real or invented native chiefs. Up until 1921, the British governed the Protectorate with only five administrators

[5] Governmental authority could be made even more fluid by competitive relations of hierarchy and dependency in the secret societies (Murphy 2007, 17).

(the District Commissioners themselves), and one circuit court judge, presiding over 1,200,000 Africans (Kilson 1966, 24–5). It was a patrimonial system of the sort discussed in the previous section, the main difference being that the British were now overlords. In the 1950s the British tried to transform this system, but in colonialism's dying days they reverted once more to a heavy reliance on chiefs (Migdal 1988, 114–15).[6] The result was 'a fragmented, weblike society with *numerous poles of power*' (Migdal 1988, 127) (my emphasis).

After independence the country's first president, Milton Margai, chose to perpetuate this loose pattern of patrimonial rule. Rather than attacking the independence of chiefs, he merely positioned himself above them, manipulating and benefiting from chiefdom conflicts (Clapham 1976; Migdal 1988, 132). After his death, this tradition was continued by Sir Milton's brother, Albert, although with considerably less skill. Patrimonial politics arguably reached its apogee, however, under the regime of President Siaka Stevens. Stevens prioritised internal security over national development, and personal loyalty over competence. He ruled the country with the aid of a notorious paramilitary police force, the Internal Security Unit, which brutally checked vociferous opposition to his regime, while filling public positions, not least the institution of chieftancy, with personal cronies. Stevens came to rely more and more for his survival on earnings from the illicit diamond trade, in which he had a large stake through his alliance with powerful Lebanese traders. In particular, he appointed his close Lebanese ally, Jamil Mohammed, as manager of the Government Diamond Office, allowing him to steer official diamond revenues into Stevens' private hands (Brown *et al.* 2005; Gberie 2005; TRC 2004). Under political protection other Lebanese were granted mining licenses, and a blind eye was turned to illicit

[6] In 1896 and 1898 both the south and north of the country rose up in the interlinked Hut Tax War and Mende Rising, initial trouble in Temne country leading to almost simultaneous attacks on government posts throughout the country, with most male British subjects in Bandajuma, Kwallu, and Sulima Districts being killed within a week (Little 1965, 350). There was evidence that the uprisings were organised through the secret societies, and some observers speculated that there was a territorial supreme council that presided over and coordinated all the *Poro*. Little, a colonial anthropologist, was sceptical of this claim, however. He believed that the initial action could have been achieved by a network of cells comprising the more senior local *Poro* officials, including chiefs, who disseminated the call to arms via bush messengers, triggering actions long rehearsed in the *Poro* bush, such as ambushes and raids. He pointed to the fact that the uprising fell apart when it became necessary to organise in more complex ways as evidence against the existence of a coordinating body (Little 1965, 361–3). *Poro* also played a part in the disturbances in northern and south-western provinces in 1955 and 1956. See Chapters 5 and 6 for a discussion of the *Poro* society.

diamond mining and smuggling. When Stevens handed the reins to Joseph Momoh in 1985, the formal state was but a shell, with real power to be found in the informal networks lying in its shadow (Reno 1995).

According to Migdal, Sierra Leonean regimes presided over a 'society of fragments' which they were hard-pressed to control: 'Appointments and manipulation, not social control and mobilization, remain the outer limits of state capabilities. The ability to enforce faithfully many types of social policy down to the level of the individual has persistently eluded those who have staffed state ministries' (Migdal 1988, 137). The politics of patrimonial rule characterised not just the civil service but also the army. Army officers were paid in rice rather than cash, which they sold on the black market for increased returns. Under Momoh, resources for fighting the war failed to reach the front, leading to disenchantment and Momoh's eventual overthrow. Under the subsequent NPRC military regime, the military hierarchy became increasingly moribund, as local army units teamed up with the rebels to victimise the civilian population. Arthur Abraham has described the generalised state of corruption in the armed forces, while Krijn Peters has written about the patrimonial relations that sustained it (Abraham 2004; Peters 2006).

Patrimonialism and patron-clientelism also structured the rebel forces. Young fighters raided the civilian population to provide booty for their commanders, who redistributed it in patronage form. There are many examples of RUF units acting on their own initiative and splintering from the leadership, especially when there were economic resources, such as diamonds, they could control (Murphy 2003, 2007). The fighting factions consisted not in well-drilled hierarchies, but in loose alliances and congeries of fighters, sometimes conflicting, sometimes colluding, and sometimes paying allegiance to a paramount leader, but with little evidence of rigorous control (TRC 2004, vol. 3A, 549–52).[7] According to anthropologist William Murphy, the constant splintering of the armed factions was a structural process informed by a local ideology of 'wealth in persons', in which ambitious individuals strive either to build up as many followers as possible, or to attach themselves to the followers of more powerful people (Murphy 2007, 19): 'The dialectic of political loyalty and disloyalty creates uncertainty, suspicions, revenge, and ruthlessness, especially when competition and conflict over resources intensifies' (Murphy 2007, 26).

[7] The TRC also notes that child Kamajors tended to follow the orders of their initiators rather than the chiefs, and that this rivalry threatened to split the entire movement (TRC 2004, 298).

The historical and social background of Sierra Leone, then, provides *prima facie* grounds for thinking that the prosecution's claim that the accused persons had established a system of effective command and control over the individual fighters who comprised the CDF was unrealistic. Backing this up, the Truth and Reconciliation Commission reported that, from its inception, the lines of command and control in the CDF were unclear. Norman clearly aspired to a position of control, but it is far from certain that his aspirations were achieved; the TRC spoke of 'virtually non-existent hierarchical controls' (TRC 2004, vol. 3A, 214). Patrimonial structures do not lend themselves to the kind of effective disciplinary control characteristic of modern military organisations. The titular leader of a territory, organisation or armed group is unlikely to wield effective control over all his supposed followers, not least because his power is always vulnerable to being undermined by subordinates establishing semi-autonomous units of their own (see, for example, TRC 2004, vol. 3A, 545). Indeed, given the terrain of Sierra Leone, the difficulty of communications, and the paucity of educated people in the movement, it was difficult to see how control could be anything but rudimentary. Consistent with this thesis, I will argue in the next section that scepticism over the superior responsibility claim was borne out by the expert evidence led at trial.

SUPERIOR RESPONSIBILITY IN THE CDF TRIAL

Expert witnesses

On 14 June 2005, Richard Mortimer Iron, a 48-year-old British Army colonel and previous head of the British army's doctrine branch, testified on behalf of the prosecution, summarising the findings of his previously prepared expert report. Col. Iron explained in court that his brief had been to discuss the dynamics of conventional and non-conventional conflict, to explain how military organisations work and are structured, and to address the area of command and control. He based his methodology on four questions: whether the CDF had a military hierarchy and structure; whether it exhibited the characteristics of a military organisation; whether the organisation was coherent (that is, whether there was a clear connection between strategic, operational, and tactical levels); and whether it was command effective (SCSL 2004e, 14 June 2005, 23–4). He used witness statements and transcripts as sources, supplementing these with visits to the field – principally in the Bo and Koribundo areas – accompanied by seven key prosecution witnesses, spending about fourteen days on the ground in total. Iron explained that an organisation's coherence could be measured 'by determining the extent to which the strategic aims of the organisation are transferred down to tactical activity on the ground' (SCSL 2004e, 14 June 2005, 24).

Iron testified that, prior to the May 1997 coup, the CDF was organised on a chiefdom basis. After the coup, 'we see the beginning of a new structure … Headquarters was established in Talia, a large centralised body of CDF fighters in Talia' (SCSL 2004e, 14 June 2005, 28–9). Talia became the base for the CDF Commander, Hinga Norman, who had a small number of support staff, and a large number of hierarchically organised CDF units. These comprised what Iron termed an 'offensive' or 'counter-attack force', which was later used for the major operations in Koribundo and Bo. In addition to this counter-attack force, the CDF continued to be comprised of 'territorial forces', dispersed in the CDF controlled chiefdoms (SCSL 2004e, 14 June 2005, 29–30).

Cohesion was imparted to the CDF through the immunisation process, which was very important in increasing solidarity and morale. In addition, Hinga Norman was a leader who inspired a great deal of personal loyalty, and the leader who wielded ultimate power (SCSL 2004e, 14 June 2005, 36–7).

Iron described the effectiveness of the CDF command as 'mixed'. At a strategic and operational level, he said, it was 'highly effective' (SCSL 2004e, 14 June 2005, 30). For example, a strategic decision was taken to assemble a counter-attack force at Talia, while operationally, the command was able to organise limited counter-offensives around the country in anticipation of support from ECOMOG (SCSL 2004e, 14 June 2005, 32). At a tactical level, that is the carrying out of orders on the ground, the CDF was less effective, mainly because of the lack of experience and training of many junior commanders (SCSL 2004e, 14 June 2005, 30).

The colonel also discussed the nature of CDF operations and the quality of communications between the CDF command and its operational units. During the junta period, Iron testified, the CDF undertook two main types of operation: dispersed and defensive ones, which took place mostly in the north and east, and appear not have been coordinated from Talia, and coordinated operations in areas of the south and west under CDF control. Here, communications took the form of messages conveyed by motorbike or moped. Alternatively, runners conveyed messages by foot along jungle paths. Iron testified that in the south and west communications appear to have been reliable, insofar as there are no accounts of messages getting lost; secure, inasmuch as they were not intercepted by the rebels; but not very timely, since they could take hours or days to transmit. Time lags notwithstanding, Iron thought that commanders at Base Zero had a good idea of what was going on at the front (SCSL 2004e, 14 June 2005, 33–5).

Another topic of testimony was discipline within the CDF. Col. Iron testified that though there were examples of top commanders being punished for not obeying orders, indiscipline in the lower ranks was neither investigated nor punished. He felt that this created a context in which indiscipline could be transferred to the battlefield:

> This is a very complex issue. At some levels discipline was harshly enforced within the CDF, at other levels it was not. So we see very strict discipline being enforced in the obeying of orders, direct orders, and if a commander failed to obey, for example, one of Hinga Norman's orders, then he could expect to be punished. But there are many other areas that – in which I would describe discipline as being lax where many what I view as wrongdoings went uninvestigated and unpunished. This was particularly so in Base Zero. And my opinion is that the environment, the culture, the ethos that was created in Base Zero transferred itself into the battlefield.
>
> (SCSL 2004e, 14 June 2005, 37.)

The report itself expanded on a number of interesting themes. On the subject of military organisation, Iron noticed that the CDF lacked units such as battalions or brigades. Rather, its fighting units were organised within chiefdom groups, with the leaders usually being respected Kamajors or hunters from before the war. These groups might range in size from 15 to 150 people, and several might band together to form larger organisations under the leadership of high-status local leaders, identified through that leader, eg 'James Kiley's [*sic*] group etc' (Iron 2005, C-4). Even when a large number of Kamajors assembled at Base Zero, there was no established rank system, although hierarchy of seniority did exist.

The organisation was provided coherence, he thought, by the exceptionally strong leadership of Hinga Norman who 'organized the military command to suit his own personality' (Iron 2005, C-4). Norman reserved the right to make all the important decisions and little authority was delegated to subordinates. By force of his dominant personality he 'exerted considerable influence and control over all the CDF forces in the south east of the country' (Iron 2005, E-1). He also possessed the power to check rank and file indiscipline at Base Zero, though for some reason he often neglected to do so (Iron 2005, E-8).

There was no fixed system of pay or promotion in the CDF, and food and munitions were always in short supply. However, senior commanders or those who had done well on missions were rewarded with increased responsibilities, and increased food supplies (Iron 2005, E-4 E-5). Norman also rewarded them with personal gifts, such as a bottle of whisky he gave Nallo for capturing Koribundo. Ordinary fighters, meanwhile, were rewarded with sexual access to captured women (Iron 2005, E-5). In addition, local Kamajor units provisioned themselves via the local population and by capturing enemy supplies.

Norman was able to decide strategy and plan operations very effectively. However, as we will see below, the organisation often lost coherence when it came to conducting operations on the ground. Iron attributes these failings to commanders' tactical inexperience and naivety, and to the culture of indiscipline that reigned at Base Zero. However, he also notices that there were personal rivalries, the role of which he downplayed by arguing that they are a feature of all military organisations (Iron 2005, B-1).

In addition to the role of Norman, Iron discussed the roles of Kondewa and Fofana. Kondewa was extremely important, he thought, to recruitment, initiation, and boosting morale, which was a vital factor in ensuring the CDF's cohesion. Meanwhile, Fofana played an important role as a supplier of logistics. According to Iron, the supply of food and weaponry was vital to maintaining the cohesion of the CDF. In his words:

> a dispersed organization such as the CDF or RUF is liable to break up as individual commanders with strong egos strive for independence from central command. This is a natural tendency in loose-knit organizations; but control can be maintained by focusing the supply of munitions without which guerrilla groups cannot operate.
>
> (Iron 2005, C-5.)

In addition, Fofana was one of Norman's trusted confidantes, and he chaired planning meetings before briefing Norman.

If Kondewa was the staff member in charge of recruitment and Fofana was the staff member in charge of logistics, the man directly responsible for military operations was Deputy Director of Operations Albert Nallo. Iron's report seems to place him on a par with Kondewa and Fofana (Iron 2005, C-4):

> The key staff branches were: logistics, headed by Director of War Moinina Fofana; recruitment and initiation, headed by Chief Priest Allieu

> Kondewa; and planning and execution of operations, conducted by the Director of Operations (in southern Sierra Leone) Albert Nallo. These key staff officers were responsible for developing plans in accordance with Norman's wishes, and then submitting them for Norman's agreement.
>
> (Iron 2005, C-4.)

Indeed, it seems only to be by virtue of a quirk in nomenclature that Nallo himself was not called Director of War, since he had a great deal more to do with fighting than Fofana did.

In rebuttal of these arguments, Dr Daniel Hoffman, Assistant Professor of Cultural Anthropology at the University of Washington in Seattle, appeared for the Defence on 9 October 2006. Hoffman, who held a PhD in cultural anthropology from Duke University, had visited Sierra Leone in 2000, 2001–2, 2003, 2005 and 2006, spending lengthy periods of time conducting ethnographic research among the Kamajors, which included interviewing more than 200 Kamajor individuals (SCSL 2004e, 9 October 2006, 24–31). With this background, Hoffman approached the question of whether or not the CDF constituted a military organisation, and the type of organisation and structure it had, writing a report informed by trial transcripts and interviews with between 20 and 25 Kamajors (SCSL 2004e, 9 October 2006, 34–6).

The report focused on the origins of the Kamajors and their evolution over time, the structure of the Kamajor/CDF movement, the aims and objectives of the CDF, the intensity of areas of fighting, socio-anthropological traits of the Kamajors that were relevant to the issue of command, and the role of children in Kamajor society. Led in court by Defence Counsel Steven Powles, Hoffman began by describing the mythical origins of the Kamajors as select individuals with the ballistic and supernatural powers to protect villages from the malign forces of the bush. He charted their increasing involvement in chiefdom based counter-insurgency operations in the early stages of the war, and then another period of expansion, in which ordinary men were recruited into the Kamajor movement by local chiefs, often from displaced communities in IDP camps (SCSL 2004e, 9 October 2006, 58–65). Another phase came following the 1997 coup, when large numbers of Kamajors began to assemble at Gendema and Bo waterside in Pujehun, following an announcement by Eddie Massalay on the BBC. Gendema came to be known as Base One, with Base Zero at Talia emerging some time later (SCSL 2004e, 9 October 2006, 65–71).[8] Hoffman testified that because

[8] Gendema is on the Liberian border, around 100km north-east of Talia.

of communication difficulties, as well as personality conflicts, there was little coordination between Base Zero and Base One, the bases being connected mainly by ECOMOG, which would send supplies and ferry important persons to both bases (SCSL 2004e, 9 October 2006, 71–3).

Base One and Base Zero were known as centres where upcountry Kamajors could go for food, supplies and munitions, he said. There was also a degree of training going on at both camps, as there was throughout the rest of the country. Hoffman disputed Col. Iron's claim that Base Zero was a forward offensive base: 'I don't think it had that level of coherence and it didn't play that role for the Kamajors, for the most part', he said (SCSL 2004e, 9 October 2006, 73).

Hoffman also questioned the degree of centralisation of the CDF. According to him, the CDF comprised:

> Different units, different groupings in different parts of the country, operating according to, if you will, directives from all kinds of authorities based on all kinds of contingencies. Some groups had easier access to Gendema. Some groups had easier access to Base Zero. There were groups that were operating largely in isolation. There were certainly efforts to reach various groupings of Kamajors, there's no question about that. But to say that direction was coming from x location, or even x individual, to my mind, overstates the case.
>
> (SCSL 2004e, 9 October 2006, 81.)

In fact, the CDF lacked the communication capacity to coordinate movements across the country – they had the bush runner system, and beyond that, announcements made on the BBC. Because of this, nobody was in a position to make decisions for the movement as a whole (SCSL 2004e, 9 October 2006, 99).

Hoffman proceeded to provide a general overview of patronage and patron-client relations, which he said were critical to West African and in particular Mende society (SCSL 2004e, 9 October 2006, 101–2). Following a logic of patronage, the term 'commander', in his view, became in the CDF a synonym for 'patron'. One became a commander by accumulating clients. Some commanders did this by simply claiming to be commanders with enough conviction to attract followers. In this situation, where patron-client relations were extremely mobile and fluid, titles connoted a sense of authority, he said, rather than a fixed list of duties and responsibilities (SCSL 2004e, 9 October 2006, 104–6).

Reflecting the lack of an effective central command, the entire movement, Hoffman testified, was shot through with local aims and concerns: 'Everyone is as concerned with those as they are with whatever the kind of overarching concerns might be' (SCSL 2004e, 9 October 2006, 87).

Hoffman concluded by providing a general critique of Col. Iron's report. First, he criticised the methodology: 'there are a lot of social nuances that are incredibly important to understanding the dynamics of the CDF which you just – nobody could possibly pick up talking to seven people over I believe it's 14 days' (SCSL 2004e, 9 October 2006, 111). Secondly, he took issue with the report's overwhelming emphasis on and characterisation of Base Zero. And, thirdly, he critiqued the universalistic claim that 'understanding any particular violent conflict, any war, allows you to understand any other war … what it ends up doing is it completely erases history. It completely erases culture, politics' (SCSL 2004e, 9 October 2006, 111). Hoffman proceeded to characterise the CDF as a 'militarised social network, or militarised social movement', distinguishing it from more conventional military organisations of which he had some experience (as a professional photographer), including UNITA, the SPLA, the American forces in Kosovo, or even Charles Taylor's forces in Liberia (SCSL 2004e, 9 October 2006, 112).

Under cross-examination by Susan Wright, Hoffman expanded on a number of themes. He highlighted the opportunities the war afforded youth to cultivate their own networks of clients, and to bypass perceived obstacles to resource accumulation (SCSL 2004, 9 October 2006, 118). He stressed that the term 'bodyguard' was more or less equivalent to 'client' (SCSL 2004, 9 October 2006, 122). And he testified to the way in which the CDF was 'an outgrowth of the expectations that came with adult manhood' (SCSL 2004, 9 October 2006, 123).

Cross-examined by Joseph Kamara, Hoffman described, among other things, how to his knowledge Moinina Fofana rose to prominence as a successful local businessman who supplied patronage to internally displaced persons. Upon becoming a member of the CDF he continued to play a similar role. Hoffman's research led him to be sceptical of the idea that Fofana had significant military responsibilities: 'Now, I would add that most people I spoke to, when they referred to him, referred to him as director, and not using that full title director of war. There were certainly instances where people did … in many of these instances, this was … told to me by combatants with a certain amount of irony and ridicule' (SCSL 2004e, 10 October 2006, 26). He testified that his research had disclosed that Fofana was in charge of food supplies at Base Zero, at least for a time, though it had not disclosed that he supplied people with weapons (though he admitted

Figure 5. Moinina Fofana upon sentencing.

that such evidence did appear in the transcript) (SCSL 2004e, 10 October 2006, 54). He rejected Kamara's suggestion that the near simultaneous attacks on Koribundo, Bo and Kenema demonstrated some higher coordination, preferring to see them as distinct events, though he admitted he had not discussed the Koribundo (SCSL 2004e, 10 October 2006, 70).

Greater detail was provided in Hoffman's expert report. On the 'meaning' of military rank in the CDF, he argued that military terms such as 'commander', 'adjutant' or 'Platoon Commander' implied 'that the individual bearing that title was a patron with client/dependents' rather than someone 'with a fixed set of responsibilities or spheres of command' (Hoffman 2006, 20). An illustration of the fact that patronage trumped military factors, was that many CDF people held the title 'commander' even though they had no military experience at all, including members of the 'War Council', most of whom were traditional leaders or politicians. The obverse of this was that titles such as 'National Coordinator', 'Director of War' or 'High Priest', while impressive, would have no corollary in a professional army (Hoffman 2006, 22).

The report proceeded to provide a detailed critique of Iron's position. Among the more salient points, it argued that Iron's methodology meant that he lacked the local knowledge to be able to interpret correctly CDF deviations from an ideal-typical military organisational norm, of which he found several (Hoffman 2006, 40). Iron misunderstood the nature of military 'appointments' such as 'Director of War' for Fofana or 'Director of Operations' for Nallo, since in the absence of a fixed military hierarchy, no such appointments could exist. Rather, 'titles were given as honorifics and to establish relative relationships rather than a list of specific job responsibilities' (Hoffman 2006, 47). The supply of munitions was not centrally controlled from Base Zero; rather, and as Iron's report in part acknowledged, 'weapons, ammunition, food, even medicine utilized by the CDF came from a variety of sources' such as ambushes of the enemy, purchases on the black market, and so on. Moreover, various individuals used the supply of weapons to increase their patronage power; the source was not just one or even a handful of individuals. In sum, 'logistics came from a variety of sources and flowed through numerous, diffuse networks largely independent of Base Zero' (Hoffman 2006, 49). Training was conducted at Base Zero, but trainings were commonplace throughout the sphere of CDF activity, 'ranging from village level tutelage by retired soldiers or experienced hunters to the larger scale trainings which took place in Telu or by ECOMOG at Base One' (Hoffman 2006, 49).

To sum up:

> the CDF was a force without a stable, centralized hierarchy capable of exerting military style command and control. The duties and obligations of CDF members to those above and below them were inseparable from the duties and obligations combatants and 'commanders' had as members of their communities. The CDF's 'many failings as a military organization' do not mean that it was just 'not a very good one.' The CDF's logic was always that of a social rather than a military institution.
>
> (Hoffman 2006, 32.)

Other evidence

The trial evidence provided some support for both viewpoints. For example, in support of Iron's report, there was evidence that, at particular points in time, several thousand Kamajors assembled at Base Zero, where they received orders and training from, among others, Hinga Norman (though there is some dispute over how long they stayed there, and there was little evidence of 'a large number of hierarchically organised units'). There was evidence of the three accused together with high- and mid-level commanders holding meetings to plan attacks on major Sierra Leonean towns. There was evidence of some of those commanders leading operations in those towns. As Iron had argued, this tended to support the idea that the CDF was to some extent effective at strategic and operational levels. In support of Hoffman's interpretation, however, there was evidence that some local commanders undertook operations of their own volition, that they provisioned themselves, that they journeyed to Gendema and Base Zero in search of supplies, and that small groups of Kamajors committed atrocities that seemed to be born out of individual greed or malice, rather than as part of any grand plan (see Chapter 2).

Iron's exclusive focus on Base Zero aside, there was substantial agreement between the two experts on the facts. It was the interpretation of the facts that differed. Whereas in Hoffman's account, it would be extremely difficult to link Kamajor crimes to the three accused, in Iron's, they could be treated as the effect of the culture of indiscipline they tolerated. The contrast was explained partly by theoretical approach and partly by methodology. Iron assumed that fighting forces were basically similar the world over, whatever the differences in the way their functions were discharged. Hoffman's anthropological approach was more inclined to see such differences as pivotal to appreciating the nature of the institution. Methodologically, Iron interviewed a small number of high- and mid-level commanders in the CDF, most of whom played prominent roles at Base Zero. Hoffman drew on an experience of interviewing hundreds of ordinary Kamajors, together with targeted interviews with some of the higher commanders too. If Iron's report almost inevitably provided the view from the top down, Hoffman's was better equipped to give a picture of the movement as a whole.

If Hoffman provided a rounded view of the movement, however, Iron's methodology was better equipped to generate data on the chain of command during specific operations or attacks. His report contained a lengthy analysis of the Bo-Koribundo campaign. Though Hoffman regarded this as atypical of CDF operations as a whole, it was nevertheless significant, since the crimes it witnessed, if successfully traced to the accused, would be sufficient to convict them of war crimes. The question that needs to be answered is whether these attacks were executed through an effective chain of command, in which the superiors had the ability to prevent or punish any crimes that may have been committed.

To answer this question we have to look closely at the evidence on the chain of command and the nature of the attack on the towns of Bo and Koribundo. Starting with Koribundo, three insider witnesses testified that in early January 1998 there was a passing out parade at Base Zero where Norman ordered an all-out offensive on junta-held towns, though he did not urge any criminal acts.[9] Fofana and Kondewa also spoke at this meeting, though there was no evidence that they urged criminal acts either. Five insider witnesses testified about a subsequent commanders' meeting. At this meeting Norman ordered Kamajor commanders, including Joe Tamidey who was to lead the Koribundo attack, to commit criminal acts such as burning the town so that only three buildings remained standing, killing enemy soldiers and civilians, as well as certain named individuals, including one Shekou Gbao.[10] Fofana and Kondewa were present at this meeting, and contributed to the discussion, though there is no evidence that they encouraged the criminal acts. There followed another meeting, at which Norman reiterated these criminal orders to Albert Nallo, saying that he should not spare even a farm or a fowl. Fofana was present, though, again, there was no evidence that he encouraged criminal acts.[11] The judges deduced from this that there was insufficient evidence to convict Fofana under Article 6(i) of the Statute either for planning, ordering, instigating or aiding and abetting crimes commited in Koribundo and Bo. They did, however, find enough evidence to convict him as a superior under Article 6(iii). To assess their verdict, we need to look closely at the evidence on chain of command for the Bo and Koribundo attacks.

In his account of the Base Zero planning meeting mentioned above, Col. Iron described Fofana directing Nallo to nominate commanders for the campaign, which Nallo did by deciding that towns should be attacked by commanders from surrounding chiefdoms. Koribundo would be attacked from three different directions, with Kamajors gathering first at Kpetewoma (Nallo's home town). Norman approved the plan, with some caveats. One was that he thought Joe Tamidey, a local Kamajor who he respected as a fighter and a herbalist, should lead the attack. By intervening, he left Tamidey's responsibility vis a vis Albert

[9] The Chamber's findings here were based on the evidence of three witnesses: former Death Squad leader Borbor Tucker, and TF2-017 and -201, the latter two of whom testified in closed session.

[10] Five witnesses: TF2-008, -011, -021, -201 and Borbor Tucker testified about this meeting, two of them in closed session.

[11] This was based on Nallo's evidence alone.

Nallo, and the other Kamajor groups involved unclear. According to Iron, 'this confusion with the chain of command may have been responsible for some of the later mishaps at Koribundo' (Iron 2005, D-3). Norman also disagreed with the choice of Kpetewoma as the operations base, preferring the village of Gbaama. Nallo apparently disagreed, though Iron is unsure whether or not he disagreed publicly, or whether he simply ignored Norman's directions and established the base at Kpetewoma anyway (Iron 2005, D-3).

Joe Tamidey then returned to his own village where he assembled about twenty-five loyal fighters. At Kpetewoma he met Albert Nallo, who introduced him to the local Kamajor leader, who placed his forces under Tamidey's command. Tamidey settled with his group for a few weeks at Kpetewoma, establishing his own system of discipline. Minor crimes such as sleeping on duty were punished by detention in a cell in the guard room, while more serious crimes, such as stealing from the civilian population, were punished by flogging (Iron 2005, D-4). Prior to the Koribundo attack, Tamidey raided the two towns of Gondama and Sembehun. This was never part of the plan, and Iron is unsure why it occurred, though he thinks it might have been an indirect response to Norman's implied criticism for ignoring his advice to base the operation at Gbaama.

On 13 February, Kamajors attacked Koribundo itself. Iron was unclear how many of the forces were assembled at Kpetewoma prior to the attack, and how many were deployed from elsewhere (Iron 2005, D-8). Reading between the lines, it must also have been unclear to him from where the fighters came, though at an earlier point Iron says they were supposed to come from Base Zero (Iron 2005, D-2). It was also unclear, according to Iron, how many of the Kamajor commanders actually attended the Kpetewoma planning meeting (Iron 2005, D-8). Further, it was difficult to determine the number of fighters involved in the attack, with estimates ranging from several thousand to several hundred, Iron finding the latter figure more plausible (Iron 2005, D-9).

The plan was to attack Koribundo from three separate directions, at staggered intervals dictated by set times (Iron 2005, D-9). Unfortunately, the plan did not work, since Joe Tamidey's group did not attack until four hours after the appointed time, and all groups were subsequently driven back (Iron 2005, D-10). Tamidey apparently thought the attack should commence at 1400 hours, whereas Nallo thought it should be 1000. The misunderstanding, thinks Iron, 'was a consequence of the confused chain of command for the Koribundo operation, where it was never precisely clear what the relationship between Nallo and Tamidey was' (Iron 2005, D-11).

In spite of this botched operation, junta forces pulled out of Koribundo that night. The following morning, Kamajor forces, 'separately entered into town'. The town's capture caused great celebrations among the Kamajors. Nallo returned directly to Base Zero, where Norman rewarded him with a bottle of whisky (Iron 2005, D-11). Other witnesses in the trial testified that when Kamajors entered the town, they went on a burning and killing spree that lasted a number of days. Some of them testified to Joe Tamidey stopping Kamajors from committing crimes, and sparing civilian individuals. Some weeks later, Hinga Norman arrived in town and, in a public meeting, chastised the Kamajors for disobeying his orders and leaving more than three houses standing. However, there was no evidence that punishment was meted out.

We saw earlier that for *de facto* control the prosecution must prove the existence of a 'goal-directed hierarchy and a general awareness of a chain of command'. According to Knoops, 'there must be a widely accepted exercise of issuing and receiving orders, as well as an expectation that insubordination will trigger disciplinary reaction'. There should be 'a mutual expectation that orders will be obeyed' and the superior 'must possess effective means enabling him to suppress an illegal act and punish the perpetrators' (Knoops 2007, 516).

What did the evidence show? It showed that Joe Tamidey was put in charge of the Koribundo operation by Norman, but that his relationship to Albert Nallo and other commanders was confused. It showed that Tamidey was able to establish his authority and a system of discipline over a group of Kamajors assembled at Kpetewoma for a few weeks. However, his authority over other groups of Kamajors who participated in the attack, who may have amounted to several thousand individuals, was unclear. After all, most of these Kamajors would have been unknown to him, and the nature of his authority over their commanders was uncertain. Because of the confused chain of command, the Koribundo operation was botched. However, upon learning of the junta's retreat, Kamajors entered the town separately the next day. Crimes ensued. There is some evidence that Albert Nallo ordered or connived in these crimes, since he claimed that 'we burned the town', though since, according to Iron, he 'returned directly to Base Zero', the degree of effective control he wielded was unclear. There was also some evidence that Tamidey tried to stop the burning and killing. After several days, the Kamajors had failed to achieve Hinga Norman's purported goals.

Bo was also supposed to be attacked from multiple axes on Sunday 15 February with units under Albert Nallo's ostensible control. However, Kamajors actually attacked on Saturday 14 February, either on the initiative of Nallo's deputy Mustapha Gubeh, or on the covert advice of Hinga Norman, before Nallo had even arrived (Iron 2005, D-13). They encountered no resistance and made merry in the town, shooting in the air, looting, burning, and searching for collaborators, making no attempt to defend their position. Nallo apparently attempted to impose order but to no avail, there being a generalised descent into lawlessness (Iron 2005, D-14). Kamajors were consequently driven from the town by a junta counter-attack on Tuesday 17 February in what Iron describes as an 'abject military failure' (Iron 2005, D-15). Nallo visited local villages to try and persuade Kamajors to join the counter-attack, but most had lost their appetite. Control was re-established the following day, however, when a force of only a few hundred retook the town, from which the junta had once again withdrawn (Iron 2005, D-16).

Again, the evidence shows confusion or contradiction in the chain of command, a lack of ability to discipline Kamajors, and problems in mobilising them too: military commanders do not normally have to 'persuade' their forces to fight.

However, Iron's report tended to minimise the significance of these facts. It concluded thus:

> a. The CDF did have a recognizable military hierarchy and structure.
> b. The CDF had most of the functional characteristics of a military organization, but in substantially different form than traditional armies.
> c. The CDF demonstrated good levels of coherence between strategic, operational and tactical levels, though much tactical activity was poorly executed.
> d. The CDF had an effective command capability at strategic and operational levels, but was weaker at the tactical level.
>
> (Iron 2005, E-9.)

Note how, in this formulation, all the CDF's deviations from a traditional military norm are presented as mere afterthoughts, rhetorically designed to minimise their impact on any conclusions the judges might draw about the effectiveness of the chain of command. However, examining the evidence through an anthropological lens, the afterthoughts would take centre stage, and be used to highlight the fact that the CDF was not strictly speaking an 'organisation'; it was not disembedded from its community roots, and consequently, formal chains of command did not function effectively.

Consider the disagreement and unclear communication – or was it mistrust? – between Norman and Nallo. Think about the miscommunication – or perhaps the conflicting agendas – between Nallo and Tamidey. Think about the lack of clear authority relations between Tamidey and the other commanders. Note the fact that it was difficult to ascertain how many Kamajors were involved in the operation – was it hundreds or thousands? – or from which directions they arrived. Consider that Nallo proceeded to burn houses, while Tamidey tried to put a stop to crimes. Note that Norman allegedly ordered the entire town burned – or was it all but three buildings burned? – and yet that only some of this burning occurred. Note that there were frictions between the Koribundo residents and residents of neighbouring Telu, and between Koribundo residents and local Kamajors (see Chapters 2 and 6 for more detail).

Consider also that the historical and anthropological evidence points to the extreme difficulty of establishing effective formal hierarchies in Sierra Leone. Think about the fact that even informal patrimonial hierarchies tend to be undermined by a social physics of centrifugal forces. Note that the top three CDF leaders had had only a matter of months to institutionalise their hierarchy. Think about the fact that two of these supposed top leaders were illiterate. Consider that communications between the different Kamajor units was by bush runner or moped.

Taking into account all this evidence, and looking at it through an anthropological lens, it seems difficult to conclude that the high command of the CDF was anything other than a tenuous patrimonial structure superimposed with only partial success upon a pre-existing social movement that had its own momentum and dynamics. Adding weight to this were Iron's findings that there was no established rank system in the CDF, that fighting units were identified by the names of their leaders, that Norman dominated the movement through force of personality, that commanders were rewarded with food and gifts, but that they also provisioned themselves – all of which tallied with Hoffman's clientelistic account. In light of this, Hoffman's portrayal of the Kamajors as a social network comprised of loosely affiliated groups all to some extent pursuing their own agendas, appears to be an interpretation that is equally consistent, if not more consistent, with the facts.

JUDGMENT AND CONCLUSIONS

The judges, however, thought differently. Drawing on the international jurisprudence, they noted that:

> a superior is someone who possesses the power or authority in either a *de jure* or a *de facto* capacity to prevent the commission of a crime by a subordinate or to punish the offender of the crime after the crime has been committed. It is thus this power or authority of the superior to control the actions of his subordinates which forms the basis of the superior-subordinate relationship'.
>
> (SCSL 2007d, 73.)

In assessing the degree of control, it argued, the test of 'effective control' should be applied; to wit, the superior must possess, 'the material ability to prevent or punish criminal conduct'.[12] Mere 'substantial influence' that falls short of effective control was not sufficient, it thought, for establishing superior criminal responsibility. Moreover, the effective control test must be satisfied even where an accused had *de jure* status as a superior (SCSL 2007d, 74). By the same token, hierarchy, subordination and chains of command did not need to be established to show effective control (SCSL 2007d, 74).

With respect to the chain of command in the CDF, they found that prior to Norman's arrival at Base Zero, the CDF structure tended to mirror the administrative structure of chiefdoms. When Norman arrived, he attempted to centralise and synchronise this structure. As well as appointing Fofana the Director of War, he appointed him a Deputy (M. Orinco Moosa), under whom was a National Director (Joseph Koroma), and Deputy National Director of Operations (Albert Nallo). It was these men who decided when and where to go to war (SCSL 2007d, 112–13). Under this tier of authority were Eastern, Northern, Western and Southern Regional Directors of Operations (the latter position again filled by Nallo). Underneath Regional Directors were District Commanders, under whom were senior battalion and battalion commanders (SCSL 2007d, 115). As well as Regional Directors, there were Regional Coordinators, who distributed food and welfare items (SCSL 2007d, 114).[13]

[12] The 'duty to prevent', it argued, arose from the moment a superior knew a criminal act was likely to be committed. An individual was also under an obligation to prevent his subordinates from committing crimes ordered by superior officers (SCSL 2007d, 77). The duty to punish arose after the superior had acquired knowledge of the commission of the crime.

[13] Note that this is my streamlined rendering of the Chamber's version, which is not quite clear.

Yet if we weigh the scholarly literature on forms of social organisation in Africa and Sierra Leone, and put it together with Danny Hoffman's expert testimony, there are reasons to be sceptical of the idea that this chain of command was effective other than on paper. Certainly, there was scant evidence to think otherwise, meaning that the emphasis was definitely on the term 'attempted'. Indeed, the Chamber expressed doubt about the effectiveness of the chain of command for the majority of CDF crime bases.[14] Nevertheless, for Bo and Koribundo, they found that the chain was effective, running from Moinina Fofana, Director of War, to Albert Nallo, Deputy-Director of Operations, to Kamajors on the ground. Given all the reasons to be sceptical that we have already mentioned, one would think a truly unimpeachable piece of evidence would be necessary to steer the judges to this conclusion. However, by their own admission, the most important piece of evidence in their decision was a single testimony, given by none other than Albert Nallo. Let us take a careful look at it:

MR TAVENER: Thank you.

Q. What was your role as National Deputy Director of Operations?

A. I was taking instructions from Hinga Norman, general and specific, and I transmitted to the war front people. Two, I collected reports for the war front, I compiled them, submit them to the National Coordinator, Sam Hinga Norman, through my Director of War, Moinina Fofana. Three, I collected arms and ammunition and I took them to the war front to the fighters. Four, I frequently visited front lines to ascertain reports and the position of the troops. I was taking interest in the fighters to make sure they lacked no logistics. I sat with Moinina Fofana to plan strategies for war operations for the southern region –

MR BOCKARIE: Your Honour, I –

THE WITNESS: – because he was illiterate …

MR TAVENER:

Q. Moinina Fofana was illiterate?

[14] For example, in Bonthe, the Chamber found that on 15 February 1998, 300–500 Kamajors launched an attack on Bonthe town. The attack was led by District Battalion Commander Morie Jusu Kamara and Commander Julius Squire. Though these men were under the *de jure* control of Albert Nallo, the Chamber doubted that they were under his effective control, 'By Nallo's own admission, he could not exercise full or strict control over all of the Kamajors in Southern Region due to their large numbers' (SCSL 2007d, 259). In consequence, the Chamber had reason to doubt that Fofana was responsible for crimes committed in Bonthe under Article 6(iii). The Chamber followed this pattern of reasoning for all the other crime bases.

A. Yes, My Lord.

PRESIDING JUDGE: Moinina Fofana was what?

MR TAVENER: Illiterate.

THE WITNESS: He couldn't read and write. Those were my roles as Director of Operations for the Southern Region.

MR TAVENER:

Q. How long did you remain at Base Zero, that is until you finally left? I am going to ask you other questions but until you finally left.

A. About six months.

Q. You mentioned you would go to the war front. How would you travel from Base Zero to the war front?

A. Well, we commandeered one Honda bike from Africa. That was what I was using, on the directives of Chief Hinga Norman.

Q. You mentioned you made reports. Did you make – how did you make those reports – were they in writing, verbal? How did you make those reports?

A. Sometimes I would write and at other times I will talk.

Q. Did Mr Fofana have any assistants?

A. Yes, My Lord.

Q. Could those assistants read and write?

A. No, My Lord. No, My Lord. Among all the directors I was the only person who could read and write.

Q. Did you ever give written reports to Mr Fofana?

A. Yes, My Lord. When I give it to him, we sit down together, I'll read it to him before we take it to the Chief, Sam Hinga Norman, the National Coordinator. Yes, My Lord.

(SCSL 2004e, 10 March 2005, 33–5.)

After a break, Nallo came back and had this to say, a description of the command structure that misses out Fofana altogether:

MR TAVENER:

Q. Mr Nallo, we were speaking about Base Zero and in your evidence earlier on you spoke about general and specific orders. Firstly, who gave these general orders?

THE INTERPRETER: Your Honour, the witness's mic is not on.

THE WITNESS: It was the National Coordinator of CDF, Chief Sam Hinga Norman. It's from him that all directives emanated.

(SCSL 2004e, 10 March 2005, 35).

Aside from the fact that there were good reasons to doubt the credibility of Nallo – to be examined in Chapter 6 – do we really get from this testimony proof that Nallo was under Fofana's effective control? If anything, Fofana's illiteracy and corresponding dependence on Nallo to translate reports for him, together with Nallo's apparent ability to bypass Fofana altogether, suggest that Nallo was the dominant party in this relationship.[15] In further support of this idea is the following exchange from 14 March 2005.

CROSS-EXAMINED BY MR BOCKARIE:

MR BOCKARIE:

Q. Mr Nallo.

A. Yes, My Lord.

Q. Yesterday in answer to Mr Yillah you said some of the responsibilities of the Director of War were assigned to you; am I correct?

A. Yes, My Lord.

Q. Can you please tell this Court those responsibilities that were delegated to you?

A. Yes, My Lord.

Q. Go ahead.

A. I used to go to the war front to collect reports, compile them, submit them to National Coordinator through the war director; general and specific instructions were given to me by the National Coordinator, Chief Hinga Norman. I used to take arms and ammunition to the war front for the fighters. I used to frequently visit the front line to ascertain the positions of troops and to report that is given to me … I and the war director had been sitting together to plan the war.

MR BOCKARIE:

Q. I will come to that, Mr Witness. Mr Witness, would you agree with me that these responsibilities you have just stated constituted the core functions of the office of the Director of War?

A. Well, I did not know his roles and responsibilities.

Q. But you'd agree with me that the functions you have just highlighted were very cardinal in carrying out the functions of the Director of War?

A. Yes, My Lord, but because he was not educated that is why I did them.

(SCSL 2004e, 14 March 2005, 50–51).

[15] Indeed, the Chamber had no trouble in accepting his contention that Joseph Koroma, Nallo's immediate superior as National Director of Operations, was, owing to his illiteracy, 'dormant' (SCSL 2004e, 11 March 2005, 59).

A few pages later, we find the following exchange, Arrow Bockarie drawing from a previous statement:

Q. At page 10186 I will read second line from the top. 'I planned strategy for the war and presented it to the War Council.' Did you tell the investigators this?

A. Yes, My Lord. I used to plan because I was the one writing it, because the Director of War was not educated. I was the one that was doing everything. He was saying it in Mende and I was writing.

PRESIDING JUDGE: He would talk to you in Mende and you would write it?

THE WITNESS: Yes, My Lord, both of us.

(SCSL 2004e, 14 March 2005, 56.)

It will be recalled that Col. Iron, in his analysis, placed Nallo in charge of the operational side of war-making, with Moinina Fofana having different but equally important logistical responsibilities, while the defence theory was that Fofana was little more than an *aide-de-camp* to Norman, and the guy who held the keys to the store. Whatever we may think about these two theories, one thing seems clear: there was little to suggest from the testimony above that Fofana had *de facto* authority over Nallo.[16] And yet the Chamber disagreed, stating confidently that:

> We find that there was a superior-subordinate relationship between Fofana and Nallo and that Fofana had authority and control over Nallo's actions. By virtue of his *de jure* status as Director of War Fofana exercised this control over Nallo, who in the hierarchical structure of the CDF organisation was his subordinate as Deputy National Director of Operations and Director of Operations for the Southern Region. Fofana also had *de facto* control over Nallo. Fofana had the legal and material ability to issue orders to Nallo, both by reason of his leadership role at Base Zero, being part of the CDF High Command, and the authority he exercised in this position as Director of War.
>
> (SCSL 2007d, 234.)

What the Chamber neglected to mention in this section was that Fofana was illiterate and, as we have seen above, dependent on Nallo to translate the situation reports for him, that the only example given of Fofana planning a strategy with Nallo was the Black December

[16] The Chamber also referenced the accounts of TF2-079, 26 May 2005, pp. 40–3, and TF2-008, 16 November 2004, pp. 46–7, which were less detailed even than this.

operation, evidence of which had earlier been thrown out of court, that the evidence of Fofana being the overall boss consisted in the closed session testimony of a single witness,[17] that the only evidence of Fofana ever giving orders to commanders was an instance of ordering Joe Tamidey not to release captured vehicles and other items before registering them at CDF HQ in case of legal claims by their owners – hardly a military instruction – that the final decision on deploying Kamajors was Norman's, and that Fofana could not dispense ammunition without Norman's say-so (SCSL 2007d, 110).

Nevertheless, the Chamber found a general chain of command that ran from Hinga Norman through Fofana to Albert Nallo, which in Koribundo also extended to Joe Tamidey and the rank and file Kamajors. In Bo, meanwhile, it found that this chain of command was partly effective, running through Norman, Fofana, Nallo, TF2-017 and James Kaillie. Again, its main justification for reasoning this way appears to have been the testimony of Albert Nallo. So what did Nallo have to say? Nallo claimed that he did all the arranging and planning for the Koribundo operation himself, which he submitted to Fofana who then submitted it to Norman. Norman then gave him specific instructions, including to burn everything and to not leave even a fowl alive. Nallo's account of the actual attack follows:

MR TAVENER

Q. When you attacked Koribundu did you have other Kamajors with you?

A. Yes, up to 700.

Q. Were there other commanders involved in that attack?

A. Yes, My Lord. Some commanders came from Pujehun, you have some from Bonthe District and Bo District.

Q. When you successfully attacked Koribundu – that means the rebels left – what happened?

A. We burnt the place. Then one of my commanders by the name of CO Lamin, when he was making up a mopping up operation, he went along Koribundu Road. That is Gbaima village in the Wunde Chiefdom –

PRESIDING JUDGE: Wait, wait. The question that was put to you was – in fact, it was a suggestion, because you hadn't even said that when you attacked the juntas ran away. That was Mr Tavener's intervention.

[17] TF2-005.

Well, what you said was the junta – or the question that was put to you was what happened after your attack and after the junta had escaped, had taken to their hills?

THE WITNESS: We took over Koribundu.

MR TAVENER:

Q. How long did you stay there?

A. We are there throughout. The only thing was that I stayed there for one day. The other day I moved to Bo on the instruction of Chief Hinga Norman.

Q. In the day that you were there what did you see?

A. We burnt houses. Then we captured some – some two soldiers.

Q. What did you do with those soldiers?

A. Well, they were with us up to when ECOMOG entered Bo. That was the time that one sergeant commander went to ECOMOG and said that we had soldiers that we had captured.

(SCSL 2004e, 10 March 2005, 82–3.)

What is not clear from this testimony, at least to this author, is whether or not Nallo led his troops into battle or how closely he followed on their heels, whether he was able to monitor and control their actions, or command their support.[18] Does this testimony really show that the Kamajors who attacked Koribundo were under Nallo's effective, material control? Under cross-examination on 14 March, he had this to say:

MR YILLAH: Yes, My Lord.

Q. Mr Witness, you said there were many commanders in Koribundu. Would I be correct to suggest that these many commanders were operating with different groups when the attack took place?

A. Yes, My Lord, but all of them were under my command. All the commands that I took from Base Zero are the ones that they had to go by for my National Coordinator so as to burn all the house in Koribundu. That they shouldn't have left even a fowl.

(SCSL 2004e, 14 March 2005, 44.)

[18] Note that the supposedly corroborating testimony of Borbor Tucker does not mention Nallo (SCSL 2004e, 10 February 2005). Interestingly, Mustapha Lumeh, a defence witness, does describe in more detail Albert Nallo's role. In Lumeh's account it *was* Nallo who provided the overall instructions for the attack at Kpetewoma (SCSL 2004e, 8 May 2006, 52–3), which included allowing soldiers and civilians to flee the town via the Bo Road. Nallo then entered Koribundo via the Sumbuya Road with Lumeh's group on Friday 13 February. They found the town empty so retreated to the bush. They returned the next day to find the town on fire, which they tried to extinguish (SCSL 2004e, 8 May 2005, 53–60). In its discussion on assessing the evidence, the Chamber singled Lumeh out as an untruthful witness. However, it was content to accept his testimony where it fitted with the story it wanted to tell.

And yet there is counter-evidence to show that Joe Tamidey, supposedly a subordinate of Nallo, intervened to stop the burning of houses and killing of civilians. And by Nallo's own admission, he himself captured some enemy soldiers instead of killing them! For these reasons, I would contend that a clear picture of responsibility in the Koribundo attack does not emerge from this testimony. This is especially the case when we weigh it against Col. Iron's observations about confusion in the chain of command, together with Iron's claim that Nallo returned to Base Zero that same day. Could a judge, treating this testimony with 'extreme circumspection' (see Chapter 6), really have concluded that all the Kamajors in Koribundo were under Nallo's, let alone Moinina Fofana's effective control? Apparently so, since, according to the Chamber, they 'were all under Albert J. Nallo's command' (SCSL 2007d, 135). Further, 'Nallo knew how the attack would proceed and who would be involved in the attack' (SCSL 2007d, 235). In support of this conclusion it footnoted three testimonies. One was Albert Nallo's response to counsel Ibrahim Yillah on 14 March 2005 (see above), another was a reference to the passing out parade at Base Zero by TF2-021, which mentions only that Jo Tamidey was the Commander in charge, and the other was from closed session witness TF2-201. It went on to conclude that Fofana 'did nothing to prevent the commission of these criminal acts by his subordinates', who were all Kamajors 'under his effective control' (SCSL 2007d, 236). The Chamber then proceeded to list the crimes ordered by Norman and committed in Koribundo that included murder, cruel treatment and collective punishments, concluding that 'all of the perpetrators of these acts were Kamajors under the effective control of Fofana' (SCSL 2007d, 239). The Chamber reasoned similarly in respect of the attack on Bo. The most significant difference was that Fofana was held responsible for only some of the crimes charged, to wit, those committed by Kamajors under the effective control of Albert Nallo.[19]

[19] The Chamber found a nexus between Nallo, TF2-017 and James Kaillie. However, the nexus between -017, Kaillie and the Kamajors killing people in Bo is not always clear to me from the evidence. But it does appear that Nallo was among a group of Kamajors who arrived at the police station, asking them to surrender their weapons (TF2-001, SCSL 2004e, 14 February 2005, 75), cited in support of this nexus (SCSL 2007d, 144, note 883). Note that Fofana was absolved of responsibility for some of the crimes committed in Bo, on account of Nallo's admission that he did not have effective control over all of the Kamajors, since there were too many, or since there were additional units outside his control. The Chamber also found that Fofana supplied arms, ammunitions, and a vehicle to three of the commanders who would lead the Bo

Did Fofana really have the authority to prevent Albert Nallo from carrying out these instructions, or to punish him after the event? Wasn't it the case that although *de jure* superior to Nallo, Nallo's *de facto* authority was greater than his? Wasn't Nallo actually possessed of significant *de facto* autonomy within a patrimonial authority network? Yet wasn't it also the case that Nallo's authority over his own putative subordinates wasn't fully effective? Wasn't the real story one of local groups of Kamajors pursuing diverse agendas in a social context where it was virtually impossible for the CDF hierarchy to exercise effective control? Robert Jackson and Carl Rosberg, acknowledged authorities on systems of personal rule, observe that, 'personal rule in Africa is characterized by the seeming paradox of relative autonomy or freedom for the ruler and his clique to make policies but great constraint or incapacity to implement or enforce them' (Jackson and Rosberg 1982, 30). These problems extend to all the institutions of state, including the military. African militaries, say Jackson and Rosberg, have been 'impregnated by African sociocultural norms', and on occasions when the military has sought to exercise power, they have been caught in the cross-currents of 'personal, lineage, clan, ethnic and other loyalties' (Jackson and Rosberg 1982, 37). To this author, this is a more realistic account of authority relations in the CDF than the one the Trial Chamber proposed.

To sum up, my anthropolitical approach shows that in cultural settings where the anthropological and historical evidence teach us that military hierarchies are rarely effective, courts need to be more cautious than this before convicting individuals. This is because there already exists a reasonable, scientific doubt over the effectiveness of the chain of command, meaning that the evidence has a slope to climb (compare Hoffman 2007). Indeed, we might argue that Prosecutors should desist from pressing charges on grounds of superior responsibility in these kinds of settings, since social scientific evidence shows that it occurs very rarely, if at all. If Prosecutors insist they have a case, judges need to subject the evidence to exra scrutiny. In the case of Moinina Fofana, I submit that this is something the Court did not do: the evidence it found

attack. However, the Chamber did not consider that this rendered him responsible for aiding and abetting it (under Article 6(i)), since he could only supply logistics under the authority of Norman. Moreover, it was not obvious that the logistics supplied had 'a substantial effect upon the perpetration of these specific criminal acts in Bo' (SCSL 2007d, 245).

for effective control would be barely convincing in a culture where we expect a close overlap between *de jure* and *de facto* roles, and it clearly did not pass the test in a context where a higher threshold of proof ought to have been required.[20]

[20] The case against Kondewa in Bonthe, discussed in Chapter 2, was stronger, but still it was not clear to me that a sufficient threshold had been met. Readers will find that I take the obverse position in the next chapter: where there is social scientific evidence to expect the efficacy of charismatic authority, the threshold for evidence of its occurrence may be slightly lowered.

CHAPTER 4

FACTS, METAPHYSICS AND MYSTICISM: MAGICAL POWERS AND THE LAW

One of the most extraordinary dimensions of the CDF trial, an aspect that made it unique in the history of international justice, was the section that dealt with supernatural forces. To be more precise, the Trial Chamber heard a considerable volume of evidence about ritual ceremonies in which CDF initiates were reportedly rendered immune to bullets by either consuming or applying occult medicines. Bullet-proofing was central to the theories of criminal conspiracy and superior responsibility advanced by the prosecution, and also to the overall strategy of the defence. In this chapter I provide some anthropological background to the use of magic and the occult in Sierra Leone, I discuss how colonial and post-colonial courts in Africa have dealt with magical phenomena, and then I examine evidence of the supernatural at trial. Ultimately, the bench acquitted Allieu Kondewa for crimes related to his mystical powers, but in this chapter I will argue from my anthropolitical perspective that their reasoning deserves a rethink.

MAGIC AND THE OCCULT IN SIERRA LEONE[1]

Most people in the West, and certainly most international lawyers, believe that the world we live in is a largely secular domain governed by the actions of men and the scientific relations of mechanical cause and

[1] Discussing 'witchcraft' in contemporary Africa distinguished Africanist Peter Geschiere describes it as: 'a very tricky topic: writing about it clearly entails the dangers of exoticizing – or even primitivizing – Africa as still beset by "traditional" forms of superstition.' Yet, having noted the centrality of witchcraft anxieties to modern African lives, he opines that: 'It would be

effect. God, if he exists at all, is assumed to be a rather distant presence, rarely revealing himself to humans and intervening only nebulously in day-to-day affairs; the same goes for other supernatural beings, such as angels, the devil or the deceased. According to this worldview, heaven and earth are distinct spheres that rarely intercalate. Even members of the Christian priesthood are thought to lack direct access to the heavenly realm: prayers are offered in the hope, rather than the expectation, that they will be answered, while most humans and objects are believed to possess no supernatural power at all (Ellis and ter Haar 1998).[2] This way of seeing things, it should be emphasised, is almost certainly a minority view – historically and globally speaking – even though it currently dominates in the West.

Certainly, for most parts of contemporary Africa, the situation is rather different. Many Africans believe in a close relation between the visible and invisible worlds, with power in the former hinging on relations in the latter. Visible and invisible spheres are constantly interacting, with beings from one world routinely intervening on the plane of another. Many humans and indeed everyday objects are thought to possess extraordinary supernatural power with the ability to act not only proximately, but at a distance also (Ellis and ter Haar 1998, 2004; Geschiere 1997; Moore and Sanders 2001). The upcountry ethnic groups of Sierra Leone are a case in point. Temne people, for example, who predominate in the Northern region, traditionally believe that space is divided into four principal regions: one for humans and animals, one for demons, one for witches, and another for ancestors, the latter three being visible only to those humans who have 'two sets of eyes' (Littlejohn 1963). For the Mende of southern and eastern Sierra Leone, humans, animals and even everyday objects are frequently believed to have 'doubles' with extraordinary powers in other dimensions. Spirits may possess the bodies of humans, especially when they sleep, or a person's spirit may leave its body during sleep or venture into the witch or spirit world; alternatively, it might possess the body of an animal. Witches or other kinds of spirit frequently sojourn in the physical world

highly regrettable if political correctness made academics avoid such an urgent topic' (Geschiere 2006, 220–1).

[2] Clearly, significant and possibly growing minorities in the West, from Christian fundamentalists to UFO spotters, do believe in regular contact between humans and extraordinary beings. However, such beliefs are not part of the mainstream, and figure barely at all in institutions of state, such as the courts. For an amusing journey through America's other-wordly sub-cultures, see Theroux (2007).

by inhabiting the bodies of animals, in particular leopards, crocodiles or chimpanzees (Ferme 2001, 32, 211).[3]

Many Africans also believe that the natural and human world can be controlled by means of special medicines. In the Mande regions of West Africa this stems from a belief that the universe has a background energy that gives life to all living things, providing momentum for every act undertaken in this world. Conceived of by itself, this energy is neutral, but it can be harnessed for immense good or harm through what Mande call *jiridon*, or 'the science of the trees':

> According to this science, most living things have useful parts that can be detached from the whole entity and combined with parts from other living things. Such recombined entities develop properties that can be used to change, to rearticulate one's environment. When made to work on the physical plane they are medicines that can cure everything from fevers to bad breath. When made to work on the supernatural plane they are amulets or secret occult devices that can perform such diverse tasks as preventing poisonous snake bites or falling in love.
>
> (McNaughton 1982, 56.)

In Mende areas of Sierra Leone, medicine and the means of using it is called *hale*.[4] Concoctions of plant, animal, and even human matter, or else Arabic inscriptions thought to condense and canalise spiritual power, are used to facilitate contact between the human and spirit worlds (Hoffman 2003, 77; Bellman 1984; Little 1965; Murphy 1980). The medicines that result may be used as lustrations, worn in amulets, buried or hung in special places, poured as libations, or activated by means of ritual incantation; they can be used for all manner of everyday and extraordinary purposes: protecting one's body, fields or property from human or spiritual attack; facilitating love affairs; pursuing political power or economic wealth; augmenting human or agricultural fertility; developing

[3] Ideas about shape-shifting and doubling are certainly not archaic aspects of local knowledge. Recently, Rosalind Shaw has described in fascinating detail the characteristics of what her Temne informants told her of 'the witch city', a malign underground space which mirrors in many respects the world of the living (Shaw 2002, 201–3). In 2004 and 2005, my Temne research assistant would speak of people who could perceive witches as having 'spiritual eyes', and told stories of a female relative confessing to offering her children to be eaten by witches in a dream. Another research assistant – a Mende graduate in economics – straight-facedly told me stories about witches who flew around at night in aeroplanes constructed from peanut shells.

[4] Remember that the Mende are a Mande-speaking people spun into Sierra Leone in the eighteenth century following convulsions in the old Mande empires of the western Sahel.

sporting or artistic prowess; and harming or helping other human beings (Bellman 1984; Little 1965; Murphy 1980; Shaw 2002; Nunley 1988; Bledsoe and Robey 1986).[5]

Medicines and charms are also used to bring success in hunting. Traditionally, Mande hunters acquired their incredible powers of invisibility, invincibility and marksmanship by communicating with forest spirits; alternatively, they approached Islamic ritual experts for powerful Arabic inscriptions (Leach 2000). The shirts they wore were typically affixed with amulets containing organic medicines or folded paper inscribed with Qur'anic verse. Sewn onto them were also parts from the animals they killed, filled with medicines. Often they were decorated with mirrors that 'flash when they catch the light, punctuating the mystery of the shirts and suggesting the vital forces and spirits that must be dealt with' (McNaughton 1982, 91). Medicines also bring success in war. Reports from late eighteenth-century Sierra Leone, for example, speak of the warrior son of a powerful Foulah, who won influence among the Mende on account of his powerful medicines, and later carved a huge kingdom from the centre of the country (Kup 1962, 155). Medicines and bullet proofing were also used in the nineteenth century, and McNaughten has claimed that hunters, with their magical powers and love of adventure, played a key role in the wars of the Mande world that led to peoples such as the Mende entering present day Sierra Leone (McNaughton 1982).

In the most recent civil war, Sierra Leone's armed factions, and especially the CDF, drew heavily on local magical beliefs. According to Patrick Muana, a scholar who was himself initiated into the movement, *Kamajoisia*, the local term for kamajor, means 'past master at doing mysterious things' (Muana 1997, 78, note 3). For Muana, the Kamajors' 'intimate knowledge of the terrain, medicinal and edible flora and fauna' contributed to the 'mysticism and near reverence that has characterised this institution'. The *Kamajoi*, he says, 'straddles and transcends the tripartite but intertwined Mende cosmological divides of man,

[5] Charms have also been popular in Freetown since at least the nineteenth century: 'The lassy-mammy charm consists in writing Arabic upon a table with an infusion or ink obtained from the bark of a tree, texts from the Scriptures of the Koran, which is then washed off and bottled. They wash themselves with it before asking favours, etc. Even the educated creoles, of both sexes, have great faith in the virtue of charms; and the possession of a "sebeh" from the Mahommedan priests is considered serviceable in times of difficulty and danger. Thieves arm themselves with it to escape detection, and prisoners at the bar put it into their mouths when defending themselves' (Clarke 1863, 353).

forest/beast, and spirit' (Muana 1997, 86–7). Kamajor dress, meanwhile, recalled the outfits of traditional hunters, comprising typically:

> a locally woven 'V' neck designed cloth sewn as a sleeveless (*kpakibaa*) ... worn with the big shorts (*mbele gutiiwai*) that reach down to the knees ... usually spotted (black) almost to resemble a leopard's coat. Caps are made of the same materials. The *Kamajoi* apparel is bedecked with cowry shells, horns, small mirrors, and talisman in woven notches. Some carry fly whisks and wear jingles on their calves. They wear an assortment of footwear: from plastic sandals to sports shoes.
>
> (Muana 1997, 91.)[6]

To become a Kamajor one needed to be initiated. According to Hoffman: 'Participation in the movement increasingly came to be predicated on an induction, a ritual and secretive "preparation" that rendered the conscript bullet-proof and was, at least in theory, meant to culminate in a public demonstration of one's capacity to repel bullets or make weapons misfire' (Hoffman 2004, 77). Presiding over these rituals were initiators such as Kamoh Brima Bangura, Mwalimu Saddam Sheriff (aka Mualemu Sheriff), Mamma Munda Fortune, and, most famously of all, a man who went by the honorific King Dr Allieu Kondewa, High Priest of the CDF (Hoffman 2004, 78–83; TRC 2004).

Prior to the war, Kondewa was apparently an amateur herbalist and travelling magician, performing 'illusions' to local audiences to the accompaniment of a cultural troupe of dancers and drummers. He was reputed to live in a house without a roof, in which he could miraculously withstand rainstorms without getting wet. He was rumoured also to be an inveterate gambler and habitual drunk.[7] Indeed, one of his detractors at Base Zero claimed that he would concoct ever more warped ideas for initiations while in a drunken stupor, saying that the ideas had come to him in 'dreams' (TRC 2004, vol. 3A, 215–16). Accounts of how Kondewa came to occupy such an important role in the movement vary. Some say that one day in 1995 three old women in Kale, a village in Bonthe, simultaneously had a dream advising the village men to pour libations

[6] While a Western journalist reporting from the recent civil war described Temne *Kapras* as: 'clad in bright, multi-coloured woollen vests and ponchos, adorned with mirrors, medicine bundles, conch shells and fetish beads, the *capras* [*sic*] looked like the paramilitary wing of the Jimmy [*sic*] Hendrix fan club' (cited in Leach (2000, 589)).

[7] One of the defence lawyers suggested that Kondewa's prodigious ability to consume alcohol was taken by some as a sign of his supernatural powers (interview with Arrow Bockarie, Bo Town, 13 June 2008).

to the ancestors following which one of them would receive a revelation. The men subsequently followed this advice, whereupon Allieu Kondewa claimed that he had received a revelation instructing him to become the Initiator for the Kamajors. Among his first initiates were Joe Timmidey and Moinina Fofana, both of whom were to climb to prominent positions in the movement, and both of whom, as we have seen, figured prominently in the CDF trial (TRC 2004, vol. 3A, 215–18).

Kondewa's reputation grew, and at some point he came to the attention of Hinga Norman, who began to use him for mass initiations at Base Zero and other areas, with as many as 5,000 people allegedly being initiated in one go. Increasingly, he became the stuff of legend. Patrick Muana, for example, provides this account of his rise to fame drawn from ethnographic work with Kamajors in wartime Bo:

> Following an RUF attack on a village in the Jong Chiefdom [Bonthe District], the rebels are reported to have massacred people in the village including a great Kamajoi and medicine man called Kposowai. His brother [Kondewah] is said to have been captured by the rebels, forced to carry looted goods and tied with 'tabay' securely for the night whilst the rebels pitched camp.
>
> As he drifted to sleep in spite of his pains, Kondewah is said to have had a vision of his brother who had been killed the day before. The ropes fell loose and the elder brother invested him with the authority to take to all able-bodied Mende men that the defence of their own lives, homes, wives, and children was a sacred duty.
>
> To assist them in that task, Kposowai is said to have shown Kondewah a secret concoction of herbs and instructed that a stringent initiation process should precede the 'washing' of the warriors in the herbs. This concoction would make them invincible in battle, impervious to bullets, and endow them with powers of clairvoyance if all taboos were kept. Kondewah is said to have slaughtered the RUF rebels, freed the other captives, and trekked several miles to a secret hiding place where he initiated the first set of men.
>
> (Muana 1997, 87–8.)

According to the Sierra Leone Truth and Reconciliation Commission, the initiations involved cannibalism, excursions in graveyards, complex taboos, and being subjected to shotgun fire using either live or blank rounds. These rituals were supposed to bestow immunity to bullets on their recipients, though there are accounts to suggest that during the rituals initiates sometimes died. Fighters, who each paid a fee to the initiators, were then deployed to the battlefield believing that they had invincible powers. The initiations appear to have been an extremely lucrative business for the initiators, and a cottage industry of initiators offering top-up initiations soon sprang up (TRC 2004, vol. 3A, 274–7, 545).

Apparently, recruits who had undergone initiation were often loath to undergo the more conventional aspects of military training offered by the CDF, charging off to the battlefield believing in their own invincibility. According to one TRC informant, Norman allowed much military strategy to be dictated by the initiators, in whose powers he firmly believed. This was a source of friction with some, Western educated members of the War Council, revolted by the macabre methods and sceptical of their supernatural claims (TRC 2004, vol. 3A, ch.3, 279–80). Tensions between Norman, the initiators and the War Council at Base Zero, appear to have been exacerbated post-1999, when the Lomé Peace Accord made the CDF redundant, and the organisation experienced further bad-tempered splits. On the one hand, initiators like Kondewa continued to stage mass initiations into ever more esoteric associations, one being called the Avondos, while on the other, Kamajor leaders competed over the spoils of demobilisation. Kondewa was eventually removed from the post of High Priest by Norman, while Norman split from other Kamajor notables, including Charles Moiwo, salvaging his position through an alliance with Joe Demby (Hoffman 2004, 132–8, 203, 279; Keen 2005, 278–9).

Before discussing its legal implications, it is worth noting that the practice of bullet-proofing is not unique to Sierra Leone. Perhaps the most famous example in Africa comes from the *Maji Maji* rebellion of southern Tanganyika in 1905–1907, the largest ever uprising against colonial rule in sub-Saharan Africa. *Maji Maji* was inspired in part by a spirit-snake cult which purported to bestow immunity to bullets upon its adherents:

> The *maji* – the water-medicine accepted by each rebel – united in common action peoples with no known prior unity. Its power was believed to be religious, or in German terms was due to witchcraft. And it inspired its recipients with a passionate courage of which the Germans had believed their subjects incapable.
>
> (Iliffe 1967, 502.)

The uprising claimed over 75,000 lives. A decade earlier, belief that bullets would turn to water via divine intervention had been reported by the British South Africa Company in the Rhodesian Risings of 1896–1897 (Cobbing 1977). More recent African examples come from late twentieth-century Liberia, where '[f]ighters from the various factions, sometimes very young and almost invariably sporting amulets supposed to make them bullet-proof, filled the streets with corpses' (Ellis 2001, 222) and Congo, where Mai-Mai militiamen, also at work during the Simba Rebellion of 1965, played a pivotal role in toppling the Mobutu regime (1997) and subsequently in terrorising parts of the north-east in the second Congo war (1998–2003):

> Their name literally means 'water-water', *mai* being the Congolese form of the Swahili word, *maji*. The name comes from a belief that bullets can be turned to water as a result of the liquid *dawa* (medicine, potion) which is poured over the body to prevent weapons from killing and maiming.
>
> (Wild 1998, 452.)

In Mozambique's 1980s civil war, a popular militia known as *Naparama* used magical concoctions to make the rebel group RENAMO's modern weapons useless against the spears, bows and arrows with which the militia were armed (Muana 1997, 85). Militiamen in Nigeria's Niger Delta are also said to have bullet-proofing powers, while in contemporary South Africa, Zulu taxi drivers not infrequently have medicines rubbed into bodily incisions, apparently to protect them from bullets (Junger 2007; Jolles and Jolles 2000). Indeed, occult forces have played a key role in African wars from Zimbabwe to the Sudan: they remain integral to the worldview of many Africans, paradoxically providing a means of interpreting and engaging with the modern world, with the consequence that mystical methods will almost certainly play a part in future conflict (Johnson 1997; Lan 1992; Comaroff and Comaroff 1993; Geschiere 1997, 2006; Ellis and ter Haar 1998; Ashforth 1998a, 1998b; Moore and Sanders 2001). Indeed, two of the cases currently being dealt with by the International Criminal Court are from countries (Congo and Uganda) where forms of mystical defence and attack have been integral to the *modus operandi* of war (Behrand 1999).

Bullet-proofing, though especially prevalent in Africa, is by no means confined to it. In the nineteenth century, various Native American groups used the technique in their struggles against settler expansion. For example, Roman Nose, the famous Cheyenne war chief, possessed a war-bonnet or head-dress, woven into which were the body of a bat and parts of particular birds, thought to make him bullet-proof. Apparently, the bullet-proofing powers would cease to function if the wearer broke a variety of arcane taboos, such as shaking hands with a person or eating food that had been taken from a dish with a metal implement (in the analysis to come we will see the importance of taboos to bullet-proofing in Sierra Leone) (Kenny 1989). Another example comes from late nineteenth-century Paraguay, where indigenous shamans searched for magical techniques that would render their people immune to settlers' bullets (Kidd 1995). In 1943, in Biak, now part of Indonesia, the Japanese navy opened fire on a huge crowd who apparently believed that bullets would turn to water. Warriors in Melanesia have also sometimes sought out magical powers to ward off bullets (Keesing 1985). In 1970s Cambodia, government soldiers loyal to the regime of Lon Nol were given amulets to make them immune to the weapons of the Khmer Rouge (Maguire 2005, 44–5). In fact, according to Brian Wilson, belief in bullet-proofing has been quite common among indigenous or third-world societies under threat (cited in Kidd (1995, 53)).

For the great French sociologist Marcel Mauss, beliefs such as these could be explained as a kind of collective wish fulfilment: societies believed in magic because they needed to feel they could influence otherwise uncontrollable aspects of their social and natural environments; magicians like Allieu Kondewa were merely the conduit for these needs: 'It is public opinion which makes the magician and creates the power he wields' (Mauss 1902 (2006), 50). Magicians prepared medicines, wove spells and performed esoteric rites that purported to satisfy these needs, and although magic itself always contained an element of artifice or simulation, this did not necessarily make the magician a fraud: 'The magician pretends because pretence is demanded of him, because people seek him out and beseech him to act. He is not a free agent' (Mauss 1902 (2006), 118). In the face of such pressure, the magician came to believe in his own illusions. For Mauss: 'the magician cannot be branded as an individual working on his own for his own benefit. He is a kind of official, vested by society with authority … He is serious about it because he is taken seriously, and he is taken seriously because people have need of him' (Mauss 1902 (2006), 119).

MAGIC AND THE LAW IN COLONIAL AND POST-COLONIAL AFRICA

The Special Court for Sierra Leone was by no means the first Western-style court to grapple with the issue of supernatural beliefs and powers. Precedents can be found in colonial Africa, where colonial courts dealt with hundreds of cases of witchcraft killings and ritual murder. In almost all of these cases, as in the CDF trial, an immanent clash of worldviews presented the judges with a profound dilemma. By aligning themselves with the magical beliefs of the accused, colonial courts risked condoning patterns of belief and action they regarded as profoundly mistaken. But by disregarding them, they handed down verdicts that seemed unjust, convicting Africans 'without regard to moral guilt' (Seidman 1965, 58). In the next section, I discuss a few colonial cases to illustrate these points.

I will begin with *Attorney-General of Nyasaland* v. *Jackson*, one of the most notorious cases in this regard. The circumstances were this: the accused, Jackson, had got into a quarrel with an elderly female relative, who had subsequently told him, 'you will not see the sun today'. Jackson interpreted this as an imminent threat of witchcraft and after an hour or so he took his bow and arrow and shot the woman. Guided by local assessors, the judge found that Jackson's mistaken fear of supernatural attack was both genuine and reasonable:

> If the accused believes in the necessity, then even if such necessity does not in fact exist, there is a mistake of fact and not of law ... In the circumstances in which the accused was placed, and believing what he in fact believed, nothing short of the actual killing of the perpetrator of the spell could avail him.
>
> (Seidman 1966, 1141.)

Aligning himself with the worldview of the defendant, the judge ruled that this was a case of homicide justified on grounds of self-defence, and Jackson was found not guilty of murder. However, this decision was later overturned by the court of appeal, which explicitly distanced itself from local beliefs. In its view:

> The test of reasonableness in itself implies an objective standard ... The test of reasonableness is one that is constantly invoked in English law. In applying it, the standard is what would appear reasonable to the ordinary man on the street in England ...
>
> On this basis, and bearing in mind that the law of England is still the law of England even when it is extended to Nyasaland, I do not see how any court, applying the proper test, could hold that a belief in witchcraft was reasonable.
>
> (cited in Seidman 1966, 1141.)[8]

[8] More flexible was the 1959 Sudanese court which found not guilty a man who had in the night mistaken an old woman dressed in black for a ghost and beaten her to death. The reasoning was that he had intended to slay a ghost, not a human being (Seidman 1966, 1146–7). A related class of cases is provided by the hundreds of medicine murders tried in Basutoland Courts, in which the accused mutilated to death an individual in order to procure body parts for medicine. The

The appeals court ruling made clear that in cases where the accused pled self-defence, the nature of the threat he or she faced must be physical, not metaphysical. As Robert Seidman has noted, it must be of the sort 'that a reasonable Englishman would recognise, not the sort which would seem frightening only to an African steeped in the culture of the bush' (Seidman 1966, 1142). This reasoning was repeated in the vast majority of colonial cases, and, as we shall see, was also significant at the Special Court. For example, in *Gadam* (Nigeria, 1954), the defendant had killed his wife because he believed she had bewitched him. His lawyer appealed to a section of the Nigerian criminal code which afforded a defence for a mistake which was 'honest and reasonable'. The court, however, held that even though witchcraft belief was common in the community, this did not make the belief 'reasonable': the test of a belief's reasonableness was whether it would seem as such to the reasonable Englishman (Seidman 1965, 50). In the 1932 Kenyan case of *Kumwaka Wa Mulumbi and 69 others*, seventy defendants admitted beating to death an old woman on account of the fact that she was a witch. Their lawyer argued that their superstition negated their *mens rea* for the crime. The court, however, was not impressed, and sentenced sixty of them to death. In the 1951 Ugandan case of *Erika Galikuwa*, the defendant was charged with murdering a witchdoctor, claiming that he acted in self-defence since he heard the witchdoctor's 'spirit voice' threatening to kill him by sucking his blood. The court, however, convicted him, stating that: 'it is difficult to see how an act of witchcraft unaccompanied by some physical attack could be brought within the principles of English Common Law' (Seidman 1965, 48–9). In the 1952 Gold Coast case of *Konkomba*, the defendant was charged with murdering a man whom a juju-man (a ritual expert) had identified to him as having bewitched and killed his first brother. When the defendant's second brother fell ill, the defendant killed the alleged witch. Lawyers argued their client believed his actions had been necessary to save the life of another, but the court found him guilty of murder nevertheless.[9]

defence that the killers acted out of necessity, in response, for example, to some pressing threat, was never tried says Seidman. Had it been so, it would probably have been rejected, he argues, on grounds one, following Jackson, that the mistake was not reasonable; and on grounds two, that the common law probably requires a value judgment to the effect that taking the life of an innocent to save another can never be justified (Seidman 1966, 1148). A fuller account of these murders and the trials that judged them can be found in Murray and Sander's marvellous book (Murray and Sanders 2005).

[9] Seidman compares this case to the English case of *Bourne* (1939), in which the defendant, a medical doctor, was charged with carrying out an abortion on a 15 year-old rape victim. The

Colonial courts were similarly disinclined to acquit on grounds of insanity. For example, in the 1956 Kenyan case of *Philip Muswi s/o Musola*, the defendant shot his wife with a bow and arrow after a long period of quarrelling from which he came to believe that she was trying to bewitch him. The court subsequently overruled the insanity defence since: 'even if [the defendant] believed that he was justified in killing his wife because she was practising witchcraft, there is again no evidence that such belief arose from any mental defect; it is a belief sometimes held by entirely sane Africans' (Seidman 1965, 51). According to Seidman, in cases like this the colonial courts applied an untenable double-standard:

> The African who commits a crime because of his pre-scientific worldview, then, falls between the two stools of mistake and insanity. On the one hand, his mistake is measured by the standard of reasonableness appropriate to Englishmen. On the other hand, his sanity is measured by a standard appropriate to Africans. An Englishman who killed another because he believed that the victim [was a] vampire … would no doubt find a safe refuge in insanity; the eleven Acholi who did the same thing were sentenced to death.
>
> (Seidman 1966, 1154.)

Except in one case defences of partial-delusion or provocation were similarly unavailing.[10]

Early on in the colonial period, J. L. Driberg lamented the situation under which what might appear to 'the African' as 'a pious duty' was called 'murder' by colonial courts, to which a death sentence attached. Some approximation between the two legal systems was called for, he thought, which 'may conduce to an administration of justice which will prove more understandable to the African' (Driberg 1934, 243). But Driberg's call was not heeded. Seidman, writing in the 1960s, argued

doctor claimed that he was acting on a psychiatrist's advice that should the pregnancy be allowed to continue, psychiatric damage to the girl might ensue. The court held the abortion justifiable. In each case the defendant honestly believed that his actions were necessary to save another, and each acted upon the advice of an expert in the relevant field. The main difference, argues Seidman, was that the tribunal believed in psychiatry, but not in witchcraft (Seidman 1965, 49). In these cases, it was the validity of the belief under which the defendant acted which determined his criminality (Seidman 1965, 49).

10 The defence of provocation was sustained in the case of *Fabiano* (Uganda, 1941), in which an old man previously suspected of having threatened a family with witchcraft was found crawling naked around the defendants' compound, ostensibly casting a spell, whereupon the defendants despatched him using a traditional Ugandan wizard-killing method, viz. stuffing green plantains up his anus (Seidman 1966, 1148).

that: 'These cases are only examples of a broad spectrum of prosecutions in which what is right and proper in indigenous society is criminal at common law' (Seidman 1965, 54). For Seidman, the common law in colonial Africa was based on a belief system 'at war with that of the indigenous population' (Seidman 1966, 1156). The common law held local people to a norm which was 'not that of the average African, but that appropriate to a civilisation thousands of miles distant' (Seidman 1966, 1150).[11] In consequence, it imposed its norms on them by 'sheer terror' (Seidman 1965, 58).[12]

Surprisingly little has been written about the way in which post-colonial courts have dealt with cases involving the supernatural, but what research there is suggests that most have been at least as insensitive as colonial courts to local belief. For example, Leigh Bienen, analysing over a hundred homicide cases in Western Nigeria, found that though judges sometimes acquitted for insanity in witchcraft-related homicides, in most cases they convicted for murder. She claims that the judges appeared impatient with stories of bewitchment. Whereas the colonial courts 'strained to find a solution for the peculiar jurisprudential dilemma presented' by simultaneously convicting and urging clemency 'Nigerian judges do not seem to consider that the problem is worth serious thought' (Bienen 1976, 234–5). In Tanzania, 'official legal policy has been aimed as much at the suppression of accusations as at witchcraft practices themselves' and '[a]ctual court cases have been rare' (Abrahams 1989). Courts have been perceived to be protecting witches, and vigilantism has flourished in the gap. In Malawi, local magistrates continue to administer colonial laws that criminalise not witchcraft, but the act of 'pretending to be a witch', even though many legal officers

11 Uneasy about the lack of moral or subjective *mens rea* in these cases, most judges upon pronouncing verdict, impleaded the executive to exercise clemency (Seidman 1965). South African courts, by contrast, tended to regard witchcraft belief as an extenuating circumstance (Seidman 1966, 1163).

12 Colonial courts were more inclined to align themselves with local beliefs in cases where a person claiming supernatural powers was charged with obtaining money by false pretences or 'larceny by trick'. Generally, the defence urged that no deception or trick was intended since the accused genuinely believed in their own supernatural powers, and colonial courts appear to have been sympathetic to this argument. To give an example, in the 1948 South African case of *Nqweshiza*, the defendant was charged with falsely pretending that she could identify a wizard by means of a piece of string to which were attached numerous thin sticks. The court exonerated her, holding that in the absence of affirmative proof to the contrary, it could not presume that she did not believe in her own power (Seidman 1966, 1150). As we shall see, this type of reasoning could easily have come into play when assessing the significance of the taboos in which Allieu Kondewa traded.

themselves believe in witchcraft.[13] The same seems to be the case in Sierra Leone. Although not referring specifically to witchcraft, a 1987 article by H. M. Joko Smart, Professor in Law at the University of Sierra Leone, implied that the national judiciary was out of step with the culture of its people. Smart observed that Sierra Leonean judges continued to rely on British court and Privy Council decisions, on the grounds that it was from Britain that the common law was transplanted. Quoting Lord Denning's judgment that 'the common law cannot be applied in foreign lands without considerable qualification', Smart believed 'the principles of law must also suit the economic, political and cultural necessities and opinion of the society in which they operate' (Joko Smart 1987, 149).

A country that provides a partial contrast is contemporary South Africa. In a remarkable article published in 2004, John and Jean Comaroff discuss the legal conundrums created by the clash of European and African modernities in postcolonial South Africa, a state where the justice minister has lamented the fact that South Africa's 'Euromodern' constitution is not better informed by 'African jurisprudence'. The difficulty of reconciling 'Afromodern' ontologies with a liberal legal framework has been revealed most starkly in cases of witchcraft crimes and witchcraft killings. Local solutions, say the Comaroffs, 'play ingeniously on the difference between the procedures of criminal and civil law' or 'ply the space between judgement and justice' (Comaroff and Comaroff 2004, 189).

The Comaroffs cite a number of cases. In one – *Netshiavha* – the defendant had killed his neighbour with an axe, believing him to be a bat, and was initially convicted of murder, But the judgment was reversed on appeal. Presiding Judge Richard Goldstone, a future Prosecutor of the ICTY, argued that:

> Objectively speaking, the reasonable man postulated in our law does not believe in witchcraft. However, a subjective belief in witchcraft may … have a material bearing upon the accused's blameworthiness … As such it may be a relevant mitigating factor … In my opinion … it offers the only explanation for the [killing].
>
> (cited in Comaroff and Comaroff 2004, 195.)

Goldstone found Netshiavha negligent but not a murderer, and commuted the sentence to four years. In another, five young men were accused of burning to death a prominent member of their village, arguing

[13] Fieldwork in Malawi, February 2008.

in justification that they believed the victim had killed their fathers and turned them into zombies. The judge convicted them for murder. However, in sentencing he took their belief in witchcraft to be a mitigating factor (Comaroff and Comaroff 2004, 194). This type of outcome, think the Comaroffs, permits *judgment* to ignore cultural difference while *justice*, viz. sentencing, is determined by it. As we have seen in this chapter, this is less of a contemporary innovation and more of a colonial-style fudge than the Comaroffs believe. In another case, a healer in Limpopo Province was indicted for performing a magic ritual to make two murder suspects invisible to the police: the charge was abetting a felony. According to the authors, the public prosecutor was not optimistic about reducing 'matters magical' to criminal forensics: 'It is going to be very interesting … to see how the courts handle evidence on whether ritual to make the boys invisible was effective. It could turn out to be a very difficult case' (Comaroff and Comaroff 2004, 200).

Another solution has been to pursue witchcraft cases in the civil courts, for example as breaches of contract. In *Mogorosi* v. *Ntebalang*, the plaintiff had paid money to a traditional doctor to procure a medicine which would drive away, or kill, her lover's wife. When the wife did not leave, the plaintiff refused to settle the fee. The doctor went to the local headman, who found against him, and then to the local chief who found in his favour, compelling the plaintiff to pay. The plaintiff then contested this judgment in the local magistrate's court. The two parties were permitted to question one another and the doctor was quizzed by two assessors, both local ritual experts. Although the case was complex and the direction of questioning took a variety of turns, the reality of occult forces was not at issue, say the Comaroffs: what seemed really to be at issue was the defendant's professional competence and traditional medical ethics. Had he and should he have procured the requisite ingredients? And, in consequence, who was under a financial obligation to whom? As the Comaroffs argue, one of the interesting features of the *Mogorosi* case was that it was tried not as a criminal conspiracy to murder, for example, but as a civil suit, a breach of contract case: 'Civil actions require different standards of evidence everywhere: They are less concerned with forensics than with circumstantial evidence that is socially and culturally sensitive to the context out of which the dispute arose' (Comaroff and Comaroff 2004, 199). This has allowed South African citizens to chart 'a new dialogue', they think (Comaroff and Comaroff 2004, 198), an insight we will do well to remember later on.

The African country that has probably gone farthest down the road of accommodating indigenous beliefs is Cameroon. There, witchcraft, previously regarded as 'an impossible offence', has been rendered illegal under section 251 of the 1967 Cameroonian Penal Code, which stipulates that:

> Whoever commits any act of witchcraft, magic or divination liable to disturb public order or tranquility, or to harm another person, property or substance whether by taking a reward or otherwise, shall be punished with imprisonment for from two to ten years with a fine of five thousand to one hundred thousand francs.
>
> (Fisiy 1998, 144.)

The law reflects the fact that the postcolonial Cameroonian elite recognises the existence of witchcraft, and indeed is often terrified of it (Fisiy 1998, 151). Fisiy discusses two cases to illustrate this point. In the case of *The People* v. *Betta Samuel and Akama Epongo*, a village man (Samuel) and chief (Epongo) were arrested after a pregnant girl (Samuel's stepdaughter) was reportedly seized by a python whilst washing in the river. Preliminary investigations revealed that Samuel had given the girl to the chief as an offering in order that he might use the river for his python (his mystic double). Samuel later died after being tortured in police custody, while the chief admitted in court that: 'I own a crocodile in the river; otherwise I would not be in the position to relate this story to you. I know that Betta captured this girl. My witchcraft is hereditary and the crocodile I control does not kill; instead it is there to counteract witchcraft practices' (Fisiy 1998, 154). Having admitted to occult practices, the chief was sentenced to two years in prison with hard labour. In *Ministere Public and Mvondo c/N. Jacqueline*, a young woman was found guilty of casting a spell that made her lover, a policeman, impotent with all women except her. She was sentenced to eight years in jail with a fine. Fisiy reports that:

> The magistrate did not hesitate to find the defendant guilty even though he claimed that witchcraft manifestations are scientifically not provable, and hence he had to rely on his own firm conviction – '*l'intim conviction du juge*.' The court took into consideration such evidence as the man's impotence with other women; the earlier threat of the defendant; the fact that she urinated in the bedroom; and her having touched her genitals with his hand. These factors were all seen as conclusive evidence of the witchcraft offense and constituted overwhelming evidence against the woman. These events, in their local context, would have measured up

> to a standard of proof to reasonable people in Batouri, Kaka land. They would have believed that these events amounted to the manifestation of occult practice.
>
> (Fisiy 1998, 157.)

In Francophone Cameroon, which follows an inquisitorial civil system, courts have even been known to employ the services of witchdoctors as expert witnesses when determining the guilt or innocence of the accused. This remarkable transformation from the colonial situation, says Fisiy, is a product of the fact that Cameroonian courts are now presided over by Cameroonian judges, who believe in witchcraft themselves, and thereby judge the cases according to the standards of the 'reasonable man' in their own communities (Fisiy 1998, 159–60).[14] Since evidence of the supernatural played such a central role in the trial of the CDF, it would be interesting to observe the extent to which the judges, two of whom were African, would evaluate the action of the defendants by reference to the standards of the 'reasonable man' in the community of international lawyers, or in West African popular society.

MAGIC AND THE OCCULT IN THE CDF TRIAL

I turn now to a discussion of the supernatural evidence at the CDF trial. Initiation, immunisation and the magical powers of the Kamajors were referred to in passing by many witnesses, and formed an unspoken background to the testimony of many others. In addition, nine witnesses – four for the prosecution, and five for the defence – testified to these processes in some detail. In the following sections I examine some of the trial's most prominent testimony in this regard.

In his testimony of 10 February 2006, former Vice-President Dr. Albert Joe Demby described the origins of initiation: 'As the war progressed, around 1996/7', he told the Court, 'some people developed mystic medicinal herbs, which when used rendered people immune to bullet wounds' (SCSL 2004e, 10 February 2006, 10–11). Initiators, he claimed, were 'like private medical doctors', whom people would visit, paying a fee to be immunised or initiated. The initiators were private individuals, men or women, under the control of neither government nor chiefs, and they

[14] In a recent article Peter Geschiere has argued that prosecuting witchcraft in Cameroonian courts has caused as many problems as it has solved, since the court has become complicit with the ambivalent figures of the local *nganga*, whose raised profile appears to have amplified popular concerns about witchcraft (Geschiere 2006).

came from all regions of the country. They included individuals such as 'Allieu Kondewa, Mama Munde the woman, Kamoh Brima, et cetera' (SCSL 2004e, 10 February 2006, 13). Frequently, chiefs would buy in the services of initiators to immunise groups of Kamajors that they had already formed. Demby himself paid 1.5 m Le to initiate the Kamajors in his chiefdom, 'because I believed that the Kamajors were doing a good job in the defence of our chiefdom, and by immunising them gave them extra protection, either really or psychologically' (SCSL 2004e, 10 February 2006, 15). In a supporting testimony, MT Collier described mass initiations in which hundreds of people would be lined up and shot at: 'When that happened everyone went clambering for him to be initiated into the society so that when there is a war, even when a gun is shot, you wouldn't be affected by it' (SCSL 2004e, 16 February 2006, 67). On 21 February 2006 a British army officer and military observer Lt General Richards testified that in his experience Kamajors were sometimes, 'almost stupidly brave' having a belief 'in their own invincibility' (SCSL 2004e, 21 February 2006, 38).

Hinga Norman, meanwhile, drew a distinction in his testimony between 'initiation', which was a period of 'segregational training' in which 'certain things are taught and certain situations develop for you to go through, so that you cannot turn tail, run away in the face of battle' (SCSL 2004e, 27 January 2006, 45) and 'immunisation' which was 'to make you even a lot bolder' (Ibid.). He argued that, in the Western world, the simplest form of immunisation was the bullet-proof vest, or iron shield, but '[t]he iron shield of the initiated Kamajor is a means by which nothing is worn, but one is safe by missile from head to sole. And I received that one. I am sure of it, I am convinced of it and I am proud of it' (SCSL 2004e, 27 January 2006, 46).

The Court heard three detailed accounts from prosecution witnesses of the immunisation process itself, all of which I will present here. The first was given by witness TF2-140, a former child soldier who fought first for the RUF and later for the Kamajors, ending his career as a ward of Sam Hinga Norman. In his testimony, he described how he was initiated into a branch of the Kamajors called the Born Naked Society, together with a variety of 'big people', 'old people' and children, each of whom had paid 15,000 Le to be initiated. The district initiator was one Mualemu Sheriff, and the money was relayed to the high priest, A. Kondewa. The process took place 'in a sacred bush' where 'charms of different types' were 'pierced into my body after going through some other ceremonies, and these charms were believed to give me protection in war' (SCSL

2004e, 14 September 2004, 74). Later, he was initiated into another sect of the Kamajors, known as the Banyamoli Society:

> In this process, this was the second contact I had in the Kamajor society. We were taken into the secret bush, but what I observed at this particular moment was that we were separated from these big guys, and especially immuned and especially cheered for in the sacred bush. 28 other small boys were with me in this sacred bush, and went for this same ceremony. What was believed of separating us was that little boys like my age at that time and others below my age were believed to be more immuned after given such medicine than the adults, for the purpose of saying that because we had no time with a woman, so the medicines acted better on children who had connection with a woman than adults. So in such a case we were specially – given special charms and these charms, we led others to war and conquest.
>
> (SCSL 2004e, 14 September 2004, 78.)

When asked to describe what was done during his initiation, he says:

> I was given also the same traditional immunisation and, as my body was pierced with blades in the sacred bush while naked, all these assorted leaves, which was dried up into charms and believed to give me traditional immunisation against the bullets, was put in my body – with the other boys, and there was a special charm made in this bush which was known as the controller, and this controller never failed us, simply because, whenever a bomb was launched, we just raised the controller and this bomb could just pass and never fail, so with such special ceremony given us, we led war.
>
> (SCSL 2004e, 14 September 2004, 78–79.)[15]

The witness described a kind of compulsive desire to fight: 'the immunisation which I had never gave me rest. Whenever I heard about war, the more I became serious to go to war, because I knew I was immune. So I had a full confidence about going to war whenever I heard about it' (SCSL 2004e, 14 September 2004, 98). He was helped by his charms,

[15] The 'controller' makes an appearance in other testimony also. Responding to a question about whether he received protection, TF2-004, for example, said: 'They gave me a sieve. They gave me a controller. They gave me a clothes, country clothes with mirrors on it to protect me' (SCSL 2004e, 9 November 2004, 77). TF2-151 described Kamajors entering Kenema with a controller: 'It was a long stick with a cross – another stick crossed on the top, and it is called the controller' (SCSL 2004e, 23 September 2004, 98), while Arthur Koroma, a Kamajor commander explained that, 'according to our own belief it normally deflects bullets or anything that – any explosive missile' (SCSL 2004e, 3 May 2006, 27).

and also a 'special oil' which he rubbed, presumably on his body (SCSL 2004e, 14 September 2004, 99).

A second initiation testimony was provided by TF2-021, another child soldier who fought for the rebels before being captured and initiated by Kamajors. His initiator was the second accused, Allieu Kondewa, or 'Papay Konde', whom the witness calls his 'sowe', the term used for a secret society priest (SCSL 2004e, 2 November 2004, 39). The witness describes, in a rather vague way, entering the bush and being marked with a razorblade, the sign that he and his co-initiates had joined the Kamajors. After a week they were taken to a graveyard, where they were told that one of their deceased relatives would come and give them something very powerful with which to fight. In the morning they returned and were given a bath. They went to the 'Society bush' and then had to run between two lines of forty Kamajors, who beat them with canes. Some people fell and collapsed. He himself had swellings on his body. A potion called *nesi* was then prepared in a drum. Each person was given a 'rubber' containing the potion, which they were told was protection for when they fought. His commander, 'German', gave palm oil, rice and white satin for him to be initiated. One Dr Gibao was registering the names (SCSL 2004e, 2 November 2004, 43). Later, he went through another initiation called 'Avondo': 'Well, what Avondo means, when you go to the warfront, as you sweat, at the same time the medicine enters your body. That is why they call the society Avondo' (SCSL 2004e, 3 November 2004, 49).

Perhaps the most detailed account of initiation and related practices came from insider witness Albert Nallo.[16] Nallo claimed to have joined the Kamajors 'for the supernatural powers that the Kamajors had … So that made us invulnerable to enemy bullets' (SCSL 2004e, 14 March 2005, 66). In the course of his testimony he narrated three episodes that linked initiation to human sacrifice. The first episode began as little more than an aside in a story about how he came to find himself to be at Base Zero, a story in which his group of Kamajors, led by Allieu Kondewa, was banished from Sogbini Chiefdom:

Q. What bad things had Kondewa been doing which caused the paramount chief to drive the Kamajors from that place?

[16] Several defence witnesses also provided quite vivid accounts of initiation. See, for example, Haroun Aruna Collier (SCSL 2004e, 12 May 2006, 13–14).

A. Well, he initiated a particular society there. When one initiate, he pass through an ambush. When he struck his eye on a tree and the eye busts.

Under questioning from counsel and judges, Nallo's story progressively unfolds. I present the different sections of this unfolding narrative below:

Description One:

WITNESS: Initiating. One of the initiates – we had one stage in our society that we had to go through which we called a Kamajor ambush when you have been initiated. In that particular ambush the man was not able to go through. During that time one of his eyes got bust. You know, he struck the eye on a palm tree. So when he struck the palm tree, Kondewa and the others took him carried him to a secluded area and they killed him. They burnt him.

(SCSL 2004e, 10 March 2005, 18.)

Description Two:

THE WITNESS: In that Kamajor society you have different stages through which the initiate will go through. So that the stage that the man reached was called Kamajor ambush. That is, all the initiates will stand in a line, they will make two straight lines and it is between that line that an initiate will walk and they had whips. During that time when he was walking – during the time when the initiate is walking in that line the other initiates would beat you seriously. And when you are beaten and you fall to the ground, then you've left the ambush. They will take you and carry you somewhere where they will kill you and burn you to ashes.

Description Three:

THE WITNESS: They will take you to a secluded area in the society bush. So that is what happened with one man. The man fell down and they took him to this bush and when they take you to this bush they had to use you as material for our society. You see, they did not find materials all the time.

PRESIDING JUDGE: Using you in what way?

THE WITNESS: They will kill him and burn him into ashes. That was what happened at Sogbini. One man was not able to go through the ambush. So when they beat him, he ran and went and hit himself

> against a palm tree and his eye bust and they held him and they killed him and turned him to ashes.
>
> (SCSL 2004e, 10 March 2005, 21–2.)

Nallo explained that: 'When a human being is burnt and turned into ashes it is called *tevie*' (SCSL 2004e, 10 March 2005, 25). The *tevie* was used, 'to mark the initiates' bodies' (SCSL 2004e, 10 March 2005, 23). They took this particular *tevie* to a town called Mokusi to initiate another Kamajor.

Later on in the trial, Nallo gave evidence of another sacrificial killing. Mustapha Fallon, he claimed, was a Kamajor from Kati Village who was murdered in the *Poro* Bush at Talia in the presence of Hinga Norman and Moinina Fofana.

> Q. Why was he killed?
> A. Allieu Kondewa said that we needed human sacrifice.
> PRESIDING JUDGE: Wait, wait, wait.
> THE WITNESS: So as to protect the fighters.
> PRESIDING JUDGE: So as to protect the fighters?
> THE WITNESS: So as to make them invisible. And we would have arranged the charm, so as to capture Koribundo, because we had attempted to go to Koribundo many times.
> MR TAVENER:
> Q: How was Mustapha Fallon chosen or picked to be a sacrifice?
> A: Well, the high priest – Dr Allieu Kondewa – said that the spirit with which he was dealing with, they had chosen Mustapha Fallon among the group as the sacrificial lamb. That was how Mustapha Fallon was chosen.
>
> (SCSL 2004e, 10 March 2005, 56.)

According to Nallo, Fallon's brothers pleaded for him to be released, but 'Kondewa said when his old spirits had laid hands on somebody he would never be released' (SCSL 2004e, 10 March 2005, 57). Nallo explained how after Fallon's throat was cut, they took his body parts and the body was burnt to ash. The liver was cooked with some medicine, which they all ate, taking an oath never to tell of the event (SCSL 2004e, 10 March 2005, 57). They reported to Kati that Fallon was killed at Koribundo. Norman gave the two brothers 300,000 Le to keep quiet, threatening that they would be killed if they did not. Finally, Nallo narrated the murder of one Alpha Dauda Kanu. Allegedly Kanu was hacked to death by the three accused in an oil plantation on the way to Mokusi. They then skinned him and removed some body parts, saying they were going to make a garment and a walking stick for Hinga Norman, 'and a fan, which is called a "controller", so as to use those things in order to become very powerful' (SCSL 2004e, 10 March 2005, 57, 60).[17]

The prosecution's theory

Initiation and immunisation played a pivotal role in the prosecution's case against the three accused, and in particular against Allieu Kondewa. In its opening address it alleged that 'Hinga Norman, Moinina Fofana and Allieu [Kondewa], schemed to take a traditional spiritual belief system and manipulated it to their own ends', namely, the seizure of power in Sierra Leone. In the context of the conflict, 'Vulnerable young men, desperate for survival in a devilish war, fell easy prey to these men' (SCSL 2004e, 3 June 2004, 16). Kondewa, the third accused, was a pivotal figure in this process, since he was the man 'responsible for the recruitment and initiation of the fighters' and '[w]ithout those fighters there were no crimes; without fighters there is no Kamajor army; and without Kondewa there were no fighters' (SCSL 2004e, 3 June 2004, 20). Kondewa, the high priest, 'prepared the fighters by purporting to protect them against bullets by means of cultish rituals. He commanded great awe and authority amongst those fighters. They believed their lives depended upon him and it is only through his blessings and approval that the battle could be won' (SCSL 2004e, 3 June 2004, 25).

Readers will recall that the prosecution charged the defendants under two different modes of liability. Under Article 6(i), it claimed they were part of a joint criminal enterprise to take power in Sierra Leone, and under Article 6(iii) it claimed they were responsible as superiors for the criminal acts of their subordinates. Bullet-proofing was important to both these modes. Under Article 6(i), the prosecution's theory was that new forms of initiation and recruitment, for which Allieu Kondewa was primarily responsible, were central to the joint criminal enterprise. Under Article 6(iii), the idea was that in virtue of the belief it bestowed in his mystical powers, initiation bound the Kamajors to Kondewa, giving him effective control over, and thus the ability to prevent or punish, their actions.

[17] Ferme writes that some Mende believe big-men acquire their power through furtive sacrifices of kinsmen, the body parts from kin sacrifices are then made into powerful medicines, in which garments are then soaked before being worn, concealed, beneath an outer layer of clothes (Ferme 2001, 182). Note that Hinga Norman denied all of these allegations.

In both theories, the prosecution appeared to be making an implicit argument about the type of authority that German social scientist Max Weber called *charismatic*. For Weber, a person with charisma was 'set apart from ordinary men and treated as endowed with supernatural, superhuman, or at least specifically exceptional powers or qualities … on the basis of them the individual is treated as a leader' (Weber 1947, 329). Charismatic authority engenders 'devotion to the specific and exceptional sanctity, heroism or exemplary character of an individual person, and of the normative patterns or order revealed or ordained by him' (Weber 1947, 301). The positions of formal responsibility that Kondewa held (High Priest and member of the War Council) were perhaps less important to understanding his significance, then, than the awe and respect he commanded. It was in virtue of this that he was responsible for all of the Kamajors' criminal acts.

In addition to these arguments about accountability, there was a third thrust to the prosecution's attack. This was the idea, a kind of commentary to the effect that, bullet-proofing was 'not real', and probably fatally dangerous. Thus, even though belief in bullet-proofing was central to the prosecution's case (without it Kondewa's authority could not be explained), the truth-value of that belief was judged negative. Miscreant Kamajors, we can infer, were viewed by the Prosecution as deeply misguided, duped via the malign influence of Kondewa, a dangerous quack. Perhaps the prosecution was also worried that a sincere belief in bullet-proofing would somehow go to the *mens rea* of the accused; thus it tried, as far as possible, to expose immunisation as a sham. Although the prosecution had to engage with local epistemologies in order to construct its case, then, it stuck to the view that these epistemologies and the ontology to which they were connected, were flawed.

The first theory was supported by various testimonies that showed initiation to be central to the Kamajors' military strategy, and thus a critical tool in the joint criminal enterprise. On 14 June expert military witness Col. Richard Iron argued:

> [T]he process of initiation aided in creating cohesion within the CDF. This cohesion in a military organisation is very important, a sense of belonging. That sense that makes you risk your life on behalf of your friends. So initiation was an important part of building the morale component within the CDF. In addition, immunisation was an important part of building the will to fight. And it is noticeable that many top-up immunisation ceremonies would take place immediately prior to attacks … In order to give fighters confidence that they are indeed immunised against bullet wounds, they would be given additional

> immunisation treatment, if that's the right word, prior to an attack … There was a great deal of personal loyalty to Hinga Norman which helped to create leadership – sorry, cohesion. And the leadership's promotion of initiation and immunisation, I think was very important.
>
> (SCSL 2004e, 14 June 2005, 36.)

To cement the claim, the prosecution tried to establish that bullet-proofing was a recent innovation. It did not lead any open session evidence on this subject, but it did have the testimony of defence witness Albert Demby, which we have already viewed, in support. It also probed Norman on this topic. On 6 February, Kevin Tavener put it to Norman that under the traditional system of hunters, 'there was no concept of being bullet-proof', the concept being introduced by Allieu Kondewa (SCSL 2004e, 6 February 2006, 78). Norman denied this, precipitating an exchange in which Kevin Tavener scornfully asked whether the traditional hunters needed to be made bullet-proof against the ducks they were hunting. The cross-examination proceeded as follows:

Q. After the coup, I suggested to the witness, a new system of Kamajor was developed, their loyalty was to him, not to the chiefs.
A. My answer was no, My Lord.
JUDGE THOMPSON: You deny that?
MR TAVENER:
Q. Just to put forward my position for the Prosecution, included in that process was Allieu Kondewa developing procedures, practices, that bound the Kamajors to you?
A. No, My Lords.

(SCSL 2004e, 6 February 2006, 81–2.)

The second theory was supported by witnesses who placed Kondewa in a position of effective control. Take, for example, TF2-008:

THE WITNESS: Allieu Kondewa. As a leader of all initiators he has command over all Kamajors that are initiated – be it in the west, be it in the south, as long as you are Kamajor – because of the power he has, the mystical power he has over these Kamajors. And after –
JUDGE BOUTET Slowly, please. So you said he has command over all Kamajors that had been initiated?
THE WITNESS: Yeah.
JUDGE BOUTET: Because?
THE WITNESS: No Kamajor will go to the warfront without his blessing.
PRESIDING JUDGE: I thought I just heard you say because of the powers he had.

THE WITNESS: The mystical power he has. Therefore he has control over all the Kamajors.

JUDGE THOMPSON: Did you say "mystical"?

THE WITNESS: Mystical, yes.

(SCSL 2004e, 16 November 2004, 49.)

This contention was expanded upon in cross-examination:

> [W]hat I'm saying here, when the Kamajors were asked to go to the warfront, I say they go to Kondewa. Already they are deployed by the Director of War, say go to warfront. Everybody will go and say, 'Yes, sir' they go and bow down and say bless them for the coup. Deployment was left purely with the National Coordinator and the National Director of War and the operations commanders. Kondewa was just to bless these people. That's what I'm saying. But, in the same, if he call and say, 'Well, you don't go.' Just as fortune teller – future teller, somebody can tell. Well, you go you have problem this time. That was not a deployment.
>
> (SCSL 2004e, 16 November 2004, 59–60.)

On 10 February 2005, when discussing preparations for the attack on Bo, Bobor Tucker testified that: 'Mr Allieu Kondewa told us that all these powers that he had in him has been transferred to us so that nothing will be wrong with us, no cutlass will strike us. He's now satisfied. So all of us will go to the war front and come back with happiness, and let no one be afraid' (SCSL 2004e, 10 February 2005, 45). In his closing statement, Kevin Tavener argued that Kondewa:

> was capable of exerting effective control over Kamajors. He was held in high regard. He had something that all Kamajors wanted; that is, the ability that they believed to make them bulletproof. And as I have mentioned, witnesses even today, or even when they gave evidence before the Court, still valued that power very highly. It was something that helped bind the Kamajors and it was an essential part of ensuring they followed the orders given to them.
>
> (SCSL 2004e, 28 November 2006, 95.)

Finally, the prosecution sought to establish that bullet-proofing was an illusion. For example, in the course of questioning Norman about his own initiation, the Court heard the following exchange:

PRESIDING JUDGE: And in a group you're being shot at, fired at?

THE WITNESS: Shots were fired at us and none of us was hit by the missiles.

MR TAVENER:

Q. Were you fired at by a shotgun?

A. Shotgun, yes, you're right.
Q. Had the cartridges been tampered with at all, do you know?
A. I don't know. That's why I was saying to Your Lordships that maybe you will like it being tested.

(SCSL 2004e, 7 February 2006, 68–70.)

Cross-examining Demby, the prosecution had this to say:

Q. … you stated in your evidence that immunisation gave them extra protection, either really or psychologically. Now in giving that answer, did you give that answer as a medical doctor?
A. Yes, because I was not initiated and I did not test those that were immunised to make sure. So I just said that.
Q. In order to be immunised, the person being immunised had to pay money to the initiator?
A. Yes, My Lord.
Q. And as a medical doctor, a scientist, would you agree that a person cannot be made bulletproof?
A. My Lord, I cannot say they cannot, because mystique, medicinal herbs are doing wonderful things which medical science cannot do. So I support that is possible. Mystique.
Q. In your answer I have just read, you said that the Kamajors who were initiated were given extra protection psychologically. By that did you mean they believed they were bulletproof, therefore they could go into battle thinking they were bulletproof?
A. That is my opinion. That may be psychological because I did not test them, I did not see them tested and I was not initiated.
JUDGE THOMPSON: But you answer is also, if I understand it rightly, that traditional medicine does wonderful things –
THE WITNESS: Yes, My Lord.
JUDGE THOMPSON: – that modern medicine cannot do.
THE WITNESS: Yes, My Lord.
JUDGE THOMPSON: All right.
MR TAVENER:
Q: Are you saying that by mystique means, the bullet, if a bullet, if fired at a person who had been initiated, would either stop, go round them, go through them without hurting them? Do you know the process by which a person – how the bulletproofness worked?
A: No, my Lord, I was not initiated, so I don't know how it goes through it.

(SCSL 2004e, 15 February 2006, 12–13.)

The exchange continued, with Tavener asking whether it was true that initiates believed they were bulletproof, to which Demby replied that 'they believed', and that belief gave them immunity. Demby also agreed that immunisation would give a man armed only with a machete the confidence to attack someone with an automatic weapon (SCSL 2004e, 15 February 2006, 13–15). Tavener then wanted to know if it was fatally dangerous for a man armed with a machete to attack a soldier armed with an automatic weapon. Demby replied ambiguously: 'My Lord, if the individual believes in his immunisation, so be it. You can do it' (SCSL 2004e, 15 February 2006, 18). Tavener pressed on whether 'the initiators had power over the initiates because they controlled their bulletproofness' (SCSL 2004e, 15 February 2006, 19). 'Not as such', replied Demby.

In another episode of this nature, Desmond de Silva cross-examined defence witness Lt General Walker on the feeling of invincibility of the Kamajors:

Q. Don't you think the benefits of these mystical qualities should be bestowed upon the British troops in Iraq?
A. At the time I did ask if we could borrow this technique.
Q. And –
A. Because it made them very brave. I watched them do things which I think British soldiers might not have done.
Q. I know. But on the whole, did the whole prospect make everybody laugh?
A. Well, I think it would be wrong and I wouldn't agree with your use of the word 'laugh'. It was a very serious business. People were fighting and dying and the CDf were, I think, known to be the bravest of those engaged in combat. And if it was a result of this belief of invincibility, I said I'd like some of this. That is about it. So I never laughed at it.
Q. Well, I hope you get some of it before you go to Afghanistan.
A. Thank you.
Q. But on the whole, you realised, of course, didn't you, that it was a form of bravery with which people paid with their lives?

(SCSL 2004e, 21 February 2006, 106–7.)

On 15 May 2006, while cross-examining defence witness Haroun Collier – who claimed to have witnessed immunisations that caused water rather than bullets to spew from the barrels of shotguns – de Silva took the unusual step of producing two shotgun cartridges in Court, one filled with shot, the other a blank. Admitting the cartridges into evidence, he insinuated that it was blanks that were fired during initiation ceremonies (SCSL 2004e, 15 May 2006, 67).

The defence case

The defence case rested on two planks. One was that there was a difference between initiation or immunisation and recruitment. Indeed, the defence was fairly successful in demonstrating that immunisation did not entail recruitment for the war effort. By driving a wedge between the two processes, they hoped to show that Kondewa played a role analogous to a modern European army priest. The second plank of the defence was that immunisation was bound up with a set of taboos that encompassed the international laws of war, as well as other prohibitions having only a local relevance. Since witnesses and the accused earnestly believed in the magical properties of these taboos, no other form of military discipline or accountability was necessary, probably the first time such a defence had been attempted under international law.[18]

I will begin by citing some sections of testimony in which witnesses confirmed their belief in the magical powers of immunisation. I then discuss some of the taboos.

On 14 September 2004, the Defence cross-examined TF2-140, the child soldier whose testimony on initiation we have already reviewed:

Q. And you believe that you are alive today because of that protection?
A. With the help of God, also. God is first and protection becomes second, but God walked through these protections.
Q. Apart from God, do you accept that you are alive today because of that particular protection?
A. Yes, My Lord.

(SCSL 2004e, 14 September 2004, 163)

On 6 June, defence counsel asked the witness TF2-080, 'Did you get any reassuring protection in being initiated into the Kamajor movement?'

A. Yes, sir. The only protection was when they said, when Kondewa passed an order that he would give me something that would protect

[18] 'Given that those who were immunised and initiated were told repeatedly that the protections would be lost if they failed to follow the rules given to them, Kondewa had every reason to believe that they would follow those rules. There is no evidence to support the contention that the immunization and initiation protected those who failed to follow the rules. Indeed, there was evidence to the contrary, that the Kamajors widely believed that those who were killed in battle had violated the rules and those who survived followed them' (SCSL 2005b, 25).

me, that would protect me during the war. That was something when they give it to you, if you believed in it then it would work.
Q. Were you given that something?
A. Yes, sir.
Q. And did you believe in it?
A. Yes, sir. I would believe it because I had joined the society.
Q. And did it work for you during the war?
A. Yes, sir.

(SCSL 2004e, 6 June 2005, 38–9.)

When it came to his own testimony, Norman explained that traditionally, hunters in Sierra Leone had 'Masonic prowess' that would make them invisible to animals. Later, these techniques were developed to make them invisible to humans in war, and invulnerable to missiles.

Q. You are saying that these were mystic powers?
A I would refer to them as mystic or Masonic, but they are powers, really, that worked.
Q. Was it supernatural?
A. Well, it depends to adjectival phrase that one would like to use.
Q. We just want to understand.

(SCSL 2004e, 27 January 2006, 39.)

Norman continued:

THE WITNESS: Immunisation was the means to strengthen to confidence of the initiate. Immunisation does not belong a right to initiates alone … immunisation is not necessarily to go to war. It is a preventive instrument whenever there is danger around, and it is based upon restrictions normally referred to as rules and regulations if, when broken, then the immunisation could not be effective … And after initiation of the fighters, and after immunisation, the test is done openly before they are admonished to battle. Openly, their village or the townspeople are invited to witness the test of the immunisation; sometimes by live snakes, sometimes by boiling water, sometimes by hot oil, sometimes by live shots from the guns. Sometimes even by the infliction of a sword strike.
Q. In what sense was this a test? All that you've mentioned, how was it a test?
A. I've said the test of immunisation was the public proof of being witnesses when these tests were performed on the initiate and on the immunised.

Q. That is to say, when the test was applied, what would show that it was an effective one?
A. That the live human beings were being paraded and into whom volumes of shots had been fired remained alive and unwounded.
(SCSL 2004e, 27 January 2006, 92–4).

On 17 February another witness, Osman Vandi, testified on the subject of bullet-proofing. Here he is being examined by Charles Margai:

Q. Were you tested after the initiation to ensure that you were immune from bullet shots?
A. Even as I'm sitting here bullet would not pierce me.
JUDGE ITOE: Were you tested? Let him answer the question.
MR MARGAI:
Q. Were you tested?
A. Many times. There was none that I was not tested with.
Q. No, what I mean is after the initiation –
A. When I was initiated and graduated there were many guns, different types. They shot me with them after I had been initiated and graduated it, right out there. It was a very short distance, like you are there and I am here.
JUDGE THOMPSON: Did he say that after initiation he was tested many times over?
MR MARGAI: Yes, My Lords.
Q. And do I take it that you were also tested on the battlefield?
A. In Freetown here there was no type of gun that stopped short of shooting at me, but even at the moment I am still alive.
Q. Thank you. Did you believe in the mystical powers of Allieu Kondewa?
A. Too much.
Q. And do you believe you are alive today because of the immunisation?
A. Yes, and through God's help.
(SCSL 2004e, 17 February 2006, 106.)

I turn now to a discussion of the laws of the Kamajors. Several witnesses testified to these laws existing, and to their breach bringing retribution in the form of death on the battlefield. TF2-140, for example, said if he went to war having broken the Kamajor laws, 'automatically I would have been a dead man' (Transcript, 14 September 2004, 171). When asked whether the Kamajor leadership punished transgressors, he responded:

> The fact was that when you refuted such commands, the best punishment was on you, because when you went to war, it was imminent that a bullet would cut you, and some had cut feet due to spoiling laws. So the best punishment is what you get in the war, was the punishment for you.
>
> (SCSL 2004e, 14 September 2004, 172.)

The Kamajor laws fell into different categories. One was a set of rules prohibiting contact with the opposite sex: 'don't have any affair with a woman, don't talk to a woman; don't tamper with a woman' (TF2-021, SCSL 2004e, 3 November 2004, 50); Kamajors 'should not sit on a chair that a menstruating woman has been sitting on'; they 'should not see a woman in town without a head tie'; 'should not be in town when a woman sits on a motor [*sic*] [probably meaning mortar]' (Albert Nallo, SCSL 2004e, 11 March 2005, 49); you 'shouldn't shake hands with a woman; you should not have an affair with a woman who is not yours' (Kenneth Koker, SCSL 2004e, 20 February 2006, 70); 'you shouldn't have an affair with a woman while wearing the Kamajor uniform' (Senesie Koroma, SCSL 2004e, 22 February 2006, 36); 'be careful of women' (Norman, SCSL 2004e, 27 January 2006, 48).

Another set prohibited consumption of or contact with certain foodstuffs: 'Don't eat nut oil' (TF2-021, SCSL 2004e, 3 November 2004, 50); 'don't eat pumpkin' (TF2-004, SCSL 2004e, 9 November 2004, 115); 'whatever crawls on its belly, you shouldn't eat it'; 'shouldn't eat the sauce called boi-boi'; 'there is a fish that electrocutes people – you shouldn't eat that either' (TF2-013, SCSL 2004e, 24 February 2005, 30); 'we should not eat bananas'; 'should not eat rice mixed with pounded okra' (Nallo, SCSL 2004e, 1 March 2005, 49); 'shouldn't eat palm kernel oil, or snake' (Senesie Koroma, SCSL 2004e, 22 February 2006, 37).

Another concerned contact with or sight of various contaminating objects or places: 'don't jump over a mortar pestle; don't sit on a pestle or a mortar' (TF2-004, SCSL 2004e, 9 November 2004, 115); 'you shouldn't enter anybody's room, or have body contact with the bed' (Kenneth Koker, SCSL 2004e, 20 Febuary 2006, 70); 'should not enter a funeral house with corpses in it'; 'should not urinate or defecate in a graveyard'; 'should not be around town around 5 o'clock'; 'should not step on a banana peel' (Nallo, SCSL 2004e, 11 March 2005, 49); 'don't see the peel of a banana' '(TF2-21, SCSL 2004e, 2006, 3 November 2004, 50); 'forbidden contact with the blood of the human being' (Norman, SCSL 2004e, 27 January 2006, 91–3); 'don't see a corpse' (TF2-21, SCSL 2004e, 3 November 2004, 50); 'you shouldn't touch the body of a dead person' (Koker, SCSL 2004e, 20 February 2006, 70).

The final set of laws cleaves more closely to international human rights law and the laws of war: 'forbidden acts of wickedness'; 'inflicting injuries on the undefended or surrendered enemies, or denying to protect the surrendered' (Norman, SCSL 2004e, 27 January 2006, 91–3); 'a very strong law that you mustn't overthrow the President the people voted for; you should not kill innocent civilians' (TF2-013, SCSL 2004e, 24 February 2005, 30–1); 'you shouldn't kill an innocent person; you shouldn't loot' (Koker, SCSL 2004e, 20 February 2006, 70); or 'take a civilian's property' (Koromo, SCSL 2004e, 22 February 2006, 37).

Norman explained the laws of the Kamajors by reference to the Bible:

THE WITNESS: Chapter 23. Deuteronomy 23, 9 to 11, My Lords. The rules of war was laid down by God, that you are protected if you don't do this, you are not if you do this. And that is the reason why specifically the Kamajor is always afraid of harming women, or touching them, when once they're prepared for war. After the admonition to go to war, and in that admonition we are told to be careful of women, and be careful of harming the innocents, be careful of theft, in war commonly referred to as looting, no immunised initiate fighter will be covered if they go against those traditional roles. So many of hunters never returned, who went against that truth, those rules. You receive your punishment in the battlefield.

MR JABBI:

Q. Just to round up on those rules and regulations as you call them, is there any other you want to mention to close it?

A. I only want to say, My Lords, that if I was a commander I only tell my men those are the rules under which you are protected. If you breach them you bear the consequences. So there is no need for physical punishment inflicted. But I'm sure, because I was not a commander in the field, their commanders – that is, the hunters' commanders – must have told them and given them admonition to battle. It is always done last you cross the line you advance to contact.

(SCSL 2004e, 27 January 2006, 48.)

Most of the witnesses who testified to this subject corroborated Norman. TF2-21 said that breaking the laws meant death by a bullet (SCSL 2004e, 3 November 2004, 50). Kenneth Koker said, 'They told us if we made any cleavage of these rules, if we went to the war front we'd be killed there …Any of the laws, if we spoiled them none – anyone who spoiled those rules would not return; he would die at the war front' (SCSL 2004e,

20 Febuary 2006, 71). Senesie Koromo testified that if you violated the rules, 'when you went to war you would be affected by bullets' (SCSL 2004e, 22 February 2006, 36–7).

The Bench's attitude

The attitude of the Bench to this type of testimony was difficult to discern. At the first mention of mystical powers it intervened to restrict the cross-examination. It appeared as though it might seek to screen out discussion of the supernatural in the same way that earlier it had screened out discussion of politics (see Chapter 2).

Q. I'm sure. And do you also agree with me that the Kamajors have mystical powers?
MR. PRESIDENT: What do you mean by that question, Mr. Bockarie?
MR. BOCKARIE: I'm sorry, sir.
MR. PRESIDENT: What do you mean by that, Mr. Bockarie?
JUDGE THOMPSON: This court needs to understand the facts.
MR. BOCKARIE: Something which is extraordinary, Your Honour.
JUDGE THOMPSON: But how does – this Court needs to ascertain facts and if you take us into the realm of metaphysics or mysticism –
MR. BOCKARIE: I will reframe.

(SCSL 2004e, 21 June 2004, 62–3).

But later on, the Bench adopted a more permissive attitude. It seemed genuinely interested in the nature and content of witnesses' beliefs, and sometimes intervened in an attempt to try and get the clearest possible testimony on the subject. At the same time, it sought to distance itself from any impression that it was aligning itself with a system of magical practice and belief, as in the following exchanges with Norman:

Q. How were you made sure or convinced of it?
A. Going through the tests. Tests of gunshots. If Their Lordships will allow perhaps, and those are performed here, I could catch the gunshot and show it to them. I'm sorry, Your Lordships.
PRESIDING JUDGE: No need to perform that. Thank you very much.
JUDGE ITOE: That is not my mission here.
THE WITNESS: Thank you, My Lords.
JUDGE THOMPSON: I concur in that observation.

MR JABBI:
Q. I am quite sure their Lordships are satisfied with your being sure of yourself in that regard. They need no further the proof of it.
A. I was thanking them for their confidence in me.
JUDGE ITOE: That was not our conclusion either.
(SCSL 2004e, 27 January 2006, 46.)[19]

We see a similar pattern in this later example, in which, as we previously saw, Norman is offering to have his immunity to bullets tested:

Q. Had the cartridges been tampered with at all, do you know?
A. I don't know. That's why I was saying to Your Lordships that maybe you will like it being tested.
JUDGE THOMPSON: Again, we want to reiterate our repudiation of that invitation.
THE WITNESS: With due respect, My Lord, I did not mean anything at all. Thank you.
JUDGE THOMPSON: Right. We're not going to be enticed.
(SCSL 2004e, 7 February, 68–70.)

Nevertheless, during parts of the trial the Bench appeared genuinely interested in the magical phenomena being described. Judge Thompson, in respect of the practice of initiators having the honorific 'Kamoh' commented 'the witness believes that we are familiar with the culture. We're not. That's why I sought clarification' (SCSL 2004e, 22 February 2006, 32–3).[20] Clearly interested in Albert Demby, he said: 'It is just to ascertain the truth, I am learning, quite frankly' (SCSL 2004e, 15 February 2006, 16). At one point he indicated that he was presiding over a clash of cultures: 'In other words, this traditional thing as against the western position' (SCSL 2004e, 15 February 2006, 15–16). But how the Bench would resolve this clash remained to be seen.

[19] On 8 May 2006, defence counsel Charles Margai also offered to be tested in court; de Silva quipped that he would be tested too, as long as he was allowed to load the gun (SCSL 2004e, 8 May 2006, 111). In an interview with Margai after the trial had closed, he assured me he did believe that immunisation worked, although it was not effective against certain sorts of bullet, for example those used by the British army. (interview with Charles Margai, 3 June 2008).

[20] Although Sierra Leonean, Thompson at various points made it clear that he was not at all at home with some of the beliefs and practices of rural Sierra Leone. To give just one example, when a witness referred to the Kamajors dancing before entering battle, Judge Thompson's frame of reference was a Nigerian novel: 'I probably recall in "Things Fall Apart", Achebe talking about the war dance', he said (SCSL 2004e, 11 May 2006, 79).

JUDGMENT AND CONCLUSIONS

Leaving aside the evidence on ritual murder,[21] by making 'mystical powers' a constitutive part of its case against the accused, the prosecution was extending international criminal law into a new domain. Arguably, it had a rationale for doing so, since there was plenty of evidence that belief in mystical powers was integral to the reality of the situation. The prosecution called witnesses who testified to Kondewa's exceptional influence within the movement, accounts that squared with the TRC's report, and with what the anthropological literature tells us about Sierra Leone, and the conflict. The defence also called witnesses who tended to reinforce this perception. Even if the theory of joint criminal enterprise were thrown out, and even if Kondewa's formal duties in the leadership structure were unclear, it was hard to doubt that he wielded sufficient charismatic authority to prevent those he personally came in contact with from committing atrocities in at least two cases. For example, evidence accepted by the Court showed that prior to the attack on Tongo Field, Hinga Norman instructed Kamajors to amputate the hands of rebel soldiers, and Kondewa subsequently gave the Kamajors his blessing: 'Kondewa then gave his blessings for these criminal acts as High Priest. The Chamber notes that no fighter would go to war without Kondewa's blessings because they believed that Kondewa transferred his mystical powers to them and made them immune to bullets' (SCSL 2007d, 221). Surely as chief initiator and High Priest Kondewa could have prevented the carrying out of this instruction by making a point of withholding his blessing?[22] Similarly, the Chamber found that prior to the attacks on Koribundo and Bo, a mass meeting was held where 'Kondewa said "I am going to give you my blessings [...and] the medicines which would make you fearless if you didn't spoil the law" Kondewa said that all of his powers had been transferred to them to protect them, so no cutlass would strike them and that they should not be afraid' (SCSL 2007d, 105). Later, Kondewa attended a planning

[21] In an interview, Kevin Tavener told me that in his view ritual murder and cannibalism were integral to the entire Kamajor movement, since they were foundational to the way in which Kondewa and the other two accused secured the loyalty of their followers through new secret societies. He claimed, however, that the judges had warned the prosecution off leading too much evidence in support of that theory (telephone interview with Kevin Tavener 20 July 2007).

[22] It is possible that the judges did not convict on Article 6(iii) here because they had already entered a conviction under Article 6(i). However, as their reasoning for Bo makes clear (see below), it seems unlikely that they would have convicted on Article 6(iii) even in the absence of Article 6(i).

meeting where Norman instructed Kamajors to kill collaborators in Bo. After this, Kondewa renewed the initiations of certain fighters at Bumpeh, for the purpose of the Bo attack (SCSL 2007d, 142). Again, it is hard to believe that Kondewa could not have prevented some offences by withholding his medicines and blessings at this stage.[23]

The defence, of course, argued that by administering his supernatural taboos, Kondewa *did* attempt in these instances to deter and punish criminal acts, and in his own mind thought he had done so. In its closing statement it argued that:

> There was only one set of laws that was spoken about all throughout these proceedings in relation to Mr Kondewa. Those laws were that you should not kill; you should not loot; you should not burn. So at a meeting, planning for an attack …, Mr Kondewa was giving admonition to Kamajors that they should not do what – anything that would affect civilians. That is the man facing charges for war crimes and crimes against humanity.
> (SCSL 2004e, 30 November 2006, 55.)

If one accepted that argument, Kondewa ought to be relieved of the charges of failing to prevent the crimes of his subordinates. But the prosecution was sceptical of this claim. It implied either that the nature of initiation changed when Kondewa took over, the taboos against harming civilians falling by the wayside, or that the taboos were manifestly ineffective, as evidenced by numerous breaches.[24] In its closing, it argued that under Kondewa's control the oathing system was so warped that Kamajors could kill police officers in Kenema in cold blood (SCSL 2004e, 28 November 2006, 98). Arguably, this is where the trial ought really to have focused. Did Kondewa actually administer these rights-oriented taboos prior to the specific attacks where crimes were committed? Did he honestly believe in their efficacy? What was his response to the mounting counterevidence? Was he, as Mauss suggested, thrust into his role by the demands of his people, acting, given his cultural background, in good faith? Was he, as the defence claimed, 'a liberator and not a villain' in the eyes of thousands? Or was Kondewa, as the Prosecution and TRC

[23] Let us remember that, according to the Court, a superior was someone who possessed the power or authority in either a de jure or de facto capacity to prevent the commission of a crime by a subordinate (or to punish the offender after a crime has been committed) (SCSL 2007d, 73).

[24] The Chamber appeared to accept this argument, noting that after the coup, 'fighters started seeking initiation individually and the rules were not highlighted to the fighters' (SCSL 2007d, 100). On the subject of the rules specifically, it appeared to have only one witness – TF2-008 – to support this point, and the foundation of his knowledge was unclear.

implied, a man who perverted 'the sacred and long-standing tradition of initiation and rites of passage' engaging in 'destruction and exploitation under the false pretences of a "secret" society' (TRC 2004, vol. 3A, 277)? In other words, was he a man who manipulated local cultural beliefs, and who at the very least turned a blind eye to the deaths of civilians, because his selfish interests demanded it?

Norman also made much of the supernatural taboos observed by Kamajors. His first line of defence was that he was not in a position of effective control over the Kamajors. But in case this defence failed, he had a fall-back position. That position, as is evident from the testimony here, was that even if he was found to be in a position of command responsibility, he could not be held accountable for failing to discipline fighters, since fighters *were* disciplined, albeit by metaphysical means. These defences threatened to throw the gulf between local and international epistemologies open wide.

In the event, the Trial Chamber issued a judgment that, while technically defensible from a legal point of view, flew in the face of the evidence. In its factual findings the Chamber observed that:

> Kondewa in his capacity as High Priest was in charge of the initiations at Base Zero and was the head of all the CDF initiators in the country. The Kamajors believed in mystical powers of the initiators, especially Kondewa, and that the process of the initiation and immunisation would make them 'bullet-proof'. The Kamajors looked up to Kondewa and admired the man with such powers. They believed that he was capable of transferring his powers to them to protect them. By virtue of these powers Kondewa had command over the Kamajors in the country. He never went to the war front himself, but whenever a Kamajor was going to war, Kondewa would give his advice and blessings, as well as the medicine which the Kamajors believed would protect them against bullets. No Kamajor would go to war without Kondewa's blessings.
>
> (SCSL 2007d, 216.)

And yet, in its legal findings, it expressed doubts about Kondewa's culpability, concluding, paradoxically, that Kondewa lacked effective control:

> Although he possessed command over all the Kamajors from every part of the country, this was, however, limited to the Kamajors' belief in mystical powers which Kondewa allegedly possessed. This evidence is inconclusive, however, to establish beyond reasonable doubt that Kondewa had an effective control over the Kamajors, in a sense that

> he had the *material* [my emphasis] ability to prevent or punish them for their criminal acts. The Chamber noted that Kondewa's *de jure* status as High Priest of the CDF gave him the authority over all the initiators in the country as well as put him in charge of the initiations. This authority did not give him the power to decide who should be deployed to go to the war front. He also never went to the war front himself. The evidence adduced, therefore, has not established beyond reasonable doubt that Kondewa had any superior-subordinate relationship with the Kamajors who operated in Bo District.
>
> (SCSL 2007d, 254–5.)

The Chamber followed this pattern for other crime bases also, acquitting Kondewa of superior responsibility for crimes in Koribundo and Kenema.[25]

In sum, the Chamber did not engage in any detail with the question of Kondewa's mystical powers. From its point of view, it needed only to mention that there were *reasonable* doubts over whether he had *de jure* authority over deployment or *material ability* to prevent or punish crimes. There are two points to note. First, the Chamber's reasonable doubt was, like the decisions of the courts in colonial Africa, almost certainly an ethnocentric one. On the basis of the evidence accepted by the Court, one could not, from an emic perspective, be in much doubt that Kondewa had an influence over the Kamajors that bordered on control. It is only from an external, etic perspective, a Western, 'rational', 'reasonable' one that the evidence might be doubted. Further, by dwelling on the materiality of Kondewa's control, the Chamber again evidenced an ethnocentric bias toward material, rather than mystical structures of power. In addition, it appeared to be operating with a naively dichotomous view of the social word in which material and ideational elements are separate and never conjoined. Neither Kondewa's mystical powers (on the existence of which

[25] By contrast, it found that he had some responsibility for some of the crimes committed in Bonthe and Moyamba, on account of more conventional indicia of superior command. For example, in Bonthe the Chamber found that Kondewa was acknowledged as the Supreme Head of the Kamajors, he issued written and oral orders, held court hearings, and threatened sanctions (SCSL 2007d, 260–1), and that there existed a nexus between Kondewa, Commander Morie Jusu Kamara, and his subordinates, some of whom committed offences. However, from the evidence, and for reasons similar to the ones discussed in the last chapter, the effectiveness of Kondewa's control is open to question. The Chamber threw out the prosecution's theory of joint criminal enterprise on grounds that the CDF's plan, to restore democracy, was not criminal. This relieved it of the obligation to consider the effect of Kondewa's mystical powers under this heading.

the Chamber was agnostic), nor the Kamajors' belief in his mystical powers (which it accepted), conferred on him the ability to control their actions effectively.[26] Thus the Chamber was able to sidestep the tricky issue of supernatural power and the law. By the same token, it dismissed out of hand – indeed, it did not even comment upon – the efficacy of Kondewa's ritual taboos, or the accused's belief in them. Thus magical beliefs proved no defence either for Kondewa's conviction on grounds of superior responsibility for crimes in Bonthe, nor Fofana's conviction for crimes in Koribundo and Bo.

In some respects, the judges were in an impossible situation here, caught in a similar jurisprudential dilemma to the colonial and post-colonial common law courts that have tried African witchcraft cases. If the judges accepted that Kondewa had effective control on account of belief in his mystical powers, they would have been under more pressure to take seriously the defence that belief in mystical powers also worked as a form of prevention and punishment. Crucially, they would have had to form a judgment on whether the ritual taboos were 'reasonable' preventative measures.[27] To get a handle on this, they would probably have had to inquire more deeply not only into the concrete circumstances in which Kondewa administered these taboos, but also into the taboos' authenticity, Kondewa's mindset, and the mindset of subordinates, among other things – all of which may have required, as in Cameroonian and South African courts, guidance from local ritual experts. And if they had acquitted on these grounds, arguing that given the context Kondewa and the other accused acted reasonably, they would have risked giving credence to a belief system with which they presumably disagreed. This would have been an unusual departure for an international court, to say

[26] This seems unreasonable, since all power, short of brute force, has an ideational component, and no individual ever has the brute force to control the actions of hundreds or thousands of others, an ability that the entire doctrine of command responsibility implies. Moreover, any implicit suggestion that Kondewa's powers were strictly ideational would be mistaken. Kondewa bestowed war medicines on the troops, material substances that gave them confidence in battle. Without these medicines, the Kamajors would not go to the front. If the Chamber took the view that the power of these medicines was illusory or fictitious, and therefore not worth taking into consideration, it thereby revealed an implicit scepticism born of its disenchanted worldview.

[27] Remember that Article 6(iii) of the Statute read: 'The fact that any of the crimes referred to in articles 2 to 4 of the present Statute was committed by a subordinate does not relieve his or her superior of criminal responsibility if he or she knew or had reason to know that the subordinate was about to commit such acts or had done so and the superior had failed to take the necessary and *reasonable* measures to prevent such acts or punish the perpetrators thereof' (SCSL 2002) (my emphasis).

the least, and would have invited the ridicule of international observers. In the circumstances, then, it is understandable that the judges sidestepped the entire issue by falling back on a 'materiality' clause. The sad consequence of this, however, was that a crucial question for international criminal justice remained unresolved, namely: how to assess credibly the responsibility of military actors who have as a significant source of their authority, imputed supernatural powers? As I discussed at the beginning of this chapter, occult beliefs are widespread throughout Africa and other parts of the world: characters like Allieu Kondewa will inevitably play a role in future conflicts and may come, in consequence, to the attention of international courts. Joseph Kony, in this respect, is only the most obvious case in point.

CHAPTER 5

WE CANNOT ACCEPT ANY CULTURAL CONSIDERATION: THE CHILD SOLDIERS CHARGE

The Special Court for Sierra Leone made jurisprudential history when it became the first international court ever to try defendants for the crime of enlisting soldiers under the age of fifteen. The figure of the child soldier, sometimes as young as seven or eight, high on drugs, wielding an AK-47, and committing atrocities such as cutting the limbs off civilians or slitting the bellies of pregnant women, loomed large in the reportage and iconography of Sierra Leone's civil war. Under its Statute, the Court was empowered to prosecute some of these soldiers, specifically those over the age of fifteen at the time the offences occurred.[1] Soon after arriving in Freetown, however, Prosecutor David Crane made it clear that he would focus not on prosecuting child soldiers, but on prosecuting those who bore the greatest responsibility for recruiting them instead (Sriram 2006, 485). So it was that Sam Hinga Norman and his co-accused found themselves charged with initiating or enlisting children, an allegation that raised controversial legal and cultural issues, each of which this chapter will discuss in turn.[2]

[1] Under Article 7.

[2] The precise wording of Count 8 of the consolidated indictment is: 'At all times relevant to this indictment: The Civil Defence Forces did, throughout the Republic of Sierra Leone, initiate or enlist children under the age of 15 years into armed forces or groups, and in addition, or in the alternative, use them to participate actively in hostilities' (SCSL 2004c, para. 29). This was an amendment of the original indictment, which charged the defendants with 'Conscripting or enlisting children' (SCSL 2002).

PRE-TRIAL PROCEEDINGS

The legal controversy, aired primarily in the pre-trial proceedings, was centred on the question of whether or not enlisting child soldiers was a crime under international law at the time the alleged offences were committed. To give a brief procedural history, the defence filed a motion on 26 June 2003 challenging the Court's jurisdiction over the crime of child recruitment. It argued that at the time of the alleged offences, international law, while *obliging states to refrain* from recruiting child soldiers, had not *criminalised* that recruitment, criminalisation coming only with the entry into force of the ICC's Rome Statute in 2002. In consequence, Article 4(c) of the Court's Statute – which empowered the Court to try individuals for this offence – violated the principle of *nullum crimen sine lege* (no crime without law). The prosecution and two *amici curiae* (friends of the Court) responded to this motion, arguing that even if codification could be dated to the Rome Statute, a *customary international norm* criminalising child recruitment had crystallised prior to that date. There followed further submissions, oral and written, and the Appeals Chamber finally ruled on 31 May 2004. The resulting decision, and the submissions that informed it, served to map the discursive terrain on which the child soldiers charge would be fought.

To grasp the legal arguments, we need only understand that international law has two main sources: treaty – for example the Geneva Convention or the Rome Statute – and custom. Custom is made up of two elements: general practice (*usus*), and the opinion (*opinio juris*) that such practice has become law. The evolution of practice into law is described by Antonio Cassese thus:

> [u]sually, a practice evolves among certain States under the impulse of economic, political, or military demands ... If it does not encounter strong and consistent opposition from other States but is increasingly accepted, or acquiesced in, a customary rule gradually crystallizes. At this later stage it may be held that the practice is dictated by international law (*opinio juris*).
>
> (Cassese 2005, 157.)[3]

[3] The International Court of Justice, meanwhile, has stressed the importance of 'settled practice' and a 'feeling' among states that they are under a legal obligation to act in certain ways (Cassese 2005, 159).

For Cassese, this does not mean that state practice must be either widespread or consistent for customary international humanitarian law to have crystallised: under the Martens Clause of the 1899 Hague Peace Conference, the usages of 'civilised peoples', 'the laws of humanity' and 'the dictates of the public conscience' may be sufficient to establish the binding value of a principle or rule (Cassese 2005, 160–1).[4]

With these principles in mind, the Appeals Chamber eventually ruled in favour of the prosecution, reasoning in the following way:

> Customary law, as its name indicates, derives from custom. Custom takes time to develop. It is thus impossible and even contrary to the concept of customary law to determine a given event, day or date upon which it can be stated with certainty that a norm has crystallised. One can nevertheless say that during a certain period the conscience of leaders and populations started to note a given problem. In the case of recruiting child soldiers this happened during the mid-1980s. One can further determine a period where customary law begins to develop, which in the current case began with the acceptance of key international instruments between 1990 and 1994. Finally, one can determine the period during which the majority of states criminalized the prohibited behaviour, which in this case, as demonstrated, was the period between 1994 and 1996. It took a further six years for the recruitment of children between the ages of 15 and 18 to be included in treaty law as individually punishable behaviour. The development process regarding the recruitment of child soldiers, taking into account the definition of children as persons under the age of 18, culminated in the codification of the matter in the CRC Optional Protocol II.
>
> (SCSL 2004d, 25–6.)

Its rhetoric suggested an ordered jurisprudential evolution of conscience into custom, custom into law, and law into punishable crime. But, in fact, the evidence for this was rather thin: the decision itself provided no evidence for a groundswell of international opinion concerning the wrongfulness of recruiting child soldiers in the mid-1980s, it notes only that the Geneva Convention and its Additional Protocols had put restrictions around the use of children in hostilities as early as 1949 and 1977, and that the Convention on the Rights of the Child was created in 1989; the supposed 'groundswell' behind the latter's adoption is not demonstrated. The paragraph's next big claim is to discern a new stage in the evolution of law, coming with the adoption of international instruments

[4] Note the 'civilising' imperative of this clause.

between 1990 and 1994. The CRC (1989/90) is one of these, the African Convention on the Rights of the Child (1990) is another, but no others are mentioned. Next comes another stage, 1994–96, in which the majority of states supposedly criminalised the proscribed behaviour. In fact, the Appeals Chamber decision gives only three examples, none of which falls within the relevant time period: Ireland (1962), Argentina (1998), and Norway (1902). In other states, the Court claims, individuals are made liable by provisions of criminal law or administrative legislation, but only four examples are given: Austria (2001), Germany (1995), Afghanistan (1976), and Turkey (1935), only the second of which falls within the relevant time period. In addition, the appeals judges assert that because of military institutional arrangements in certain countries, the recruitment of children is in practice 'impossible', citing England, Switzerland and Mauritania [*sic*] as examples.

None of which is to say that, in legal terms, the Chamber was mistaken; it is merely to point out that the story was rather more complicated than the one it chose to present.[5] The rhetoric disguised the reality that international law proceeds haphazardly in fits and starts, conditioned not by the gradual evolution to maturity of mankind's collective conscience, but on contingent, particular, personal and political choices, in which individuals and even whole communities may from time to time find themselves subjected to another culture's norms. Indeed, this very decision was itself heavily personally accented, since one of the judges – Renate Winter – had earlier been subject to a recusal motion filed by the defence based on her alleged bias – citing as evidence her previous work

[5] Rosen states that the international law on child soldiers is inscribed in several key documents, which have fitfully expanded the prohibitions on involving children in warfare. The 1949 Geneva Convention addressed the question of child soldiers only obliquely, but its 1977 Additional Protocols I and II were more explicit. Protocol I, which regulated international armed conflict (of which the Sierra Leone conflict, incidentally, was ruled to be one), provided a rather weak admonition to state parties to take all 'feasible measures' to ensure that under-fifteens did not take 'a direct part in hostilities' and to 'refrain from recruiting them into their armed forces', leaving open the possibility of 'voluntary enrolment'. Additional Protocol II, which applied to internal armed conflicts was stronger, providing that, 'children who have not attained the age of fifteen years shall neither be recruited in the armed forces or groups nor allowed to take part in hostilities' (cited in (Rosen 2007, 300–1). The 1989 United Nations Convention on the Rights of the Child, while raising the threshold of childhood to the age of eighteen, repeated the weak language of Additional Protocol 1 however. It was not until the 1998 Rome Statute established the ICC in The Hague that 'conscripting or enlisting children under the age of fifteen years into the national armed forces or using them to participate actively in hostilities' was clearly criminalised in both international and domestic conflicts. The age of prohibition was raised to eighteen in the year 2000 by the Optional Protocol to the Convention on the Rights of the Child on the Involvement of Children in Armed Conflict (Rosen 2007, 301–2).

on the child soldiers issue with UNICEF – and since the decision was accompanied by strong rumours of personal splits on the Appeals Bench (Cockayne 2004).

The picture was complicated further by the fact that the indictment charged the defendants not with recruiting child soldiers, but with initiating and *enlisting* them. As Judge Geoffrey Robertson noted in a dissenting opinion, when the Rome Statute codified the criminalisation of child recruitment in 1998, it distinguished between three different dimensions of recruitment: conscription, which implied some measure of force; enlistment, for example enrolment as a volunteer; and using children to participate actively in hostilities. According to UNICEF, the wording of the Statute merely clarified what was already intended, namely, that recruitment could have both compulsory and voluntary dimensions, and that both were illegal (SCSL 2004b). For Robertson, however, the category of *enlistment* extended the crime of recruitment 'in a considerable and unprecedented way' (SCSL 2004f, 5), with the result that:

> what had emerged, in customary international law, by the end of 1996, was an humanitarian rule that obliged states, and armed factions within states, to avoid enlisting under fifteens or involving them in hostilities, whether arising from international or internal conflict. What had not, however, evolved, was an offence cognizable by international criminal law that permitted the trial and punishment of individuals accused of enlisting (ie accepting for military service) volunteers under the age of fifteen.
> (SCSL 2004f, 26.)

What was ultimately at stake in these wranglings was the principle of non-retroactivity, or *nullum crimen sine lege*. As the decision pointed out, the principle exists to protect those who, in good faith, act in ways which they believe to be lawful. Thus, as the Chamber noted, of critical importance was the question of whether it was foreseeable and accessible to the defendants that their acts could be criminally punished (SCSL 2004d, 15). The majority judges ruled that, because of the number of international organisations and treaties condemning child recruitment, and because of the fact that some states explicitly criminalised the practice, it was. Robertson argued that because of ambiguity in the criminal status of the category of enlistment, it was not.[6] I will argue in this chapter, however, that from an anthropolitical

[6] The confusion surrounding the status of the law was not lost on the UN Secretary General. When, in the year 2000, he was advising the Security Council on the drafting of the Special

perspective both sets of judges rather missed the point. Immersed as they were in the precepts of international law, they were oblivious to another very powerful reason for thinking that the defendants could not have foreseen that their actions were punishable: namely, the cultural context in which they operated.

CONCEPTIONS OF CHILDHOOD IN SOUTHERN SIERRA LEONE

Many scholars now accept that although all societies have a 'concept' of childhood, actual conceptions differ across cultures. Conceptions of childhood may differ in their boundaries (when a child ceases to be a child), dimensions (legal, ethical, metaphysical), and divisions (infancy, adolescence, etc) (Archard 1993). Southern Sierra Leone is a case in point. In the scholarly literature, childhood there is represented as a dangerous condition. Anthropological studies tell us that when born, children are thought to have entered into this world from a realm of spirits, where their supernatural 'doubles' often remain. Children are 'liminal beings between the world of animality and madness' (Ferme 2001, 198). Like animals, they cannot control their behaviour or bodily functions; nor can they keep secrets, a fundamental criterion of adulthood. Their closeness to the world of spirits implies 'loyalties in conflict with the world of the living' (Ferme 2001, 198). Children may also be channels for bringing spirits, often unpredictable, unruly and malefic into the human world, and they are always vulnerable, through death, to re-entering the spirit domain: 'Infants are suspected of lacking a commitment to live among humans, because of their links with powerful agencies in the world of spirits, where they are thought to exist before birth' (Ferme 2001, 199). For that reason, social norms caution parents against getting too emotionally close to their offspring. Although in practice mothers coddle and spoil their infants, and their private anguish may be very real, the Mende do not publicly mourn the deaths of young children (Bledsoe 1990; Ferme 2001, 200).

Court statute, he suggested it employ the terminology 'abduction and forced recruitment', being uncertain whether or not enlistment, in 1996, was a crime. As Robertson opined: 'If it was not clear to the Secretary General and his legal advisers that international law had by 1996 criminalized the enlistment of child soldiers, could it really have been any clearer to Chief Hinga Norman or any other defendant at that time, embattled in Sierra Leone?' (SCSL 2004f, 6). For a critique of Robertson, see Smith (Smith 2004).

Children must learn to be humans through experiencing hardship. Caroline Bledsoe, for example, has written of how Mende children are often denied food – 'starved' in local parlance – as punishment for wrongdoing. Corporal punishment is also widely used:

> After the initial two or three years of closeness with the mother ... Mende children are constantly chastised and corrected, frequently bullied and deprived of food. Children are non-persons without rights. They are rarely admired and their feelings or preferences are hardly considered.
>
> (Boone, cited in Bledsoe (1990, 73).)

When they reach 'the age of sense (6 to 8)' many children, often the most promising ones, are farmed out through the widespread local practice of 'fostering' (Bledsoe 1990, 74).[7] They are placed with distant relatives or contacts as a means of teaching them discipline, of extending the reach of their parents' social networks, and in the hope of giving them access to benefits such as modern schooling. In a fostering relationship, it is not uncommon for children to work hard, preparing food, cleaning, washing and performing other forms of labour for the foster family's household, such as farming, petty trading, or even digging diamonds. Throughout this period the child may be granted only miniscule amounts of food, subjected to verbal or physical abuse, visited only rarely by his or her parents – who will display little emotion upon seeing them – and granted only limited access to the supposed pay-offs of fostering, for example modern education (Bledsoe 1990) see also Stovel (2005, ch. 7).[8]

Relationships such as this, which would doubtless be regarded as neglectful or abusive in many societies, are legitimised in southern Sierra Leone by a local ideology anchored on the belief that there is 'no success without struggle'. In this worldview meritorious children are thought to rise to the top by demonstrating 'unflinching loyalty to their "trainers" in the face of severe punishment' (Bledsoe 1990, 80). Indeed, the ability to endure suffering is thought crucial to building the personal qualities that will allow a child to navigate the universe of highly unequal patron-client relations she or he is bound to encounter later in life. Forms of deprivation that are similar, if not even more severe, are found in rural Islamic schools (Bledsoe and Robey 1986).

[7] Bledsoe cites figures of between a third and a half of all children being given to these fostering relationships.

[8] The Mende 'hardship ideology' is certainly not unique, with analogues to be found in Puritan England and America (Bledsoe 1990). For debates among historians about the idea of childhood in the West, see Cunningham (1998).

Suffering is also a critical component in the process of *Poro* and *Sande* initiation. In Mende, uninitiated children 'are referred to as *kpowanga* (pl.), a term that also means "mad" and "mentally deficient"' (Ferme 2001, 200). Bledsoe writes that: 'Seeing spoiling as leading to ignorant, untrained children and hardship as leading to knowledgeable, trained adults, the hardship theory emerges most graphically in the *Poro* and *Sande* secret societies of the region, which are known for their severe initiations' (Bledsoe 1990, 77). It is through initiation that children acquire the status of full human beings, or adults (Hoffman 2003, 300). As part of this life-cycle transition, *Poro* initiates are ritually 'killed' and 'eaten', only to be reborn in the stomach of the *Poro* 'bush devil', from which they emerge into the town as men. During their period of seclusion they are scarified by a razor that signifies the tooth marks of the devil, and they witness the brutalisation and killing of fowl, demonstrations of the fate that befalls them should they break the secrets of the *Poro* society. In *Sande* initiation, girls undergo the pain and mutilation of circumcision (Bellman 1984; Ellis 2007; Murphy 1980).

Arguably, the practice of child soldiering represents a logical extension of these types of initiation and patron-client relationship. Paul Richards, for example, has written that child abduction into the RUF mirrored to some extent the ritual kidnapping suffered by *Poro* initiates. He also compared the harsh instruction and ideological indoctrination of rebel recruits to the period of seclusion in the *Poro* Bush (Richards 1996, 81, 160). In the CDF, recruitment tended to have a more voluntary character, but, as we saw in the previous chapter, the analogues with initiation were even stronger. Indeed, where normal social structures were dissolving, it appears that initiation in an armed faction was one of the only ways through which children could be humanised. Hoffman reports a media interview with Hinga Norman in which the latter spoke about the CDF's experience of rescuing orphans: 'A lot of these kids witnessed the slaughter of their parents and were so traumatized that they were living like beasts in the bush. We had to catch them and bring them back into the fold as human beings' (cited in Hoffman 2003, 301). In this context, military initiation supplanted the transitions to adulthood normally enabled by the secret associations: 'as conflict disrupts the cycles of male initiation, participation in combat – initiation into the militia – becomes the passage into manhood. It is no coincidence that to become a Kamajor one must be initiated, and that during the war to become a man one needed to become a Kamajor in much of the rural Mende-dominant region' (Hoffman 2003, 303).

The links to patron-clientelism are even clearer. Before the war, a local idiom of clientelism was 'being for' someone. This meant that, 'you have made yourself subject to the person. You work for him, fight for him, etc. And he is in turn responsible for you in all ways [such as court fines, clothes, food, school fees, or bridewealth]' (Bledsoe 1990, 75) – a description that clearly resonates with Murphy's take on the fighting factions, in which children's subordination to adults was based on, 'a cruel mixture of brutality, personal benevolence, and reciprocity' (Murphy 2003, 65). Child soldiers were often 'fiercely loyal to their commanders', commanders themselves spoke of their 'role as protectors or surrogate fathers of youths made destitute by the war' (Murphy 2003, 70). In other cases parents offered their children to armed groups as a means to ensure their security, or even their personal advancement (Murphy 2003, 74). With this in view, it is easy to see that warlord politics represented merely 'a new and harsher form of patrimonial politics' than existed hitherto (Murphy 2003, 68). In fact, in these networks children often rose to the status of patrons themselves, lording themselves over other children and adult civilians.

To summarise, then, local culture regards children as dangerous, half-wild beings, who do not enjoy the rights of adulthood. Transition to adulthood comes through hardship and suffering, which is also linked to learning the role of 'client' in a network of patron-client relations, and to secret society initiation. In the context of war, military patronage networks frequently substituted for civilian ones, while ritual initiation into fighting groups became a vehicle for transition into adulthood. Viewed from this angle, child soldiering, while hardly a welcome development, is not necessarily aberrant, showing strong continuities with pre-war forms of social organisation. While the abduction and forced recruitment practised by the RUF doubtless transgressed the line of local norms, even as it drew upon them, initiation into the CDF self-defence militia, by contrast, was probably seen by local chiefdoms as a natural response to insecurity. Outreach workers in the CDF strongholds of Bo and Kenema, for example, explained to me that most people initiated their children into the CDF not in order for them to fight but in order for them to gain immunity to bullet wounds. However:

> If some young fellow of thirteen or fourteen years is very courageous and says 'let me go and fight' no-one is going to stop him. The community doesn't think anyone should be held responsible for that. In any case, in our traditional culture we have our secret societies, and when one is initiated into that, you are considered to be an adult! In fact a boy is an adult when he can do three things: when he can climb a palm tree and pick

> palm fruits, so he can earn money; when he has been initiated into the secret society; and when he can have sexual intercourse.[9]

Views such as this clearly have a bearing on whether or not the accused knew they were committing wrong acts, or transgressing the law.

CHILDHOOD AND COMMUNITY IN INTERNATIONAL LAW

As I have already mentioned, the judges at the Special Court were ignorant of these local ideas. 'Childhood' in the decision and its supporting documents is scripted as a state of being measured or demarcated by biological age. For example, the African Convention on the Rights and Welfare of the Child defines a child as 'a human being under the age of eighteen'.[10] The Convention on the Rights and Welfare of the Child Optional Protocol II makes do with an implicit definition of children, the relevant sections applying to 'persons under the age of eighteen'.[11] In other conventions, it appears axiomatic that under-fifteens are children. The Geneva Convention Additional Protocols, for example, refer to 'children who had not attained the age of fifteen', the ICC and Special Court Statute to 'children under the age of fifteen years'.

Similarly incongruent with local ideas is the decision's portrayal of childhood as a pristine state of psychological innocence and vulnerability.[12] The Toronto Amicus Brief, for example, claimed that the war was responsible 'for shattering the lives of a generation of Sierra Leonean children' (SCSL 2003c, 1), the metaphor suggesting, rather unrealistically, that an originary state of wholeness had been rendered into pieces. It proceeded, in a section entitled *Statement of Facts*, to devote the first eight paragraphs of its brief to a description of children that portrayed them as passive victims devoid of agency:

> Children in Sierra Leone *were recruited* and trained as combatants by both the armed opposition and forces fighting in support of the government … Some … joined out of desperation or disaffection, *but remained because of fear* … They *were forced*, often under the influence of drugs and alcohol,

[9] Interview with outreach workers, names withheld, in Kenema town, 13 June 2008.

[10] Begging a question, needless to say, about the social construction of 'humanity'.

[11] The editors of a recent volume on the politics of childhood regard the Convention on the Rights of the Child as a pivotal document, since it seeks to subsume the almost infinitely varied concrete experiences of children under a single universal programme. As such, it is inherently aspirational and political (James and James 2005).

[12] Compare Rosen, who gives an overview for international law in general (Rosen 2007).

> to commit crimes ... Women and girls *were also forcibly conscripted* into the rebel fighting forces ... The crimes that these children *were forced to commit*, at once turned them into the perpetrators and victims. (my emphasis)
>
> (SCSL 2003c, 3–6.)

That this is a more or less accurate description of some of the events in the war is not in doubt. But in other cases, as suggested by the academic literature cited above, children exercised a much more complex agency and responsibility. In the few cases where this was acknowledged in the Toronto brief, it was quickly clawed back in clauses and qualifiers that downgraded the agency of children: 'Children were specifically recruited because rebel and government commanders *considered them* to be compliant and *believed them* to be aggressive fighters.' And: 'Though feared for their ruthlessness and brutality, child soldiers *were subjected* to a process of physical and psychological abuse and duress that exacted *a devastating toll* on their physical and mental integrity' (my emphasis) (SCSL 2003c, 5). In the appeals decision itself, the figure of child victim was perpetuated, the 'grave consequences' of recruitment supposedly having 'the most atrocious consequences for the children' (SCSL 2004d, 16–17) with the consequences for adults not even meriting thought.

According to the prosecution and its *amici*, the prohibition on using child soldiers in warfare was the product of unanimous universal opinion. The prosecution, for example, spoke of acts that were against 'the dictates of the public conscience' and 'universally regarded as abhorrent' (SCSL 2003b, para. 2); the Toronto submission pointed to 'international resolutions and instruments expressing outrage' (SCSL 2003c, para. 6); UNICEF spoke of 'universal acceptance' that child recruitment was a criminal offence (SCSL 2004b, para. 7); the Chamber itself referred to 'the common standard of behaviour in the international community' (SCSL 2004d, 14). This chorus of opinion gave a powerful impression of universal agreement on the ontological properties of childhood, and on the moral wrongness of enrolling children in military service, providing a foundation for the idea that a crime in international customary law had crystallised.

But what was this universal opinion and public conscience of which the decision spoke? A closer look reveals it to be a construction, a mythology, an artefact of the imagination born out of several centuries of economic and social development in the West, subsequently adopted by elite classes in the Third World (Boli-Bennett and Meyer 1978; Cunningham

1998).[13] Operating on the discursive plane of international law, all the citations the decision provides in support of its reasoning are from international conventions, international organisations (UN bodies, tribunals, commissions, the occasional statesmen, NGOs) and national states. The international community of which the decision speaks, then, is not a real community, but a loose conglomeration of international organisations, international tribunals, transnational NGOs, globetrotting consultants, journalists and academics who concern themselves with humanitarian issues – the people and organisations that Alex de Waal has described as 'the humanitarian international' (De Waal 1997). The ICTY and ICTR, for example, figure far more frequently than does Sierra Leone.

Underwriting this mythology is the idea that the individual states out of which the international community is predominantly comprised exercise a sovereign authority and ideological legitimacy in their own territories. But to a scholar of African politics, this idea seems extraordinarily naive. This is because many African states are desperately dependent on international approbation (loans, grants, investment, intervention) for their very survival, and sign up to international treaties for reasons of *realpolitik*. Being what Robert Jackson has called 'quasi-states' or 'pseudo-states', they are anxious to win the trappings of statehood and the economic advantages of membership in the international community (Jackson 1990). As Mark Drumbl has noted: 'national governments may welcome [legal] transplants for any number of self-serving reasons that have nothing to do with their merit or endogenous resonance within local communities' (Drumbl 2007, 126). This is especially the case in a country such as Sierra Leone, depicted in much policy and academic discourse as an archetypal 'failed state', where the writ of the government, especially in war time, runs barely beyond Freetown (Clapham 1996; Clapham 1999; Jackson and Rosberg 1982; Reno 1997, 2000). Because

[13] Many authors credit Philippe Ariès with the discovery that: 'childhood is, in large measure, a social construction that can vary in time and space' (Hiner and Hawes 1991). Archard argues that: 'Ariès is at least right to observe that the most important feature of the way in which the modern age conceives of children is as meriting separation from the world of adults. The particular nature of children is separate; it clearly and distinctly sets them apart from adults. Children neither work nor play alongside adults; they do not participate in the adult world of law and politics. Their world is innocent where the adult one is knowing; and so on. We now insist upon a sharp distinction between the behaviour demanded of children and that expected of adults; what is thought appropriate treatment of children is distinct from that of adults … Other cultures … see children as differing from adults in a far less dramatic and obvious fashion' (Archard 1993, 29). See also Rosen, who provides an overview of the cross-cultural role of children in armies (Rosen 2007).

of this, it cannot be taken for granted that treaties signed by the Sierra Leone government have significance for people in rural areas, nor that the knowledge of the government's legal experts in Freetown is shared or even accessible nationwide.[14]

The rhetorical subsumption of local Sierra Leonean communities under the mantle of an idealised international community allowed the Appeals Chamber majority to reason, quite unreasonably, that: 'Citizens of Sierra Leone, and even less, persons in leadership roles, cannot possibly argue that they did not know that recruiting children was a criminal act in violation of international humanitarian law' (SCSL 2004d, 26). In doing so, they ignored the fact that conceptions of children in rural Sierra Leone differ greatly to those preferred by the international community; that military operations were allegedly planned from a base deep in the countryside, surrounded by hostile rebel forces and a national army who habitually used child soldiers themselves; and that prior to the war Kondewa was an illiterate herbalist and masked dancer, confined to the southern regions of Sierra Leone.[15] What is more, they gave no weight to the fact that in 1996, when reporting to the Committee on the Rights of the Child, even the Sierra Leonean government's legal expert referred only to the fact that, pursuant to the Geneva Convention, children may not be *conscripted* into the armed forces; nor to the fact that under a Sierra Leonean military forces act, recruitment was legal at any age with parental consent (SCSL 2004f, 24–5).

The Appeals Chamber, then, was either oblivious to or brushed aside empirical realities in Sierra Leone. In consequence, its decision set the stage for a trial that would unfold as a predominantly technical exercise in establishing whether or not the defendants had transgressed an international law, instead of a test of whether the defendants *knew* they had transgressed an international law, let alone a dialogical exercise inquiring first into whether or not a local norm had been infringed, and

[14] An alternative take on this is to suggest that we are living in a period of transnational legal pluralism, in which the norms and laws of international law interpenetrate and exist in parallel to local beliefs (Merry 1988, 1992; Wilson 2000). In support of this idea, Richard Wilson reports from a workshop to prepare for Sierra Leone's TRC that: 'No division emerges between western human rights advocates and Africans demanding respect for local culture customs or religion … relativism is dead here' (Wilson 2001, 22). Yet, as the anthropological evidence I present shows, these ideas are far from generalised throughout the population; they are more properly the preserve of a small, albeit increasingly influential, transnational elite.

[15] Note that Fofana was also illiterate and that Norman himself had enrolled in the British army at the age of fourteen.

only then into the liabilities and penalties that should be imposed.[16] To some extent the judges themselves were not to blame: it was the entire edifice of international law that was problematic, built as it is on relations between states, with little regard for the beliefs and mores of the communities underlying them.

CHILD SOLDIERS IN THE CDF TRIAL

When it came to the trial itself, the prosecution concentrated on showing that the CDF included children, that these children participated in hostilities, and that the accused knew about this. They called an expert, ordinary civilians, CDF commanders and three child soldiers as witnesses.[17] The Court heard evidence that Kondewa used children as bodyguards at Base Zero; that at Base Zero there was a Kamajor named Junior Spain who was between twelve and fifteen years old; that a child referred to as 'Small Hunter' shot witness TF2-035; that children manned checkpoints in Daru, carried a stick called 'a controller' into battle, and were known to dance in front of the Kamajors as they walked into battle; that by mid-August 1998, over 300 children from the Kamajor society had been demobilised at Bo, that in 1999, the CDF registered over 300 children aged under fourteen for demobilisation in the Southern Province, and that at a meeting at Base Zero, Norman complained that child combatants were outperforming the adult fighters (SCSL 2007d, 207–8).

The defence countered with a number of tactics. To begin with, it challenged the age of some of the child witnesses. Next, it challenged the ability of witnesses to know the age of the children they allegedly saw. For example, when asked about how one distinguished children of different age in local areas of Sierra Leone, former Vice President Dr Albert Joe Demby told the Court that, for the Mende, a child is considered 'grown up', and thereby liable to more severe punishments, when his arm is long enough to reach behind his head and touch his opposite ear, which usually happens between the ages of seven and nine (SCSL 2004e, 10 February 2006, 6). In addition, the defence tried rather unconvincingly to suggest that the Kamajors themselves had certain prohibitions on

16 In seventy-nine pages'-worth of oral argument, heard in court on 6 November 2003, the question of culture or local beliefs did not arise once (SCSL 2003d).

17 The relevant witnesses were TF2-005, TF2-021, TF2-032, TF2-033, TF2-042, TF2-061, TF2-082, TF2-201, TF2-017, TF2-079, TF2-140 and EW2.

recruiting children under eighteen.[18] The Kondewa team devoted considerable energies to demonstrating that initiation and recruitment were not synonymous, as evidenced by the fact that many people being initiated did so simply to protect themselves from being hit by bullets, never intending to go to the front line. But it was clear from the testimony that some of the initiates, youths included, were intending to fight. Norman, on one occasion, pointed out that it was not illegal under Sierra Leonean law for children to defend their communities. In addition, elements of a cultural defence were included in the expert testimony of anthropologist Danny Hoffman (SCSL 2004e, 9 October 2006, 107–9), though they were not a major focus of the defence case, the defendants reasoning, perhaps, that the pre-trial decision had made those arguments unwinnable.[19] Most commonly, and least believably, the defendants tried the ruse of ignorance, denying all knowledge of child soldiers. Thus it was that the cultural realities of the CDF child soldier phenomenon were largely ignored.

Some of the ambivalence of the social processes surrounding child soldiering did, however, inevitably emerge. In illustration of this, I discuss next the testimony of the two child soldier witnesses who testified in open session. The first is the frightening story of TF2-021, upon whose testimony the Trial Chamber's decision eventually hinged. The second is the remarkable testimony of TF2-140, a witness who gave an account of being captured and initiated by Kamajors, taking part in fighting, and later being adopted by first accused Hinga Norman as his 'son'. Both witnesses evidenced the types of patron-client relation of which the anthropological literature speaks.

18 As we saw in Chapter 2, this strategy ran aground when their witness admitted under cross-examination that his own grandson, a Kamajor, was initiated when under eighteen.

19 Another indicator of this can be found in the Norman motion for acquittal, submitted at the end of the prosecution's case in August of 2005. In the motion the Norman team, instead of addressing the concept of the child, or local cultural practices surrounding children, stuck to the legal issues demarcated in the Appeals Chamber decision. For example, it argued that there was no evidence of Norman conscripting or forcibly recruiting children (para. 147). It then argued that active participation in hostilities required combative missions and using a firearm; not, for example, the mere manning of checkpoints (para. 148). It then submitted that guilt required Norman to both know and *actively approve* the conscription or enlistment (para. 149). The prosecution successfully rebutted these points, not by mentioning anything about the situation in southern Sierra Leone, but by reference to the Court's indictment, to the Geneva Convention, and to an explanatory note in the Statute of the ICC (SCSL 2005c, 14). Several defence testimonies also pointed to the fact that, post-1998, Norman had taken steps to rehabilitate child soldiers.

The testimony of TF2-021

In the next chapter I will raise some serious question marks over the reliability of TF2-021's evidence, but in this one I will focus instead on what his testimony reveals about the child-soldiering phenomenon. According to TF2-021, he was abducted by rebels in Kailahun in 1995, when he was nine years old. Two years later, at age eleven, he was captured by a Kamajor named German who forced him to carry looted property. Later, German took him to Base Zero where he and about twenty other young boys were initiated by Allieu Kondewa. Kondewa gave them a potion to rub on their bodies, with the advice that it would make them strong for fighting. Later, German taught 021 how to use a gun. He began going on missions. In the first of these he shot an unarmed woman whom he took to be an assailant, looted various goods, and captured women who were transferred to Base Zero. At a later date, he participated in attacks on SS Camp and Kenema, in screening people at checkpoints, and in the January 1999 defence of Freetown. During his account of Kenema, he gave a chilling and fairly vivid description of eating people at the CDF's *Yamorto* base. In 1999, when 021 was thirteen, he was initiated by Kondewa into the Avondo society (SCSL 2004e, 2 November 2004).

Having been separated from his parents at a young age and captured by the rebels, TF2-021 was a candidate for the 're-humanisation and reintegration through initiation' thesis advanced above. What emerged fairly clearly from his testimony was that, following capture, he became the junior party in a harsh patron-client relationship of the type we earlier examined in the anthropological literature. Specifically, he was a client to his captor-patron-commander German. Indeed, he comes close to admitting this when, under cross-examination, Dr Jabbi puts the following theory to him: 'It seems to me, after the loss of your parents for at least two years before you were captured by German, German, therefore, was a virtual substitute parent to you when he captured you?' To which the witness responds:

> 'Well, that is the way I felt'.
> 'Did you, yourself, take him as a sort of parent?' asks Jabbi.
> Yeah, I took him to be a brother.
>
> (SCSL 2004e, 3 November 2004, 12.)

German even gave the child his own real name. Under cross-examination he agrees with Dr Jabbi that he was happy when the CDF 'freed' him

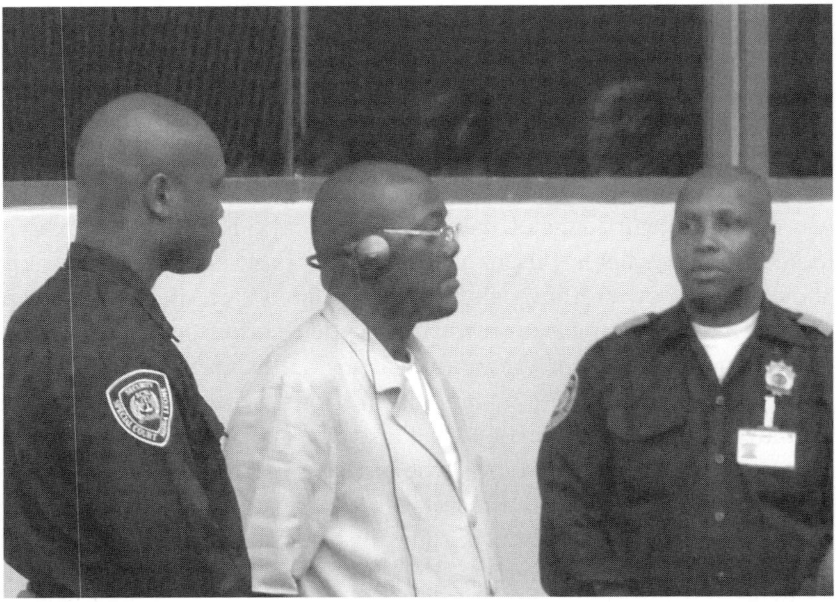

Figure 6. Allieu Kondewa upon sentencing.

from the rebels (SCSL 2004e, 3 November 2004, 6, 8), and he describes his initiation in the following terms:

> Well, the man that captured me at – German – were there for some days, and he told me he was going to initiate me into the Kamajors. Then I told him that I'm afraid of being initiated into the Kamajors. Then he held my hand, he took me to the gate, and said, 'You see the small boys? They are all Kamajors.' He said, 'So I don't see anything why you should be afraid.' That gave me the zeal. He held my hand and took me to the bush.
>
> (SCSL 2004e, 2 November 2004, 37.)

Was TF2-021 forced here to join the Kamajors, or did he do so voluntarily? Was it wrong, from a local point of view, to prepare a young person like this to participate in hostilities?[20] Would or could Kondewa have known that his actions were liable to attract criminal prosecution? The

[20] TF2-021 goes on to commit atrocities that almost certainly did transgress local norms, such as cannibalism. These are actions about which the witness, 'wasn't feeling good' because 'the things we were doing were things I was not supposed to be doing' (SCSL 2004e, 2 November 2004, 105). But those 'things' were criminal acts captured by other provisions of local and international law, and should be distinguished from the act of enlisting in the Kamajors itself.

answer is that we will never know. The Appeals Chamber had already pre-determined the answers, adjudging the first two questions irrelevant and the third affirmative – not by recourse to empirical realities in Sierra Leone, but by reference to the practice of national states, international organs, and NGOs.

The testimony of TF2-140

TF2-140 was the son of an English teacher, born in 1983. In 1996, when he was thirteen years old, rebels invaded his town, beat, and then burned his father alive. The witness was then taken to an RUF base where he underwent training, and was later 'used' by the RUF as manpower and in attacks. During one attack in 1997 he was captured by the CDF who placed him in a cage of palm fronds where they tortured him. Eventually, he was released from the cage, and, fearing for his life, he assisted his captors on various missions in which they succeeded in capturing some RUF ammunition. By now trusting that he would not run away, his Kamajor commander, Sandi, decided to have him initiated. By this stage he was fifteen.[21]

He was initiated into the Born Naked Society with some other 'small boys', who were thought, by virtue of their youth, to be especially suited to immunisation. Two weeks later he set out for Mano Junction, engaging in some very fierce fighting on the way. Once there, he was initiated into another society – *Banyamoli* – by High Priest Allieu Kondewa, who gave the children special charms to take to war. After initiation, he decided to leave to pick up his special clothing: 'I decided to come back to collect my immuned attire … ' (SCSL 2004e, 14 September 2004, 80). On the way he passed through Koribundo which had just been attacked by the Kamajors. He saw dead bodies, houses on fire, Kamajors looting, he heard the cries of captured rebels and collaborators, and he saw children, 'security' for a Kamajor commander named Joe, standing at a checkpoint.

After getting his attire he went to Bo, where he stayed in a house close to the compound of Moinina Fofana. One day, out of curiosity, he went to investigate the compound, and saw Hinga Norman there. He gradually became acquainted with the security officers at the compound, until they trusted him enough to carry Hinga Norman's bag: 'So now I was in charge of taking the bag from the room to the vehicle whenever

[21] Most of TF2-140's testimony was deemed legally irrelevant by the Court, since it failed to establish a clear link between the witness and the defendants during the period when the former was from the point of view of international law, a child. Nevertheless, I am discussing it here because of the light it throws on the complex nature of young soldiering in Sierra Leone.

the chief was ready to travel' (SCSL 2004e, 14 September 2004, 89). Later, he carried Norman's gun for him. At a subsequent time, he travelled to Freetown with Norman, back to Bo, and from there to Guinea. In Guinea he attended a meeting with Norman, President Kabbah, Vice-President Albert Demby, and British High Commissioner Peter Penfold. He described Kabbah giving Demby Le 32 million to assist Norman and the CDF.

From Guinea he returned to Freetown, where he stayed at the Brookfields Hotel (Kamajor HQ), together with other boys below his age. From Brookfields he went to various locations where his immunity gave him the desire and strength to fight. Thereafter, he returned to Freetown where he once again stayed with Hinga Norman. There were some other small boys there whom Norman was trying to rehabilitate: 'Shortly after we left Guinea, Chief Norman had a decision to say that all small boys were exempted from war' (SCSL 2004e, 14 September 2004, 100). He was handed over to a child protection agency, but the programme failed, so he returned to Norman. He describes one more incident in which he is rounded up by one Pa Binda for an operation in which a pick-up truck is looted, and then his narrative ends.

In the testimony, which for the time being we will treat as being true, age and authority are treated in interesting ways.[22] Initially, during the process of initiation, the witness depicts himself as a small boy, though at fifteen years old he is an adolescent, and is already legally entitled to fight. When he is in Guinea, at age sixteen, he is not spoken to, because 'I was to the gathering to be a very small boy', and at the Brookfields hotel, 'Some were of small rank and some were of my age rank, some big guys, age-able fellows, we were all there' (SCSL 2004e, 14 September 2004, 97). However, earlier on in his testimony, just after his initiation, he describes being stopped at a checkpoint where: 'I showed my identity and I was known to be a CDF man.' In the context of CDF initiation, then, he is a small boy; in a meeting with the President, he is 'a very small boy'; whereas in a context where the CDF has just stormed a rebel held town, he is 'a CDF man'. These nuances point beyond the sociological commonplace that identities are situationally structured, to a more specific point about the nature of age, size and authority in Sierra Leonean and indeed many

[22] Under cross-examination it emerged that, on first meeting the prosecution, the witness had claimed that he was born in 1986, not 1983. Serious doubts were also raised about the account of his trip to Guinea. It also emerged that he had received a million and a half Leones from the Court, in addition to other benefits.

other African cultures. In Africa, signifiers of size generally speaking denote authority, more than they do age (see, for example, Bayart 1993; Nugent 1995; Schatzberg 2002). A 'small boy' can be a person of any age, so long as he is in a position of relative powerlessness. Conversely, a man of importance and influence is a 'big man'. Africa being a gerontocratic society in which the powerful eat well, 'small boys' are often younger and thinner, and 'big men' are often older and fatter, but we cannot assume a unidirectional mapping of small onto young and big onto old. Getting unambiguous evidence on the age of child soldiers then, was a difficulty for the Court.

The testimony also contains some interesting references to agency and emotion that I think highlight the ambivalence of the child soldier phenomenon. For instance, the invasion of his village and the murder of his father are clearly traumatic memories for the witness, and after narrating this episode he has to take some time to compose himself. Shortly after, he describes himself as being 'used' by the RUF. Further, after capture by the Kamajors, he clearly states that he assisted them because he had no choice, knowing that he would otherwise be killed. However, after gaining the trust of the Kamajor commander, there is a shift in authorial voice. Initiation is described in faintly proud tones, and he describes recording the names of 'all of those *who also wanted* to go under the same process of initiation' (my emphasis). Though arduous, initiation is portrayed as an attractive, empowering experience. After initiation, the witness appears fairly free to decide his own fate: 'I decided to come back and collect my immuned attire.' Moreover, once in Bo, he is able to just wander into Moinina Fofana's compound. There, he is able to commit himself to the plan of attaching himself to Hinga Norman, a really big man: 'I then became totally committed to them and I joined the security panel' (SCSL 2004e, 14 September 2004, 89). Still, he has to wait a bit longer before he is properly part of Norman's entourage: 'At that time I was not fortunate to be one of his boys ... ' (SCSL 2004e, 14 September 2004, 90). However, soon he is able to 'express myself personally to him that I was a war-affected child' and consequently 'he got pity of my existence, so he took me as a personal son of his, so he took me [a]llong. He had the confidence to take me' (SCSL 2004e, 14 September 2004, 90). At another point, when he describes his experience of fighting, he appears to be moved by two springs: first, his own intentionality, but secondly something deeper, the immunity itself, which acts as a kind of inner impulsion: 'We fought war, because, I mean, the immunisation which I had never gave me rest. Whenever I heard about war, the more I became serious to go to war, because I knew I was immune. So I had a full confidence about going to war whenever I heard about it' (SCSL 2004e, 14 September 2004, 98).

Later on, the witness spends time at a rehabilitation centre for child soldiers, where, 'we were taught to forget about war, forget about all the past things, think about something good' (SCSL 2004e, 14 September 2004, 101–2). And, asked by the prosecuting attorney how he feels about fighting for the CDF, he gives a rather ambiguous reply:

> The circumstances I went through were unavoidable and for the mere sense I could say that these things were not in place – some of these things were not in place, but at the moment I could not have never denied or voiced it out, because I would have been referred to as a traitor, and some of these things did not go down well with me, like, critically thinking, about how my own father was brutalised, and when I saw the people, it was a sort of hell, you know, I was in a position of hell. Yeah, so these are memory times I will never forget in my life.
>
> (SCSL 2004e, 14 September 2004, 103.)

On the one hand, he suggests that he was caught in unavoidable circumstances and forced to do things he did not want to do (whether with the rebels or the CDF is unclear). Some of the things were out of place or out of order, yet he was unable to voice his objections. My reading of the next part of the statement is that the witness is trying to say that, by thinking critically, he can project his feelings about what happened to his father onto what happened to other people, and that by doing so he realises that he was in 'a position of hell'. By speaking this way he leaves open the ambivalent possibility that some of the things in his experience as a child soldier *were* in place. Perhaps, in the absence of 'thinking critically', things went down 'ok' with him. This hints at the possibility that it is only after exposure to a church-run NGO that he has come to realise his life as a child soldier was hellish.[23]

The ambivalence grew stronger under cross-examination. In an astonishing exchange, Norman tenderly asked the witness if he could still call him 'his son', to which the witness agrees, going on to admit that he still considers himself such (SCSL 2004e, 14 September 2004, 102). Norman then delicately mentions that he had not heard the story about the boy's

[23] The allure of the child soldiering phenomenon in neighbouring Liberia is discussed in (Utas 2005).

father being killed before, thereby showing sympathy with the witness, but also raising a faint question mark about the story's authenticity. He then refers, in oblique terms, to a misdemeanour the witness perpetrated on a Catholic priest to whose care he was entrusted. Although the witness claims not to remember the event clearly, Norman is able to hint that the witness may be untrustworthy, and at the same time to portray himself, once again, as his guardian and advocate. So familiar is he with the young man, that he adopts a conversational approach to cross-examination, for which he is reprimanded by the judges (SCSL 2004e, 14 September 2004, 116). Interestingly, a hint of bitterness emerges when the witness speaks about his rehabilitation: 'Since I was with you and you pushed me to this programme and it be – it happened to be a failure, so I had no other option after fully telling you about my plight' (SCSL 2004e, 14 September 2004, 123). It appears from his phrasing 'you pushed me' that he enrolled on the programme reluctantly, under duress, perhaps preferring to have remained a soldier under the protection of Chief Norman, his adopted 'father', than to be rehabilitated. Note the surprising contrast with the positively accented tones in which initiation and fighting are referred to. Norman later recovers from the witness's mild aspersion of betrayal by eliciting that he continues to pay the boy's school fees, and telling him he is looking forward to seeing his examination results.

Under cross-examination, John Wesley Hall tried to get the witness to say that he fought for the CDF voluntarily. But his response suggested something more complex:

Q. Do you consider yourself a patriot to Sierra Leone?
A. Yes, I can so, but being a patriot, it was unavoidable. I was forced to be a patriot. I would never have been of such if it was not the circumstances being unavoidable.
Q. You would not have joined the Kamajors on your own?
A. Or any armed conflict, because my father never would have allowed me if it was not the circumstance of his death that forced me to join the revolution.
Q. And that was two years before you came in the Kamajor?
A. Yes.
Q. Were you forced into joining the Kamajors, or did you do it voluntarily?
A. If I –
Q. They had seized you; correct?

A. I was with them, tightly with them. Being a small boy that time, that's why they spared me.

(SCSL 2004e, 14 September 2004, 133–4.)[24]

He is a patriot, but only by force of circumstance. In different circumstances he would not, nor would he have been allowed, to join a war. But given the situation that prevailed, he was 'tightly with' the Kamajors, grateful, in a way, for being spared by them. TF2-140's testimony provides a poignant insight into the realities of being a child soldier in wartime Sierra Leone. Initially abducted in the most horrific of circumstances, he is first made to fight for the group that killed his father, then captured by another armed faction that tortures him. Nevertheless, he comes to identify himself with this faction, acquiring some power and agency within it. He yearns to better himself, and works hard to get attached to a big man in the movement, becoming part of his entourage, a client in his personal network, his adopted 'son'. With the war drawing to a close, he is 'pushed' to a church-run rehabilitation programme that ends in failure, and from there, he finds himself in the care of the Special Court, testifying against his former guardian. The confusion of his life as a child soldier is reflected in the curious mix of helplessness, self-importance, pride, agency, regret and loyalty that are expressed in the testimony, heightened by a heteroglossic voice that includes RUF military argot, the dutiful voice of a client or son, and Christian images of hell. His opportunism, a personality trait perhaps responsible for him still being alive to tell his story, is meanwhile suggested by his shifting loyalties, the question marks surrounding the veracity of his account, together with the large sums of money he has received from the Court. TF2-140's testimony suggests some of the complexity of the child soldiering phenomenon, then, a moral ambivalence ignored by the international community's chorus of outrage

JUDGMENT AND CONCLUSIONS

Over the past few centuries, childhood in the West has developed sociologically and legally into a condition surrounded by a variety of protections. Ideologically, these protections serve to protect the 'innocent' and 'vulnerable' child from the manipulative, dangerous, exploitative or corrupting influences of the adult world (Boli-Bennett and Meyer 1978). Notwithstanding its poor verisimilitude, the idea persists that legally

[24] Note that, as the son of a schoolteacher, the witness was in a social class likely to be spared the 'success through struggle' ideology of poorer Mende families (Bledsoe 1990).

children need a space in which to mature before they can confront grown-up hazards. In Sierra Leone, as we have seen, the situation is quite different. Although, legally, the Sierra Leonean state is a signatory to the various conventions that protect the lives of children, children in southern Sierra Leone are actually regarded as unruly beings who must be fashioned into adults through unequal relationships and arduous life cycle rituals; an experience of labour and hardship en route to maturity is prescribed. For the poor in southern Sierra Leone, the economy permits little else in normal times, and in a context of war, enrolment in a military faction may have been the only way for children to survive. Even where enrolment was non-voluntary, we can see from the testimonies above that it was capable of generating complex feelings of empowerment and loyalty. But the Appeals Chamber at the Special Court was oblivious both to local ideologies of childhood and the empirical realties of wartime Sierra Leone, and its pre-trial decision cast a long shadow over the subsequent trial.

Assessing the evidence, the Trial Chamber found ample evidence that the CDF knowingly recruited children and used them in hostilities. Nevertheless, it acquitted Moinina Fofana, failing to find a clear link between him and the child soldiers the evidence described. It reached different conclusions with respect to Allieu Kondewa. Here, it relied entirely on TF2-021's testimony (summarised above), in which the witness claimed that at age eleven he was initiated by Kondewa before being sent to battle. The Chamber, while accepting the defence's argument that initiation was not identical to enlistment, found in this instance that: 'the evidence is absolutely clear that on this occasion, the initiates had taken the first step in becoming fighters'. Moreover, 'Kondewa knew or had reason to know that the boy was under fifteen years of age, and too young to be enlisted for military service' (SCSL 2007d, 287).[25] 'Thus', the Chamber concluded, 'this evidence has established beyond reasonable doubt that Kondewa committed the crime of enlisting a child under the age of 15 into an armed force or group' (SCSL 2007d, 287).

Was the Chamber right? Was it true that Kondewa, 'knew or had reason to know ... that the boy ... was too young to be enlisted for military service'? If we follow Geoffrey Robertson's dissenting opinion from the pre-trial proceedings, there are question marks over whether anyone would know that such a person should not be enlisted, since the law on

[25] The witness also had a membership card, bearing Kondewa's stamp, which listed his age (incorrectly) as 12. Given that Kondewa was illiterate, it is difficult to know how much weight to attribute to this.

enlistment was unclear at the time. But, even putting this to one side, I have argued that the idea that someone of Allieu Kondewa's background would or should know the proper state of international law is unrealistic. This is not only on account of his illiteracy and physical isolation from the heartlands of international law, but also because the local cultural context was so heterodox. At the very least, Kondewa's knowledge should have been proved, not assumed.

I am not, let me make clear, endorsing Kondewa's actions. Only the most fanatical of cultural relativists would argue that equipping very young persons to fight in wars is a good thing. Yet only an equally unyielding universalist, I contend, could believe that locking up men for acts they did not know were wrong should be the solution, or that making examples of such men would be the most humane way to reform the practices of a culture. By throwing out the defence motion on jurisdiction, and by subsequently entering a conviction, this, unfortunately, is just what the Court managed to do. Kondewa, there are reasons to think, was convicted on this charge without regard to moral guilt. Just like the colonial Africans we discussed in the previous chapter, he was held accountable not to the norms of his own culture, but to those of a society thousands of miles away. And if this is not enough to make international lawyers think that there was something wrong with the way this case was brought, they should consider that the wider ambitions of transitional justice surely require that judicial decisions make sense to the communities in which they are made.

The Trial Chamber's decision, it should be noted, was later overturned on appeal. The majority judges acquitted Kondewa on what can best be described as a technicality, specifically, that the time of TF2-021's enlistment should be fixed to the moment at which he was forced to carry looted goods for the Kamajors, not to the moment at which he was initiated by Kondewa (SCSL 2008b, 50). This relieved Kondewa of the legal guilt for enlisting child soldiers, although the imputed moral wrongness of his actions remained. As Justice Winter opined in a sentiment with which the other judges would sadly have probably agreed: 'Not being a domestic court [the Special Court for Sierra Leone] cannot also accept any cultural consideration as excuses for criminal conduct' (SCSL 2008b, partially dissenting opinion of Justice Renate Winter, 1).[26]

[26] Justice Winter, unsurprisingly, dissented from the majority opinion, arguing, *inter alia*, that Kondewa's actions substantially furthered the process of TF2-021's enrolment and acceptance into the armed group (SCSL 2008b, partially dissenting opinion of Justice Renate Winter, 4).

CHAPTER 6

'HE'S NOT VERY FORTHRIGHT': FINDING THE FACTS IN A CULTURE OF SECRECY

As the judges in Trial Chamber One were fond of saying, the Special Court for Sierra Leone was an institution dedicated to finding the facts, and determining the truth or falsity of the charges against the accused.[1] Making this task more difficult, however, was that communication at the Court frequently ran into problems. Sitting in the public gallery during the opening months of the trial, one of the most interesting features of courtroom encounters was, from my observations, their inconclusiveness. Cross-examination in particular was often an extremely laboured affair, counsel frequently failing to get straight answers to their questions. In this chapter I posit that these and other fact-finding difficulties stemmed in part from a cultural valorisation of furtiveness and dissimulation, complicated by other features of the social and cultural context, such as dissonant notions of space and time, inter-ethnic misunderstandings, orality, and the material poverty of many witnesses, not to mention problems of trauma and memory lapse.

SECRECY AND AMBIGUITY IN SIERRA LEONE

The great German sociologist Georg Simmel thought that secrecy was one of mankind's greatest achievements (Simmel 1906, 462). A universal human attribute, secrecy was distributed differently in different types

[1] Some lawyers would be more cautious about the idea that courts can unveil the 'truth' of past events. What they focus on instead is whether the court can establish a level of proof conventionally sufficient to convict the defendants.

of society. In less developed societies, public offices were often enveloped in secrecy and mysticism, while private individuals, because they tended to live in close proximity to one another, were exposed to a great degree of public prying (Simmel 1906, 468).[2] Secrecy was often used to protect groups that were immature or otherwise insecure, and in new societies, a select group would often establish its dominance by recourse to some secret or lie, which thereafter conferred solidarity and collective efficacy (Simmel 1906, 471, 446). By contrast, in developed societies he thought there was a strong social prohibition against lying, a phenomenon he attributed to the importance of faith and trust in sustaining economic and social relations that were impersonal and highly differentiated; he also thought the morality of honesty grew in tandem with democracy (Simmel 1906, 445–7). Meanwhile, another theorist of secrecy, James C. Scott, has written that dissimulation and trickery are often the tactics of choice for politically weak or vulnerable people (Scott 1990).

Whatever we may think of these generalisations about the differences between developed and less developed societies, there is a consensus among anthropologists of the Sierra Leone culture area, a region that is sometimes also known as the '*Poro* cluster', that the practice of secrecy is central to its social organisation, most obviously in its secret associations. The *Poro* or *Sande* secret societies are social sodalities with a centuries'-old history. Anthropologists have described them as vehicles through which men and women communicate with the spirit world in the interest of governing the society's political and economic affairs, in the process of which some society members take on the persona of spirits, like the famous 'bush devil' (Ellis 2007, 223–37). The societies are also organs of education, judicial forums, vehicles for collective action, purveyors of social services, and guardians of gerontocratic power, making them among the most important social institutions in modern Sierra Leone. They are not secret in the sense of people being unaware of their existence, since prior to the most recent war almost all adolescent rural Sierra Leoneans would have been initiated into them. Rather, they are secret in the sense that they are repositories of knowledge that can only be revealed to certain categories of member (for example elders), and never to non-members; elders control secrecy, and in particular the secret knowledge of medicines, in order to reproduce their power (Little 1965; Bellman 1984; Murphy 1980). Writing about Kpelle society in Liberia,

[2] Extrapolating from this we might posit that the greater a society's exposure to public prying, the more incentives for people to develop means of dissimulation and disguise.

for example, anthropologist William Murphy remarked that it had a special ambience, combining 'a perplexing mixture of public actions managing surface appearances and hidden actions conducting the important transactions of the society' (Murphy 1980, 195). Like a set of Chinese boxes, secrecy was constructed at multiple levels with each level working to obscure the next. Secrecy surrounding the *Poro*'s mystical powers, in addition to endowing the cult with political legitimacy, provided a 'sacred veil' behind which more mundane yet nonetheless important decisions affecting the community were manipulated (Murphy 1980, 203).

Poro members have a variety of strategies for preserving the 'secret' of their society. For example, *Poro* activities are typically shielded from normal view by being located in the bush, behind high fences, protected by medicines hung from the leaves of trees (Little 1965; Murphy 1980). Members of the *Poro* inner circle meet in the forest: 'the area of greatest secrecy, privacy, and mystery' (Murphy 1980, 197). When the *Poro* spirits come to town, their impersonators are disguised by masks, raffia, capes and other accoutrements and non-members must stay indoors (Wallis 1905, 186; Little 1965, 354). The voice of the *Poro* 'bush devil' is disguised via either flutes or reeds, or else he speaks so esoterically that interpretation is required (Bellman 1984; Little 1965; Murphy 1980). The *Poro* initiation process is a schooling in the arts of concealment, in which the importance of keeping secrets is inscribed with a knife on the initiate's body (Ferme 2001, 180). The initiator wears a mask, concealing his identity and allowing him to assume a powerful alter ego. Masks hypostatise spirits, protect identities, keep knowledge secret and shield the wearer from supernatural attack; esoteric Arabic inscriptions are concealed on its interior (Ferme, 2001, 2) (Hart 1986; Jedrej 1986; Nunley 1988). More generally, *Poro* business is always discussed in the obliquest terms. Initiates are taught: 'the meaning of various signs and symbols and to use certain pass words that are secret to the *Poro*; most allusions to society business are so cloaked in proverbial language as to be obscure to an outsider' (Little 1965, 357).[3]

[3] *Poro* and *Sande*, it should be noted, are not the only secret societies in this culture area. Murphy reports that for the Liberian Kpelle, whenever there is some important skill, it is appropriated by a secret society. So for example there is a 'horn society' to control the activities of witchcraft; a 'spirit society' that knows how to drive away the potentially troublesome spirit of a recently deceased person; a 'snake society' that can cure snakebites (Murphy 1980). Beryl Bellman found that the *Poro* existed alongside and overlapped in membership with twelve other secret societies. The latter involved beliefs in various magical phenomena such as bush spirits with the power of flight, witches that demanded human sacrifices, a society that could strike an enemy with lightning, people who could appear at night as animals, mermaids that entered into sexual relations

Secretive arts extend into other areas also: one example is the use of Arabic literacy. Among the Mende, Islamic *Morimen* sometimes write Arabic verses on paper or on a wooden board, then dissolve them in water: 'The moriman blesses the amulet or liquid and gives his client instructions for its use. The client may wear the amulet or bury it, or he may drink the *nesi* or rub it on himself. Sewing up the Arabic writing in a leather pouch or dissolving it in water lends an air of secrecy to the event by concealing the letters' (Bledsoe and Robey 1986, 210). *Morimen* also use their powers to contact powerful spirits (*jinai*) in dreams, using them to intercede with ancestors and fellow spirits. Bledsoe reports of *jinai* that, 'like the Mende, all are obsessed with secret knowledge. *Jinai*, in fact, have their own secret society (*jinai hinda*: '*jinai* matters') much as humans do'! (Bledsoe and Robey 1986, 211).

According to William Murphy, magic and secrecy are also integral to the exercise of political power. In the Mende political imaginary, 'extraordinary public accomplishments of Mende political actors may evoke the presence of enabling mystical powers', while politics depends on 'secret arrangements for engineering public outcomes and effects' (Murphy 1998, 568). Mende political actors who succeed in outwitting their opponents by staging public appearances that dissimulate private, clandestine strategies, are regarded with awe and a certain sort of uneasy admiration:

> The Krio term for politics (*politiki*) shares the meaning of tricks and deception also denoted by the Mende term *kabande*. Indeed *kabande* is often used as a Mende translation of the Krio term for politics. These dual meanings of *kabande* as 'deception' and 'wonder' convey the semantics of a process and product logic: the process of strategically creating public deceptions produces political outcomes that are surprising and wondrous.
>
> (Murphy 1998, 570.)

This emphasis on secrecy and concealment is reinforced by a number of popular sayings and proverbs. Across the border in Liberia, the Kpelle say: 'A *Poro* man is in your abdomen', meaning 'everything must remain inside of you. It means that a man does not talk what he hears or sees; he

with men, vengeance-seeking ancestral spirits, and a society that could cure people of bites from a spirit snake, among others (Bellman 1984). Other ethnic groups also have additional secret societies existing alongside *Poro*. For example, in the late colonial period some Temne communities had a *Ragbenle* society, composed of both human and masked-spirit members, through which the chief obtained 'the supernatural sanctions of his power' (Dorjahn 1959, 157). Even in Freetown, the Krio community has adopted Freemasonry as an analogue of *Poro* (Cohen 1971).

must know to whom he is talking and he must know himself' (Murphy 1981, 670).[4] Ferme writes of the Mende in Sierra Leone that: 'a person who communicates directly what he or she desires or thinks, or who draws unmediated inferences from sensory data and texts, is considered to be an idiot or no better than a child. Instead, ambivalence in prized' (Ferme 2001, 6–7). While an expression common throughout Sierra Leone is '*Tok Af Lef Af*', a Krio proverb which 'refers to the importance of defending yourself by always keeping something back from others as a precaution against their using what you tell them against you' (Shaw 2000, 38), a practice which can be observed in various spheres of everyday life.

Recourse to the arts of political disguise is often found among politically vulnerable classes and communities (Scott 1990) and is common throughout Africa, as well as in other parts of the world (Ellis and ter Haar 2004, 70–89). That they appear so acute in Sierra Leone has been traced by anthropologists to several centuries of war and instability. Ferme links a 'cultural order of dissimulation' to a 'violent historical and political legacy' (Ferme 2001, 1), while in Shaw's view, traditional suspicion – even of friends and relatives – derives from 'the shifting alliance and enmities, as well as to the use of spies, which characterized the habitus of war' (Shaw 2000, 39). Murphy argues that it is also embedded in a cultural logic of patronage relations, wherein 'public social realities are controlled and manipulated by less public forces' (Murphy 2003, 76), a logic in which powerful patrons provide clandestine assistance 'behind' or 'in back of' their clients, meaning they can publicly deny responsibility when the actions of their clients earn public disapprobation in national or international spheres. Indirectness, obliqueness, dissembling and circumspection are practised arts that function then to protect individuals from the possibly malign intentions of others. According to Ferme: 'among the Mende and other people of the Upper Guinea Coast of West Africa these common strategies unfold in the absence of ideals of transparency' (Ferme 2001, 6–7).

Interestingly, these anthropological observations echo a long-standing set of European anxieties about truth telling in this culture area. For example, Robert Clarke, a medical doctor and long-term resident of the

[4] Knowledge, thoughts, emotions and cleverness are thought to exist in the 'back region' of one's abdominal cavity. The most powerful, dangerous people, are said to have 'deep abdomens' (Murphy 1981, 669–70). It is perhaps significant that most of the reports of cannibalism in the Sierra Leone civil war concerned cases of eating the liver and intestines.

colony, wrote in the mid-nineteenth century that the locals' worst fault was 'a propensity to untruthfulness' (Clarke 1863, 332), while in Graham Greene's novel *The Heart of the Matter*, the main protagonist, a colonial police officer, reflects affectionately on the ability of local people to paralyse 'an alien form of justice' by the simple method of lodging false complaints against one another (Greene 2004 [1948], 128).[5]

The socially sanctioned tendency to conceal the truth from others obviously creates problems in certain social contexts, for example courtrooms. Consequently, indigenous Sierra Leonean courts, and common law magistrates' courts have developed practices for counteracting it. For example, in customary settings, plaintiffs are sometimes asked to take an oath on a 'swear', which is a device which brings illness and/or death by supernatural means to the person at which it is aimed. Writing in the early colonial period, Braithwaite Wallis, a British district officer, described the use of swears in local courts in Mendeland:

> the natives have the means not only of almost compelling witnesses to speak the truth, but of arriving at a more or less correct conclusion as to who is prevaricating and who is committing wilful perjury. This is done through the agency of the TOR-TOR BEHOR, or medicine-man, upon whose fetish the litigants have to swear in the Court … If a person is required to take an oath, he does so upon one of these medicines, which is usually in the keeping of the TOR-TOR BEHOR. The breaking of this oath would to them mean either death, sickness, or at any rate, prolonged ill-luck, which is supposed sometimes to extend even to the relations of

[5] The full passage is as follows: 'From eight thirty in the morning until eleven he dealt with a case of petty larceny; there were six witnesses to examine, and he didn't believe a word that any of them said. In European cases there are words one believes and words one distrusts: it is possible to draw a speculative line between the truth and the lies; at least the *cui bono* principle to some extent operates, and it is usually safe to assume, if the accusation is theft and there is no question of insurance, that something has at least been stolen. But here one could make no such assumption: one could draw no lines. He had known police officers whose nerves broke down in an effort to separate a single grain of incontestable truth; they ended, some of them, by striking a witness, they were pilloried in the local Creole papers and were invalided home or transferred. It woke in some men a virulent hatred of a black skin, but Scobie had long ago, during his fifteen years, passed through the dangerous stages; now lost in the tangle of lies he felt an extraordinary affection for these people who paralysed an alien form of justice by so simple a method' (Greene 2004 [1948], 128).

I should state for the record that while in my own experience I have noticed people in Sierra Leone being economical with the truth, I am not aware of being often lied to, leading me to regard these colonial sources as exaggerations. Nevertheless, I reference them here as colourful illustrations of an anxiousness about truth telling that, in my experience, preoccupies Sierra Leoneans also.

> the offender. The use of these medicines is therefore a powerful factor towards the settlement of cases in these Courts.
>
> (Braithwaite Wallis 1905, 403.)

Similar methods remain important today. In 2002, supporters of Sierra Leone's Truth and Reconciliation Commission commissioned a report into cultures of confession in the country. It found that various ethnic groups used swearing and cursing to help ensure that perpetrators and witnesses told the truth (Manifesto 99 2002, 5). Typically announced by a town crier or cult leader in ritual garb, the purpose of curses was to strike terror into the hearts of witnesses. It observed that:

> In oath taking, the strong belief that God and the ancestors would not tolerate perjury influences the culprit to own up or the witness to give true testimony. The fear of death, disease, death of children or any other misfortune when the cult system is employed to cast a spell (or curse) on the culprit persuades the guilty party to confess their crime even at the eleventh hour.
>
> (Manifesto 99 2002, 23.)

To take two examples, it found that the Mende had a number of curses, such as *Sasa*, *Ngegba* and *Tilei*, dealing with offences such as stealing, adultery, sexual offences and defiling the bush. The breaking of these oaths led to reprisals in forms such as bronchitis, death by thunderbolt, diphtheria or insanity. For the Temne, it found that curses such as *Poron* or *Sakabana*, *Ehsasa*, *Oren* or *Ch*, were applied to cases of defiling the bush, miscellaneous crimes, burglary, murder or other heinous crimes. These could bring down retribution in the form of oral cancer, death by thunderbolt or 'death to the entire family by sequence' (Manifesto 99 2002, 22). In an earlier study, Dorjahn reported that swears engendered a drying or wasting of the victim's body (Dorjahn 1959, 167).

In 2005 I conducted a study of local courts in Magburaka, Tonkolili District, which, under Sierra Leone's bifurcated legal system, administer the local version of customary law (Kelsall 2006a). They employed a combination of adversarial and inquisitorial procedures in an atmosphere that was relatively informal (compare Ferme 1998). Although not without their problems, they dispensed justice fairly efficiently, and I was told that local people preferred them to the nearby magistrates' court because of their more relaxed protocol.

On one occasion I observed a case in which a disgruntled party threatened to bring a ritual practitioner to court to make his opponent swear that his story was a truthful one. In the nearby magistrate's court, the

Figure 7. Local court, Magburaka.

magistrates told me of a case where a plaintiff had refused to reclaim property that was legally hers, since the accused had threatened to put a swear on her. The former local court chairman, Pa Kaibie, who was also a leader in the local *Poro* association (whose sacred bush lay just beyond the local courthouse, or *barri*), accompanied me to a village in the chiefdom in which there lived a concentration of ritual practitioners who duly showed and discussed with me their 'swears', a diverse range of macabre paraphernalia, including an old bottle of indeterminable medicinal ingredients; a crib of twine, feathers and quills; a wreath of plastic and metal bangles, cowrie shells, and old leather bits (see Figure 8).[6] Pa Kaibie had presided over the use of such swears in the local court, but the current court chairs in Magburaka did not favour them. In consequence they were relegated to

[6] I took the opportunity of photographing some of these objects, and when it came to the final one, I was surprised to observe some lines of interference on the viewing screen of my digital camera. I took a few pictures but the lines steadily multiplied until the screen turned white, then black, before the camera ceased to function completely. My informants explained to me that this was because of the hesitation I had shown in 'giving kola' (a small monetary fee) to the swear. About a mile's distance from the village, the camera began to work again. Uploading the photos to my computer, I was interested to find that the lines of interference are dimly visible, raked across the picture of this particular swear.

Figure 8. Ritual expert with swear, Tonkolili District.

the informal or auxiliary legal system, presided over by paramount chiefs, section chiefs, village headmen and juju men, who form the most accessible level of the justice system for many people (Alterman *et al.* 2002).

At the turn of the twentieth century, Braithwaite Wallis observed that:

> Native Courts are certainly different from any legal tribunal I know of in Europe, and their procedure is distinctly contrary to our ideas of a fair trial. Nevertheless, the Mendi [*sic*] Courts have, many times, proved themselves capable of just and impartial decisions, while numbers of their laws are excellent and eminently adapted to the requirements of the country. And it would surely be strange if this were not the case, for they have been gradually evolved after countless generations by a people who possess an African civilization and a distinct philosophy of their own.
>
> (Braithwaite Wallis 1905.)

Although the work of historians and legal anthropologists has taught us to be wary of such romanticised claims, the fact that some of the local practices observed by Wallis have endured in one form or another to this day, suggests that they are too important to be ignored.

In the absence of these practices, common-law magistrates' courts, by contrast, appear to have developed more rough and ready methods of getting clear responses from witnesses. On the occasions when I sat in on the magistrates' court in Magburaka, I observed that the local magistrate, Mr Fidawi, screamed at witnesses who were reticent or who dissembled, threatening them with contempt of court. When I asked about this practice – by which I was initially shocked – the magistrate explained to me that: 'Sometimes they categorically dodge the question … Sometimes you have to put it straight to them … You have to put it hard to him so he can understand that we mean business.' Certainly he succeeded in loosening tongues (Kelsall 2006a).

PROBLEMS WITH EVIDENCE AT THE CDF TRIAL

Secrets and lies

Given this background, the stage at the Special Court seemed set for a clash between a Western-style technology of truth recovery and a local culture in which guarding secrets and dissimulating the truth was a well practised skill. Indeed, Sierra Leoneans' special concern with secrecy was manifested in several ways in the CDF trial, some small and some large. For example, until prohibited by the Bench, Norman would sometimes introduce witnesses to Kamajor talk by asking if they recognised various bodily postures, presumably coded signs of identification or communication of the type also found in the secret societies. Early on, one witness asked Norman: "Well are we here to expose societies?" (SCSL 2004e, 21 June 2004, 58). Some witnesses were reluctant to speak about their experience of initiation, for fear of exposing secrets. Albert Nallo claimed he was afraid that, by divulging Kamajor secrets, the medicine with which he was initiated would turn him to ashes (SCSL 2004e, 11 March 2005, 33–4). Tamba Gbeki, Assistant to the Head of Investigations, told me that when conducting witness interviews they often had to break down a deep reluctance to speak about the Kamajors based on belief that doing so would cause initiates' stomachs to swell until they died, an affliction with analogues in secret society culture.[7] Witnesses claimed that Norman and his co-defendants conducted meetings in 'Walehun I', a secret location reminiscent of secluded meetings in the *Poro* bush. MT Collier, a key witness for the defence, was reluctant even to admit to the presence of a *Poro* Bush in Talia, and refused to speak in any detail about its functions.

[7] Interview with Tamba Gbeki, Special Court, June 2003.

One of the exhibits described the CDF as a 'Sierra Leone secret society'. Norman claimed that there were certain details about ECOMOG which he could not divulge, implying his links to powerful patrons. Similarly, the claim that all along President Kabbah was in charge of the Kamajors was presented by the accused as a kind of 'veiled defence' (SCSL 2007d, 212). One of the key pieces of evidence against Norman concerned a speech he gave at the parade ground in Talia prior to the attack on Tongo, in which his injunctions to Kamajors to commit atrocities were, as we shall see, decidedly oblique.

Nevertheless, some witnesses did divulge secrets of the Kamajor society. As we saw in Chapter 4, there was little reluctance to talk about certain dimensions of initiation and the Kamajor taboos. Further, some witnesses seemed happy to provide details of Norman and his co-accused ordering and committing international crimes. Possibly these kinds of revelation were facilitated by the fact that an aura of secrecy hung around the entire trial on account of protective measures which screened witnesses from the audience, their identities concealed by pseudonymous masks, and which prevented them from mentioning the names of some of the key protagonists and places in the stories they told. Indeed, as we saw in Chapter 2, protective measures became a controversial issue when Norman decided to boycott proceedings until the screen was removed. He claimed witnesses were under no compulsion to tell the truth while protected from public scrutiny by a screen (SCSL 2004e, 20 September 2004, 85–6). Equally likely, perhaps, was that the concealing properties of the screen furnished precisely the environment witnesses needed to speak openly.

Interestingly, the presence and absence of a visual screen set up a reverse parallelism in the nature of witness testimony. Many witnesses who testified behind the screen provided more or less precise accounts of atrocities they had witnessed or suffered. While these details – as we will see below – were often sketchy and open to challenge, they were at least details. Defence testimonies, given by witnesses without the protection of a screen, were strangely empty by comparison. They tended to focus on simply denying knowledge of the prosecution's charges, or of narrating details that were of only tangential relevance to the indictment. The witnesses' own agency was often occluded or elided in these testimonies, and they remained largely silent on the details of what the defendants were actually doing if, as they claimed, they were not doing what the prosecution alleged. Their reticence suggested either that the accused were more or less guilty as charged, or, more intriguingly, the presence of a transcript that remained hidden from court.[8]

In addition to these allusions to a culture of secrecy, there were other context-dependent difficulties in assessing the credibility of witnesses and their evidence. To begin with, their stories were often rather vague with respect to detail, and in particular with respect to details of time and place. Second, cross-examination of witnesses was often an extremely laborious affair, suggesting either that witnesses distrusted the Court, or that they had something to hide. Cross-examinations were especially difficult on the subjects of witness payments and contradictions between prior statements, problems that stemmed not only from the '*Tok Af Lef Af*' cultural syndrome, but also from the fact that the trial was taking place in an impoverished economy with a predominantly oral culture, and that the quality of the investigation had been poor. Taken together, these problems often made it difficult to assess whether or not a witness was telling the truth.

In some previous international tribunals, the difficulties of interpreting witness testimony in a foreign culture have been acknowledged. For example, in the ICTR *Akayesu* case, an expert testified that:

> It is a particular feature of the Rwandan culture that people are not always direct in answering questions, especially if the question is delicate. In such cases, the answers given will very often have to be 'decoded' in order to be understood correctly. This interpretation will rely on the context,

[8] In a 1997 fieldwork based article, Patrick Muana reported that: 'The Kamajoi command structure is rigidly hierarchical. The head of the whole structure is called the Grand Commander, but the identity of the individual is a matter of secrecy amongst the *Kamajoisia*. It is thought that he is the founder of the movement and he resides somewhere in the Bonthe District – Bomu liehun. He is represented in different sectors by lieutenants who have been apprenticed to him and who have been granted license to initiate other *Kamajoisia*. It is thought that he heads a "super council" of Chiefdom and sector representatives. These sector commanders are called "Chief Kamajoi" and they liaise with the traditional chiefs, initiate, deploy, and command the *Kamajoisia* in their own sectors. Most are resident within hotels in Bo and Kenema. In consultation with the chiefdom authorities and at short notice, they can deploy men in areas to be fortified, conduct preliminary trials for former RUF combatants and then refer them, where necessary, to the chiefdom authorities. They are linked to the Deputy Defence Minister, through the chiefs, who maintain very close but questionable relations with this force' (Muana 1997, 89). This might refer to an earlier period of the war, or it might be mythology, but it is certainly a story different from the one that was told in the Special Court. Further, Muana states that it is the *Kamo*, or initiator, who is the operational commander of each local force (Muana 1997, 90). In 2004, Paul Richards noted that: 'Hidden from public view, the cryptic command structure of the CDF still stands … there is a sense in some quarters that they represent a threat to state authority (this threat might become real if their external leader, Sam Hinga Norman, is convicted by the Special Court)' (Richards, Vincent, and Bah 2004, 12).

the particular speech community, the identity of and relation between the orator and the listener, and the subject matter of the question.

(cited in Cryer 2007, 1.)

In Part V of the judgment, the Special Court judges devoted twelve pages to explaining the assessment of evidence, drawing on international jurisprudence, especially that referenced in the prosecution's final trial brief; surprisingly, they neglected to make any special reference to the cultural context in which the evidence was heard:

> In assessing the credibility and reliability of oral witness testimony, the Chamber has considered factors such as the internal consistency of the witness' testimony, its consistency with other evidence in the case, any personal interest a witness may have that may influence his motivation to tell the truth, as well as observational criteria such as the witness' demeanour, conduct and character. In addition, the Trial Chamber has considered the witnesses' knowledge of the facts on which they testify, and the lapse of time between the events and the testimony.
>
> (SCSL 2007d, 80.)

In an appendix, Judge Thompson expanded on these principles:

> Equally important for the evaluation of evidence as to its probative value were these factors: i) internal consistency and detail, ii) strength under cross-examination, iii) consistency against prior statements of the witness, iv) credibility vis-à-vis other witness accounts or other evidence submitted in the case, to wit, corroboration; and v) possible motives of the witness.
>
> (SCSL 2007d, C-17.)

Were these techniques adequate? And was the Chamber true to its word? In the following sections I discuss some of the problems with evidence in the CDF trial, and provide some examples of how the judges sought to deal with these difficulties.

'All I can say here is what I remember': ambiguous evidence

Much of the testimony in the CDF trial was ambiguous. Witnesses often gave accounts of events that were disjointed, entangled or contained small or large inconsistencies or ellipses; often they were vague with respect to their location in space and time. To give an example, on 27 September 2004, Witness TF2-152, a 29-year-old trader from Kenema, gave a section of testimony connected to the subject of cannibalism. The testimony concerned an incident in which, having been arrested by Kamajors, the witness and his friend were led across town in the direction of a base known as Yamortor. On the way to the base, having stopped off at the market to buy onions and pepper, they reached a checkpoint where one of the Kamajors, who went by the name of Yamorto, slit the side of the witness's friend with a knife and pulled out the intestines. The intestine was then strung across the road to make a checkpoint. Yamorto next tore into the witness's friend's chest with a knife and removed the heart, which he placed in a black plastic bag and gave to the witness to carry. He then cut the witness on his neck and began drinking his blood. The testimony was inconsistent in two respects: first, the witness said twice that the intestine was 'tied' to a stick to form a checkpoint, but on two other occasions in cross-examination, it was merely 'turned into a checkpoint' or 'made into a checkpoint', and finally 'they did not tie it to the stick. They put something on top of it' (SCSL 2004e, 27 September 2004, 114–17, 152–3). Second, there was an inconsistency between the testimony and the witness's prior statement, which I will return to a little later on.

What were the reasons for these ambiguities? It is obvious that minor gaps and inconsistencies in accounts such as this can be caused by trauma, imperfect perception and memory lapse. The witness may not have had a good view of the checkpoint, he may have repressed details of the scene, several years after the events, his memory may have faded. In addition, for many victims of displacement, violence and torture, it has been noticed that 'life all but ceases to be narratable' (Jackson 2002, 91). Nadezha Mandelstam, interviewing survivors of Soviet gulags for example, noticed that '[p]laces, names, events and their sequence were all jumbled up in the minds of these broken people, and it was never possible to disentangle them' (cited in Jackson 2002, 91). On other occasions, says Jackson, 'speech is sometimes so flooded by affect and fragmented by flashbacks that it resists lineal ordering' (Jackson 2002, 99).

However, for the sake of the defendants, we have to also consider a more troubling possibility, which is that the account was fictitious. Sierra Leone, like several other African countries, is a society in which the social life of rumours is strong (Ellis and ter Haar 2004, 33–49). Historically, for example, rumour and cannibalism are intimately linked and tend to increase during periods of social stress. Rumour was especially prevalent during the war, when reliable information was scarce. Moreover, in its investigations the prosecution sometimes found that potential witnesses would claim to have seen something, which later turned out to be hearsay.[9] Now, given the number of accounts

[9] Interview with David Crane, Special Court, 15 June 2004.

circulating about Kamajors (and other armed factions) using entrails as checkpoints, it is probable that this did happen in some places during the war. But did it happen in Kenema on this day? And did it happen to this witness? Was it fanciful to think that this witness might have heard such a story, claimed it as his own in a meeting with the prosecution and then, for reasons perhaps of embarrassment, or else learning of the financial rewards that came from testifying, decided to stick to it all the way into court? There was no forensic evidence to support his testimony, and no corroboration either.[10] And for what it is worth, the Special Court Outreach officers I spoke to in Kenema, one of whom claimed to have been present throughout the war, said they had never heard of a Yamorto Base in Kenema. Yamorto existed at Base Zero, they thought.[11]

The Chamber, however, dismissed inconsistencies like these as irrelevant: 'Minor inconsistencies in testimony do not necessarily discredit a witness. The events in question took place several years ago and, due to the nature of memory, some details will be confused, and some will be forgotten' (SCSL 2007d, 82). So irrelevant, in fact, that in its factual findings they are cleverly made to disappear. In this case: 'Colonel Biko cut open the stomach of TF2-152's friend and created a checkpoint by *stringing this person's guts between two sticks*' (SCSL 2007d, 183). To take another example, there was an inconsistency, or an ellipsis in the testimony of TF2-086, who narrated being assaulted by Kamajors and later awaking to find herself lying beside her friend Jitta's dead body. However, in the hearsay account TF2-086's brother – TF2-071 – TF2-086 had awoken to see Jitta's head cut off and placed on a stick (SCSL 2004e, 11 November 2004, 76). The Chamber found that 'the Kamajors took Jitta to the bush *and killed her*' (SCSL 2007d, 172). In another case, TF2-108 and TF2-109, two female witnesses described three killings at Talia, but there were discrepancies over whether one of the victims – Lahai Lebbi – was burned on the ground or whether a platform was made for him (Transcript, 30 May 2005, 12–14). The Chamber found that 'Lahai Lebbi was tied up by Kamajors and *burnt to death*' (SCSL 2007d, 189). In each of these examples, accounts which are different or inconsistent in

[10] TF2-021 did give an account of eating people at the Yamortor base in Kenema, but given the problems we will encounter with this witness, that ought perhaps to be taken with a grain of salt. In a separate incident, another witness, TF2-144, also mentioned a Kamajor named Yamorto piercing a man's chest with a knife. See (SCSL 2007d, 182).

[11] Moreover, I have been unable to find any reference to a Yamorto base in the main TRC report or the transcripts from the Kenema hearings (TRC 2004).

their detail are subsumed under a more general, less detailed account. In this manner the ambiguities in the testimony are elided by a more general description, a rhetorical strategy of concealment that confers the impression of a confident truth.

My next, more serious example, which we previewed in Chapter 2, also comes from Base Zero. The witness, TF2-222, was a 57-year-old farmer and former schoolteacher, who claimed to have been a former guardian of RUF leader Sam Bockarie. He was also an amateur playwright, and had previously scripted a satirical account of the war entitled 'Sierra Leone in a Dilemma' (SCSL 2004e, 17 February 2005, 75). He later helped create the War Council at Base Zero, and provided this account of a parade ground meeting in early December 1997, prior to the CDF attack on Tongo. In this meeting, Norman gave orders for the attack on Tongo Field. According to the witness, Norman said 'the attack on Tongo will determine who the winner or the looser [*sic*] of the war would be' and that 'there is no place to keep captured or war prisoners like the juntas, let alone their collaborators'. The witness testified that he felt uncomfortable with this command because it was like telling the Kamajors 'not to spare the vulnerables [*sic*]'. Norman also said that '[if] the international community is condemning human rights abuses ... then I take care of the human left abuses', meaning that 'any junta you capture, instead of wasting your bullet, chop off his left [hand]'. He also told the fighters to 'spare the houses of those men who burnt down your own house', which TF2-222 interpreted as an indirect instruction to burn houses. Now, here comes the crucial bit. Apparently, after Norman had finished speaking, Fofana stepped up to address the crowd, and said: 'you've heard the National Coordinator ... any commander failing to perform accordingly and losing your own ground, just decide to kill yourself there and don't come to report to us' (SCSL 2004e, 17 February 2005, 110–20).[12] As the defence pointed out in its closing argument, this account appears to include an ellipsis, since Fofana's statement, 'you've heard the National Coordinator ... any commander failing to perform accordingly and losing your own ground' seems to refer not to Norman's statement about burning down houses or cutting the hands off of perpetrators, but to some sort of instruction about troop positions or movements, which is lost in the narrative.

[12] The Chamber claims that the account of this meeting was corroborated by TF2-005, on p. 106 of a closed session, and by Norman himself, but the words themselves appear to be uncorroborated.

In the judgment's *legal* findings, this episode is re-presented thus:

> At a passing out parade at Base Zero between 10 and 12 December 1997 Norman gave instructions for the Tongo and Black December operations. Norman said that the attack on Tongo would determine who wins the war. He also said there was no place to keep captured prisoners like the juntas, let alone their collaborators. He directed the Kamajors that instead of wasting bullets, to chop off the left hand of any captured junta as a signal to any group that would want to seize power through the barrels of the gun and not the ballot paper. *He also told the fighters not to spare the houses of the juntas.* After hearing Norman's instructions, Fofana addressed the Kamajors saying that any commander failing to perform accordingly and 'losing your own ground', should kill himself and not come to report to Base Zero.
>
> (my emphasis) (SCSL 2007d, 217.)

The Chamber proceeded to find that 'Fofana's speech at the passing out parade in December 1997 when the attack on Tongo was discussed was clearly an encouragement and support of Norman's instructions to kill captured enemy combatants and "collaborators", to inflict physical suffering or injury upon them and to destroy their houses' (SCSL 2007d, 217). There are a number of points to note here. First, the Chamber has chosen not to give any weight to the idea that, because of the ellipsis in the witness account, Fofana may have been encouraging something other than instructions to kill collaborators. Second, if Norman had ever given such an instruction, it was an oblique one, as was the instruction to burn houses. Third, Norman allegedly gave explicit instructions to amputate the left hands of the enemy but there was no evidence of such acts ever having been committed; instead, there was evidence of Kamajors hacking at three people with a cutlass, cutting a man's right hand, hacking a man in the neck, and shooting a man five times (SCSL 2007d, 228). By parlaying Norman's specific instruction to cut off left hands into the more sweeping instruction to 'inflict physical suffering and injury', the Chamber rendered his words more consistent with the evidence on Count 4 (cruel treatment). It then re-presented these as 'criminal acts explicitly included in Norman's order' (SCSL 2007d, 223). Taking these points into consideration, then, there are grounds for thinking that the nexus between Fofana and the allegation of aiding and abetting murder, cruel treatment, and collective punishment, on which he was ultimately convicted under Article 6 (i) of the Statute, was more rhetorical than real.[13]

[13] Note that even the Appeals Chamber thought Fofana's words were 'ambiguous and may be interpreted not as approving Norman's unlawful orders, but rather as an appeal to each of the

My next example was also crucial to the trial. On 8 November 2004, TF2-096, a 37-year-old woman, described her experiences at Talia Yawbecko. One of the episodes she narrated involved her fetching water at a well in the centre of Talia, where she saw a procession of Kamajors coming towards her led by two men dancing with an effigy on their heads. Also present was Allieu Kondewa and another initiator Kamoh Boni. 'When they passed the well where I was fetching the water', testified the witness, 'then Konde stretched his arm and took the gun from Kamoh Boni. I saw him shoot one of them; then he fell.' Later, her mother-in-law told her that the two dancers were 'town commanders', their 'people' from a neighbouring area. Next day, a Kamajor pointed out two graves to her, and told her that this was where the men were buried (SCSL 2004e, 8 November 2004, 24–8).

Unfortunately, there was not a lot of detail to this testimony. The timeframe given for the incident – 'toward the end of 1997' – was imprecise. The witness did not report the 'killings' to any authority. There was no corroboration or forensic evidence. The witness's vantage point on the shooting of one man was not fully explained, she did not witness the shooting of the other man, and she did not see either of them die (Kondewa's defence counsel missed the opportunity to cross-examine on this aspect, preferring to use the 'figment of your imagination' approach instead). That the victims were buried in Talia was hearsay. More generally, and as the Kondewa defence complained in its closing:

> very few of the witnesses called by the Prosecution gave names of the perpetrators whose acts they described, and even fewer gave details about dates and locations. Whilst understandable, given the time which has passed and the nature of the events being recounted, it seriously limits the ability of the accused to identify and interview potential witnesses to the events described, in order to test the credibility of the account given.
> (Transcript, 30 November 2006, 44.)

Nevertheless this level of evidence was deemed sufficient by the Trial Chamber to convict Kondewa for the commission of murder: 'the Chamber finds that it has been proved beyond reasonable doubt that Kondewa is individually criminally responsible … for committing

commanders to fight hard and not loose [*sic*] his ground' (SCSL 2008b, 23), suggesting that he might have successfully appealed this conviction.

murder' (SCSL 2007d, 278) (although this was sensibly overturned on appeal) (SCSL 2008b, 69–70).[14]

In fact almost all the witnesses in the CDF trial had difficulty in knowing, remembering, or divulging precise deictic markers, that is, details that could anchor an event in space and time. The following, by no means exceptional example, is taken from the testimony of the trial's second witness, TF2-157, given on 16 June 2004. It concerns the meeting in Koribundo where Hinga Norman allegedly claimed responsibility for the crimes of the Kamajors. The example is interesting because the witness is unable to provide a precise date for a meeting he alleged he attended. He is also unable to say unequivocally the time of day that the meeting was held. Neither is he able to say clearly how long he stayed at the meeting:

Q: Now did that meeting continue for long?
A: The time that I witnessed in that meeting, the meeting lasted – it lasted for – when I was there – I can't tell you how long it lasted, but it lasted but it lasted on to the time I left the place and I stayed there for quite a considerable time. I can't tell you how long it took after I left.
Q: Can you say how long you were there?
A: I can't tell you that because I hadn't a wristwatch on me.

(SCSL 2004e, 17 June 2004, 14.)

Cross-examination then moved to the witness's account of a second meeting:

Q: I will also briefly and finally deal with another meeting that you said was held, when was that?
A: It was in the same month, towards the end of that particular month.
Q: You were a bit specific about the first one; that it was in the first week of March. Can you specify the week in March when this second meeting was held?
A: That was what I told you. I said it was at the end of the month. If any man tells you at the end of the month – if the moon is going to the end

[14] Note also that a defence witness, JD Murana, in whose compound the corpses were supposedly buried, denied the allegations (Transcript, 12 October 2006). To take another example of a thinly detailed testimony, TF2-187 testified to her uncle being murdered by Kamajors in Gambia Village. However, the defence were not even given the uncle's name, there was no corroboration, there was no body or grave (SCSL 2004e, 1 June 2005). The Chamber accepted the testimony as fact, although it stopped short of convicting the accused because of uncertainty about the timeframe of the events (SCSL 2007d, 264).

of – to completion, then that's the end of the month. I can't tell you the exact date.

(SCSL 2004e, 17 June 2004, 14.)

Arrow Bockarie, Counsel for the second accused, tried again:

Q: Now you said there was a meeting held in [Koribundo] some time in March which was addressed by Chief Norman. Am I correct?
A: Yes.
Q: For how long did this meeting last? The first meeting, how long did it last?
A: It started when the sun has come up and it was almost daylight. I didn't have a watch on my wrist. And he spoke, and even when I went away he continued to talk and it lasted for long. Whatever he said in my absence, I didn't hear.
Q: As a muslim, the meeting commenced before the afternoon prayers or before [*sic*] the afternoon prayers?
A: That was before the afternoon prayers, that was when the meeting started.
Q: Now, was it before 12 o'clock or after 12 o'clock?
A: I didn't have a watch and you are asking me about 12 o'clock. If I had a wrist watch then I would have told you, but that was when the sun was really up, that was when the meeting started.

(SCSL 2004e, 17 June 2004, 41.)

Interestingly, Bockarie has elicited a potential inconsistency here. At first the witness says that it was 'almost daylight' when the meeting took place; later he says the sun was 'really up'.[15] This vagueness calls into question the accuracy of the witness's recollection of events, but by this time the Bench had grown impatient, intervening with 'Get along', 'This man keeps saying, "I didn't have a watch," "I didn't have this," I mean, we keep coming back to that' (SCSL 2004e,17 June 2004, 41.).

Nor was it surprising that the details of place and time were sketchy, since there is an anthropological literature that suggests that local and Western notions of space differ radically. For example J. Littlejohn, writing in 1963, claimed that Temne people (Sierra Leone's second largest tribe) believed the earth to be 'a flat, circular object resting on the head of a giant', the hair of whose head was the earth's trees and plants, and the

[15] William Murphy has suggested that the apparent contradiction between 'almost daylight' and 'the sun was really up' might be a problem stemming from the translation of Mende adverbs into English. Personal Communication.

lice in which were the people and beasts (Littlejohn 1963, 1). Ordinary Temne space was 'neither arithmetically measured nor geometrically analysed', being broken into units such as 'the space between two villages', 'a day's journey' or 'within earshot' (Littlejohn 1963, 4). Summing up, he stated that:

> Temne space is not the featureless container of things it us for us, analysed through ideal forms and bearing systems of numerical measurement; instead it falls round them in meanings read off from the physiognomy of landscape and the human body, combined with images embodying notions of good and evil.
>
> (Littlejohn 1963, 14.)

More prosaically, the details at trial of an event's location were often simply vague. Witnesses could usually identify the town or village, and sometimes the streets in which events took place, but beyond this details were often sketchy. With the exception of a scale model of Base Zero, both defence and prosecution made virtually no use of maps, diagrams or sketches that would help the Court assess the reliability of witness accounts of events.

Temporal markers were even thinner. Most witnesses hailed from communities in which the rhythms of the agricultural season and the march of the sun across the sky were more important than clock time and the Roman calendar.[16] While some witnesses could remember days of the month and years, others could not testify to any of these: 'I'm a Mende person. I don't count months', said one (SCSL 2004e, 8 May 2006, 106). Counsel would often try and locate stories in time by reference to other well-established events, such as the election, overthrow or restoration of the Kabbah regime, but they were not always successful. Some witnesses claimed to be able to remember the date and the year when an event took place, but their stories did not match those of other witnesses. Sometimes witnesses changed their mind on the stand. As we have seen they often gave rather general temporal markers – such and such happened 'towards the end of the year', or, 'towards the beginning of the month', or 'not too long after that'. Witnesses were rarely in the possession of wristwatches, and unsurprisingly had only vague ideas of the duration of often traumatic episodes. Perhaps more surprisingly, witnesses were usually reluctant to give any kind of an estimate of the

[16] This is not to gainsay that many people in these communities would have some familiarity with these referents, even if they preferred or could not afford to use them, or that some people would be perfectly comfortable with them.

time that elapsed between events. Many seemed to be fearful of telling lies under oath, or of being caught out by defence counsel, and their reticence on this score considerably impeded the progress of the Court.

When they could not get temporal details, prosecution and judges often resorted to describing witnesses as 'illiterate', 'unsophisticated' or 'relatively unsophisticated'. On 3 June 2005, for example, Judge Thompson remarked that 'this kind of encounter or impasse would convince me that this Tribunal is right in adopting a flexible approach to admission of these statements made by persons who are not as sophisticated as us and who may not have been too familiar with the process and method of investigation' (SCSL 2004e, 3 June 2005, 46). On another occasion, defence counsel Margai admitted: 'So I am taking the cue from the Bench by not confining my questions to specific periods, because I am assuming that the witness is not sophisticated enough to remember dates' (SCSL 2004e, 17 June 2004, 53). In this way Court officers tried to mask their inability to engage productively with witnesses by alluding to the latter's social and intellectual inferiority. It implied that the Court should not expect too much from people who were uneducated, tapping into now largely discredited attitudes about the mental deficiencies of non-literate peoples (Gee 1996, 26). Indeed, witnesses often acquiesced in this, stressing their unlettered credentials. The following quote, from TF2-157, who described himself – in a way to make most modern anthropologists blanche – as 'a primitive man from the bush' (SCSL 2004e, 16 June 2004, 25) is typical:

> Yes. For dates, for those that I can remember I will talk about them here, but I am not a learned person. So if you are talking about dates and asking me if I can remember that particular, if you know that's the correct date, tell me that's the correct date. All I can say here is what I remember. If you say that's the date and you remember the date, then say it. I don't remember dates. I'm telling you those dates that I remember.
>
> (SCSL 2004e, 17 June 2004, 40.)

Here it might be useful to consider William Murphy's observations about a similar vernacular dichotomy – between 'country' and 'civilised' – in Liberia. According to Murphy:

> the application of civilized and country categories is more an outcome of actors' definitions and purposes than a reflection of some immutable reality … a person can manipulate the categories to serve certain purposes in certain contexts. An educated Kpelle man might emphasize his civilized status is some village affairs while emphasizing his country status in others; or he may act like a civilized person in his village, yet find

> it advantageous to lay claim to a country status in his dealings with the government in Monrovia.
>
> (Murphy 1981, 675.)

Insofar as this observation applies also to Sierra Leone, we can see that witness's self-effacing confessions exonerated them from providing precise details of the events on which hung the defendants' fate. In fact none of the Koribundo witnesses testifying in open session was able to give a precise date for either of the meetings at which Norman was said to have incriminated himself. Such a date might have helped the Court determine whether or not these witnesses were actually present at the meeting, or whether they had heard about it from someone else. Neither were the witnesses able to give a very clear indication of how long they stayed at the meeting. All seem to have left before it ended, leaving open the possibility that Norman's remarks were taken out of context. And although the Bench showed suitable caution in not entering convictions for significant sections of the prosecution's case – such as the charges relating to Black December and much of the evidence for offences around Talia – on grounds that it could not locate them precisely within the timeframe of the indictment, the general disadvantage at which the defence investigations were put was not addressed.

'Would the witness answer the question directly?' Laborious cross-examinations

As I mentioned in the introduction to this chapter, one of the things that struck me most about the CDF trial was its laborious nature. Some of this was probably the result of innocent translation difficulties or intercultural misunderstanding.[17] But we also have to consider the more

[17] The language of the Court was English, which was spoken by the Bench and the legal teams. However, few of the witnesses chose to testify in English, most choosing Krio, Mende, Temne or Limba. Nor was English spoken well, if at all, by two of trial's accused. Consequently, the Court relied on simultaneous translation. As the barristers and judges spoke to the witness, the translation was piped into the headphones of the witness and accused in a language of their choosing, and the answer was piped in English to the Court and public gallery. For the most part translation proceeded smoothly. However, there were sometimes problems caused by technical glitches, overlapping microphones, either counsel or witness speaking too quickly, and issues of interpretation. The pace of direct and cross-examination was considerably slowed by the need to translate the testimony simultaneously, a drag that undoubtedly interrupted some of the courtroom's cut, thrust, and natural flow. Since several members of the legal teams spoke native languages – indeed Jabbi was a linguist by training – disagreements about the precise translation being rendered came up repeatedly. In the case of TF2-159 on 9 September, Judge Itoe went so far as to say 'Do you want us to have another interpreter for another interpreter?' (SCSL 2004e, 9 September 2004, 65–6).

troubling possibility that witnesses were either consciously or unconsciously dissembling, either because they were afraid, or because they had something to hide. A few illustrations follow.

TF2-162 was a 75-year-old resident of Jaiama Bongor chiefdom, who testified to being in the mosque in Koribundo when the town was attacked by Kamajors on 13 February 1998. He witnessed the Kamajors setting fire to a house, and he also spoke about Norman's public meeting where he allegedly claimed responsibility for Kamajor atrocities. The cross-examination of this witness was a drawn-out affair, fraught with difficulty, mostly because the witness gave most of his answers in a non-committal conditional tense. In this snippet, the defence lawyer is cross-examining the witness about the presence or absence of certain key figures at a meeting the witness has testified he attended:

Q. But was [Kosseh Hindowa] present at the Barri in the meeting we discussed this morning after the taking of Koribundu?

A. I did not see him there.

Q. And Joe Tamidey?

A. I know him very well.

Q. Was he at the Barri?

A. Even if he was there, I did not see him, because you would meet with people, but if you did not see the person, you can't say he was there.

JUDGE THOMPSON: Would the witness answer the question directly. The – probably we want counsel for the prosecution that we don't want commentaries or hypothesis, because I am finding it extremely difficult and the evaluation of witnesses' evidence is crucial to the determination of findings of facts and the truth, and perhaps he needs to be advised that when a direct question is asked, a direct answer is required and not a hypothetical or commentary or analysis.

MR BANGURA: I take the point, Your Honour. I will endeavour to get the witness to answer questions directly, but Your Honour will also appreciate that he is, by his disposition already shown to this Court, he is a kind of person given to too much talking.

JUDGE THOMPSON: Yes, but the Court needs to be able to work out a compromise. I mean, he cannot impose his own peculiar way of narrating style. We are not here in a kind of story-telling context where this might be permissible. I am just trying to say that we are here to ascertain the truth, and when you have a convolution of facts and hypothesis, and commentary and analysis, it becomes inextricably difficult to be able to separate them.

(SCSL 2004e, 8 September 2004, 82–5.)

My next example comes from the testimony of TF2-176. This witness was also in the Koribundo mosque when the town was attacked on 13 February. He fled the town but on returning he found that his house and twelve others had been burnt. He was tied, beaten and robbed by a Kamajor, but later released by a Kamajor commander. He also attended Norman's meeting in Koribundo. In the example below, Yada Williams, counsel for the third accused, is trying to elicit evidence about a certain Kamajor commander, presumably because his actions have a bearing on the general character of the Kamajors, and the nature of command and control:

Q. I would – I want to ask you your opinion about Xxxx. Was he a good commander?
A. Yes, he told me so.
Q. That's what he told you?
MR. PRESIDENT: Ask the question again.
BY MR. WILLIAMS:
Q. Yes, was he a good commander?
A. Yes.
Q. And you felt very safe when he was around? I mean, because, I mean, you have mentioned that you were a little bit afraid, you were panicked because of what had happened. Right. Did you feel at ease? Did you feel comfortable when he was around?
A. Yes.
Q. Did he discipline soldiers? Sorry, did he discipline Kamajors who did wrong to the people of [Koribundo]? I mean –
A. I don't understand.
Q. Did he discipline Kamajors who – or people who did wrong to residents of [Koribundo]? Okay, let me ask you this. I mean the – the ordinary Kamajors at [Koribundo], did they have a lot of respect for him?
A. I don't understand your question.
Q. It is a simple and straightforward question.
MR. PRESIDENT: To you, Counsel, not to him. Take your time, have some patience with him.
MR. WILLIAMS: As My Lord –
MR. PRESIDENT: Reframe your questions, you know.

MR. WILLIAMS: Yes, My Lord. I don't know whether it's interpretation that is faulty, but, I mean, I cannot –

MR. PRESIDENT: Take your time. It demands a lot of patience, you know, examining a witness who is illiterate. We have all gone through those experiences. Take your time, please.

MR. WILLIAMS: Yes.

BY MR. WILLIAMS:

Q. The ordinary Kamajors, I mean, the lower rank Kamajors, did they have a lot of respect for Xxxx as commander?

A. That I would not know because I am a civilian.

(SCSL 2004e, 18 June 2004, 47–8.)

The next excerpt is from the cross examination of TF2-007, a 26-year-old male from Fengehun in Bo District, who, in examination-in-chief, spoke to the murder of his father by Kamajors. The witness claimed that one day he was arrested by Kamajors who took him to where they were holding his father captive. His father had been tortured, part of his ear cut off. The Kamajors told father and son to bid one another farewell before throwing the father in a burning hut. Later, they decapitated the body, placed the head on a stick, and danced with it. The defence, however, had a counter-theory, in this case that the boy's father had fled the village because he was a junta informer. Accordingly, they were trying to find evidence of a grave.

MR. KOPPE:

Q. My question, Witness, is: Is your father buried at the cemetery of the town?

A. I have told you just now that when he was killed, I didn't know whether – [interpretation interrupted]

PRESIDING JUDGE: Answer the question. Was your father buried in the cemetery in the village? Simple question. We have heard your explanations, but answer that question. It is very simple.

THE WITNESS: I didn't know whether he was buried there.

PRESIDING JUDGE: You don't know. I mean, stop answering questions in a twisted manner. You have a cemetery in your village which is what counsel is referring to. You have said that when somebody dies in the village, he's buried in the cemetery. Was your father buried in that cemetery?

THE WITNESS: I didn't see him being buried there.

PRESIDING JUDGE: You didn't see him being buried there, but was he buried there?

THE WITNESS: Whether they buried him there, I didn't see it happen.

Later on, Yada Williams cross-examined the witness on whether or not his father owned a gun. In the example here, he is trying to connect him to a death in the village, but the witness evades him:

MR WILLIAMS:
Q. I mean your father, did he ever own a single-barrel gun?
A. Whether he had it, I didn't see it with my own eyes.
Q. Did he ever go out hunting? Did your father ever go out hunting?
A. Well, even if he went, I didn't know.
Q. You were staying at your father's house; is that correct?
A. Sometime – sometimes I lived there, but I was learning the Koran, so that is where I stayed.
Q. Will you answer the question, please. Did you stay at your father's house?

For a further twelve pages'-worth of testimony the witness frustrates Williams. Take, for example, the following episode. Acting on information from investigations, Williams is trying to get the witness to admit that on a previous occasion several people in the witness's village were taken by soldiers to Bo, whereupon they were killed, and that it was the witness's father who orchestrated these events:

MR WILLIAMS: Yes.
Q. And the four people you said you knew who were taken to [Bo], did any of them ever return to your village?
A. Those four people up to now, I've not seen them.
Q. Do you know what happened to them?
A. I don't know.
Q. Were you ever told what happened to them?
A. Whether they told me what happened to them? Yes, I heard it. But I was not there.
Q. I know you were not there, Mr Witness.
A. Mm-hmm.
Q. Tell the Court what you were told – tell the Court exactly what you were told that happened to them.
A. They said that they have been killed by soldiers, but I didn't see it, and I didn't go there.
Q. Let me ask you this, Mr Witness: Could you tell the Court how these people were removed from your village to [Bo]?
A. I didn't know that.

Q. Mr Witness, I'm putting it to you that you're not speaking the truth. You are not speaking the truth.
A. What am I – what I saw is what I talk about. What I didn't see, I wouldn't talk about.
Q. Your father was in [Bo] when these people were killed. Is that correct?
A. When they killed these people –
Q. Your father was in [Bo] when they were killed.
A. That's what I didn't know. Whether when they killed them, my father was in [Bo]. I didn't know that. I didn't know where he was. I didn't know that.

PRESIDING JUDGE: Is the evidence that they were killed in [Bo]?
MR WILLIAMS: Yes, My Lord.
PRESIDING JUDGE: That they were killed in [Bo]?
MR WILLIAMS: Yes, My Lord.
PRESIDING JUDGE: I see.
MR WILLIAMS:

Q. You know that these people were killed in [Bo]. Is that correct? You know they were killed in [Bo]?
A. Yes.
Q. And your father, you know very well that your father was in [Bo] at the time? You know very well?
A. I heard that he was in [Bo]. But I didn't know whether he was in [Bo] Town because we didn't see each other. Where he was, I didn't go there.
Q. I'm putting it to you, Mr Witness, that you know very well that it was your father who orchestrated for the killing of those people. You know very well.
A. Even if he did it, I didn't see. What I saw is what I'm talking about.
Q. Mr Witness, I'm not saying that you were in [Bo]. I'm saying that you were told, you were informed subsequently – you could not have been present in [Bo]. My question is this: That you were informed, you knew, through some other means, secondary means or whatever it is, that it was your father who orchestrated for the killing of those people.
A. Now, who told me?

(SCSL 2004e, 3 December 2004, 28–31.)

Giving conditional responses to questions was a not uncommon feature of witness testimony. To give another example, Haroun Collier, when asked whether he was proud of the actions of the Death Squad, responded variously that he 'can', 'could' or 'would' be proud of it, which prompted the following exchange:

JUDGE THOMPSON: Can I ask the interpreters, why do we get an answer in the subjunctive to a question about the past? Why do we get that answer when the question was, 'were you proud of it', and then we get a response, 'I would be.' That is subjunctive.

THE INTERPRETER: Yes, Your Honours, it's the way we get the answers in Mende.

JUDGE THOMPSON: I see, in other words, the subjunctive answer comes in response to a question asked in the past tense, or referring to the past tense?

THE INTERPRETER: Yes.

JUDGE THOMPSON: Is that how it is in Mende?

THE INTERPRETER: Yes, that's what we get from the witness.

JUDGE THOMPSON: I see.

PRESIDING JUDGE: But in Mende, you cannot say, 'I was'?

THE INTERPRETER: No, you can.

JUDGE ITOE: Or to say 'I am proud,' is there nothing in Mende that can be translated to, 'I am proud'?

THE INTERPRETER: Yes, there is.

(SCSL 2004e, 15 May 2006, 42–3.)

To help us get a handle on these difficulties, we can turn to the rich literature on intercultural understanding and translation, to the historiography and anthropology of Sierra Leone, and to legal discourse analysis. In respect of the first, the scholarly literature on the subject of intercultural misunderstanding draws our attention to the importance to communication of cultural frames.[18] John Gumperz, for example, has analysed a number of situations in which communication stalls, partly because of different cultural expectations of what a situation is about, and partly because of culturally conditioned differences in prosody, which Gee defines as: 'The ways in which words and sentences of a text are said: their pitch, loudness, stress, and the length assigned to various syllables, as well as the way in which the speaker hesitates and pauses'

[18] Gee's work, for example, has shown how differences in cultural and class background can affect activities such as the style of composing oral narratives and interpreting texts. To take an example of the latter, he explains how the cigarette packet term 'Lung cancer death rates are clearly associated with an increase in smoking' (Gee 2005, 42) is grammatically susceptible to at least 112 different constructions of meaning. Nevertheless, the vast majority of people who read it, situated in a particular culture and context, unhesitatingly ascribe to it only one.

(Gee 1996, 94; see also Locke 2004). Drawing on a study by Erickson of a series of student-counsellor sessions, for example, Gumperz reports that each conversation appeared to be introduced by a phase in which participants probed each other for evidence of a shared perspective or common background of experience. If these initial manoeuvres were successful, the session was more likely to continue smoothly as 'a well-coordinated sequence of exchanges' (Gumperz 1982, 142). Conversational engagement was maintained by means of 'indirect inferences which build on background assumptions about context' (Gumperz 1982, 2) as well as habitually used 'contextualization cues' or 'constellations of surface features of message form' that conversationalists use to signal the precise import of their utterances and the desired response (Gumperz 1982, 131). Where either of these is not shared, communication has a tendency to break down, even among grammatical speakers of the same language. In the student-counsellor sessions referred to above, the ability to find a common rhythm was a function, among other things, of similarity in ethnic background, while ethnic difference was fertile ground for miscommunication (Gumperz 1982, 177–203). Given that lawyers and witnesses at the court tended to come from rather different national, cultural, and class backgrounds, it is hardly surprising that their exchanges were infrequently smooth.

The potential for cross-cultural miscommunication was magnified by the fact that the conversation was conducted in two languages, mediated by an interpreter. Scholars have known about the potential pitfalls of this situation for some time. Based on a study of Spanish interpretation in American courtrooms, Susan Berk-Seligson, for example, has debunked the myth that the court interpreter 'is nothing short of a machine that converts the English speech of attorneys, judges, and English-speaking witnesses into the mother tongue of the non-English speaking defendant or witness' (Berk-Seligson 1990, 2).[19] Her study shows how interpreters often unconsciously skew speakers' intended meanings, by failing to mirror the 'pragmatics' of speech.

Doubtless difficulties were also caused by the sheer unfamiliarity of the setting for many witnesses. Legal discourse analysts have also shown that court procedures produce exchanges that are 'highly unusual from a conversational point of view' (Conley and O'Barr 1998, 21). Lawyers

[19] Although minor disagreements over translation were not uncommon, see for example the transcript of 9 May 2006, pp. 33–4, Dr Jabbi, counsel for Norman and also a trained linguist, said to me in an interview after the trial that he did not think that translation had caused insuperable difficulties (interview with Dr Bu-Buakei Jabbi, 11 June 2008).

must form all their utterances as questions, while witnesses are restricted to providing answers to whatever questions are asked. As in the above case of TF2-162, exchanges at the Special Court can consequently be viewed as a struggle or contest over testimonial style. Judges frequently admonished counsel to 'control your witness', complaining that evidence was 'not sequential' or 'entangled', and they sometimes admitted to being 'totally confused'. There were further exhortations to get at the 'truth' or 'the facts': 'Remember, if we don't find the facts, we will never be able to even apply the law' (Judge Thompson, SCSL 2004e, 17 June 2004, 53). 'Take control of him', said Judge Thompson in the case of Haroun Collier, 'Let's have the classic example of question and answer and then the examination-in-chief will be more focused. You know your case. Really the narration thing is more akin with the oral tradition … we're not in a folklore setting here' (SCSL 2004e, 12 May 2006, 47). But rather than lawyers successfully dominating witnesses (Conley and O'Barr 1998, 22–31), court encounters often produced a kind of stalemate or confusion, as illustrated by the examples above.

As might be expected, prosecution and defence lawyers tended to have different explanations for these communicative difficulties. In its opening statement, the prosecution informed the audience that: 'the vast majority of the testimony … comes from persons who are illiterate and from very simple backgrounds. Individuals native to the rural areas of southern and eastern Sierra Leone … [T]hey are a simple people whose nature is anything but violent' (SCSL 2004e, 4 June 2004, 30).[20] The idea that witnesses were all good natured, simple country folk reflected stereotypical views about the simplicity of rural, non-literate people. With this image in mind, the prosecution argued that their witnesses – in contrast to most witnesses in Western courts of law – 'were completely without their own agendas … they were without artifice … in a way they were like human cameras … they just said what they saw'.[21]

Saying just what they saw often came across in Court as a form of extreme circumspection. Circumspection, of course, can also be a form of evasion, since by being circumspect one avoids the prospect of saying anything that might get one into trouble: 'I have taken an oath on the

[20] Though in earlier days Sierra Leone was known as the Athens of West Africa, a sobriquet earned by virtue of having Africa's first university (established at Fourah Bay College in 1827), literate education has always been the exclusive preserve of its elite. In 2004, the country had an adult literacy rate of just 35 per cent. Unsurprisingly, this statistic was reflected in the type of witnesses who appeared before the Special Court.

[21] Kevin Tavener, telephone interview, 20 July 2007.

Koran and on the Bible. What I'm saying here is the truth. If it didn't happen in my presence, I would not say it. I would not say what did not happen in my presence. I am only saying what happened, and what I saw', said one witness (SCSL 2004e, 11 May 2006, 73). We can see this by looking back at the examples above. TF2-162's equivocation over whether or not Joe Tamidey was at the Koribundo meeting, is a hedge that protects him from the possibility that Tamidey was actually there. TF2-176 chose not to venture an opinion on the character of the kamajor commander's authority in Koribundo, but it is quite probable that he had one. Turning to the example of TF2-007, my best guess is that the witness is well aware that there is an opinion in his village that his father played a part in these murders, but for reasons best known to himself, he is circumspect about this.

Defence lawyers I spoke to suspected that witnesses behaved like this because their stories were made up: '[They were] incredibly evasive ... they wouldn't answer questions directly ... they wouldn't make eye contact ... their stories were not linear ... there was nothing to get hold of ... there were no details of times or dates ... they lied about the amount of money they received ... it was incredible.'[22] My own sensitivity to this possibility has been heightened by Marco Jacquemet's close analysis of the Italian Camorra trials. Jacquemet shows how insider witness testimonies which on the surface were plausible, and which were used in an initial set of trials to convict defendants, were upon scrutiny filled with hedges, stalls, and ambiguities that invited a more sceptical reading (Jacquemet 1996, see especially 95–130). The prosecution, however, had a different interpretation. After the trial ended, I interviewed prosecution counsel Joseph Kamara and asked him about what I saw as the tendency of some witnesses to be difficult under cross-examination. His explanation was this: 'It comes from the background of these people ... they have barely been exposed to this kind of justice system ... as soon as they identify that these [lawyers] are the "bad guys", they don't want to give them what they want, even if it's the truth!'[23]

The following is an example, taken from the testimony of TF2-159, a 28-year-old farmer and businessman, given on 9 September 2004. The witness gave testimony about the Kamajor attack on Koribundo, the looting and burning of houses, murder, decapitation, evisceration, and cannibalism, proving to be one of the most important witnesses

[22] Quincy Whitaker, telephone interview, 14 June 2007.

[23] Interview with Joseph Kamara, Special Court for Sierra Leone, 11 June 2008.

for the Koribundo crime base. Mostly this testimony was quite clear and quite compelling, but under cross-examination, the witness refused to give straight answers. Defence counsel Yada Williams at one point complained that 'the witness has been going on a frolic' (SCSL 2004e, 9 September 2004, 152), and Judge Boutet commented that: 'There really is a suggestion of impasse with the witness.' The following excerpt, which addresses the subject of the witness's previous meeting with Court investigators, provides an example:

MR WILLIAMS

Q. So tell the Court what transpired at the first meeting, the very first meeting you had with the investigators. Tell the Court what transpired between you and them.

A. When they came and met me in [Koribundo][24] or when I came here; which one are you talking about?

Q. It has to be at some place. So you tell us what transpired at the first meeting.

A. Isn't that what I talked about this morning?

Q. I want you to say it again.

A. That Friday?

Q. You know what I am saying. Do you know who is an investigator?

A. What do you mean by what you are saying?

(SCSL 2004e, 9 September 2004, 155).

One interpretation of this exchange is that the witness is having difficulty understanding what the lawyer wants, a difficulty compounded by translation perhaps. Another, equally plausible, interpretation is that the witness is being evasive, using the primary tactic of deflection. In the opening question, Williams asks clearly about the *first* meeting. The witness responds by shifting the focus from *sequence* to a query about *place*. Williams tries virtually the same question again. This time, the witness attempts to wriggle out of the situation by asking, rhetorically, whether he hasn't already spoken of it. Williams says he wants the witness to 'say it again'. He dodges this by introducing a query about time, a deictic marker so vague – 'that Friday?' – that it cannot possibly be of help to the Court. Williams, getting impatient, presses, 'You know what I am saying', a form of words which the witness picks up on and inverts, 'What do you mean by what you are saying?' eliding, in the process, the original question. Later on in this testimony, when the witness was being

[24] Note that the place name is redacted in the transcript.

re-examined on the issue of a potential inconsistency between his pre-trial and oral testimony, Judge Thompson instructed the prosecution: 'Probably you should advise your witness that the sort of responses we are having may well persuade an imaginary judge from space, perhaps, to think that he is trying to hide something' (SCSL 2004e, 10 September 2004, 38). Clearly, the strain was beginning to show.

On many occasions witnesses seemed determined to hedge their responses. Take the example of defence witness Moses Bangura here:

Q: Mr. Witness, I suggest to you that there was some training going on at Base Zero; do you agree with me?
A: Well, I cannot deny that, but I would not accept that. I only saw the field, and I did not know whether, before I went there, there had been training there, or they had not been training there. I did not know.
Q: I am talking about while you were there, Mr Witness, the three-month period you were there. I am suggesting to you there was training going on at Base Zero very frequently.
A: I and my group, see, we were not trained there. They did not train us there. Because, since we did not go there on a training mission, we went there for the purpose for which we went there.

(SCSL 2004e, 17 October 2006, 27.)[25]

To understand what was happening here, it is useful to consider the adversarial nature of the proceedings, something with which most witnesses would be quite unfamiliar. As Conley and O'Barr have noticed, cross-examination in an adversarial system is experienced as a hostile environment for both lawyer and witness. As Judge Thompson made clear: 'witnesses who volunteer to come and testify must be ready to subject themselves to aggressive and vigorous cross-examination in order to

[25] Watching the children's movie *Shrek 3* recently, I was reminded of some of the circumlocutions heard at the Special Court by a scene in which Prince Charming interrogates Pinocchio, who, because of his protean nose, is unable to lie:

PRINCE CHARMING: You! You can't lie! Where is Shrek?
PINOCCHIO: Well, uh, I don't know where he's not.
PRINCE CHARMING: You don't know where Shrek is?
PINOCCHIO: On the contrary,
PRINCE CHARMING: So you do know where he is!
PINOCCHIO: I'm possibly more or less not definitely rejecting the idea that I undeniably
PRINCE CHARMING: Stop it!
PINOCCHIO: Do or do not know where he shouldn't probably be. If that indeed wasn't where he isn't!

ascertain the truth, and we'll do nothing on the Bench to depart from that tradition' (SCSL 2004e, 17 June 2004, 48). It is arguable, however, that in the Sierra Leonean context these aggressive procedures did not serve the truth. With more than one witness, the Bench had to intervene to calm things down: 'Perhaps we should ask Dr Jabbi to ask his witness to be less confrontational. It's a search for a truth. It's not really a fighting match' (SCSL 2004e, 2 June 2006, 53). As Arrow Bockarie, counsel for Moinina Fofana, said to me:

> the witnesses perceived us as being enemies ... that is generally the thinking of rural Sierra Leoneans ... here if somebody testifies against another it really creates some bad blood ... they had that at the back of their minds ... that these are not our friends ... so unless you are very certain of your answer, you are not going to get cooperation.[26]

As we have seen, Sierra Leone scholars have argued that Sierra Leone's cultural order of dissimulation is linked to a history of insecurity (Ferme 2001; Shaw 2000), and it seems probable that witnesses responded to the adversarial setting by drawing on a fund of dissembling strategies provided by their historical experience and cultural background: to feign ignorance or misunderstanding; to be cautious, circumspect, and indirect.[27]

The judges recognised this was a problem, but as the trial wore on they seemed to be minimising its significance by treating it as an innocent idiosyncrasy of local speech genres. For example, in the course of TF2-007's equivocations, referred to above, Judge Itoe intervened with the following remarks:

PRESIDING JUDGE: There's a traditional way of translating Mende into English. I'm sure that's the way the Mende people reply to questions. Dr Jabbi? Mr Bockarie?

MR BOCKARIE: My Lord, not all of them.

Pressing on regardless, he opined:

PRESIDING JUDGE: He's a real traditional man. He was born and raised in that village and he has lived through the traditions. So you can see his answers, you know, they're never direct. Yes, Mr Koppe, you can move along.

[26] Interview with Arrow Bockarie, Bo Town, 13 June 2008.

[27] I should stress that I am not blaming the witnesses for this outcome. The lawyers must bear some responsibility for not getting the best out of witnesses.

MR KOPPE: Last question on the matter of the cemetery. Is there, Witness, maybe –

PRESIDING JUDGE: In fact, the sooner we can leave that cemetery the better. Yes?

(SCSL 2004e, 2 December 2004, 80.)

Shortly after this exchange, the judges made another comment:

JUDGE THOMPSON: Many times he seems to be saying 'even if.' He's virtually disclaiming. Even if it happened, I don't know. That seems to be the –

PRESIDING JUDGE: He's not very forthright.

JUDGE THOMPSON: No, that's his approach. Everything is prefaced with 'even if.'[28]

PRESIDING JUDGE: That's what Mr Williams is missing, for being born and bred in an OAU village. And that's why you should not get angry with witnesses like this. They don't mean any harm at all to you. That's their way. We've seen many of them through our passage in this business.

(SCSL 2004e, 3 December 2004, 35.)

In the final judgment, the judges accepted most of the evidence from prosecution witnesses, whether or not they had been difficult on the stand. It made no reference to the problems it had remarked upon during trial, stating as we have seen that it had evaluated the evidence on the basis of a number of factors, including strength under cross-examination. But was strength under cross-examination in this context an appropriate test? While it is true that witnesses were not weak, in other words, like TF2-007, they did not capitulate to the probing and insinuation of opposite counsel, they were rarely strong in the sense of providing clear answers, clarifying details or giving convincing elaborations. Rather, they were slippery, dodging questions with a rope-a-dope style, until counsel, having failed to land the knockout blow, threw in the towel.[29]

[28] Note that this exasperated comment suggests that Thompson, an urbane Sierra Leonean who had been living for years in America, is as much out of his depth as are the non-Sierra Leonean members of the Court.

[29] According to my methods, 64 per cent of the open session prosecution witness testimonies and 79 per cent of the defence witness testimonies contained one or more episodes of inconsistency, evasive speech genres, serious ambiguity or entanglement, or problems with statements, either singly or in combination.

The Chamber also stated that where internal inconsistencies in testimony or contradictions with other evidence demonstrated a 'poor, selective, or tainted' recollection of events, then corroboration was required. Following this principle, it made explicit mention of rejecting the evidence of one prosecution witness, and accepting another's only when corroborated (SCSL 2007d, 89). The Chamber also mentioned that: '[s]ome Defence witnesses were clearly testifying with the objective of assisting one of the accused.' Other witnesses, the Chamber thought, seemed to want to mislead the Court. Brima Tarawally, for instance, was 'deliberately obstructive', while Mustapha Lumeh 'was hesitant in answering questions, [his] attitude and behaviour in court led the Chamber to conclude that assisting the Chamber with the discovery of truth was not his primary reason for testifying' (SCSL 2007d, 90). This kind of evidence was entirely rejected. The Chamber also found that some defence witnesses, though corroborating each other, had come with 'stock' answers to refute the charges against the accused.

But it is not clear that these standards were consistently applied. For example, in its factual findings the Chamber admitted TF2-007's testimony (above) (SCSL 2007d, 163), even though it was not corroborated by anyone.[30] To take another example, we saw that TF2-159 was a very uncooperative witness, there were inconsistencies in his testimony, and at one stage Judge Thompson insinuated that he might have something to hide. Nevertheless, large chunks of his testimony found their way into the final judgment, including the damning allegation that two women were skewered on sticks before having their entrails eaten.[31] Even though there was no forensic evidence, only the women's Christian names were known, and there was no corroborating testimony, this evidence was used to convict Moinina Fofana of superior responsibility for murder (SCSL 2007d, 136). And where testimony *was* corroborated, a very weak form of corroboration appeared sometimes to suffice. Take TF2-159 again. Supposedly corroborating the part of his testimony where he describes Kamajors singing songs as they beat, wounded and mutilated alleged

[30] Although TF2-007's account of his father's murder was accepted by the judges, neither of the accused was ultimately found responsible for it. This was the right decision, I suggest, made on the wrong grounds, since the finding seemed to stem not from any concerns about whether or not the witness's father had actually been killed, or if he had, whether or not this was a local revenge murder, but from Albert Nallo's admission that he could not control all the Kamajors in Bo District (SCSL 2007d, 242–55).

[31] His written statement said the women were killed with a cutlass (SCSL 2004e, 9 September 2004, 108).

junta collaborators, including two men named Sarrah and Momoh, is an account given by former child soldier TF2-140. However, upon inspection, the section of TF2-140's testimony cited by the Chamber refers to some collaborators being beheaded in another town at another time (though the name of the town is redacted from the trial transcript) (SCSL 2004e, 14 September 2004, 73). What the Chamber in fact appears to be referring to is a section of testimony eight pages later where the witness, describing his entry to Koribundo[32] states: 'I saw houses on fire. Then I saw dead bodies lying around, lying on the ground, beheaded bodies' (SCSL 2007d, 81). This, however, falls some way short of corroborating testimony of Kamajors singing songs as they mutilated specific people. Moreover, the name of the road at which this scene was observed has been redacted from the trial transcript (the reason is unfathomable) making it difficult even to know whether or not there was a possibility, let alone a likelihood, that the bodies referred to belonged to Sarrah and Momoh, or perhaps to some other civilians, or even to enemy soldiers killed in combat. Although this appears, then, to be at best a piece of weak corroboration, it was strong enough at the Special Court for Sierra Leone, to help convict Fofana for murder.

'I can't just answer a question like that': witness payments

Problems in communication became particularly acute when cross-examining witnesses on the subject of witness payments. Witnesses were often brought to Freetown for around a month at a time, during which they were provided lodging and received allowances of up to 20,000 Leones a day, medical treatment, allowances to support their families, replacement farm labour and other perks, such as clothes in which to appear in court. In 2004, the UNDP's Human Development Report estimated Sierra Leone's annual GDP per capita in 2004 as $520, which translates into 3,848 Le per day. Taken together with Sierra Leone's high income disparities, and minimal access to rural health care, we can see that witness allowances were very generous in local terms, and they formed a more or less constant theme in the opening two sessions of the trial. For example, on 8 September, John Wesley Hall established that TF2-162 had received Le 833,000 (SCSL 2004e, 8 September 2004). On 13 September, Quincy Whitaker told the witness (TF2-032) that the Court had given him more than 1 million Leones. TF2-140 had

32 In the transcript the name of the town has been redacted, but it appears in the Berkeley War Crimes Studies Center monitoring reports of the proceedings. In general, redaction appears to have been a rather random process.

received over Le 1.5 million (SCSL 2004e, 14 September 2004). TF2-021, another child soldier, received over 2 million Leones (SCSL 2004e, 2 November 2004). However, getting the witnesses to agree to these facts was extremely laborious. In the following section, I provide a few examples to support these points.

The first comes from TF2-162, a 75-year-old resident of Jaiama Bongor chiefdom, who we encountered in a previous section. On 8 September 2004 he got into an exchange with defence lawyer Michiel Pestman on the subject of whether or not the prosecution had ever paid him medical expenses (SCSL 2004e, 8 September 2004, 71–8):

Q. Can I repeat my question? Did you receive anything else from the Prosecution apart from the food, accommodation and the dress you are wearing?
A. Yes.
Q. Like what?
A. Yes. If I am sick, they would take me to hospital. They would give me medicine, and that is what I use to heal myself.
Q. And did they give you money to go to hospital?
A. Yes, they take me to the hospital and they would buy all the medicines and give it to me if I am sick.
Q. And how often did they give you medicine?
A. That was when I fall ill. If I fall ill and I tell them, then they will take that action.
Q. How often did that happen?
A. I have not fallen ill so many times. Even if they are doing it to some other people, they have not done it to me so many times, but when I am ill, they would do that – they would take that action.
Q. How often did you go to hospital?
A. No, if I do not fall ill, I wouldn't go to the hospital, but if I fall ill, they would take me to the hospital, because it was their responsibility.
Q. Why do you say it was their responsibility?
A. Because it was they who brought me here.
Q. Was that part of the deal?
A. Even if that was not an agreement, but if they brought me here and I fall ill, then definitely they would take it as a responsibility.
Q. Did you ask them to take you to hospital in return for giving evidence in Court?
A. So that they can take me to the hospital? If I fall ill and they did not take me to the hospital, how could I have come here? If they take me

to the hospital and I get well, then I will have to come here. No, they won't allow that.

Q. So you didn't ask them to take you to hospital in return for giving evidence today in Court?

A. No, they didn't take me to hospital in return for giving evidence. They knew why they brought me here, so if I fall ill, it is their responsibility. So if they send me to do any job for them, I will do it.

Q. Apart from visiting the hospital, getting medicine –

JUDGE BOUTET: I don't think the witness has said that he has visited the hospital. There seems to be some confusion there.

(SCSL 2004e, 8 September 2004, 71–2.)

The exchange continues in similarly laboured vein for another six pages, in which we see a dismal failure by the officers of the Court to establish rapport with the witness. The communicative exchange is unclear and inconclusive as a result: court officers and witness appeared to be talking about two different things throughout.

My next example comes from TF2-012, a 56-year-old farmer who testified to events in Koribundo. Defence lawyer John Wesley Hall has some difficulty in getting the witness to agree that he has received some 660,000 Leones in payments. This is particularly interesting since the previous day, the witness denied receiving any payments at all.

BY MR. HALL:

Q. We asked you about these payments yesterday, you did not volunteer that. Could you tell us why?

A. Are you asking me if I can tell the Court why I didn't answer yesterday?

Q. Yes, I am?

A. Yes, I'm not here – I was here to testify. I didn't know I was going to talk about any monetary matters. What I knew is what I spoke about and that is exactly what I did yesterday. That is why I didn't answer the question.

Q. The question was put to you directly and you just choose not to answer it, is that it?

A. When you ask me a question, I can only answer the question that I'm able to answer. If I'm not able to answer a particular question, I won't answer it.

Q. You were paid 600,000 Leones and you just forgot it?

A. No, I can't forget about money matters.

Q. You swore to tell the truth when you came in here, did you not?
A. Yes.
Q. You also swore to tell the whole truth, did you not?
A. Yes.
Q. When you were asked about the money you did not tell the whole truth; did you not?
A. Yes, I can't just answer a question like that.
MR. HALL: That's all I have, [Thank] You.

(SCSL 2004e, 22 June 2004, 1–5.)

As with other exchanges, communications on the subject of witness payments were often fraught with misunderstanding. By raising the issue, the defence was insinuating that witnesses had a financial incentive to testify, plus an incentive to massage their stories to fit the theory of the prosecution, on whom they were dependent in a patron-client type of way. Witnesses meanwhile appeared to be doing their best to wriggle off the hook of this insinuation, not by giving straight answers, but by dissembling. In support of this interpretation is not only the anthropological literature on Sierra Leone, which would lead us to expect such a response, but also the fact that communication difficulties were far more common under cross-examination than under examination-in-chief. Norman was not exaggerating when he complained: 'You see, My Lord, as an accused person, I am observing the witness. Every time the witness has come to give evidence in chief, they are not difficult. But when [we] question, then they become non-understanding, non-educated' (SCSL 2004e, 9 September 2004, 79). Faced with this kind of intransigence, defence lawyers would sometimes, after prolonged ineffectual attempts to get clear answers, simply give up. Meanwhile, it was difficult to know what weight the Bench would place on these payments. On the occasions when the defence's insinuations became too bold, the Bench shut them down, as on 2 December 2004, when counsel for the second accused was asked whether he was calling the integrity of the judicial proceedings into question (SCSL 2004e, 2 December 2004, 89–93). It was perhaps for this reason that this strand of cross-examination fell away from the Third Session onwards. Ultimately, the Chamber made no reference to witness payments in its judgment, and we can thereby infer that it regarded the payments, some of which amounted to more than five times the national average annual income per capita, as insignificant.

Tok Af Lef Af: problems with statements

Giving *prima facie* support to the suspicion that witnesses were changing their stories in order to please the prosecution was the fact that some witnesses had met with the prosecution several times, changing their statement more than once. In fact, there were discrepancies between witnesses' written, pre-trial statements and their *viva voce* courtroom testimony in a large proportion of cases. Sometimes the inconsistencies were trivial, but sometimes they went to the heart of a witness's testimony and credibility. This created difficulties for the Court, since discrepancies might stem not only from the potential for witness payments to provide an incentive to lie, as the defence alleged, but also from an incompetent investigation, or from a local cultural order that encouraged witnesses to be economical with the truth. In the following section I provide some illustrations of these difficulties.

We have already encountered witness TF2-012 in connection with witness payments and ambiguities in dates and times. There were also issues raised by his statement. For example, when discussing the Koribundo public meeting, he had said in his statement that the Koribundo people had expressed their thanks to Hinga Norman, something which potentially put the testimony on Koribundo in a different light. However, in Court, he denied this: 'I didn't hear that one … I've told you I didn't say that' (SCSL 2004e, 22 June 2004, 52). In his written statement, the witness claimed, on two separate occasions, that Hinga Norman had told the assembled Kamajors that he had ordered them to leave just four houses in Koribundo unmolested. But in his oral testimony, he insisted it was three houses. There was another inconsistency as well. In an earlier statement, he claimed to have seen Moinina Fofana at the meeting, but in a later statement he corrected this. In spite of cross-examination on the subject, it was unclear whether that retraction was because of a memory change, or because of an error in the translation or transcription of the first interview. In response, the Court tried over and over again to get the witness to say whether or not the statement he made was read back to him in Mende. The best answer it got was the following:

JUDGE BOUTET: When they were finished with writing something on a piece of paper, did they read to you what was written on that piece of paper and did they do so in Mende?

THE WITNESS: No. They would just ask me and I'd answer; they would ask me and I answer; they would ask me and I'd answer, and when

I finished asking [*sic*] the questions, they thanked me. And that's the end.

(SCSL 2004e, 22 June 2004, 21.)

On 27 September TF2-154, a 29-year-old woman, testified to the Kamajor invasion of Kenema in February 1998. She narrated how Kamajors surrounded her house, accused her father (who was not present) of being 'a junta', then fired a grenade into the house. Next a tenant of her father's was shot in the foot and thrown, still alive, into the burning building. A second tenant, the first tenant's younger brother, was then hacked with a machete, dragged towards a swamp, sprinkled with petrol and set alight. Under cross-examination, the witness was adamant that this was the way events transpired. However, in three written statements the witness was quoted as saying: 'I saw one of the Kamajors shot, the older one on his foot. The older one was tied and an old motor tyre was dropped on his neck and a liquid which they had in a rubber was sprinkled on the tyre and the tyre was set on fire. And I heard and saw the older one crying and struggling to die' (SCSL 2004e, 27 September 2004, 63). There is also a statement from 7 November 2003 which says of the younger brother: 'His battered body was taken by the Kamajors and thrown into the fire' (SCSL 2004e, 27 September 2004, 71). This inconsistency might lead one to believe that the witness did not have as clear a view of events as she claimed; or maybe that she did not even witness the events herself; or even, if one wanted really to be sceptical, that the events never happened at all. The witness herself had scant explanation for the discrepancy, except to say: 'maybe there's a mixup with the names – the names. By their names I identified them' (SCSL 2004e, 27 September 2004, 67).

Another example comes from the testimony of TF2-152, which we discussed earlier in relation to its ambiguous account of Kamajors using human entrails as a roadblock. Readers will remember that, after narrating the story about the roadblock, the witness testified to Yamorto tearing into his friend's chest with a knife, removing the heart, and placing it in a plastic bag for the witness to carry. However, on cross-examination, it was revealed that in his pre-trial statement, the witness spoke of the victim's *liver* being removed and bagged. Pressed on the discrepancy, the witness's explanation was that 'Probably the person that wrote the statement didn't get me clear' (SCSL 2004e, 27 September 2004, 154).[33] The Chamber

[33] William Murphy has informed me that this may be a translation error, since the Western cosmology of the heart as the seat of emotions is often expressed in Sierra Leonean Mande

appeared to accept this kind of explanation, since in the judgment discursive modulations are used to cover up the discrepancies. In the case of TF2-154, for example: 'Although both young men protested that they were not part of the junta, *they were killed by the Kamajors* (my emphasis) (SCSL 2007d, 177). Similarly, in the inconsistency between TF2-152's statement and his oral testimony, the ambiguity is ironed out thus: '*Various organs* were removed from TF2-152's friend's torso' (my emphasis) (SCSL 2007d, 183). Both testimonies were accepted as factual findings, even though they were uncorroborated and inconsistent with earlier statements.

The difficulties posed by witness statements are even more acute in the next example. On 10 February 2005, Bobor Tucker, aka Jengbema, appeared in Court. Tucker, allegedly a member of the CDF's 'Death Squad', was a key insider witness for the prosecution. He provided incriminating evidence on several of the indictment's counts, and, more importantly, he gave key testimony to support the prosecution's theory of command responsibility, implicating Norman, Fofana, and Kondewa in the planning and order of CDF attacks. However, on this crucial issue, there was some discrepancy between his testimony and his statement. While his testimony portrayed Norman as the ultimate source of authority on the battlefield, his statement had implicated the CDF War Council.

Q. The war council gave direction to the Death Squad; isn't that correct?
A. No, sir, I received instructions from Pa Norman directly himself. That is why he had a private place where he talked to me. They called the place Walehun II.

This response was inconsistent with four sentences from his statement of 9 May 2003, read in court by John Wesley Hall:

Q. 'We got our orders directly from the war council. Mr Lome would bring the orders to us. They know what their organisation was; I don't know. The orders we would get were always from Lomé' And
Q. 'Whatever the war council would say we would do'
(SCSL 2004e, 10 February 2005, 78–9.)

We should recall at this point that anthropological knowledge of the Sierra Leone culture area would lead us to expect many witnesses not

cultures through the idiom of the 'liver'. William Murphy, personal communication, 7 March 2007. Giving weight to this, the terms liver and heart seem to be frequently interchanged in the Taylor trial.

to give the full story, or the full truth, in their initial encounters with Prosecutors. The Krio saying *Tok Af Lef Af* encapsulates the idea that only a foolish, untrustworthy or downright reprehensible person will divulge everything they know in a first encounter, meaning that many people will withhold some portion of the truth, talking half, leaving half, not least because the person they are dealing with might constitute a threat. Tucker's subsequent explanation for this discrepancy is in fact a perfect exposition of this:

A. I used to say those words to the investigators. But during the time that I made those statements I was in deep fear because, because I knew that I myself was somebody who took part in the war. Then the Special Court has come played over the fighters. I was not really free with them until recently when I made the last statement, the one which I saw for myself which I gave to them. All the other statements I made were under fear. I was really afraid.
Q. So you admit to lying to the investigators then to protect yourself.
A. I was not telling lies. I was really afraid and when you are scared you do not know how to position yourself.

(SCSL 2004e, 10 February, 79.)

Albert Nallo, the prosecution's star witness, was another insider who talked half and left half. He provided seventeen separate statements to the prosecution, his story growing more elaborate over time. Pressed on this, Nallo explained to the Court that he did not tell the full truth to the prosecution in his first encounters since he was afraid that he himself would be apprehended. Also he was afraid that the oath of silence he had taken would cause him to spontaneously combust (SCSL 2004e, 10 March 2005, 34). In June 2008, I asked prosecution counsel Joseph Kamara about the *Tok Af Lef Af* phenomenon. 'Of course we encountered *Tok Af Lef Af*', he said:

> On first encounter, whatever [a witness] tells us, they are so far away from the truth … there is a process of building trust. So a witness will have two, three, four statements and he will be changing along the line as he moves closer to the truth as his confidence grows. They want to know about their security … [34]

As we have seen, this interpretation was quite consistent with the anthropological literature. But we must also consider the alternative

[34] Interview with Joseph Kamara, Special Court for Sierra Leone, 11 June 2008.

possibility, which is that witnesses were moving further from the truth as they became aware of the material benefits it would bring.

In this vein, the defence normally sought to use inconsistencies to impeach the credibility of the witness, but here the problems were multiplied by the fact that many witnesses, not being literate, often could not recognise the statement sheet with which they were presented, consequently they could not identify a statement as their own, which proved an obstacle to entering it as an evidential exhibit. John Wesley Hall put his finger on the problem when cross-examining TF2-006:

> Part of the problem, Your Honour, is that the witness says he does not remember the document, he does not know how many times he marked the document, he can't read this document to tell us that this is the one, but it was one that was given to us by the Prosecution as his statement. So I am hamstrung in my inability to get him to identify this document.
> (SCSL 2004e, 9 February 2005, 25.)

Charles Margai identified a similar problem when cross-examining TF2-088:

> You see, because this is not the first time witnesses are saying to this Court, when it suits them, that a portion which they find disturbing was not what they said, and that leaves us with no option but to seek an order from this Court for the investigators to appear in this Court and be examined as to the method of adopting – taking the statement.
> (SCSL 2004e, 26 November 2004, 102.)

As Margai suggested, the logical next step was to try and shed further light on the matter by calling and interviewing the investigators who took the statement, but this option was ruled out by the Bench:

> Well, don't think that we are going to be calling every single investigator that did this because we are not prepared to do that
> (SCSL 2004e, 14 February 2005, 31).

This was in spite of their believing that, as Judge Thompson said, 'it is becoming evident that we are confronted with some kind of problem as to how these statements were recorded' (SCSL 2004e, 14 February 2005, 32). The Bench went on to argue that the Court should relax the strict principles governing the admission of prior inconsistent statements into evidence, since currently it 'runs against this roadblock where a witness says "I never told him that," so the question is what does a tribunal do? Do we pack our bags and go home and say well, no' (SCSL 2004e, 14 February 2005, 35).

The prosecution, understandably, was grateful for the opportunity to attribute inconsistencies between statements to problems with the statement taking process, rather than with the witnesses themselves: 'Your Honour, the Prosecution certainly takes a similar view to Your Honour. There clearly was some problem in taking statements from witnesses' (SCSL 2004e, 14 February 2005, 35). As Joseph Kamara explained to me, part of that problem was that witnesses were difficult to take statements from:

> It has to do with the naivety of our people ... our witnesses are not like witnesses elsewhere. They have a system of telling a story ... a witness will always prefer to tell the story his own way ... you see a huge statement with a lot of irrelevance and also the issue of exaggeration ... so we had to do confirmation trips ... going back as lawyers to the witnesses and trying to dress down statements to the bare bones.[35]

The issues were thrown into sharp relief by the testimony of TF2-021, the child soldier whose testimony proved pivotal to the Trial Chamber's conviction of Allieu Kondewa (SCSL 2007d, 286–8). Under cross-examination, defence counsel identified numerous and serious inconsistencies between his oral testimony and written statement. The witness's response was to disown the statements. For example, the witness claimed in his oral testimony that he was nine years old when captured by rebels, but in his written statement, he had clearly claimed he was five. The witness responded: 'Well, that particular statement is not my statement' (SCSL 2004e, 2 November 2004, 130). The witness's statement said that he saw Foday Sankoh in Kailahun, but in Court he denied this. The statement said that he saw a rebel by the name of Savage shoot an old woman: 'No, I did not tell them then – that's not my statement' (SCSL 2004e, 3 November 2004, 55). The statement said that, while in Kenema, the witness spent most of his time indoors: 'I did not tell them that', (SCSL 2004e, 3 November 2004, 57). As the inconsistencies mounted, Michiel Pestman, counsel for the second accused, summed up the issues: 'Either the investigators made up a statement, or the witness is lying, so it's quite interesting' (SCSL 2004e, 4 November 2004, 8).

Much of the investigation for the CDF trial was conducted by English-speaking expatriates accompanied by Sierra Leoneans. Since many languages are spoken in Sierra Leone, the local investigator would sometimes rely on a local interpreter. At its most complex, a statement might

[35] Interview, Joseph Kamara, Special Court for Sierra Leone, 11 June 2008.

be given in a local vernacular language, translated by a local interpreter into *Krio*, the *lingua franca*, translated by the Sierra Leonean investigator into English, and then transcribed in English by the expatriate investigator.[36] If literate in English, the normal procedure was for the witness to then read and sign the statement; if not, to have the statement read back to him or her, to affirm it, and then affix a thumbprint. The former method provided a reasonable guarantee that what the witness said had been accurately recorded. The second method was less certain, since discrepancies could occur when translating a statement from the vernacular into Krio, and from Krio into English. Mistakes could also occur during the transcription into English. It was difficult to check the latter kind of errors, since miscommunication could also occur when translating a transcribed English statement back into Krio or tribal language for the witness. In the event of inconsistencies between the written statement and the *viva voce* testimony in court then – and there were many – it became impossible to determine whether the inconsistency was a result of poor translation and transcription on the part of court staff, or poor memory or mendacity on the part of the witness.

On 2 March 2005, Victoria Chitanda, a Zimbabwean investigator previously employed by the Special Court, responded to a *subpoena* with testimony relating to TF2-021's statement. Chitanda explained the process of interviewing, translation, checking with the witness, and finally getting the witness to sign or affix a thumbprint. In this case, she had met the witness once and then, on their second meeting, taken a statement from him. She told the Court that the interpreter had an association with the witness, though she had made the mistake of forgetting to record his name on the cover sheet. Defence counsel pointed out all the inconsistent portions of the statement to her, and she confirmed that the witness did in fact make those statements. She went on to say: 'As I explained earlier on, I had a standard procedure for taking a statement. That procedure was carried out in this situation, culminating in the statement being read back to the witness in Krio, the witness agreeing that this was said, and proceeding to put his thumbprint on it' (SCSL 2004e, 2 March 2005, 20). She believed the statement was a true reflection of what was said.

[36] In addition, a source in the translation unit told me that the Prosecutor was insufficiently responsive to concerns that the statement taking process was vulnerable to translation problems. Other sources in the prosecution criticised the Head of Investigations for spending too much time on the Charles Taylor issue, and not enough time supervising investigators in the field.

A huge amount hung on whether the judges believed Chitanda, who was standing in for virtually the entire investigative process. If the judges took her on trust, then they would have to assume that every inconsistency in a statement signalled mendacity or memory failure on the part of the witness. If they disbelieved her, then the statements amounted to nothing, and the trial had to be judged on the oral evidence alone. But if they did this, they removed corroborating evidence for a crucial plank of the defence case, the perfectly plausible charge that some witnesses came to court with massaged or made up stories on account of the handsome benefits that accrued.

When it came to the judgment, the Chamber sided with the witnesses. In spite of its inconsistency with prior statements, TF2-021's testimony, was 'highly credible and largely reliable', it found (SCSL 2007d, 89). This finding threw the competence of the entire investigation into doubt,[37] a difficulty the Chamber got around by stating that it had a preference for 'orality', effectively neutralising any statement-based challenges.[38] In fact, the judgment provides no examples of testimony thrown out because of its incompatibility with previous statements.

Insider witnesses

The Chamber also discussed the credibility of the trial's ten insider witnesses.[39] The evidence of these witnesses, many of whom could be considered 'co-perpetrators' or 'accomplices', was treated with 'particular caution' and the 'utmost circumspection', it said (SCSL 2007d, 88). Did the Chamber follow its own rules of thumb? To throw light on this question, I turn now to an analysis of some of the testimony of Albert Nallo,

[37] Sources in the prosecution, for example Kevin Tavener, were also quick to attack the incompetence of the investigators, which raised an interesting question. If the investigation was incompetent, how could the prosecution be sure it had arrested and charged the right men? Surely a flawed investigation could lead to a flawed theory of responsibility, and the investigation should be redone with a fresh set of eyes? It seems, however, that the prosecution was confident that it had the right men – they were, after all, the *de jure* leaders – and strenuous efforts were made to re-interview and proof witnesses to ensure that their stories placed the accused in the responsibility frame.

[38] The Chamber stated that it was permissible to find a witness credible and reliable in respect of some parts of testimony, but not in others, and that it could reject the evidence of a witness in part or in whole (SCSL 2007d, 81). To reinforce this point, it argued that minor inconsistencies, which could be explained by lapses in memory, did not necessarily discredit a witness. Moreover, it stated its preference for oral testimony, not expecting the former to be identical to evidence given in prior statements. It claimed that uncorroborated evidence was subjected to special scrutiny (SCSL 2007d, 82–7).

[39] Albert J. Nallo, Borbor Tucker, TF2-017, -201, -005, -008, -011, -079, -082, -223.

described by the Chamber as the 'the single most important witness in the Prosecution case, especially against Fofana' (SCSL 2007d, 88).

I provided a description of Albert Nallo in Chapter 2. I will now examine in detail a few episodes of Nallo's testimony which were of special importance to the trial. The first concerns the CDF command structure. On 11 March, Kevin Tavener for the prosecution steered his examination in chief towards the command structure of the CDF:

MR TAVENER:
Q. You've spoken about the War Council and they made recommendations. To whom did the War Council make recommendations?
A. To the national coordinator of CDF Chief Hinga Norman.
Q. You've spoken about Allieu Kondewa. To whom did he report to?

At this point Nallo utters a long 'Errrr'.

A. There were three persons. I wouldn't know who was reporting to whom. When this one speaks it will go to the other one. It's like the Son and the Holy Spirit.

Visibly chortling, Judge Itoe intervenes at this juncture to put words into Nallo's mouth:

PRESIDING JUDGE: The Holy Trinity.
THE WITNESS: Yes, My Lord. It's the trinity.

Chuckling a little himself, Tavener gratefully seizes on this:

MR TAVENER:
Q. Who were in the trinity?
PRESIDING JUDGE: Please, hold on. Wait, Mr Witness. Wait. Yes.
MR TAVENER:
Q. Who were the persons in the trinity?
A. Well, Chief Hinga Norman was the boss – God. Chief Hinga Norman was the God, sorry. Moinina Fofana the Son.

Again, unable to contain his enthusiasm, Itoe interjects:

PRESIDING JUDGE: And Kondewa the Holy Spirit.
THE WITNESS: And the high priest is the Holy Spirit.
(SCSL 2004e, 11 March 2005, 23–5).

In this exchange Nallo appears to be momentarily floundering, perhaps unable to give a precise description of the relations at the apex of the CDF. He thus begins to speak in metaphors. Surprisingly, he is assisted in this diversion by Judge Itoe, who heartily helps him along. In the final judgment, this metaphorical and metaphysical notion of command responsibility appears without commentary:

> Norman, Fofana and Kondewa were regarded as the 'Holy Trinity'. 'Norman was the God, … Fofana was the Son, and [Kondewa] was the Holy Spirit.' The three of them were the key and essential components of the leadership structure of the organisation and were the executive of the Kamajor society.
>
> (SCSL 2007d, 108–9.)

Another controversial episode of Nallo's testimony was his narration of events in four villages surrounding Base Zero, where he claimed he had been sent by Norman to punish collaborators. In this testimony Nallo gave a reasonably vivid description of the torture and mutilation of one Joseph Lansana in Sorgia Village: 'We cut off his ear, lit a plastic and we were dripping it on his body', said Nallo. 'We tortured him. When we are torturing him we are beating him up. We cut off his ear, we putting fire on him and tied him up' (SCSL 2004e, 10 March 2005, 48–9). Later, Nallo described killing Lansana's mother: 'the old woman was chopped … When she was chopped, we left her naked as she was born … We took petrol along, about two gallons, and set ablaze their compound. We took the old woman and threw into the fire. That's where she died' (SCSL 2004e, 10 March 2005, 49). Yet later on in the trial the defence produced Joseph Lansana of Sorgia Village, who denied the events, and who was clearly in possession of both of his ears. As Steven Powles, summing up for the defence said: 'Joseph Lansana came and totally disavowed, totally undermined the truthfulness and veracity of Nallo's evidence. He came and he said "Yes, it was the CDF who killed my mother but not when Nallo said it happened, some years before. And "No, they didn't cut off my ears, here they are, two ears for Your Honours to see" (SCSL 2004e, 29 November 2006, 61–2). Obviously, Nallo's account was either the result of an acute memory defect or else an attempt to mislead the Court. In light of a mistake as serious as this, or the possibility of perjury, one might reasonably question the credibility of Nallo's other testimony. But this, the Court chose not to do. Indeed, it concealed the seriousness of the discrepancy by mentioning in the judgment only that the time-frame for the killing of Lansana's mother was in doubt, and by rejecting this specific portion of evidence (SCSL 2007d, 89).

In fact, reading the transcript, one could be forgiven for thinking that the judges had allowed themselves to get too close to Nallo. For example, at the end of Nallo's examination-in-chief, the judges cautioned the defence that, because they were nearing the end of the trial session, they should keep their cross-examinations brief and to the point, a warning they repeated on several occasions. Then there was the warm send-off Nallo received from Presiding Judge Itoe, a fond farewell that showed little sign of caution:

PRESIDING JUDGE: All right. Well, thank you very much for coming to assist this Chamber with your evidence.
THE WITNESS: Yes, My Lord.
PRESIDING JUDGE: It has been long, but it has revealed many things which will assist the Chamber to determine the truth in this matter.
THE WITNESS: Yes, My Lord.
PRESIDING JUDGE: I think the Chamber would like to commend one thing, and that is that you came to testify in order to ensure that there is, you know, lasting peace in this country.
THE WITNESS: Yes, My Lord.
PRESIDING JUDGE: That is the purpose of the justice which we have come to administer in this country.
THE WITNESS: Yes, My Lord.
PRESIDING JUDGE: We thank you very much for coming ... We wish you a safe journey to wherever you live. And if we have to see you next time, that will be fine. If not, well, we hope, the world being a small village, we may see you somewhere, somehow, someday. So thank you very much.

(SCSL 2004e, 15 September 2005, 140.)

As he left the stand and returned to the witness protection unit's antechamber, the Court's videographer caught up with Nallo. Ebullient, shaking hands with a member of Court staff, he can be heard proclaiming: 'I think I have done a very good job for this country.'[40] In its overall assessment of the insider witnesses, the Chamber had this to say:

> Nallo's frank and public admission of his personal role in the war, including the commission of criminal acts, and his willingness to testify openly (presumably at considerable personal risk) about the activities of his fellow leaders and commanders are important factors that have added to his overall credibility. For the greater part, Nallo testified without hesitation, unambiguously, and, in the Chamber's opinion, through a genuine desire

[40] Video Summary, Prosecutor vs. Norman, Fofana Kondewa Prosecution Case, 7–16 March 2005: http://www.sc-sl.org/Videos/Video-SCSL15.wmv.

> that the truth be known. Parts of his testimony were collaborated by TF2-017, one of Nallo's subordinates. Occasionally, however, Nallo appeared equivocal or exaggerated in his responses to questions. The Chamber has rejected those portions of his evidence.
>
> (SCSL 2007d, 88.)

The fact that Nallo had been living in Freetown for two years at the expense of the Court, presumably with plenty of time to get his story straight, was not accorded any weight. Nor was the fact that he admitted, in a classical example of *Tok Af Lef Af*, that he had failed initially to tell the full truth to the investigators, adding more and more detail as it became clear to him that only those at the 'apex' of the CDF would be prosecuted. That Nallo subsequently admitted to ordering and committing war crimes, including human sacrifice, in several areas was not thought to compromise his character. The fact that Nallo chose to testify in public was taken as a token of his credibility, whereas a student of Sierra Leonean culture might think the fact that he was testifying in an open forum militated strongly against the full truth being told. The Chamber presumed that by testifying openly Nallo was assuming considerable personal risk to himself. Actually, by testifying openly he made it more likely that the Court would be obliged to relocate him and his family to a more developed country, where he could start a new life. That the defence suggested that he had been investigated on various occasions for looting and corruption seems to have been regarded as irrelevant, as were the circumstances surrounding his expulsion from his post in the CDF. Given this problematic background, we might be forgiven for thinking that Nallo's testimony, far from being motivated by a genuine desire that the truth be known, was more likely a case of *Kabande*, the practice of 'strategically creating a public deception that was surprising and wondrous' (Murphy 1998), both to settle a score with the defendants and save his own skin.

CONCLUSIONS

Exchanges at the Special Court were frequently difficult and inconclusive. Sometimes that difficulty appeared to be simply because witnesses and lawyers did not understand one another. On other occasions it appeared to be because witnesses were hedging, equivocating, evading or dissembling. These problems contributed to it being a difficult, drawn-out affair. Added to this, testimonies were sometimes sketchy in their detail, making them difficult to disprove or definitely corroborate, and there was virtually no forensic evidence. To cap it all, there were often discrepancies between witnesses' prior statements to the prosecution, and what they said in Court – some minor some serious. As well as being caused by the trauma of the witnesses' experiences and the inevitable passage of time, I have suggested in this chapter that these problems also stemmed, at least in part, from the cultural context of the trial. Many witnesses were unused to using calendar dates or clock time; many were economical with the truth in their first statements to the prosecution; many were not literate, making it difficult to link them conclusively to statements; many were wary of the adversarial courtroom, and drew on a fund of culturally prized dissembling techniques to protect themselves; and for many, the handsome allowances offered by the witness protection unit arguably gave them incentives to tell lies. It all added up to a laborious trial in which finding the facts proved an immense struggle, culminating in a decidedly shaky evidential base.

As I argued early on in this chapter, local legal organs in Sierra Leone have developed special techniques to combat problems like these, but the judges at the Special Court were dependent on more conventional means. They claimed they would evaluate evidence on the basis of its internal consistency and detail, strength under cross-examination, consistency against prior statements, corroboration and possible motives of the witness. This chapter has questioned whether those techniques were in this context sufficient, and it has also queried whether they were consistently applied. Sometimes the Chamber accepted without corroboration evidence that was inconsistent or lacking in clear detail. It also admitted evidence from witnesses who, in parts of their testimony, had been shown to be seriously mistaken or lying. It claimed to use the principle of corroboration to test witness testimony that was in some way suspect, but we have seen that on some occasions, a very weak form of corroboration sufficed. The Chamber also accepted evidence from witnesses who were equivocal under cross-examination, neglecting to comment on the unique challenges posed by such testimony. Further, the judges failed to take seriously the special challenges to witness credibility posed by witness payments, and by the fact that some of the insider witnesses had at least as great a responsibility for crimes as did some of the accused.

CHAPTER 7

CULTURAL ISSUES IN THE RUF, AFRC AND CHARLES TAYLOR TRIALS

The neo-traditional, or Afromodern elements in the origins, ideology, and organisation of the CDF ensured that cultural issues would be particularly visible in the CDF trial, but they were also apparent in the Special Court's three other trials. This chapter provides an overview, summarising the nature of the charges in the trials of the RUF, AFRC and Charles Taylor, before proceeding to discuss issues of superior responsibility, child soldiers, witness credibility, and forced marriage.

In March and April 1993, the Court indicted Issa Sesay, Morris Kallon and Augustine Gbao as co-conspirators in the RUF case. Their trial began in June 2004. The prosecution alleged that the three were senior members of a joint criminal enterprise orchestrated by Foday Sankoh and the then Liberian rebel leader Charles Taylor, that invaded Sierra Leone in 1991, planning to take control of the territory and especially its diamond wealth by any means necessary, including by terrorising and punishing the civilian population. First accused Issa Sesay was alleged to be have held a variety of senior positions in the RUF, rising to acting head of the movement by the time of Foday Sankoh's incarceration in May 2000; second accused Morris Kallon was another senior commander, and by early 2000 was subordinate only to Sesay; meanwhile third accused Augustine Gbao was a senior officer and commander, becoming Overall Intelligence and Security Commander for the AFRC/RUF from mid-1998 (SCSL 2006b).

In March and September 2003 the Court indicted Alex Tamba Brima, Ibrahim Bazzy Kamara and Santigie Borbor Kanu as co-conspirators in the AFRC case, their trial beginning in March 2005. The prosecution alleged that the three were part of a group of soldiers who overthrew the elected government of Ahmad Tejan Kabbah in a military coup on 25 May 1997. Subsequently, they released Major Johnny Paul Koroma from Pademba Rd prison and made him their leader. Koroma subsequently became the chairman of the Armed Forces Revolutionary Council, and invited Foday Sankoh's RUF to join him in a junta to govern Sierra Leone. As a reward for their services, the three accused were appointed to senior positions in the AFRC, referred to as 'Honourables', and appointed to its Supreme Council; Brima and Kamara were made Public Liaison Officers, with various ministries and parastatals placed under their control. Their objectives were to stay in power at all costs, even if that meant the commission of criminal acts. In February 1998, the AFRC was dislodged from power by a combination of CDF and ECOMOG forces, and Johnny Paul Koroma subsequently travelled abroad. SAJ Musa became the acting leader of the AFRC, but after he was killed in December 1998, first accused Alex Tamba Brima assumed the overall command, with Kamara his Deputy Commander and Kanu his Chief of Staff. Thereafter, the three accused were the most senior commanders of the AFRC (SCSL 2005a).

In June 2003, the Court unsealed the indictment of Charles Taylor. He subsequently evaded the Court's jurisdiction by going into exile in Nigeria. After a change of government in Liberia, and intense diplomacy on the part of the Court, Liberian President Ellen Johnson Sirleaf requested Taylor's extradition, and he was finally flown by helicopter to the Special Court for Sierra Leone on the evening of 22 March 2006, after attempting to flee Nigeria. He was later transferred to a branch of the Special Court in The Hague, his trial commencing properly on 7 January 2008. The prosecution's indictment alleged that, from the late 1980s, Taylor was the leader of the National Patriotic Front of Liberia, in which role, or else later as President of Liberia, he assisted and encouraged, acted in concert with, directed, controlled or was super-ordinate to members of the RUF, AFRC or Liberian fighters, who committed a variety of violations in Sierra Leone (SCSL 2007b).

The RUF accused were charged with eighteen counts of crimes against humanity, war crimes and other serious violations of international humanitarian law, including terrorising the civilian population and collective punishments, unlawful killings, sexual violence, physical violence, use of child soldiers, abductions and forced labour, and attacks on UNAMSIL personnel. The AFRC accused were charged on fourteen counts under the headings of terrorising the civilian population and collective punishments, unlawful killings, sexual violence, physical violence, use of child soldiers, abductions and forced labour, and looting and burning, while Charles Taylor was charged with eleven counts, incorporated under the broad headings of terrorising the civilian population, unlawful killings, sexual violence, physical violence, child soldiers, abductions and forced labour, and looting (SCSL 2006b, 2005a, 2007b).

The AFRC trial concluded in December 2006, the Trial Chamber passed judgment in June 2007, and in February 2008 the Appeals Chamber upheld guilty verdicts and sentences of fifty years for Brima, forty-five years for Kamara, and fifty years for Kanu. The RUF trial concluded in August 2008, and at time of writing the judges were still deliberating their verdict. The trial of Charles Taylor in The Hague was ongoing.

In the following sections, I turn to some interesting cultural aspects of these trials.

SUPERIOR RESPONSIBILITY

As in the CDF case, the issue of command or superior responsibility loomed large in the Court's other trials. For reasons of economy, I will concentrate here on the AFRC case. According to the prosecution, the AFRC, although not a perfect military organisation, had a recognisable military hierarchy and structure, the functional characteristics of a military organisation, internal coherence and a strong command capability; consequently, it exercised effective command and control over its members (SCSL 2007a, 168). By contrast, the defence argued that, in the years prior to 1997, the Sierra Leone Army (SLA) had been approaching almost total breakdown as a military organisation, and that since the AFRC consisted mainly in former soldiers of the SLA, it too had 'only a semblance of a military structure and hierarchy' (SCSL 2007a, 168). Moreover, by February 1998, when the junta was chased from Freetown, it had split into several separate groups, over which no-one exercised effective control. In addition, at no time was there an elaborate enough structure with a sufficient span of command positions to maintain control, its operational units were not standardised, recruitment and promotion was haphazard, and there was virtually no training (SCSL 2006c, 61–91). Consequently, the defence submitted that the AFRC was an irregular military force without the strong, clearly defined chain of command sufficient to establish the superior responsibility of the accused.

The Court heard from two expert witnesses on the issue of command structure in the AFRC: Colonel Richard Iron – whom we have already met in the CDF case – for the prosecution, and Major-General Prins of the Royal Netherlands Marine Corps for the defence. Of these experts, Trial Chamber II found Colonel Iron to be the most convincing, partly because of his greater experience with ground troops, and also because he had interviewed members of the AFRC of similar rank to the accused. Prins' report, the Chamber averred, drew mainly on secondary sources. However, both reports, the Chamber thought, were of limited use in determining the responsibility of the accused, since both applied the criteria of well-developed military organisations to the AFRC, where such characteristics were evidenced 'in only rudimentary form' (SCSL 2007a, 171). According to the Chamber, the AFRC:

> had a command structure, although this underwent change as the authority of the key personalities, including RUF commanders when the two groups worked together, waxed and waned. Rules and systems facilitating the exercise of control existed, yet these rules and systems were legitimated not by law but by the authority of the individual commanders.
> (SCSL 2007a, 167.)

The expert reports, in consequence, could only be the starting point for an analysis of superior responsibility (SCSL 2007a, 167).

Drawing on the reports, the Chamber focused on three 'generic' structural features of military organisations that it found critical to facilitating control. These were: a functioning chain of command; a sufficiently developed planning and orders process; and a strong disciplinary system. The Chamber proceeded to apply these criteria to the evidence from four phases, corresponding to major changes in the AFRC as it moved from district to district in Sierra Leone (SCSL 2007a, 173). During some of these periods, the Chamber recognised, the AFRC had split into separate factions in different geographical locations. Consequently, it only considered the evidence pertinent to locations where the accused were in command. At the end of this exercise it determined that in Kono District, the AFRC had a chain of command and a planning and orders process; in Bombali it had a well-developed chain of command, a planning and orders process, and a disciplinary system, although this was selectively applied; while in Freetown and the Western Area there was a chain of command and a functioning planning and orders process until the AFRC lost control of State House several days after its capture on 6 January 1999, whereupon the chain of command and planning process were interrupted, and commanders issued orders only to those troops within their proximity.

The Chamber proceeded to link the accused, where the evidence allowed, to crimes charged in the indictment under Article 6(3) of the Statute. It found Brima guilty of superior responsibility for crimes committed by his subordinates in Bombali District, Freetown and other parts of the Western Area; Kamara was guilty as a superior for crimes in Kono, Bombali, Port Loko, Freetown and other parts of the Western Area; while Kanu was guilty of the same in Bombali, Freetown and other parts of the Western Area. The Trial Chamber found that the accused had the material ability to prevent or punish the crimes of their subordinates on account of, among other things, the fact that they issued orders, made binding decisions, participated at a senior level in military operations, participated in decision-making, did not distance themselves from decisions that were made, and received reports from the field (see SCSL (2008a, esp 80–8).

The AFRC judgment represented an advance over the CDF judgment, since it commented explicitly on the expert witness reports, and provided a description of authority within the AFRC – founded on shifting personal authority relations – that was coherent with the analysis of neo-patrimonialism we discussed in Chapter 3. In addition, its 'three generic structural characteristics' were a good starting point for assessing whether *anyone* within the organisation had effective control (although these criteria would not have been sufficient to capture the kind of charismatic authority wielded by a man like Allieu Kondewa). On appeal, the defence, while not explicitly disputing these criteria, questioned whether the evidence adduced by prosecution witnesses was actually sufficient to place the accused in the structure of effective command the Chamber had claimed to identify; the prosecution, who prevailed, argued that it was. I will not comment on the plausibility of the Chambers' findings here, except to reiterate that where there is background evidence of a historical and cultural nature to cast doubt on the functioning of a conventional command structure – to suggest something else, like a neo-patrimonial structure, in other words – then witness testimony on the subject of superior responsibility should be subjected to an extra degree of scrutiny, as should witness credibility overall.

CHILD SOLDIERS

The AFRC, RUF and Charles Taylor were also charged with conscripting and using child soldiers, raising some similar and different issues to the CDF trial. For reasons of economy, I will limit my discussion here to the evidence in the AFRC trial. Briefly, the prosecution alleged that the AFRC made systematic use of child soldiers: 'Thousands of children were abducted from all over Sierra Leone; [t]housands of children underwent military training at AFRC/RUF camps; [c]hildren were formed into Small Boys Units and Small Girls Units; and Armed Small Boys Units and Small Girls Units were used in combat' (Final Trial Brief, cited in SCSL (2007a, 351)). In support of this allegation, it called an expert witness, five witnesses who had been child soldiers, and several other witnesses who testified to having seen or trained child soldiers. Most crucially, it called witnesses TF1-157 and -158. The latter were aged thirteen and ten years old respectively when AFRC fighters attacked their village, hacked their father to death and abducted them. They were subsequently forced to carry loads, underwent military training, one was force-fed drugs, and both were made to fight.

The defence did not dispute that the AFRC recruited child soldiers. Instead, it called an expert witness, Mr Osman Gbla, a Sierra Leonean political scientist, to argue that in Sierra Leone, the definition of childhood was flexible: 'the ending of childhood [in the traditional African setting] has little to do with achieving a particular age and more to do with physical capacity to perform acts reserved for adults' (cited in SCSL (2007a, 225)). He argued that the armed forces in Sierra Leone had recruited persons under fifteen for many years, and claimed that much of the recruitment was voluntary, with children often joining their family members in the AFRC in order to escape victimisation by civilian communities. The defence consequently argued that the accused would not necessarily have known their acts were unlawful, so that Count 12 should be dismissed on grounds of 'mistake of law'.

The Trial Chamber had little time for this. Rejecting 'any defence based on cultural distinctions regarding the definition of "childhood"' (SCSL 2007a, 353), it reasoned that, whatever cultural constructions the defence put upon the phenomenon, a child was defined in Sierra Leonean national law as a person under sixteen years of age (SCSL 2007a, 226). As for the contention that recruiting children into the armed forces was formerly commonplace, the Chamber referred to the Appeals Chamber ruling that we have discussed at length in Chapter 5. Enlistment and conscription of child soldiers had already crystallised as a crime in customary international criminal law during the period of the indictment, and the previous practice of any particular state was therefore rendered irrelevant. Because of this, the accused could not credibly argue the defence of mistake of law (SCSL 2007a, 226).

It went on to find that 'the AFRC fighting faction used children as combatants because they were easy to manipulate and program, and resilient in battle ... most if not all the children were forcibly abducted from their families or legal guardians' (SCSL 2007a, 361). This, thought the Chamber, was a 'particularly egregious' form of conscription (SCSL 2007a, 362). Brima, Kamara, and Kanu were sentenced to fifty years, forty five years and fifty years respectively (SCSL 2007c, 36).

In this author's view, the defence was right to argue that the definition of childhood in Sierra Leone was flexible, it was also correct that the accused would not necessarily know that conscripting young persons was illegal, and it was also plausible that many under-fifteens enrolled voluntarily, although the defence did not advance any evidence of this. But what the accused must have known, since it clearly transgressed a local norm, was that abducting a young person from their family and community, often after having killed their parents, and then forcing them to fight, was wrong. And for this reason, it was right that the accused should be held to account. Unfortunately, the elements to which the accused were held accountable, namely that:

> The perpetrator conscripted or enlisted one or more persons into an armed force or group or used one or more persons to participate actively in hostilities; [s]uch person or persons were under the age of fifteen years; [t]he perpetrator knew or should have known that such person or persons were under the age of 15 years; and that [t]he conduct took place in the context of and was associated with an armed conflict...
>
> (SCSL 2007a, 225)

fitted poorly the nature of the crime, being so expansive that they could easily incorporate other acts which, as we saw in the case of the CDF, would locally have seemed quite legitimate. It is arguable, then, that the prosecution should have dealt with these heinous acts under the headings of abduction, forced labour, or enslavement.[1]

WITNESS CREDIBILITY

We saw in the previous chapter that communicative interactions in the CDF trial were often laboured affairs, with witnesses frequently hedging,

[1] Although the latter two were not free from cultural controversy either.

dodging or giving ambiguous answers, especially to the questions of opposing counsel. If anything, these issues were even more pronounced in the RUF, AFRC and Taylor trials, providing further evidence that this was not an idiosyncratic effect of the individuals who testified in the CDF case, but rather at least in part an effect of holding the trial in a context where a culture of ambivalence is prized. Indeed, in his closing statement, RUF defence lawyer John Cammegh described witness credibility as 'the most spoken about feature in this trial' (2004g, 5 August 2008, 68).[2] Prior to the trial's close, I interviewed Cammegh, counsel for Augustine Gbao, and Wayne Jordash, counsel for Issa Sesay, about the differences between witnesses at the Special Court, and the witnesses they were familiar with from the British justice system. The two lawyers echoed sentiments about the propensity of Sierra Leoneans to tell the truth that were a recurrent concern for colonial observers, and which have been discussed – with greater sensitivity and nuance – by modern anthropologists. In 'my own sad experience', Cammegh claimed, 'I have found that there is a culture of lying in this country … it's almost like a computer that goes on default such that, if in doubt, lie',[3] making 'qualitative assessments almost impossible to achieve … you're standing on sands that are permanently shifting'.[4] For Jordash, meanwhile: 'There's not the same fear [here] of the consequences of lying or pursuing an alternative agenda … there's less of an adherence to the discipline of truth exploration … to the notion that the account is supposed to adhere to what happened, that what happened should drive the narrative forward ….'[5] According to Cammegh: 'If we look at the demeanour of these people there was a lot of listlessness, lack of eye contact, a lack of delivery, confidence and conviction – all the hallmarks of someone not necessarily telling the truth, or fulfilling the role of telling certain individuals what they think they want to hear.'[6] In the AFRC trial, meanwhile, first accused Alex Tamba Brima complained about witnesses that had been brought to court to tell lies against him, while the prosecution claimed that Brima himself was an 'incredible liar' and that defence witnesses had come to court to lie to protect their former commanders and brothers in arms. One defence witness had been

[2] The full reference is SCSL 2004g.

[3] I should state again for the record that, in my experience with Sierra Leoneans outside the Court, I have not encountered what I would call 'a culture of lying'. However, I have noticed the tendency to conceal information in a *Tok af Lef Af* kind of way.

[4] Interview with John Cammegh, Special Court for Sierra Leone, 16 June 2008.

[5] Interview with Wayne Jordash, Special Court for Sierra Leone, 11 June 2008

[6] Interview with John Cammegh, Special Court for Sierra Leone, 16 June 2008

so brazen as to lie to the Court about his leg being hacked off by rebels, when in reality it had been amputated at a hospital for leprosy prior to 1994![7] Jordash had expected that the power of the UN tribunal would make the witnesses fearful of not telling the truth, but in fact, he thought, it had had the opposite effect, a sentiment John Cammegh echoed.[8]

Lawyers in the RUF trial also commented on the tendency of witnesses to dodge the questions of opposing counsel. According to Jordash:

> In the West witnesses have a linear logic of A to B to C to D. In an English court you can lead the witness to where you want to go … even if they don't go to the final conclusion, then it doesn't matter because the logical inference remains. Here, you could do that and it did work sometimes, but it wasn't the only approach … sometimes the witness would see the logic but would divert you from it with the most absurd propositions – the most amazing and ludicrous answers when they had spotted where they didn't want to go.[9]

Cammegh, meanwhile, claimed that:

> In examination-in-chief they might have sounded quite convincing … but when cross-examination came, they were undone by persistent, repetitive refusal to answer a straight question with a straight answer, the request for questions to be asked again, while they thought of the right answer … any kind of stalling tactic to parry the defence. You would catch them contradicting themselves and they would deny making the contradiction or deny that they had made that statement.[10]

As we saw in the CDF trial, witnesses often responded badly to the adversarial setting. In the AFRC trial, one of the witnesses, an amputee, exclaimed: 'It seems as if this lawyer is trying to provoke me' prompting Judge Sebutinde to step in with the advice, 'none of these two sides is your enemy … keep your temper down, keep your

[7] Prosecutor vs. Brima, Kamara, Kanu Closing Arguments, 7–8 December 2006. Available at www.sc-sl.org/video.html.

[8] Compare this rather sweeping assessment from colonial lawyer J. L. Driberg: 'Lying is also a kind of defence mechanism which the African employs when he is embarrassed by our odd procedure and by formalities so different from his own. He generally lies because he does not understand and therefore thinks it safer to lie' (Driberg 1934, 240–1, note 1).

[9] Interview with Wayne Jordash, Special Court for Sierra Leone, 11 June 2008.

[10] Interview with John Cammegh, Special Court for Sierra Leone, 16 June 2008. For an example, see the testimony of General John Tarnue (SCSL 2004g, 13 October 2004).

cool.'[11] Jordash claimed that, because of this, he had to modify his style of cross-examination: 'There was a definite dislike of an adversarial approach, it was best to approach the witness in the gentlest of terms', and that he was forced to think of new stratagems for dealing with Sierra Leonean witnesses: 'I would use more open-ended questions so the witness wouldn't understand where I wanted them to go … Once the witness didn't understand what I wanted, there was less of an adversarial dynamic.'[12]

As in the CDF trial, inconsistencies in witness testimonies were a prominent theme in the RUF and AFRC trials. In his closing statement, Cammegh pointed to twenty-nine material inconsistencies relating to Augustine Gbao in the testimony of TF1-366 alone (SCSL 2004g, 5 August 2008, 61–2). In the AFRC trial, all three defence teams questioned the credibility of prosecution witnesses in their closing statements. In particular, they pointed to inconsistencies within and between testimonies, especially of insider witnesses. They found these issues sufficiently serious that they raised them again at the appeals stage, arguing that the Trial Chamber had erred in law and fact by not properly addressing issues of credibility and inconsistency (although these were claims for which the Appeals Chamber had little sympathy). In his closing statement in the RUF trial, Cammegh claimed that the prosecution witnesses had a tendency to better their statements over time: 'It's a bit like a layer cake; you put another layer on. The icing on the top in 168's case was: Gbao is the overall top commander. I saw him every day. Roll back three years and it was "I saw him once"' (SCSL 2004g, 5 August 2008, 71). In another example, witness TF1-368 apparently gave six statements to the prosecution before mentioning that he saw Augustine Gbao ordering the killing of Kamajors. When queried on why they did not mention such events earlier, the stock answer was apparently: 'I wasn't asked.'[13] A good example came in the testimony of General Tarnue, one of the prosecution's key witnesses, whose first reference to Issa Sesay accompanying Sam Bockarie on a significant visit came in a statement given in July 2004, just a few months before he was due to testify. When asked why he did not mention this important piece of evidence before, he explained that he had not been previously asked about Sesay (SCSL 2004g,

[11] Special Court for Sierra Leone video summary, 5–15 April 2005, available at www.sc-sl.org/video.html.

[12] Interview with Wayne Jordash, Special Court for Sierra Leone, 11 June 2008.

[13] Interview with John Cammegh, Special Court for Sierra Leone, 16 June 2008.

11 October 2004, 16ff). The AFRC trial's second witness, explained to the Court that: 'When a man recollects, you have phase one, phase two, maybe phase three will be the final one.'[14]

The AFRC lawyers claimed that witnesses were motivated by a desire to protect themselves, by personal grudges, and by money.[15] Cammegh, meanwhile, believed there was 'very strong evidence to suggest that certain witnesses were told they had a particular job to do'. While Jordash thought: 'There's no doubt that witnesses change their stories in response to payments and perks. Look at what they know two years before the trial, then as they get closer to the Court their memories improve. And I saw that with Defence witnesses also.' In Jordash's experience, 'Very few failed to understand that the more valuable they became in terms of testimony, the more money they stood to make', explaining: 'We've all lived in Sierra Leone and we all know that money is a hugely motivating factor. The sort of cash the Prosecution and Witness and Victim Support [Unit] hand out makes a real difference. And the Prosecution had its own unsupervised budget. The Prosecution can't or won't explain this' (see also Kelsall 2008, 21).[16]

Further light was shed on this issue by *voir dire* hearings held during the summer 2007 trial session, which examined the admissibility into evidence of statements that Issa Sesay had made in 2003, while being held by the Office of the Prosecutor during a period in which investigators were trying to 'turn' him into a prosecution witness. The hearings, together with subsequent research by the Berkeley War Crimes Studies Center, revealed to a worrying degree that the investigations had been *ad hoc*, uncoordinated and unsupervised, providing opportunities for the use of threats, incentives and arm-twisting in the statement taking process. According to Sesay, the then deputy Chief of Investigations, Gilbert Morissette had visited him in detention in between statement taking sessions:

> He would come and say, 'Issa, we are just trying to help you. But what we have been hearing, if you don't confirm these things, how will we be able to help you?' He said, 'So you have to confirm the things that we have heard. That's the only way we'd be able to help you, so that you will be out of this problem'.
>
> (cited in Van Tuyl 2008, 21.)

[14] Video Summary, AFRC Trial, 7–16 March 2005, available at www.sc-sl.org/video.html.

[15] Prosecutor vs. Brima, Kamara, Kanu Closing Arguments, 7–8 December 2006, available at www.sc-sl.org/video.html.

[16] Interview with Wayne Jordash, Special Court for Sierra Leone, 11 June 2008.

Insofar as this was true, and the procedure applied to other potential insider witnesses, we have an explanation for why allegations against the accused tended to increase across statements, and why witnesses, like Sesay, began to tell 'half-truths' to the investigators (Van Tuyl 2008, 21). Sesay's defence lawyer claimed that Sesay was particularly vulnerable to this type of inducement because he had had no schooling beyond the age of thirteen, because he had spent most of his formative years in a jurisdiction without a functioning legal system, and therefore was not properly cognisant of his rights. We might add that the cultural context, with its valorisation of practices like *Tok Af Lef Af*, might have also made telling half-truths the path of least resistance. According to the judges, however, 'the cultural background of the accused [wa]s not relevant' to this matter (cited in Van Tuyl (2008, 28).

Even in cases where witnesses were not coerced, the *ad hoc* nature of the operation made it a sloppy one. The OTP had hired Corinne Dufka, the Human Rights Watch representative in Sierra Leone, to advise them on matters of Sierra Leonean history and context. Much of the investigation, meanwhile, was done by professional investigators from Canada and Switzerland. They had little or no experience either of international law, the history of the conflict, or the cultural context of Sierra Leone. Dufka tried to prepare them by providing briefing packs, but, according to her, many investigators did not bother to read them. In the absence of a more rigorous training programme, they went into the field unprepared, with little sense of how to follow leads specific to the context, how to build a case relevant to its nature, or how to elicit information from Sierra Leonean witnesses without leading them (Van Tuyl 2008, 41–4). The result was that many of the original statements they took were misleading, and witnesses subsequently had to be re-interviewed or proofed.

The Berkeley report also confirmed in more detail information that Kevin Tavener, Senior Trial Attorney on the CDF case, had given to me in a July 2007 interview.[17] Van Tuyl writes that:

> He found that investigators working during the pre-indictment phase had almost uniformly produced witness statements with little or no corroboration. There was no cross referencing between witness statements and police diaries, no photographs of scenes or the individuals who had been interviewed, no cross-referencing investigations with maps, and extremely scarce forensic evidence.
>
> (Van Tuyl 2008, 44.)

[17] Telephone interview with Kevin Tavener, 20 July 2007.

For John Cammegh, this was a shocking oversight: 'And here the prosecution has really let everyone down because you think they would have tried to produce incontrovertible forensic evidence to anchor allegations ... It's beyond an impossible bad dream that they can construct this case out of these kinds of witnesses and testimonies ... '[18]

The credulity of the Court was stretched to its limit in the trial of Charles Taylor, where the judges heard extensive evidence of a culturally unfamiliar practice, cannibalism, told by witnesses whose mode of address was sometimes elliptical, and who had presumably received significant inducements to testify. To provide some background, there is evidence to suggest that, historically, human sacrifice may have played a restricted role in *Poro* society initiations in this region and that in post-war Liberia practices like this came unfastened from their traditional moorings and began to play a part in competition between modern politicians (Ellis 2007, 220–80).[19] There is also historical evidence that during warfare, body parts and, in particular, the hearts of defeated enemies would sometimes be consumed by the victors in the belief that some of the victim's power would be transferred to them, and that these practices were re-invented by various fighting factions in Liberia's most recent civil war. However, it is also true that while it may be more culturally familiar, cannibalism is not necessarily less shocking to Sierra Leoneans and Liberians than it is to Europeans, and that stories of cannibalism consequently exert a powerful grip on the popular imagination, with moral panics in this region often expressed in terms of rumours of cannibalism, and cannibal talk used as a metaphor for other, more prosaic forms of exploitation and the abuse of power (Richards 1996, 80–1; Shaw 2001). Because of this, establishing whether or not particular cannibal stories are true is a challenging task.

These difficulties are illustrated in the case of Joseph, aka 'Zigzag' Marzah, allegedly Charles Taylor's Chief of Operations, who, at the time of writing, had been the prosecution's most dramatic witness. Marzah, an ethnic Gio, was born in Nimba County, Liberia, in 1958. He joined the army in 1978, but went into exile in 1985 during the reign of Samuel Doe, since Doe was victimising members of the Gio. Marzah claimed that while in Ivory Coast he was contacted by one Prince Johnson, who told him of a certain Charles Taylor, who was planning to redeem the people

[18] Interview with John Cammegh, Special Court for Sierra Leone, 16 June 2008.

[19] There have also been widespread rumours of political ritual murder in post-war Sierra Leone, and a few court cases. See Shaw (2002, 247–62), and also TRC 2004 (Appendix 3, Part 3, 6).

of Nimba County. Marzah subsequently became one of seventeen members of Charles Taylor's National Patriotic Front of Liberia, who invaded Liberia from Ivory Coast on 24 December 1989. He went on to explain how he was part of a second group of Liberians and Sierra Leoneans who, led by Foday Sankoh, crossed the border into Sierra Leone in March 1991, acting under instructions from Taylor. Marzah proceeded to give evidence poignant to several of the prosecution's charges, including that Taylor arranged arms shipments to Sierra Leone, that RUF commanders ferried diamonds from Sierra Leone to Taylor, and that Taylor ordered numerous executions of his enemies in both Sierra Leone and Liberia. Marzah claimed that he personally had carried out hundreds of executions on Taylor's orders, including the murder of babies and the slitting of the bellies of pregnant women. He described one particular incident in which he had participated in the murder, beheading and dismembering of RUF commander Denis 'Superman' Mingo. Mingo's hand was cut off and taken to Taylor; afterwards, Marzah ate Superman's heart in a banana plantation at the house of Benjamin Yeaten, Taylor's chief of security. As with Albert Nallo in the CDF trial, Marzah never missed an opportunity to exonerate himself and implicate his former boss, with almost every criminal act in Liberia and Sierra Leone being 'on the instruction' or 'at the direction' of Charles Taylor (SCSL 2003e, 12–13 March 2008).

During cross-examination, defence counsel Courtney Griffiths asked Marzah to describe in detail the murders of babies, the belly-slitting, the acts of cannibalism, and the burying alive on the beach outside Taylor's house in Monrovia of a pregnant woman. Griffiths asked these questions in a tone of mild incredulity, as if to say: 'These stories are preposterous, fantastic, and cannot be true.' In particular, he asked Marzah about the practice of human beings eating other human beings. Marzah explained that, under the reign of Samuel Doe, ethnic Krahn had sometimes come to Nimba County and killed and eaten Nimbalians. Subsequently, Charles Taylor encouraged the people from Nimba to avenge themselves on the Krahn in the same way (SCSL 2003e, 13 March 2008, 5994–5).[20] Griffiths then asked whether Taylor had ordered Marzah to eat people in Sierra Leone as well, and Marzah responded that Taylor had instructed them to kill Nigerian ECOMOG soldiers and white UN officials in Sierra Leone and to eat them as food, 'like pork' (SCSL 2003e, 13 March 2008, 5998).

[20] The full reference is SCSL 2003e. The Prosecutor of the Special Court v. Charles Ghankay Taylor. Case No. SCSL-2003–01-T. Trial Chamber II. Freetown: Sierra Leone.

A little later, Griffiths asked Marzah to give a description of how it was he ate people:

Q. So help me, please, just how do you prepare a human being for a pot?
A. I am sorry there's no way to demonstrate here because we are sitting.
Q. Just describe it to us?
A. Okay. The way we do it, the way you're standing, sometimes we lay you down, slit your throat and butcher you and take out your skin, your flesh, throw your head away, your intestines, your flesh, we take it and put it in a pot and cook it and eat it. The way you're standing, you cannot stay like that and we eat you. We would kill you first and take those parts that are not good for us and this your palm, your two palms [in video recordings Marzah is shown placing his hands together as though in prayer at this point],[21] we would put them together and clean inside your intestine and wrap it around, because it's not correct. It's a hard bone. Charles Taylor knows that. That's how we eat them.

(SCSL 2003e, 13 March 2008, 5999–6000.)

Readers will appreciate that this piece of testimony, although remarkable, is not particularly clear. Griffiths continued to press Marzah about whether Taylor himself had actually ordered people to be eaten and killed. Marzah responded in a typically convoluted and elliptical way, forcing us to read between the lines to get the meaning, which even then, I submit, is not entirely clear:

Q. Was there ever a time when you stood in front of Charles Taylor physically like now and he said to you, 'Zigzag, I want you to go out and eat a human being' or a part of a human being?
A. Apart from Superman?
Q. Anyone. Anybody?
A. Okay, thank you.
Q. Whether he be white –
A. Thank you, I understand. It happened twice when Gbarnga fell. I stood physically before Charles Taylor at the time Robin White was interviewing him. They were standing beside a jeep and he was telling the man that he was in his yard. That is the time he telephoned the Death Squad for me to carry out that execution. Anywhere there are human beings, you should eat them. They are no longer human beings. I was not in position to eat them raw, rather than to cook them

[21] Video summary, prosecution witness Zigzag Marzah, www.sc-sl.org/video.html.

with pepper and salt and fix some barbecue with them. It was from Gbarnga.

(SCSL 2003e, 13 March 2008, 6002).

At a later stage, Griffiths quizzed Marzah about the burial alive of a pregnant woman on the beach outside Charles Taylor's home, over whom the blood of a slaughtered ram was showered in what was allegedly an old warrior ritual intended to terrify the other members of Taylor's power-sharing government. Griffiths wanted to know why it had taken Marzah two years before he mentioned such a dramatic incident to the prosecution, and whether it was actually possible to tear a sheep to pieces with one's bare hands. Over eight pages of transcript, Marzah gave unclear and convoluted answers, full of retorts, side-avenues and shifts in temporal perspective (SCSL 2003e, 13 March 2008, 6004–12). 'You are supposed to know, as a African, when we are talking about the warrior ceremony and moreover to fight over a living animal … Mr Lawyer, you are supposed to know. You are from Africa', Marzah chuckled. 'It is not something I was used to in Kingston, Jamaica', was Griffiths' cool retort (SCSL 2003e, 13 March 2008, 6011).

The cross-examination reached a dramatic climax on its second day. Among other things Griffiths probed Marzah on details of illegal arms shipments to Sierra Leone, he accused Marzah of receiving instructions on his mobile phone from someone outside the Court and taking messages in the toilet, he suggested that Marzah had been shipping arms across the Guinean border to line his own pockets, and that he had been telling the investigators what they wanted to hear in order to profit for himself. He then put it to Marzah that he was a liar, and that he was not close to Charles Taylor at all, an allegation that released a flood of information about Taylor's instrumentalisation of the *Poro* society:

Q. I further suggest that you have never sat with Charles Taylor or been in his presence to receive orders from him? Furthermore I suggest that you have never spoken to him on either the telephone, or by radio?

A. Should I answer?

PRESIDING JUDGE: Yes, please answer.

THE WITNESS: I talked to Taylor on so many occasions, and even before Taylor established the Poro society, during which we ate people's livers which we experienced with him, I – since you don't have things to put across to me, let me just break open everything so that you will know the truth.

PRESIDING JUDGE: Slowly, slowly.

THE WITNESS: My first time to – for you to believe me that I sat with Mr Taylor, let me give you the proof the reason why Mr Taylor had the trust and confidence in me. No matter, the Poro society law maybe I will spoil it here. I don't have any problem with that. Let me be bold to tell you. I started sitting with Mr Taylor during the death of Theodore when we took his liver and we used it at a ceremony and he shared with us. We all ate it. And the same things happened in the case of Sam Dokie. The death of Sam Dokie, his liver was taken away by us and then we carried it and it was cooked by this lady. I will call the woman's name. Annie Yenni. Annie Yenni. Annie Yenni. Annie Yenni cooked it and Charles Taylor shared it with us. I am not talking about the ceremony that took place behind his house. Those were things that we did in Monrovia. At that time we had not yet been in Monrovia and when we came to Monrovia to clarify to you the reason why Charles Taylor trusted me and that, because I kept secrets. And even at the time he escaped from Ghana when we arrested Cooperville along with Moses Blah, we arrested those two people, and he was there in Ben's veranda. Ben and I were sitting down and he said we should 'control those people's hearts until I get there'. Then we took out those two guys' livers and then, after we had kept it in Ben's freezer for a long time, when Charles Taylor arrived we cooked it and all of us shared it together. Since then he trusted me as a full member of the Poro society. I am sorry to say this now, but once I have been pushed to the corner I am going to say the truth. I am saying the truth nothing but the truth. And now too much of the questioning that you are bringing you have let me disclose to you the secrets of my Poro society and that means at any time I move from here I will no longer be member of that society. That is a secret and that made him Dankpannah.

MR GRIFFITHS: I think, your Honours, that the society is called Poro P-O-R-O.

PRESIDING JUDGE: Poro society. Yes, that is the common spelling, Mr Griffiths.

MR GRIFFITHS: I am grateful, your Honour.

JUDGE SEBUTINDE: Mr Witness, your last statement which you said 'and that made him Dankpannah', what do you mean?

THE WITNESS: Any big person who is part of that Poro society from whom you take instruction is commonly known as Dankpannah, but that Dankpannah name is a society name for him.

JUDGE SEBUTINDE: What does it mean?

THE WITNESS: The big boss. The big boss. He is over all the bosses, in which case when he got up whilst he was coming closer to you when you look at his face you will be shrouded in fear. That is he had authority, yes.

MR GRIFFITHS:

Q. Because of what?

A. For to hear the voice from us to be able to control the Republic, which we did

A. We did it and it was because I was afraid and I was part of it and that was the culture for us to control the country.

Q. No, you did it, Mr Marzah –

A. Yes.

(SCSL 2003e, 14 March 2008, 6153–6.)

At this point Marzah appeared shaken and made the gesture of a cross over himself.

Q. Why are you crossing yourself, Mr Marzah?

PRESIDING JUDGE: Repeat your question.

MR GRIFFITHS:

Q. Why are you crossing yourself? You just crossed yourself in the chair. Why? Is it because you are lying under oath?

A. I have broken the laws of my Poro society. This is not something that I am supposed to expose but, because Charles Taylor did not give you notes to tell you that we should forget about that area and he is sitting down there and you continued to ask me, I have already spoilt my law and even down to him, his very self, everything has been exposed.

(SCSL 2003e, 14 March 2008, 6157).

It was difficult to know what the Court would make of all this. Were these events that seemed so incredible, fabrication and rumour? Or were they explicable against a background of Liberian history and political culture? Were Marzah's circumlocutions tokens of his mendacity, or were they just indicative of a culture-specific elliptical mode of address? Was his final revelation about Taylor eating hearts in the *Poro* the truth, forced out under pressure? Or was it, to borrow a phrase from William Murphy, 'a kind of dazzle by bluff' (Murphy 1998, 568)? At the very least, one expects, the judges would have a difficult job making up their minds.

FORCED MARRIAGE

During the Sierra Leone conflict hundreds if not thousands of women were abducted from their homes by rebel forces, raped, and forced to become 'wives' of rebel combatants or commanders. Locally, these women were known as 'bush-wives', with the epithet 'bush' signifying the illegitimacy of the marriage (Coulter 2008, 55–6). Sensitised to this evidence, in March 2006 the prosecution applied to amend its indictment to include the crime of 'Forced Marriage', which was charged for the first time in an international court as an Other Inhumane Act and crime against humanity. From the point of view of the prosecution, forced marriage, which they defined as 'forced conjugal association by the perpetrator over the victim … forcing a person into the appearance, the veneer of a conduct (ie marriage), by threat, physical assault or other coercion … ' (cited in SCSL (2008a, 61) was a unique crime which, while usually involving sex, was distinct from the other charges of sexual violence contained in the indictment, and thus worthy of additional prosecution and penalties. It was to become one of the most controversial cultural issues of the AFRC trial. In this section I explore the anthropological and legal background of forced marriage, and the way it was discussed at the Special Court for Sierra Leone.

Dating from at least the mid- to late-nineteenth century, the extended family or patrilineage has formed the basis of social organisation in rural Sierra Leone (Richards, Vincent and Bah 2004, 2). Typically, each community will have a single founding family that claims ownership of the land and the political prerogatives of chieftancy (a situation institutionalised by the British colonial practice of indirect rule). The ruling family will dominate the area's main village or town and establish a network of economic and political power through alliances with other powerful families, for example skilled warriors (in the pre-colonial period), or merchants. These powerful families will also be linked to weaker families, and families of (former) slaves, who are likely to inhabit the area's more far-flung and less hospitable villages. Crucial to maintaining the entire social network are marriage alliances. Ruling families exchange daughters laterally with other powerful families, while poor families try to marry their daughters 'up' to more powerful lineages. In the former case, bridewealth is waived, but in the latter case, the powerful lineage is liable to make a series of payments to the poorer household which help sustain it economically and cement its place in a pattern of patron-client relations. Meanwhile, the son of a poor family who marries the daughter of a rich one is likely to labour on his father-in-law's farm in lieu of bridewealth (Richards, Vincent, and Bah 2004, 2–3): 'Men become indebted to their in-laws: they must offer gifts, work-prestations, and take on financial burdens in case of family crises' (Ferme 2001, 99). The marriage contract also provides the template for a gendered division of labour within the household.

Poor families try to marry their daughters off at a young age to the (usually polygamous) men of wealthy households, meaning that 'Village girls threaten to defeat strategies of lineage alliance by finding lovers where they choose' (Richards, Vincent, and Bah 2004, 5), while the ruling families try to make sure that young men marry their daughters, for a high bride-price.[22] Individual choice in relations of marriage thus threatens the entire system, and considerable pressure is applied to both girls and boys to conform: 'In many cases, girls are destined to a union to which they have not consented, which may be called a "forced marriage"' (Bélair 2006, 569), while 'Some villages try to force young men to marry, and apply steep fines to young men "playing the field"' (Richards, Vincent, and Bah 2004, 5). Some young men liken marriage in rural Sierra Leone to a situation of slavery. Indeed, before and after the abolition of domestic slavery in Sierra Leone in 1927, many former slave lineages were incorporated into ruling households by means of marriage ties, and idioms of slavery still pervade the marriage relation (Ferme 2001, 82).[23]

Individual autonomy in marriage is thus subordinated to the interests of the family, and to the reproduction of an entire structure of (unequal) rural economy. Variants of this system, sometimes called a lineage mode of production, exist all over Africa (see, for example, Meillassoux 1972; Henn 1986), and social scientists have often observed a corresponding diminution in the importance of the individual in African social institutions and political ideology. Charles Piot, for example, writes that: 'Persons [in West Africa] do not "have" relations; they "are" relations' (Piot 1999, 18), while Chabal and Daloz claim that:

> Not only do Africans not conceive of themselves as discrete individuals in the Western mould, but few would accept that their own identity as citizen should be circumscribed politically as it is in the West …

[22] If a poor family cannot marry its daughter up, it is also likely to try and extract labour from the son of another poor family.

[23] Domestic slavery was abolished in a series of ordinances drafted between 1926 and 1927 (Ferme 2001, 81).

> individuals are not perceived as being meaningfully and instrumentally separate from the (various) communities to which they belong.
>
> (Chabal and Daloz 1999, 52.)

The effects are manifest in the status of marriage in Sierra Leonean customary law. Bélair reports that marriage serves the purposes of procreation, the provision of domestic labour by the woman, and the creation of an alliance between two families: 'In fact, customary marriage has traditionally been considered the union of two families rather than two individuals. While the consent of the wife's family is necessary for a valid marriage, that of the wife is not' (Bélair 2006, 568). In addition, there is a corresponding lack of recognition of women's sexual autonomy: 'under customary law, the man has the right to beat his wife if she "misbehaves." The concept of marital rape does not exist in customary law, and women have a duty to submit to their husbands' sexual desires, with few exceptions' (Bélair 2006, 570). Further underlining the subordination of the individual female to the interests of the family Bernath finds that:

> In cases of sexual assault and rape the customary practice is for the families of the victim and of the perpetrator to settle these cases by compensating the victim's family with money and/or goods. The main focus is to salvage the reputation of the victim's family rather than bring the rapist to justice or provide redress for the victim.
>
> (AI 2005, 6.)

In practice, the daughter of a strong lineage who is married to a man in another strong lineage is likely to be well protected by her brothers. Mariane Ferme's study of marriage relations in a Mende village reveals considerable strategising among individuals and families in the field of marriage, adultery and divorce, and in some cases wives, backed by their families, prevailed (Ferme 1998, 81–111). However, in the case of a weaker lineage, a woman may be vulnerable to mistreatment, either because it is dependent on continued bridewealth payments from the richer family, or because it cannot afford to redeem the daughter by repaying bridewealth that has already accrued: 'The poor keep quiet about injustices because they know the extent to which their livelihoods are meshed with those of the leading families through marriage' (Richards, Vincent, and Bah 2004, 4–5). Thus while it would be quite wrong to think of customary marriages as forms of sexual slavery, in some cases they are vulnerable to forms of abuse that approach it: 'customary law tolerates many features or practices that, when put together in certain marriages, take the shape of sexual slavery' (Bélair 2006, 576). This was recognised by the Truth and Reconciliation Commission, which also believed that the inferior status of women in traditional Sierra Leonean society contributed to the patterns of violence against them during the war:

> [t]he abductions and use of young girls and women as bush wives and sex slaves by armed groups during the war could be attributed to the traditional beliefs that governed this issue prior to the war. Some of the armed groups did not consider it an aberration to rape young women or use them as sex slaves.
>
> (TRC, 3b, 103, cited in Bélair (2006, 595).)

These issues were addressed in the AFRC trials by a series of witnesses who described their experience of forced marriages, and by two expert witness reports; I will concentrate here on the latter. The prosecution called Zainab Bangura, a renowned Sierra Leonean civil society and women's rights activist, as its expert witness. Bangura, in her expert report and testimony, drew a distinction between traditional arranged marriages, and the type of forced marriage practised during the war. According to Bangura, in traditional Sierra Leonean society there was no stipulated age for girls to be married: 'it's when somebody has a breast and … started menstruating and normally, they choose a husband for you' (SCSL 2004h, 3 October 2005, 64). Customarily, marriages were arranged by the families of the girl and the man to be married: 'the wife herself is the last person to know about the marriage' (SCSL 2004h, 3 October 2005, 64–5). Indeed, consent of the families: 'is very paramount, fundamental to the marriage institution in Sierra Leone' (SCSL 2004h, 3 October 2005, 70). The bride's consent was also important, but typically she was placed under considerable duress to comply: 'Eventually you have to agree, because you can't take the pressure off' (SCSL 2004h, 3 October 2005, 70). Within a marriage, wife and husband would be expected to perform certain roles: 'you have to cook, you have to take care of him, you have to listen to what he says, you have to ask his permission for everything' while 'when you are married to the man, he's the one who protects you at any time' (SCSL 2004h, 3 October 2005, 55, 58). If a wife was mistreated in a marriage, she could fall back on her family to protect her: 'during the process of marriage, the family gives conditions that you can't beat my daughter, you can't do this … if he treats you badly, he flogs you, he doesn't give you food … you always have a fall back … Somebody will come and sit with him and say, "No, you cannot do this"' (SCSL 2004h, 3 October 2005, 72).

Forced marriages, by contrast, occurred during war time, when a rebel soldier or commander would seize a woman, often in the course of an attack, and claim her as his wife:

> When he comes to the house, when he captured [you], he said, "You now me wife" ... So I am taking you, you are my wife. So the – right from the beginning of the entire relationship with him he identifies you as his wife, which means you belong to him. You are with him and you are part of his property
>
> (SCSL 2004h, 3 October 2005, 52.)

Typically, the woman would have no choice but to consent to this initial act of appropriation: 'You were not given a choice. He grabs you and says, "You are my wife"' (SCSL 2004h, 3 October 2005, 129). Later on, she might appear to have a choice, but the alternatives – gang rape, destitution, death – were so unattractive that she would invariably opt to remain with her husband: 'You see the alternative and you realise that you are better off where you are, and you continue to hope that you will stay there' (SCSL 2004h, 3 October 2005, 131). As in a traditional marriage, husband and wife would be expected to perform certain roles: 'when you become a wife of a rebel, it means you service him alone, you take care of him, you do his laundry. And he of course takes care of you, he protects you, and you belong to him, so nobody else among the other rebels can tamper with you, can either attack you or rape you' (SCSL 2004h, 3 October 2005, 54).

Bangura found that some bush wives sought to escape and reintegrate into their communities after the war, others appeared to remain with their husbands because of the absence of other viable options, while others were grateful to their husbands, loved them, and voluntarily remained:

> I said to them, 'Why are you still with him?' You know, and some of them said, 'Well, I have children. What am I going to do with these two children? You know, nobody is going to marry me any more'. Some of them said, 'Well, he saved me ... this person was going to kill me.' So, for them it was – this person had demonstrated some amount of love ... Some of them tell you ... 'I love him and I just want to stay with him'.
>
> (SCSL 2004h, 3 October 2005, 60–1, 75–6.)

For Bangura, the harm caused by forced marriage was the loss of family support, loss of dignity, and psychological trauma:

> You are at his mercy ... you don't have a fall back position ... Your life is ruined ... a lot of the women who finally went and settled in Kailahun,

> most of them are disconnected from their families … for those ones who finally were integrated, their problem is more … psychological … the way you feel about yourself as a human being, because you have been not only psychologically but sexually abused … it takes away from the self-dignity as a woman.
>
> (SCSL 2004h, 3 October 2005, 71–4.)

In addition, some were stigmatised and rejected by their communities, which for Bangura, 'is one of the worst experiences that an individual can face in Sierra Leone' (SCSL 2004h, 3 October 2005, 79).

Her views were summarised in this section of her expert report:

> The fundamental difference between an early or arranged marriage in times of peace and a forced 'marriage' during war is that family members were not involved in the arrangement of the latter so-called 'marriage', no official ceremony of any form took place and nor was the consent of the parents sought. Instead, girls were forcefully abducted from their homes, schools, or hiding places and taken to the bush where they were informed that they had become 'wives'. Moreover, rebel 'husbands' did not show their 'bush wives' respect. They were constantly flogged, physically and psychologically abused and their husbands always had the final say. Because it was a marriage without consent and no intermediaries were present, the 'wives' had no protection or family support they could count on. Some of these bush 'wives' had actually lost their parents who were trying to prevent their abduction. Forced marriage during the conflict had no security. The 'husband' could abandon his 'wife' whenever he wanted to and get a new one whenever he felt like it. The 'wives' were led to believe that their 'husbands' had a right to kill them, without fear of any repercussions. There were no formal or informal institutions available to address the brutality of the 'husbands'. The 'bush wife' was at the mercy of her rebel husband and had no justice neither could she seek redress.
>
> (cited in SCSL 2007a, 577.)

Cross-examining Bangura, the defence appeared to be driving at the idea that there was little distinction between traditional marriage and forced marriage, Mr Knoops putting it to her that: 'it's fair to say that forced marriage has always been a part of the system of Sierra Leone' (SCSL 2004h, 3 October 2005, 115). Bangura, however, preferred to differentiate between forced marriages 'wherein the consent of the family is not taken and the normal tradition and ceremony … does not apply' and arranged marriages, 'something that was done without your consent but it has the respectability of the community and the participation of the family … So it's not forced marriage' (SCSL 2004h, 3 October 2005,

115–16). Mr Knoops's response was to focus on the issue of individual consent: 'Do you agree that from the point of view of the women who do not consent, who do not consent in a marriage, there isn't really a difference?' A contention that Bangura rejected in the following way: 'If they felt it didn't matter they wouldn't have wanted to take their husbands to be accepted by their families' (SCSL 2004h, 3 October 2005, 118).

The next day, Mohamed Pa-Momo Fofanah for the Defence continued to press this theme, arguing that in normal Sierra Leonean society many girls under the age of eighteen married without giving their consent, and were thus victims of forced marriage, citing a UNICEF fact sheet in support. He asked Bangura whether, as an activist, she accepted that fact. Her response was the following:

> Well, I have to take – even as an activist I work within my environment. There are certain basic things you cannot accept because you know it is impossible to deal with it at that particular time. As an advocacy [*sic*] who works in it, you know there are certain things you can't take head on in your own community because you are not going to be able to make any result. It's like we fight … FGM, you can't make any result in Sierra Leone at the moment.
>
> (SCSL 2004h, 4 October 2005, 19).

The defence also opined that forced marriage was an oxymoronic notion, 'a flat contradiction in terms' and that 'the marriages you referred to as forced marriages … were mere relationships, social relationships' (SCSL 2004h, 4 October 2005, 38). Knoops thought it was 'more a matter of being forcibly abducted instead of forcibly married' (SCSL 2004h, 3 October 2005, 134), while Graham and Fofanah thought that the concept didn't exist in Sierra Leonean or indeed international law: 'in 2004, in fact, May 2004 the Special Court had created a new offence that bordered on forced marriage' (SCSL 2004h, 4 October 2005, 40) claiming that 'the phrase "forced marriage" is a new phenomenon' (SCSL 2004h, 4 October 2005, 62).

The defence also called its own expert witness, Dr Dorte Thorsen, who had worked extensively on gender relations and marriage in West Africa. Thorsen argued that the prosecution's methodology was ill-suited to uncovering the considerable nuance that existed in so-called forced marriages, and that it gave insufficient attention to the obligations of husbands within the marriage, the ability of women to strategise, and indeed the significant power that these marriages sometimes conferred. Thorsen claimed that the terms 'bush wife' and 'bush husband' related to:

> Bundles of obligations and rights inherent in [an] implicit conjugal contract. Consequently, when a Sierra Leonean man told (an abducted) girl that she would be his wife, he forced her into the relationship but also indicated that he was willing to taken [*sic*] on (some of) the responsibilities ascribed to a young husband.

She pointed out that academic studies of the Liberian conflict had shown that a considerable degree of choice often entered into women's relationships with combatants, and that: 'the degree of freedom in such choices is impossible to estimate since they depend both on the situation in which girls find themselves and on the alternatives available to them.' Since the institution of bush wife implied a bundle of rights and obligations, 'the position as a "bush wife" was not only drudgery and sexual abuse but also the base of power' (cited in SCSL (2006c, 22–3). For these reasons, the defence argued, the practice of forced marriage neither met the elements of the crimes of sexual slavery, nor was sufficiently grave as to qualify as an Other Inhumane Act, both of which were charged as crimes against humanity. Alternatively, they argued that perpetrators should have recourse to a defence of 'mistake of law' (SCSL 2006c, 22–3).

After all the evidence had been heard, the Trial Chamber reasoned that the phenomenon of forced marriage would need to contain criminal elements distinct from the counts of sexual violence contained elsewhere in the Statute to qualify as an Other Inhumane Act,[24] and it found, to the disappointment of the prosecution, that it did not. However, to the defence's chagrin, the majority judges also found that the elements of forced marriage did fall under the crime of Sexual Slavery:

> the totality of the evidence adduced by the Prosecution as proof of 'forced marriage' goes to proof of elements subsumed by the crime of sexual slavery ... the use of the term 'wife' by the perpetrator in reference to the victim is indicative of the intent of the perpetrator to exercise ownership over the victim, and not an attempt to assume a marital or quasi-marital status ... in the sense of establishing mutual obligations.
>
> (SCSL 2007a, 219.)

The majority pointed out that none of the trial's witnesses gave any evidence to indicate that having the status of 'bush-wife' added anything unique to their suffering:

[24] Article 2(g) of the Special Court Statute elaborates the crimes of: 'rape, sexual slavery, enforced prostitution, forced pregnancy and any other form of sexual violence.'

> Not one of the victims of sexual slavery gave evidence that the mere fact that a rebel had declared her to be his wife had caused her any particular trauma, whether physical or mental. Moreover, in the opinion of the Trial Chamber, had there been such evidence, it would not by itself have amounted to a crime against humanity.
>
> (SCSL 2007a, 219.)

In a concurring opinion, Judge Sebutinde stressed that forced marriages were not really marriages, no ceremony normally having been held, and that they could not be equated with arranged marriages, though they do 'mimic peacetime situations in which forced marriage and expectation of free female labour are common practice' (SCSL 2007a, 576). While arranged marriages were in violation of a variety of international conventions, they were not criminal, whereas forced marriage was 'clearly criminal in nature and … liable to attract prosecution' (SCSL 2007a, 577).

Judge Theresa Doherty dissented from the majority. In her opinion, forced marriage was a coercive relationship with both sexual and non-sexual elements that had 'little or no similarity to traditional marriage' (SCSL 2007a, 587). The non-sexual elements, and in particular the very fact of being labelled and forced to perform the duties of a 'wife', imparted an added degree of moral and mental suffering:

> Serious psychological and moral injury follows 'forced marriage'. Women and girls are forced to associate with and in some cases live together with men whom they may fear or despise … further, the label 'wife' may stigmatise the victims and lead to their rejection by their families and community … prolonging their mental trauma.
>
> (SCSL 2007a, 590).

Although some women benefited from these 'marriages', the overwhelming environment of coercion meant that this was a relative benefit only, and it in no way diminished the severity of the acts (SCSL 2007a, 589). Moreover, forced marriage could be considered criminal at international law because of the prohibitions against it in international human rights treaties ratified by Sierra Leone, and because of its explicit criminalisation in a variety of national jurisdictions:

> I consider that international treaties and domestic law provide that marriage is a relationship founded on the mutual consent of both spouses. In 'forced marriage' the consent of the victim is absent. In the absence of such consent, the victim is forced into a relationship of a conjugal nature with the perpetrator thereby subsuming the victim's will and

> undermining the victim's exercise of their right to self-determination ... By vitiating the will of one party and forcing him or her to enter into and remain in a marital union the victim is subject to physical and mental suffering the phenomenon of forced marriage transgresses the internationally accepted conventions that both parties must consent to a marriage. It is contrary to principles of criminal law shared by common law and civil law systems alike, as well as Islamic law and the legal systems of some Asian and African states.
>
> (SCSL 2007a, 594.)

The issue was revisited on appeal. Interestingly, the Appeals Chamber found that the Trial Chamber had erred. It was a mistake to think that, in order to qualify as an Other Inhumane Act, forced marriage must be considered absent its sexual content, and it was a mistake to subsume the criminal elements of the phenomenon under the count of Sexual Slavery. The evidence had clearly shown, it thought, that forced marriage was an offence which, while having a sexual component, also had distinct ingredients: 'The trial record contains ample evidence that the perpetrators of forced marriages intended to impose a forced conjugal association upon the victims rather than exercise an ownership interest and that forced marriage is not predominantly a sexual crime' (SCSL 2008a, 62). It caused great harm to its victims, equivalent in gravity to other crimes against humanity, and its perpetrators could have been in no doubt that their actions were criminal:

> the perpetrators intended to force a conjugal partnership on the victims, and were aware that their conduct would cause serious suffering or physical, mental or psychological injury to the victims. Considering the systematic and forcible abduction of the victims of forced marriage, and the prevailing environment of coercion and intimidation, the Appeals Chamber finds that the perpetrators of these acts could not have been under any illusion that their conduct was not criminal.
>
> (SCSL 2008a, 66.)

The Chamber reflected 'society's disapproval', it said, by recognising that 'forceful abduction and use of women and girls as forced conjugal partners as part of a widespread or systematic attack against the civilian population' was criminal conduct, an ' "Other Inhumane Act" capable of incurring individual criminal responsibility in international law', although it declined to enter convictions on this count (SCSL 2008a, 66).

I turn now to a discussion of the issues from the anthropolitical perspective that I have adopted throughout this book. I will argue that, as with the child soldiers issue in the CDF case, the Court read the evidence wrong. It was wrong because it tended to mistake the nature of the transgression of forced marriage, and also, to some extent, the nature of its harm. On the first, the nature of the transgression, both defence lawyers and judges appeared overly preoccupied with the extent to which forced marriage was a consensual act on the part of the so-called 'wife'. Cross-examination and discussion revolved around whether there was more or less consent than in a traditional marriage, whether there was room for manoeuvre, whether benefits accrued to the wife. All the judges concluded that the relationship was coerced, and that consent was illusory. Judge Doherty and the Appeals Chamber went further, using the evidence on consent to establish that the practice was criminal under international law. But this was to mistake the issue. From a local perspective, well-represented by Zainab Bangura's testimony, the crucial issue was not whether the girl had consented, but whether the girl's *family* had given its consent. It was the fact that the family had not given its consent that made this a transgressive act in local eyes, not that the 'wife' was a non-consenting partner. The fact that individual consent was the paramount consideration in the numerous human rights treaties referred to by Judge Doherty, some of which had been ratified by the state of Sierra Leone, was, as I have argued in the case of child soldiers, neither here nor there from the point of view of local communities. As the evidence at trial showed, the real parties to a marriage in Sierra Leone were the families of the bride and groom, not the individuals themselves.

And what of the nature of the harm or suffering caused? If we extract the violent and sexual aspects of the phenomenon, it seems clear from the evidence that what made the institution of forced marriage harmful was the fact that the marriage was not consented to by the families, that it was not legitimated ceremonially, that women did not enjoy the safety net of their families around them, that their husbands may even have murdered their families, and that all these facts were likely to have powerful symbolic, moral and psychological effects. Bangura gave expert evidence that, in some cases, women had tried to repair the damage done by seeking their families' acceptance of the union, and that in at least one case, a man had laboured on his in-laws' farm with a view to this. This strongly suggests that, from a local perspective, forced marriage was seen as an offence against the family, and that the remedies were restorative, not retributive. Indeed, it was undoubtedly the case that unions of this sort were unlawful under customary law, meaning that the Court might have addressed the issue most appropriately by incorporating some customary maxims and means of redress into its statute, acquiring, in the process, a more genuinely hybrid character.

Finally, when it comes to the question of *mens rea*, it is clear that the perpetrators would have known that their actions were wrong, but not necessarily for the reasons the Court thought. This is because young men would have known that it was impermissible to abduct a girl and force her into marriage without the consent of her parents. They would also have known that it was wrong severely to mistreat a woman. But unfortunately they would not necessarily have known that it was wrong to have sex with a woman you consider your wife without her consent, or that to do so would cause her grave psychological harm. Again, for the law to be fair, the husbands of forced marriages should not have been held accountable to human rights instruments about which they probably knew nothing. They should have been held accountable to local, customary laws, or to well-understood norms of transgressive violence. It also bears repeating that the prosecution was at pains to stress that forced marriage did not always involve non-consensual sex or coerced domestic labour. In consequence, criminalising forced marriage invited the unwelcome possibility that men who had rescued women from potentially violent situations, protected them, and subjected them neither to extraordinary levels of abuse or violence, or even to any abuse at all, might be found guilty of a crime against humanity. What such men were guilty of, I submit, was a lesser offence of entertaining marriage-like relations outside the bounds of a union legitimated under customary law.

Obviously, in many cases, forced marriages involved types and levels of non-consensual sex and violence that would be regarded as illegitimate in a traditional marriage, or in any other type of relationship. There can be little doubt that women from any culture would suffer greatly in such circumstances. It was therefore fitting that where violence and sexual coercion crossed such lines, those responsible should be held to account under appropriate provisions of the Special Court statute, such as 'sexual slavery'. This is what the majority judges in the Trial Chamber decided, and what was unfortunately overturned on appeal.[25]

CONCLUSIONS

It is a sad and unsettling fact that women are sometimes forced into traditional marriages in Sierra Leone, sometimes beaten, and sometimes

[25] To be precise, the trial chamber judges took a more extreme line, regarding the totality of the evidence on forced marriage as evidence of sexual slavery, which was surely to overstate the case.

coerced into having sex, and that customary law does not provide adequate safeguards against this eventuality. While these facts are to some extent explained by the need for social reproduction within a stratified agricultural community, it is clear that in contemporary Sierra Leone many young people are straining to escape these strictures. During the course of fieldwork in Tonkolili District in Sierra Leone in 2005, I attended a village meeting at which a representative of a paralegal NGO was discussing human rights issues. The issue of non-consensual sex in marriage came up, and the paralegal warned the men against it, exclaiming 'woman is not a slave!' and threatening, emptily as it happened, to charge offenders with rape in the criminal court. The women in the audience, mostly leaning into the Court *barri* from the outside, murmured approvingly, and one or two echoed enthusiastically 'woman is not a slave!', events that I found quite moving. On this anecdotal evidence, reform of social institutions, the customary legal system, and the entire relationship between customary and common law would be welcome to some Sierra Leoneans, and to this author as well. However, as I will argue in the next chapter, it should not have been the job of the Special Court to use international law to engineer social change of this sort, nor to hold an international human rights prism, with its ethnocentric notions of individual autonomy, self-determination and sexual freedom, over practices that were best viewed through a local lens (compare Bélair (2006)). A similar argument can be applied to the child soldiers charge. In the case of the AFRC and RUF, the child soldier phenomenon was, generally speaking, characterised by a greater degree of compulsion than in the CDF case, and it was this element of abduction and compulsion that made it transgressive, not the phenomenon of using children in hostilities itself. The allegations of superior responsibility for the criminal acts of subordinates were also, as in the CDF case, problematic. Commendably, Trial Chamber II did at least attempt to formulate some more robust indicia of the phenomenon than Trial Chamber I, whatever the doubts about how well these were applied. Finally, we have seen in this chapter that anxieties about witness credibility were just as acute in these trials as in the trial of the CDF. The problems of statement changes, equivocation, witness payments, not to mention the sometimes scarcely believable nature of the allegations, remained the same.

CHAPTER 8

CONCLUSION: FROM LEGAL IMPERIALISM TO DIALOGICS

I wrote in the preface to this book that the Special Court was rather like a Mercedes Benz, crawling at a pitiful pace along Sierra Leone's potholed roads: prestigious, maybe, but ill-adapted to the local terrain. Pushing the analogy further, we could be forgiven for thinking that in the case of the CDF, it was so ill-suited that one of the defendants was taken to the wrong place, while another got locked in the vehicle through little fault of his own.[1] In the subsequent chapters, I have tried to show that this was because the legal doctrine of superior responsibility was unsuited to the realities of Sierra Leonean social and military organisation; I have argued that Western legal precepts and procedures were unsuited to judging adequately the actions of a man whose power stemmed from occult beliefs; I have suggested that crimes such as forced marriage and enlisting children for military service were inappropriate to the Sierra Leonean cultural context; and I have pointed to a range of difficulties that the encounter of two unfamiliar cultures created for the task of assessing witness credibility. In this, the book's conclusion, I suggest some ways in which this situation might be repaired. I will begin by discussing some practical reforms, then some ethical issues, then some epistemological quandaries, before finally advocating a more pluralistic justice approach.

[1] Norman, of course, died before the vehicle reached its destination. As I hope to have shown, issues of cultural difference made the trial very laborious, but I would not go so far as to blame them for Norman's death.

PRACTICAL REFORMS

I argued in Chapter 6 that the quality of evidence elicited at the Special Court was generally poor. This was for a variety of reasons. The trial was taking place in a culture where ambivalence is prized, which may have encouraged witnesses to tell only half truths in their statements to investigators; many witnesses were illiterate; many were unaccustomed to using Western calendar and clock-time; statements were taken in translation; there was no supporting forensic evidence; witnesses reacted badly to the adversarial ecology of the courtroom; and witness payments provided an incentive for them to massage the truth. Fortunately, these kinds of problems could have been addressed – and could be addressed in future international trials – by way of some fairly straightforward practical reforms. Investigators should spend more time building trust with potential witnesses before taking statements from them, for example. They must be especially careful not to lead them. The Court must devise a system of witness compensation that does not provide incentives for witnesses to massage the truth. Investigators must be accompanied by a trained translation team, and they should film statements where witnesses are illiterate. Special efforts should be made to collect forensic evidence, linking witnesses to crime scenes, and to excavation of gravesites. And where a murder has been witnessed but no body found strenuous efforts must be made to corroborate the story. The cumulative effect of these reforms would, in all probability, lead many witnesses and much evidence to fall by the wayside, leaving behind a smaller, tighter, more efficient case, in which the evidence would be more difficult to controvert. Once in court, meanwhile, staff need to devise measures to counteract the tendency of witnesses to hedge or dissimulate. This might mean a more relaxed inquisitorial style, as in the customary courts, or it might mean a much harsher, more demanding adversarial style, as I observed in the magistrates' court. In either case, local legal traditions ought to feed more explicitly into courtroom ecology.

Critics might argue that reforms such as these will be unfeasibly expensive, adding to costs that were already astronomically high in local terms. However, if the international community wants a Western-style trial with a high standard of evidence, it is better to have the all-terrain vehicle than the Mercedes Benz, or so at least I would contend.[2]

[2] Although inexpensive by international standards, the Court was incredibly dear in local terms, its staff budget being greater than that for the entire civil service of Sierra Leone (Gberie 2006).

NORMATIVE ISSUES

The normative position driving this book and in particular Chapters 5 and 7, has been that the law ought not to be an instrument of cultural imperialism. Unfortunately, a proper defence of that position is beyond the scope of this book; suffice to say, the idea that representatives of one culture ought not to take punitive action with a view to changing the practices of another has support from moral philosophers of various stripes, including not only moral relativists and post-colonial theorists but also cosmopolitans, Rawlsian liberals and value-pluralists (Gray 2000; Galston 1999; Jones 2006; Crowder 1994). Unfortunately, this is just what the judges at the Special Court did when they entered convictions on charges of enlisting child soldiers and forced marriage, criminalising elements of local culture which, from a local perspective, were not obviously illegitimate. To avoid making it an imperialist imposition, then, international criminal law ought to grow out of a social consensus that is not merely aspirational, but instead, empirically genuine. It should hold individuals to account who have deviated from international norms that are well understood locally; it should express the moral outrage and fulfil the desire for retribution only of communities that are real.

Some readers will doubtless think that I am romanticising local communities here, but I am not. All communities are to some extent mythological constructions of conflicted empirical realities. They are never homogeneous, they always contain relatively oppressed minorities and they always suppress dissent; they condemn certain modes of life while valorising others; some will make our toes curl. Nevertheless, local communities – by which I mean aggregates of individuals who share a common lifeworld – are empirically real in the sense that they educate and socialise individuals, providing their epistemological outlook and moral compass. The international community, to wit the human rights NGOs, international lawyers, and national statesmen who determine the fundamental principles and treaties of international law, is not a real community in this sense. Its ideas barely penetrate the empirical communities on its periphery, and have yet to be internalised by actors in places such as southern Sierra Leone. Until they have been, until dissonant norms have been understood and accommodated, they ought not to be enforced.

This normative standpoint should resonate not only with the diverse philosophical schools referred to above, but also with many students and practitioners of the law. After all, there is a tradition in the common law itself, embodied in cardinal principles such as *nullum crimen sine lege* and concepts like *mens rea*, that holds that individuals ought not to be convicted without regard to moral guilt. In other words, the law should deliver to the offender his or her deserts for transgressing a norm of which he or she could reasonably have been aware. The forced marriage and child soldiers charges at the Special Court, when applied in particular to the accused in the case of the CDF, did neither of these. Instead, they criminalised the actions of men who were, in all probability, not aware they were committing bad acts since, by the lights of their own community, these acts were normal or condonable.

As the world becomes a more integrated place, it is possible to imagine that ethical systems will tend toward a universal norm. With that in mind, I am not particularly opposed to human rights lawyers trying to expedite that process by proselytising against the kinds of acts they perceive as wrong. Indeed, in a place like rural Sierra Leone they might already find some – though I suspect not much – sympathy for the idea that under-fifteens should never be enlisted in the defence of their own communities. They would probably find considerably more support for their condemnation of the institution of non-consensual marriage, which, as I have mentioned earlier, is increasingly unpopular with young people. But that level of unpopularity has probably not yet reached a level, I suspect, where anything like a majority believe it to be wrong, and until that point has been reached, I contend, it would be untoward to enforce it as law.

What I am advocating, in short, is a dialogical approach to legal institution building. This implies a genuine engagement with the worldview of the Other. Instead of imposing its own, ultimately metropolitan, norms on local communities, the international community should take more peripheral norms seriously, engaging in an extended dialogue, testing whether convergence or consensus can be found. In Mikael Bakhtin's words:

> [Only] a dialogic and participatory orientation takes another person's discourse seriously, and is capable of approaching it both as a semantic position and as another point of view. Only through such an inner dialogic orientation can my discourse find itself in intimate contact with someone else's discourse, and yet at the same time not fuse with it, not swallow it up, not dissolve in itself the other's power to mean.
>
> (Bakhtin 1994 [1963], 94.)

EPISTEMOLOGICAL QUANDARIES

I have argued in this book that international law doctrines were unable properly to capture the nature of authority in Sierra Leone, and alternatively that the judges interpreted the doctrines with insufficient imagination and sensitivity. To a large extent this was a problem of knowledge, since the doctrine of superior responsibility has grown out of cultural contexts in which legal-rational, bureaucratic forms of authority have been predominant (even if, as in the case of the former Yugoslavia, such forms had begun to collapse). The doctrines were not developed to deal with a country like Sierra Leone, a society with numerous poles of power in which bureaucratic authority has always been extremely weak, and in which patrimonial and charismatic authority has been correspondingly strong. In Chapter 3 I argued that historical and sociological writing on Sierra Leone provides *prima facie* grounds for scepticism that any of the accused would have been able to wield conventional military control over their subordinates. To a large extent, and in particular in the CDF case, this scepticism was borne out by the evidence, and the defendants were acquitted of these charges in the majority of crime bases. Nevertheless, the judges seemed determined to find evidence for superior responsibility at least somewhere, relying mainly on *de jure* criteria, plus dubious insider witness testimony of *de facto* authority, to do so.

As I argued in Chapter 3, the judges were insufficiently sensitive to the cultural context here. As every anthropologist knows, similar actions can have different meanings in different cultural contexts (Geertz 1973). Letters of appointment to superior positions, written orders, and oral testimony of orders being given, which might be convincing tokens of a superior's effectiveness in a strong organisational culture, are less convincing in a culture like Sierra Leone. The evidence needs to be interpreted in context, and in locations where there are *prima facie* grounds for thinking that conventional superior responsibility does not exist, a more exacting standard of proof ought to be required.

Knowlegde of context ought also to have a bearing on prosecutorial strategy. Readers will recall that the Court's mandate was 'to prosecute those who bear the greatest responsibility' for crimes committed during the civil conflict in Sierra Leone. As we have seen, the armed factions in Sierra Leone were not like conventional militaries and neither were they like mafia organisations, authority being far more fluid and diffuse. For this reason, it was probably a mistake to think that, by prosecuting those at the top of notional military pyramids, one would be capturing those most responsible for conflict-based crimes. In diffuse-authority contexts like this, it would actually make better sense to concentrate on other modes of liability – committing, instigating, aiding and abetting – and on commanders closer to the ground. In the case of Sierra Leone, this might have led to the prosecution of several score direct perpetrators of the worst atrocities, in addition to some, though not all, of the existing accused. This would mean a greater volume of trials, but also cases that would have been slimmer and easier to prove.[3] Not incidentally, such a strategy would also have been in better harmony with local understandings of what responsibility in this context really meant.

Another welcome effect might have been to relieve some of the pressure on insider witnesses to tell lies. As things were, insider witnesses had an incentive to admit to committing atrocities, but to deny responsibility for those atrocities by implicating people higher up the putative command chain, lest they be found to bear 'greatest responsibility' themselves. The result was that a few figureheads were imprisoned for crimes over which they had little control, while lower-level commanders – often the direct perpetrators of atrocities – walked free, their pockets bulging with payments from the Court. This was unsatisfactory both legally and morally. Had, by contrast, all of these insiders been prosecuted, and had telling the truth about superiors stood to gain them at most a reduced sentence, then not only would the worst perpetrators have been held accountable, but the incentives to fitting up their bosses would at least have been reduced.

I switch now to another epistemological quandary, the issue of magical powers. Just what should the Court have done about a man like Allieu Kondewa? I argued in Chapter 4 that although Sierra Leone provided an unpropitious context for the exercise of conventional military control, a background belief in occult forces made it more likely that some individuals would be able to wield significant charismatic power.[4] In this context,

[3] This has some resonance with the advice contained in (Boas 2007) and appears to be the approach favoured at the ICC (Clark 2008).

[4] Mariane Ferme has pointed out to me that not every Kamajor in the country believed in the powers of Kondewa, and that Kamajors frequently questioned the respective merits of different initiators. But to my mind the fact that so many believed or wanted to believe in the initiators, and that even if sceptical they returned again and again for 'top-up' initiations, shows that immunisation and the background structure of occult belief was crucial to understanding the movement (Mariane Ferme, personal communication, June 2008). To provide an analogy from my own culture, I may be sceptical of any number of car mechanics, but this does not mean I call mechanical laws into question.

it is hard to believe that Allieu Kondewa did not have the authority to prevent the Kamajors with whom he personally came into contact from committing atrocities, or that he could have punished – or arranged the punishment of – those who had done so. Because of this, my own view is that the prosecution were justified in alleging superior responsibility in his case, and that the judges could have found him guilty on this charge. The tricky business comes when we examine Kondewa's defence. As with the witchcraft cases we have discussed for colonial Africa, this raised difficult questions not only about the background structure of cosmological belief, but also about the *mens rea* of the accused. Were Kondewa's medicinal taboos, by emic standards, genuine? Did he, in the face of a mounting civilian body count, really think that his medicines deterred Kamajors from committing war crimes? Was this belief reasonable? Doubtless, such questions would have been difficult to resolve. Were the judges really qualified to assess the credibility of a man who claimed mystical powers? By whose standards of reasonability would Kondewa be judged? Who would guide them, Western psychiatrists, or local ritual experts? By whose standards would the judges assess the credibility of this advice? No wonder the judges sidestepped these issues, given the epistemological worm-can they threatened to open. Issues like these must be confronted, however, if international courts are to rule meaningfully. By cleaving rigidly to international practice, international courts are currently unable to get a handle on the occult, creating an unbridgeable gulf between their worldview and that of the people they are trying, not to mention the many victims they claim to speak for.

And then there is the problem of categories of law. I have argued that, had the judges been more open-minded, Kondewa could have been found guilty under Article 6(iii) of the Special Court Statute. But perhaps this did not adequately or exhaustively capture the real nature of his offence. We currently have very little idea of how provincial Sierra Leoneans, some of whom entrusted themselves and their relatives to his care, some of whom suffered at the hands of Kamajors, and some of whom were liberated by Kamajors he had initiated, viewed his actions. Perhaps they regarded him as a home-grown hero, producing locally legitimate solutions to a local conflict. Or perhaps, as the TRC contended and the prosecution claimed, he was a charlatan, a quack, guilty of perverting a traditional belief system for personal ends. This, arguably, is the charge on which the evidence should have been heard, and around which the legal arguments should have revolved, producing a trial that could have stimulated a useful dialogue about the entire structure and uses of occult belief in Sierra Leone.

PLURALISTIC ACCOUNTABILITY FOR POST-CONFLICT SOCIETIES

The case of Allieu Kondewa shows that if international criminal law is to be meaningful in non-Western communities, it will need to adjust its outlook quite radically. This means either opening the door to local precepts and procedures, or else accepting that the role of the criminal law should be both more limited, and better integrated with a diverse range of accountability mechanisms. The latter option would imply instituting Western-style courts side-by-side, and yet in dialogue with, non-Western accountability mechanisms, building on the full range of justice mechanisms extant in present-day Sierra Leone, and melding them with a few elements of international expertise, support, and imprimatur. It would imply, to return to our vehicular metaphor, a revamped version of the uncomfortable, dangerous, yet efficient minibuses that ply the local roads. This is already an option that has some support in the transitional justice literature. Mark Drumbl, for example, has written eloquently about how international justice should give 'qualified deference' to local justice mechanisms. He has urged that we 'integrate non-Western legal traditions into globalized understandings of the adequacy of due process' and that we 'insert comparative law methodologies more deeply into the international jurisprudence' (Drumbl 2007, 207). He advocates multivalent and polyphonic justice solutions, meaning that 'the process of justice might look different in Sierra Leone than it does in Cambodia, and the process of justice in Cambodia might differ from that in Kosovo' recognising the potential need for 'international lawyers to become more familiar with comparative methodologies, particularly from the developing world' (Drumbl 2007, 19). Kieran McEvoy meanwhile has urged international lawyers to move beyond legalism toward a 'thicker' understanding of transitional justice, deploying resources to skill up partners in the community, civil society, or even the private sector (McEvoy 2007), while Eric Stover and Harvey Weinstein have advised a more modest role for international trials, paying attention instead to a broad range of extant justice ideas, and suggesting that prosecutions be embedded within an ecological approach to social reconstruction (Stover and Weinstein 2004a).

All of this implies a more pluralistic strategy. In the case of Sierra Leone, this might have involved a commission of inquiry that was much more open to local epistemologies and local justice practices than the Sierra Leonean TRC, followed by a period of reflection in which it was decided how best to hold the culpable to account.[5] This might then have been followed by a variety of institutional initiatives in assessing the facts, apportioning blame, and meting out punishment, providing space for both international and local narratives, and opportunities for both retributive and restorative justice drawing on legal approaches both formal, informal, customary and international; in other words, it would have been a genuinely hybrid approach.[6]

Interestingly, there is already a legal organisation in Sierra Leone that works in this spirit. *Timap for Justice* is a Sierra Leonean NGO that receives funding from the Open Society Justice Initiative. It specialises in paralegal services that straddle the country's dualistic legal system. The organisation has one qualified lawyer and thirteen paralegal officers working in Freetown and in six provincial chiefdoms. *Timap* uses a wide range of methods to tackle a broad range of justice issues, and will litigate if required. It employs what it describes as a synthetic, pragmatic approach to the legal system. The NGO's staple fodder tends to be disputes relating to the obligations of the extended family, and in particular child maintenance and custody cases. However, it has also been involved in land cases, contract and employment disputes, government corruption cases, abuses of the court system, assaults by government officials on ordinary people, witchcraft cases, unlawful female circumcision, illegal detention, immigration and repatriation cases, and many more (Maru 2006).

The NGO's approach has been described in a recently published paper by *Timap* co-founder Vivek Maru. Though the NGO works within the law, there are aspects of its work which can only be described as legal in the loosest sense, he says. For example, in one case a 26-year-old woman was brought to the *Timap* office having been abandoned by her family after her first three children had died and she confessed to dabbling in

[5] For critiques of the TRC's ethnocentricity, see Kelsall (2005) and Shaw (2005, 2006). For a more sanguine view, see Stovel (2005).

[6] Some would argue that the Special Court already marked an advance on previous international tribunals in terms of the scope of its outreach efforts and attempts to dialogue with local communities. Yet these efforts were always underfunded, and largely conducted after the mandate and indictments had been drawn, meaning that they inevitably had a monological and didactic bent. According to Kerr and Lincoln's research: 'The overriding impression of the first set of outreach events, conducted by the then Registrar, Robin Vincent, and Prosecutor, David Crane, was of Court staff flying in to remote regions on helicopters and travelling ("hurtling") along in white UN jeeps, with large entourages, arriving at the venue and giving a short presentation, answering a few questions, which had often been prearranged, and then leaving very quickly without looking back. This left behind an impression of superiority and difference' (Kerr and Lincoln 2008, 21).

witchcraft. As it happened, a member of *Timap*'s Community Oversight Board was a part-time diviner, and this woman offered to exorcise the witch, which she attempted to do by preparing a ceremony and purgative meal. According to Maru: 'Here the problem did involve human rights – Macie B's right to basic health and food – but the partial solution we could offer did not involve law at all' (Maru 2006, 447). *Timap* drew on a traditional practice, perhaps bizarre or even offensive to many transitional justice practitioners, in order to create an aperture for Macie's reintegration.[7]

In another example, a mother visited *Timap*'s office claiming that her 4-year-old daughter had been abducted by the local secret society (the women's arm of which is called *bondu*), taken to the bush against her mother's will, and circumcised. At the time female circumcision was not outlawed in Sierra Leone and had strong support from the President's wife, as well from many local power brokers. *Timap*'s paralegals judged that securing redress through the police and courts would not be an option. However, circumcising a pre-adolescent child without familial consent *is* a violation of local customary law. *Timap* decided that the best course of action was to intervene with the Paramount Chief, securing the return of the girl, an exemption of fees for the mother, and a fine for the society leaders. This then was a successful example of securing redress for the violation of traditional constraints surrounding a traditional practice. Subsequently, the NGO has sought to try and reform the practice itself, trying to identify female *bondu* members who have mixed feelings about female circumcision with a view to opening a dialogue about the practice within the society. According to *Timap*: 'the only kind of reform that is plausible in the medium term is one that involves an evolution of norms, and, perhaps, a renegotiation of power relations within the communities in which the practice occurs' (Maru 2006, 463).

Timap's flexibility and pragmatism in these cases, the reason it is able to take traditional dispute resolution methods seriously, is explained by the fact that its local staff share traditional beliefs: all of them believe firmly in a world where witchcraft and magic are real forces with which ordinary people must contend. Moreover, the organisation as a whole believes that customary institutions are entitled to respect, both because of their link to tradition and because of their relevance and accessibility to most

7 The ceremony was apparently a success and Macie and her family went to live with her husband's family again, where they appeared to prosper. However, in January 2006, Macie's fourth child tragically died, apparently from choking. Although the community has not accused her of witchcraft, she was once again expelled from the family of her husband.

ordinary people. That is not to say that it regards indigenous practices as beyond criticism. Maru describes the origins of *Timap's* moral compass as mixed, drawing on Christian and Muslim beliefs, as well as traditional Sierra Leonean values, modified by ideals of the international human rights movement. Its core methodology centres on mediation, and a set of standard techniques which will be familiar to ADR practitioners worldwide. However, it also does much more than this, and its success depends not so much on a set of tools, as on a certain sensibility and sensitivity towards local realities. Its primary concern is to help improve the lives of poor people, using the law as a tool where appropriate, and using other methods where they stand more chance of success. Maru describes the NGO's methodology as dialogical, and insists that: 'We are not legal missionaries who would banish customary darkness with formal legal light' (Maru 2006, 461).

Of course, most of the time *Timap* is not dealing with cases of murder, cruel treatment, looting or any of the other offences that make up the compendium of war crimes. I am not for a moment claiming that these offences can all be satisfactorily addressed by small paralegal NGOs. It is, rather, in its sensibility that *Timap* provides a useful model. Transposed into the international realm, such a sensibility would imply a greater openness to a broader spectrum of local belief, to locally researched ideas about the nature of offences committed and the categories of new and old law required to capture them, to local research and ideas about who ought to be held to account, a more flexible approach to the procedural modes and forms of evidence best able to try such offences, and a more consultative approach to the types of sentence, forms of punishment, or forms of compensation meted out.[8]

As I finish writing this book, there are encouraging signs that support for a more pluralistic and dialogical approach to international justice is

[8] In 2005 I spent five weeks in Magburaka town, Kholifa Rowalla Chiefdom, where *Timap* has an office. I accompanied Michael Luseni, its paralegal officer, to cases in local courts, to client mediation sessions, and to awareness-raising dialogues in local villages, into which the organisation was hoping to expand. *Timap* staff often trod a fine line between legal evangelism and respect for local beliefs in these encounters, and its success, like that of other institutions in Sierra Leone, was founded as much on a sense of esoteric mystery – in this case surrounding the law – as it was on ideals of transparency. Moreover, the NGO was engaged in low-level power struggles with other justice service providers in the community such as chiefs, with whom it had to tread carefully. That said, *Timap* was undoubtedly a popular local institution, with some success in widening poor people's access to the law, and it was to some extent expanding the realm of the law and exposing people to human rights talk without in most cases riding roughshod over local belief. And it was doing all this at a modest cost (Kelsall 2006a).

gaining ground. Indeed, through a combination of accident and design, it might actually be implemented in the case of northern Uganda. As we saw in the Introduction to this book, the ICC indictments of five LRA leaders in October 2005 generated widespread controversy. The upshot of those indictments, according to Marieke Wierde and Michael Otim, has been to place accountability for the LRA firmly on the agenda, with subsequent peace talks in Juba discussing not whether the LRA should be held accountable, but how. After submissions from the government, the rebels, local NGOs, and the ICC, the parties are now proposing a process in which LRA members accused of serious crimes will be tried by a special division of the Ugandan High Court. In addition, the country will embark on a truth commission type process, establishing a 'commission of inquiry into the past and related events'. Reparations will be provided by the government, while an alternative justice and reconciliation process will be established, in which traditional justice will be key (Otim and Wierde 2008, 25). While authors such as Tim Allen remain sceptical about the authenticity and applicability of traditional justice mechanisms (Allen 2008), and international human rights NGOs including Amnesty International and the International Federation for Human Rights have urged Uganda to respect its obligations to the ICC (Otim and Wierde 2008, 25), it is my hope that after the cross-examination of culture in international trials presented here, they and other commentators will be more aware of the pitfalls to trying a case of this kind in a western-style international court. Culture matters, and for justice to be done, the international community must adapt to this fact.

REFERENCES

Abdullah, Ibrahim. 2004a. Bush path to destruction: the origin and character of the Revolutionary United Front (RUF/SL). In *Between Democracy and Terror: The Sierra Leone Civil War*, edited by I. Abdullah. Dakar: Council for the Development of Social Science Research in Africa (CODESRIA).

ed. 2004b. *Between Democracy and Terror: The Sierra Leone Civil War*. Dakar: Council for the Development of Social Science Research in Africa (CODESRIA).

Abraham, Arthur. 1974. Bai Bureh, the British, and the Hut Tax War. *International Journal of African Historical Studies* 7(1): 99–106.

1978. Mende Government and Politics under Colonial Rule. Oxford: Oxford University Press.

2004. State complicity as a factor in perpetuating the Sierra Leone civil war. In *Between Democracy and Terror: The Sierra Leone Civil War*, edited by I. Abdullah. Dakar: Council for the Development of Social Science Research in Africa (CODESRIA).

Abrahams, Ray. 1989. Law and order and the state in the Nyamwezi and Sukuma area of Tanzania. *Africa* 59(3): 356–70.

AI. 2005. Briefing paper: Sierra Leone: 'No-one to turn to: women's lack of access to justice in rural Sierra Leone'. AFR51/011/2005. London: Amnesty International.

Allen, Tim. 2006. *Trial Justice: The International Criminal Court and the Lord's Resistance Army*. London: Zed Books.

2008. Ritual (Ab)use? Problems with traditional justice in Northern Uganda. In *Courting Conflict? Justice, Peace and the ICC in Africa*, edited by N. Waddell and P. Clark. London: The Royal African Society.

Alterman, Owen, Aneta Binienda, Sophie Rodella and Kimyia Varzi. 2002. *The Law People See: The Status of Dispute Resolution in the Provinces of Sierra Leone in 2002*. Freetown: National Forum for Human Rights.

Archard, David. 1993. *Children: Rights and Childhood*. London and New York: Routledge.

Arendt, Hannah. 1963. *Eichmann in Jerusalem*. London: Penguin.

Ashforth, Adam. 1998a. Reflections on spiritual insecurity in Soweto. *African Studies Review* 41(3): 39–68.

1998b. Witchcraft, violence and democracy in the new South Africa. *Cahiers d'Etudes africaines* 38(152): 505–32.

Avruch, Kevin and Beatriz Vejarano. 2002. Truth and reconciliation commissions: a review essay and annotated bibliography. *Social Justice* 2(1–2): 47–108 (with B. Vejarano). Republished in *The Online Journal of Peace and Conflict Resolution*, Issue 4.2, Spring 2002; at www.trinstitue.org/ojpcr/4_2recon.html.

Baines, Erin K. 2007. The haunting of Alice: local approaches to justice and reconciliation in Northern Uganda. *International Journal of Transitional Justice* 1(1): 91–114.

Bakhtin, M. M. 1994 [1963]. Problems of Dostoevsky's poetics. In *The Bakhtin Reader*, edited by P. Morris. London: Arnold.

Bangura, Yusuf. 2004. The political and cultural dynamics of the Sierra Leone war. In *Between Democracy and Terror: The Sierra Leone Civil War*, edited by I. Abdullah. Dakar: Council for the Development of Social Science Research in Africa (CODESRIA).

Bass, Gary Jonathan. 2000. *Stay the Hand of Vengeance: The Politics of War Crimes Tribunals*. Princeton and Oxford: Princeton University Press.

Bayart, Jean-Francois. 1993. *The State in Africa: The Politics of the Belly*. London: Longman.

Behrand, Heike. 1999. *Alice and the Holy Spirits: War in Northern Uganda*. Oxford: James Currey.

Bélair, Karine. 2006. Unearthing the customary law foundations of 'forced marriages' during Sierra Leone's civil war: the possible impact of international criminal law on customary marriage and women's rights in post-conflict Sierra Leone. *Columbia Journal of Gender and Law* 15(3): 551–607.

Bellman, Beryl L. 1984. *The Language of Secrecy: Symbols and Metaphor in Poro Ritual*. New Brunswick, NJ: Rutgers University Press.

Berk-Seligson, Susan. 1990. *The Bilingual Courtroom: Court Interpreters in the Judicial Process*. Chicago and London: University of Chicago Press.

Berman, Bruce. 1998. Ethnicity, patronage and the African state. *African Affairs* 97(389): 305–41.

Berry, Sara. 1993. *No Condition is Permament: the Social Dynamics of Agrarian Change in Sub-Saharan Africa*. Madison: University of Wisconsin Press.

Bienen, Leigh. 1976. The determination of criminal insanity in Western Nigeria. *Journal of Modern African Studies* 14(2): 219–45.

Bledsoe, Caroline H. 1990. 'No success without struggle': social mobility and hardship for foster children in Sierra Leone. *Man* New series 25(1): 70–88.

Bledsoe, Caroline H. and Kenneth M. Robey. 1986. Arabic literacy and secrecy among the Mende of Sierra Leone. *Man* New series 21(2): 202–26.

Boas, Gideon. 2007. *The Milosevic Trial: Lessons for the Conduct of Complex International Proceedings*. Cambridge: Cambridge University Press.

Boli-Bennett John and John W. Meyer. 1978. The ideology of childhood and the state: rules distinguishing children in national constitutions, 1870–1970. *American Sociological Review* 43(6): 797–812.

Braithwaite Wallis, C. 1905. In the court of the native chiefs in Mendiland. *Journal of the Royal African Society* 4(16): 397–409.
Branch, Adam. 2004. International justice, local injustice. *Dissent* (Summer): 22–8.
Bratton, Michael and Nicholas Van de Walle. 1997. *Democratic Experiments in Africa*. Cambridge: Cambridge University Press.
Brenneis, D. 1988. Language and disputing. *Annual Review of Anthropology* 17: 221–37.
Brown, Taylor, Richard Fanthorpe, Janet Gardener, Lansana Gberie and M. Gibril Sesay. 2005. *Sierra Leone Drivers of Change*. Bristol: The IDL group for DFID.
Burman, Sandra B. and Barbara E. Harrell-Bond (eds.). 1979. *The Imposition of Law*. New York and London: Academic Press.
Carothers, Thomas (ed.). 2006. *Promoting the Rule of Law Abroad: In Search of Knowledge*. Washington DC: Carnegie Endowment for International Peace.
Cassese, Antonio. 2005. *International Law. 2nd edn* Oxford: Oxford University Press.
Chabal, Patrick and Jean-Pascal Daloz. 1999. *Africa Works: Disorder as Political Instrument*. Oxford: James Currey.
2006. *Culture Troubles: Politics and the Interpretation of Meaning*. London: Hurst.
Clapham, Christopher, 1999. Sovereignty and the Third World state. *Political Studies* 47(3): 522–37.
Clapham, Christopher. 1976. *Liberia and Sierra Leone: An Essay in Comparative Politics*. Cambridge: Cambridge University Press.
1985. *Third World Politics: An Introduction*. Madison: University of Wisconsin Press.
1996. *Africa and the International System*. Cambridge: Cambridge University Press.
Clark, Phil. 2008. Law, politics, and pragmatism: the ICC and case selection in Uganda and the Democratic Republic of Congo. In *Courting Conflict? Justice, Peace and the ICC in Africa*, edited by N. Waddell and P. Clark. London: The Royal African Society.
Clarke, Robert. 1863. Sketches of the colony of Sierra Leone and its inhabitants. *Transactions of the Ethnological Society of London* 2: 320–63.
Cobbing, Julian. 1977. The absent priesthood: another look at the Rhodesian Risings of 1896–1897. *Journal of African History* 18(1): 61–84.
Cockayne, James. 2004. Special Court for Sierra Leone – decisions on the recusal of Judges Robertson and Winter. *Journal of International Criminal Justice* 2(4): 1154–62.
Cohen, Abner. 1971. The politics of ritual secrecy. *Man* 6(3): 427–48.
Collier, J. F. 1975. Legal processes. *Annual Review of Anthropology* 4: 121–44.

Comaroff, Jean and John L. Comaroff. 1993. *Modernity and its Malcontents: Ritual and Power in Postcolonial Africa*. Chicago and London: University of Chicago Press.

Comaroff, John L. and Jean Comaroff. 2004. Criminal justice, cultural justice: the limits of liberalism and the pragmatics of difference in the new South Africa. *American Ethnologist* 31(2): 188–204.

2006. Law and disorder in the postcolony: an introduction. In *Law and Disorder in the Postcolony*, edited by J. Comaroff and J. L. Comaroff. Chicago: Chicago University Press.

Conley, John M. and Wiliam M. O'Barr. 1998. *Just Words: Law, Language, and Power*. Chicago and London: University of Chicago Press.

Coulter, Chris. 2008. Female fighters in the Sierra Leone war: challenging the assumptions? *Feminist Review* (88): 54–73.

Crane, David M. 2006. White man's justice: applying international justice after regional third world conflicts. *Cardozo Law Review* 27(4): 1683–8.

2007. The spaceship has landed: who's justice anyway? Justice in situations of ongoing conflict – a prosecutor's point of view. Expert paper 'Workshop 2 – Justice in Situations of Ongoing Conflict'. ICTJ Workshop on Building a Future on Peace and Justice. Nuremburg.

Crowder, George. 1994. Pluralism and liberalism. *Political Studies* 42(2): 293–305.

Cryer, Robert. 2007. A long way from home: witnesses before international criminal tribunals. *International Commentary on Evidence* 4(1): 1–4.

Cryer, Robert, Hakan Friman, Daryl Robinson and Elizabeth Wilmshurst. 2007. *An Introduction to Criminal Law and Procedure*. Cambridge: Cambridge University Press.

Cunningham, Hugh. 1998. Histories of childhood. *American Historical Review* 103(4): 1195–208.

De Waal, A. 1997. *Famine Crimes: Politics and the Disaster Relief Industry in Africa*. Oxford: James Currey.

Dorjahn, Vernon R. 1959. The organization and functions of the 'Ragbenle' society of the Temne. *Africa* 29(2): 156–70.

Dougherty, Beth K. 2004. Right-sizing international justice: the hybrid experiment at the Special Court for Sierra Leone. *International Affairs* 80(2): 311–28.

Driberg, J. H. 1934. The African conception of law. *Journal of Comparative Legislation and International Law* 16(4): 230–45.

Drumbl, Mark A. 2005. Collective violence and individual punishment: the criminality of mass atrocity. *Northwestern University Law Review* 99(2): 539–610.

2007. *Atrocity, Punishment, and International Law*. Cambridge: Cambridge University Press.

Duffield, Mark. 2001. *Global Governance and the New Wars: The Merging of Development and Security*. London: Zed Books.

Ellis, Stephen. 2001. Mystical weapons: some evidence from the Liberian war. *Journal of Religion in Africa* 31(2): 222–36.

2007. *The Mask of Anarchy. The Destruction of Liberia and the Religious Dimensions of an African Civil War. Revised and updated 2nd edn.* New York: New York University Press.

Ellis, Stephen and Gerrie ter Haar. 1998. Religion and politics in sub-Saharan Africa. *Journal of Modern African Studies* 36(2): 175–201.

2004. *Worlds of Power: Religious Thought and Political Practice in Africa.* London: Hurst.

Elster, Jon. 2004. *Closing the Books: Transitional Justice in Historical Perspective.* Cambridge: Cambridge University Press.

Fanthorpe, Richard. 2001. Neither citizen nor subject? 'Lumpen' agency and the legacy of native administration in Sierra Leone. *African Affairs* 100(400): 363–86.

Ferme, Mariane. 1998. The violence of numbers: consensus, competition, and the negotiation of disputes in Sierra Leone. *Cahiers d'Etudes africaines* (150–152): 555–80.

2001. *The Underneath of Things: Violence, History and the Everyday in Sierra Leone.* Berkeley: University of California Press.

Fisiy, Cyprian F. 1998. Containing occult practices: witchcraft trials in Cameroon. *African Studies Review* 41(3): 143–63.

Fletcher, Laurel E. and Harvey Weinstein. 2004. A world unto itself? The application of international justice in the former Yugoslavia. In *My Neighbour, My Enemy: Justice,and Community in the Aftermath of Mass Atrocity*, edited by E. Stover and H. M. Weinstein. Cambridge: Cambridge University Press.

Forges, Alison des and Timothy Longman. 2004. Legal responses to genocide in Rwanda. In *My Neighbour, My Enemy: Justice and Community in the Aftermath of Mass Atrocity*, edited by E. Stover and H. M. Weinstein. Cambridge: Cambridge University Press.

Foucault, Michel. 1980. *Power/Knowledge: Selected Interviews and Other Writings 1972–1977.* New York: Pantheon Books.

Galston, William A. 1999. Expressive liberty, moral pluralism, political pluralism: three sources of liberal theory. *William and Mary Law Review* 40 (March): 869–907.

Gberie, Lansana. 2005. *A Dirty War in West Africa: The R.U.F. and the destruction of Sierra Leone.* London: Hurst and Co.

2006. A court, a war hero, and a baffled country. *Concord Times*, 14 March, available at www.concordtimessl.com/features/htm.

Gee, James Paul. 1996. *Social Linguistics and Literacies: Ideology in Discourses.* London and New York: Routledge.

2005. *An Introduction to Discourse Analysis: Theory and Method.* New York and Abingdon: Routledge.

Geertz, Clifford. 1973. *The Interpretation of Cultures.* New York: Basic Books.

1973. Thick description: toward an interpretive theory of culture. In *The Interpretation of Cultures: Selected Essays*, edited by C. Geertz. New York: Basic Books.

1983. Local knowledge: fact and law in comparative perspective. In *Local Knowledge: Further Essays in Interpretive Anthropology*, edited by C. Geertz. New York: Basic Books.

Geschiere, Peter. 1997. *The Modernity of Witchcraft: Politics and the Occult in Postcolonial Africa*. Charlottesville and London: University Press of Virginia.

2006. Witchcraft and the limits of the law: Cameroon and South Africa. In *Law and Disorder in the Postcolony*, edited by J. C. Comaroff and J. L. Comaroff. Chicago: Chicago University Press.

Gibbs, James L. Jr. 1963. The Kpelle moot. In *Law and Warfare: Studies in the Anthropology of Conflict*, edited by P. Bohannan. Austin and London: University of Texas Press.

Gluckman, Max. 1964. The judicial process among the Barotse. In *Law and Warfare: Studies in the Anthropology of Conflict*, edited by P. Bohannan. Austin and London: University of Texas Press.

Gray, John. 2000. Pluralism and toleration in contemporary political philosophy. *Political Studies* 48(2): 323–33.

Greene, Graham. 2004 [1948]. *The Heart of the Matter*. Vintage: London.

Gumperz, John J. 1982. *Discourse Strategies*. Cambridge: Cambridge University Press.

Hart, W. A. 1986. Aron Arabai: The Temne mask of chieftancy. *African Arts* 19(2): 41–5, 91.

Hayner, Priscilla. 2001. *Unspeakable Truths*. London: Routledge.

Hazan, Pierre. 2006. Evaluating transitional justice: a difficult but indispensable task. A paper prepared for the conference, 'Beyond the Toolkit: rethinking the paradigm of transitional justice', Bellagio, Italy, November 2006.

Henn, Jean Koopman. 1986. The material basis of sexism: a mode of production analysis with African examples. Working Paper 119: Boston University African Studies Center.

Hiner, N. Ray and Joseph M. Hawes. 1991. Standing on common ground: reflections on the history of children and childhood. In *Children in Historical and Comparative Perspective*, edited by N. R. Hiner and J. M. Hawes. New York and London: Greenwood Press.

Hirsch, John L. 2000. *Sierra Leone: Diamonds and the Struggle for Democracy*. Boulder: Lynne Rienner.

Hoffman, Daniel J. 2006. Expert report on the Kamajors of Sierra Leone prepared for the Fofana Defense Team. Seattle: University of Washington.

2007. The meaning of a militia: understanding the Civil Defence Forces of Sierra Leone. *African Affairs* 106(425): 639–62.

Hoffman, Danny. 2003. Like beasts in the bush: synonyms of childhood and youth in Sierra Leone. *Postcolonial Studies* 6(3): 295–308.

2004. The Kamajors of Sierra Leone: New magic and the war machine. Unpublished PhD Thesis, Anthropology Department, Duke University, Durham.

Humphreys, Macartan and Jeremy Weinstein. 2004. What the fighters say: a survey of ex-combatants in Sierra Leone. CGSD Working Paper No. 20. Freetown: PRIDE with the support of The Earth Institute at Columbia University, and UNAMSIL.

Huyse, Luc and Mark Salter (eds.). 2007. *Traditional Justice and Reconciliation After Violent Conflict: Learning from African examples*. Stockholm: Institute for Democracy and Electoral Assistance.

ICG. 2003. *Africa Briefing: The Special Court for Sierra Leone: Promises and Pitfalls of a New Model*. Freetown/Brussels: International Crisis Group.

ICTJ. 2007. What is transitional justice? www.ictj.org/en/tj/.

Iliffe, John. 1967. The organization of the Maji Maji rebellion. *Journal of African History* 8(3): 495–512.

Iron, Richard. 2005. *Military Expert Witness Report on the Civil Defence Force of Sierra Leone*. Norfolk, Virginia: Directorate General of Development and Doctrine/Allied Command Transformation.

Jackson, Michael. 2002. *The Politics of Storytelling: Violence, Transgression, and Intersubjectivity*. Copenhagen: Museum Tusculanum Press.

Jackson, Robert H. 1990. *Quasi-States: Sovereignty, International Relations and the Third World*. Cambridge: Cambridge University Press.

Jackson, Robert H. and Carl G. Rosberg. 1982. *Personal Rule in Black Africa: Prince, Autocrat, Prophet, Tyrant*. Berkeley: University of California Press.

Jacquemet, Marco. 1996. *Credibility in Court: Communicative Practices in the Camorra Trials*. Cambridge: Cambridge University Press.

James, Allison and Adrian James. 2005. Introduction: the politics of childhood – an overview. In *The Politics of Childhood*, edited by J. Goddard, S. McNamee, A. James and A. James. Basingstoke: Palgrave.

Jedrej, M.C. 1986. Dan and Mende masks: a structural comparison. *Africa* 56(1): 71–80.

Johnson, Douglas H. 1997. *Nuer Prophets: A History of Prophecy in the Upper Nile from the Nineteenth and Twentieth Centuries*. Oxford: Oxford University Press.

Joko Smart, J.M. 1987. Recent trends in law reform in Sierra Leone. *Journal of African Law* 31(1/2): 136–50.

Jolles, Frank and Stephen Jolles. 2000. Zulu ritual immunisation in perspective. *Africa* 70(2): 229–48.

Jones, John R. W. D., and Steven Powles. 2003. *International Criminal Practice*. 3rd edn. Oxford: Oxford University Press.

Jones, Peter N. 2006. Toleration, value-pluralism, and the fact of pluralism. *Critical Review of International Social and Political Philosophy* 9(2): 189–210.

Junger, Sebastian. 2007. Blood oil. *Vanity Fair* February 2007, pp. 112–22.

Kahn, Paul W. 1999. *The Cultural Study of Law*. Chicago and London: University of Chicago Press.

Kaldor, Mary. 2006. *New and Old Wars: Organized Violence in a Global era*. 2nd edn. Cambridge: Polity.

Kandeh, Jimmy. 2003. Sierra Leone's post-conflict elections of 2002. *Journal of Modern African Studies* 41(2): 189–216.

Kaplan, Robert D. 1994. The coming anarchy: how scarcity, crime, overpopulation and disease are rapidly destroying the social fabric of our planet Atlantic Monthly 1994 [cited February 1994], 44, available at www.theatlantic.com/politics/foreign/anarchy.htm.

Keen, David. 2005. *Conflict and Collusion in Sierra Leone*. Oxford: James Currey.

Keesing, Roger M. 1985. Killers, big men, and priests on Malaita: reflections on a Melanesian troika system. *Ethnology* 24(4): 237–52.

Kelsall, Michelle Staggs. 2008. Report on the tenth session of the RUF trial, Special Court for Sierra Leone. Berkeley: UC Berkeley War Crimes Studies Center.

Kelsall, Michelle Staggs and Shanee Stepakoff. 2007. 'When we wanted to talk about rape': silencing sexual violence at the Special Court for Sierra Leone. *International Journal of Transitional Justice* 1(3): 355–74.

Kelsall, Tim. 2005. Truth, lies, ritual: preliminary reflections on the Truth and Reconciliation Commission in Sierra Leone. *Human Rights Quarterly* 26(2): 361–91.

2006a. Law and Legal Institutions in an Upcountry Sierra Leonean Town. Freetown: National Forum for Human Rights with Timap for Justice.

2006b. Politics, anti-politics, international justice: language and power in the Special Court for Sierra Leone. *Review of International Studies* 32: 587–602.

Kenny, Maurice. 1989. Roman Nose, Cheyenne: A brief biography. *Wicazo Sa Review* 5(1): 9–30.

Kerr, Rachel and Jessica Lincoln. 2008. The Special Court for Sierra Leone: Outreach, Legacy and Impact. London: War Crimes Research Group King's College London.

Kidd, Stephen W. 1995. Land, politics and benevolent shamanism: the Enxet Indians in a democratic Paraguay. *Journal of Latin American Studies* 27(1): 43–75.

Kilson, Martin. 1966. *Political Change in a West African State: A Study of the Modernization Process in Sierra Leone*. New York: Atheneum (originally published by Harvard University Press).

Knoops, Geert-Jan Alexander. 2007. The transposition of superior responsibility onto guerilla warfare under the laws of the international criminal tribunals. *International Criminal Law Review* 7: 505–29.

Kpundeh, Sahr. 2004. Corruption and political insurgency in Sierra Leone. In *Between Democracy and Terror: The Sierra Leone Civil War*, edited by I. Abdullah. Dakar: Council for the Development of Social Science Research in Africa (CODESRIA).

Kup, A. P. 1962. *A History of Sierra Leone 1400–1787*. Cambridge: Cambridge University Press.

Lan, David. 1992. *Guns and Rain: Guerrillas and Spirit Mediums in Zimbabwe*. London: James Currey.

Langston, Emily. 2004. The superior responsibility doctrine in international law: historical continuities, innovation and criminality: can East Timor's Special Panels bring militia leaders to justice? *International Criminal Law Review* 4: 141–83.

Laughland, John. 2007. *Travesty: The Trial of Slobodan Milosevic and the Corruption of International Justice*. London: Pluto Press.

Leach, Melissa. 2000. New shapes to shift: war, parks and the hunting person in modern West Africa. *Journal of the Royal Anthropological Institute* 6(4): 577–95.

Lemarchand, Rene. 1972. Political clientelism and ethnicity in Tropical Africa: competing solidarities in nation-building. *American Political Science Review* 64(1): 68–90.

Leonard, David K. and Scott Straus. 2002. *Africa's Stalled Development: International Causes and Cures*. Boulder CO: Lynne Rienner.

Little, Kenneth. 1965. The political function of the Poro, Part 1. *Africa* 35(4): 349–65.

Littlejohn, J. 1963. Temne space. *Anthropological Quarterly* 36(1): 1–17.

Locke, Terry. 2004. *Critical Discourse Analysis, Continuum Research Methods*. London: Continuum.

Lutz, Ellen. 2006. Transitional justice: lessons learned and the road ahead. In *Transitional Justice in the Twenty-First Century: Beyond truth versus justice*, edited by N. Roht-Arriaza and J. Mariezcurrena. Cambridge and New York: Cambridge University Press.

Maguire, Peter. 2000. *Law and War: An American Story*. New York: Columbia University Press.

2005. *Facing Death in Cambodia*. New York: Columbia University Press.

Manifesto 99. 2002. Traditional Methods of Conflict Management/Resolution of Possible Complementary Value to the Proposed Sierra Leone Truth and Reconciliation Commission. Freetown: Manifesto 99.

Maru, Vivek. 2006. Between law and society: paralegals and the provision of justice services in Sierra Leone and worldwide. *Yale Journal of International Law* 31: 427–76.

Mauss, Marcel. 1902 (2006). *A General Theory of Magic*. London: Routledge.

McEvoy, Kieran. 2007. Beyond legalism: towards a thicker understanding of transitional justice. *Journal of Law and Society* 34(4): 411–40.

McGowan, Winston. 1990. The establishment of long-distance trade between Sierra Leone and its hinterland, 1787–1821. *Journal of African History* 31(1): 25–41.

McNaughton, Patrick R. 1982. The shirts that Mande hunters wear. *African Arts* 15(3): 54–91.

Médard, J-F. 1982. The underdeveloped state in Tropical Africa: political clientelism or neo-patrimonialism. In *Private Patronage, and Public Power: Political Clientelism in the Modern State*, edited by C. Clapham. London: Pinter.

Meillassoux, Claude. 1972. From reproduction to production: a Marxist approach to economic anthropology. *Economy and Society* 1(1): 93–105.

Merry, Sally Engle. 1988. Legal pluralism. *Law and Society Review* 22(5): 869–96.

1992. Anthropology, law, and transnational processes. *Annual Review of Anthropology* 21: 357–79.

Migdal, Joel S. 1988. *Strong Societies and Weak States: State-society Relations and State Capabilities in the Third World*. Princeton NJ: Princeton University Press.

Minear, Richard H. 1972. *Victors' Justice: The Tokyo War Crimes Trial*. Princeton, NJ: Princeton University Press.

Minow, Martha. 1998. *Between Vengeance and Forgiveness: Facing History after Genocide and Mass Violence*. Boston: Beacon Press Books.

Mitchell, Don. 1995. There's no such thing as culture: towards a reconceptualisation of the idea of culture in geography. *Transactions of the Institute of British Geographers* 20(1): 102–16.

Moghalu, Kingsley Chiedu. 2005. *Rwanda's Genocide: The Politics of Global Justice*. Basingstoke: Palgrave Macmillan.

Moore, Henrietta L., and Todd Sanders, eds. 2001. *Magical Interpretations, Material Realities: Modernity, Witchcraft and the Occult in Postcolonial Africa*. London: Routledge.

Moore, Michael S. 1985. The moral and metaphysical sources of the criminal law. In *Criminal Justice: NOMOS XXVII*, edited by J. W. Chapman and J. R. Pennock. New York and London: New York University Press.

Moore, Sally Falk. 1969. Law and anthropology. *Biennial Review of Anthropology* 6: 252–300.

1992. Treating law as knowledge: telling colonial officers what to say to Africans about running 'their own' native courts. *Law and Society Review* 26(1): 11–46.

Muana, Patrick K. 1997. The Kamajoi militia: civil war, internal displacement and the politics of counter-insurgency. *Africa Development* 22(3/4): 77–100.

Murphy, William P. 1980. Secret knowledge as property and power in Kpelle society: elders versus youth. *Africa* 50(2): 193–207.
1981. The rhetorical management of dangerous knowledge in Kpelle brokerage. *American Ethnologist* 8(4): 667–85.
1998. The sublime dance of Mende politics: an African aesthetic of charismatic power. *American Ethnologist* 25(4): 563–82.
2003. Military patrimonialism and child soldier clientalism in the Liberian and Sierra Leonean civil wars. *African Studies Review* 46(2): 61–87.
2007. The powerful presence of the past: historical dimensions of integration and conflict in the Upper Guinea Coast. Conference paper. Max Plancke Institute for Social Anthropology, Halle/Saale, Germany.
Murray, Colin and Peter Sanders. 2005. *Medicine Murder in Colonial Lesotho: The Anatomy of a Moral Crisis*. Edinburgh: Edinburgh University Press.
Nicolson, Donald. 1994. Truth, reason and justice: epistemology and politics in evidence discourse. *Modern Law Review* 57(5): 726–44.
Nugent, Paul. 1995. *Big Men, Small Boys, and Politics in Ghana: Power, Ideology, and the Burden of History, 1982–1994*. London and New York: Pinter.
Nunley, John. 1988. Purity and pollution in Freetown: masked performance. *TDR* 32(2): 102–22.
Oomen, Barbara. 2005. Donor-driven justice and its discontents: the case of Rwanda. *Development and Change* 36(5): 887–910.
Opala, Joseph A. 1994. 'Ecstatic renovation!': street art celebrating Sierra Leone's 1992 revolution. *African Affairs* 93(371): 195–218.
Osiel, Mark. 1997. *Mass Atrocity, Collective Memory, and the Law*. New Brunswick NJ: Transaction Publishers.
Otim, Michael and Marieke Wierde. 2008. Justice at Juba: international obligations and local demands in Northern Uganda. In *Courting Conflict? Justice, Peace and the ICC in Africa*, edited by N. Waddell and P. Clark. London: The Royal African Society.
Paul, Robert A. 1990. What does anybody want? Desire, purpose, and the acting subject in the study of culture. *Cultural Anthropology* 5(4): 431–51.
Peters, Krijn. 2006. *Footpaths to Reintegration: Armed Conflict, Youth and the Rural Crisis in Sierra Leone*. PhD Thesis, University of Wageningen, Wageningen.
Peters, Krijn, and Paul Richards. 1998. 'Why we fight': voices of youth combatants in Sierra Leone. *Africa* 68(2): 183–210.
Phillips, Nelson and Cynthia Hardy. 2002. *Discourse Analysis: Investigating Processes of Social Construction, Qualitative Research Methods Series 50*. London: Sage Publications Ltd.
Piot, Charles. 1999. *Remotely Global: Village Modernity in West Africa*. Chicago and London: University of Chicago Press.
Pospisil, Leopold. 1981. Modern and traditional administration of justice in New Guinea. *Journal of Legal Pluralism* 19: 93–116.

Prunier, Gerard. 1995. *The Rwanda Crisis: History of a Genocide: 1959–1994*. London: Hurst and Co.

Rashid, Ismail. 2004. Student radicals, lumpen youth, and the origins of revolutionary groups in Sierra Leone, 1977–1996. In *Between Democracy and Terror: The Sierra Leone Civil War*, edited by I. Abdullah. Dakar: Council for the Development of Social Science Research in Africa (CODESRIA).

Reno, William. 1995. *Corruption and State Politics in Sierra Leone*. Cambridge: Cambridge University Press.

1997. War, markets, and the reconfiguration of West Africa's weak states. *Comparative Politics* 29(4): 493–510.

2000. *Warlord Politics and African States*. Boulder: Lynne Rienner.

Richards, Paul. 1996. *Fighting for the Rainforest: War, Youth and Resources in Sierra Leone*. Oxford: IAI and James Currey.

2004. The Emotions at War: Atrocity as Piacular Rite in Sierra Leone. Wageningen: Social Sciences Department, University of Wageningen.

2005. To fight or to farm: agrarian dimensions of the Mano River conflicts (Liberia and Sierra Leone). *African Affairs* 104(417): 571–90.

Richards, Paul, James Vincent and Khadija Bah. 2004. Social capital and survival: prospects for community driven development in post-conflict Sierra Leone. In *World Bank Working Paper Series, No. 12*. World Bank, available at www.worldbank.org/conflict.

Robertson, Geoffrey. 2002. *Crimes Against Humanity: The Struggle for Global Justice*. London: Penguin.

2007. General editor's introduction to essays on fairness and evidence in war crimes trials. *International Commentary on Evidence* 4(1): 1–5.

Roht-Arriaza, Naomi. 2006. The new landscape of transitional justice. In *Transitional Justice in the Twenty-First Century: Beyond Truth Versus Justice*, edited by N. Roht-Arriaza and J. Mariezcurrena. Cambridge and New York: Cambridge University Press.

Rosen, David. 2007. Child soldiers, international humanitarian law, and the globalization of childhood. *American Anthropologist* 109(2): 296–306.

Rosen, Lawrence. 1985. Intentionality and the concept of the person. In *Criminal Justice. Nomos XXVII*, edited by J.R. Chapman and J. Rolaud Pennock. New York: New York University Press.

Rudolph, Christopher. 2001. Constructing an atrocities regime: the politics of war crimes tribunals. *International Organization* 55(3): 655–91.

Sandel, Michael J. 1992. The procedural republic and the unemcumbered self. In *The Self and the Political Order*, edited by T.B. Strong. Oxford: Basil Blackwell.

Sands, Philippe (ed.). 2003. *From Nuremburg to the Hague: The Future of International Justice*. Cambridge: Cambridge University Press.

Schabas, William. 2006. *The UN International Tribunals: The Former Yugoslavia, Rwanda and Sierra Leone*. Cambridge: Cambridge University Press.

Schatzberg, Michael. 2002. *Political Legitimacy in Middle Africa: Father, Family, Food*. Bloomington: Indiana University Press.

Scheppele, Kim Lane. 1989. Foreword: telling stories. *Michigan Law Review* 87(8): 2073–98.

Scott, James C. 1990. *Domination and the Arts of Resistance: Hidden Transcripts*. New Haven and London: Yale University Press.

SCSL. 2002. The Statute of the Special Court for Sierra Leone. Freetown: Special Court for Sierra Leone.

2003a. The Special Court for Sierra Leone. Promotional Booklet. Freetown: Special Court for Sierra Leone.

2003b. Prosecution Reply. Preliminary Motion Based on Lack of Jurisdiction: Child Recruitment. SCSL-2003-8-54. 7 July 2003. Freetown: Special Court for Sierra Leone.

2003c. Amicus Curiae Brief of University of Toronto International Human Rights Clinic and Interested International Human Rights Organizations. The Prosecutor v. Sam Hinga Norman. Fourth Defence Motion Based on Lack of Jurisdiction (Child Recruitment). Appeals Chambers. SCSL-2003-08-PT. 29 October 2003. Freetown: Special Court for Sierra Leone.

2003d. Motion Re Child Soldiers. Appeals Chamber. The Prosecutor v. Sam Hinga Norman, Sitting In Open Session. Case No. SCSL-2003-08, 6 November 2003. Freetown: Special Court for Sierra Leone.

2003e. The Prosecutor of the Special Court v. Charles Ghankay Taylor. Case No. SCSL-2003-01-7. Trial Chamber II. Freetown: Special Court for Sierra Leone.

2004b. Amicus Curiae Brief of the United Nations Children's Fund. Fourth Defence Preliminary Motion Based on Lack of Jurisdiction (Child Recruitment). SCSL-2003-08. 21 January 2004. Freetown: Special Court for Sierra Leone.

2004c. Indictment. The Prosecutor Against Samuel Hinga Norman, Moinina Fofana, Allieu Kondewa. SCSL-03-14-1. 4 February 2004. Freetown: Special Court for Sierra Leone.

2004d. Decision on Preliminary Motion Based on Lack of Jurisdiction (Child Recruitment). In the Appeals Chamber. Prosecutor Against Samuel Hinga Norman. Case No. SCSL-2004-14-AR72(E), 31 May 2004. Freetown: Special Court for Sierra Leone.

2004e. Transcript. The Prosecutor of the Special Court v. Sam Hinga Norman, Moinina Fofana, Allieu Kondewa, SCSL-04-14-T. Freetown: Special Court for Sierra Leone.

2004f. Dissenting Opinion of Justice Robertson. In the Appeals Chamber: Decision on Preliminary Motion Based on Lack of Jurisdiction (Child Recruitment). Prosecutor Against Samuel Hinga Norman. Case No. SCSL-2004-14-AR72(E). 31 May 2004. Freetown: Special Court for Sierra Leone.

2004g. Transcript. The Prosecutor of the Special Court v. Issa Sessay, Morris Kallon, Augustine Gbao. Case No. SCSL-2004-15-T. Freetown: Special Court for Sierra Leone.

2004h. Transcript. The Prosecutor of the Special Court v. Alex Tamba Brima, Brima Bazzy Kamara, Santigie Borbor Kanu. Trial Chamber 2. Case No. SCSL-2004-16-T. Freetown: Special Court for Sierra Leone.

2005a. Further Amended Consolidated Indictment. The Prosecutor Against Alex Tamba Brima, Brima Bazzy Kamara, and Santigie Borbor Kanu. Case N. SCSL-2004-16-PT. 18 February 2005. Freetown: Special Court for Sierra Leone.

2005b. Motion for Judgment of Acquittal of the Third Accused Allieu Kondewa. The Prosecutor Against Samuel Hinga Norman, Moinina Fofana, and Allieu Kondewa. Case No. SCSL-2004-14-T. 4 August 2005. Freetown: Special Court for Sierra Leone.

2005c. Decision on Motions for Judgment of Acquittal Pursuant to Rule 98. Prosecutor Against Sam Hinga Norman, Moinina Fofana, Allieu Kondewa. Case No. SCSL-04-14. 21 October 2005. Freetown: Special Court for Sierra Leone.

2006a. Decision on Motions by Moinina Fofana and Sam Hinga Norman for the Issuance of a Subpoena Ad Testificandum to H.E. Alhaji Dr Ahmad Tejan Kabbah, President of the Republic of Sierra Leone. SCSL-04-14-T. 13 June 2006. Freetown: Special Court for Sierra Leone.

2006b. Corrected Amended Consolidated Indictment. The Prosecutor Against Issa Hasan Sesay, Morris Kallon And Augustine Gbao. Case No. SCSL-2204-15-PT. 2 August 2006. Freetown: Special Court for Sierra Leone.

2006c. Public Version, Kanu – Defence Trial Brief. The Prosecutor Against Alex Tamba Brima, Brima Bazzy Kamara, and Santigie Borbor Kanu. Case No. SCSL-2004-16-T. 8 December 2006. Freetown: Special Court for Sierra Leone.

2006d. Public Prosecution Final Trial Brief. SCSL-14-747. 27 November 2006. Freetown: Special Court for Sierra Leone.

2006e. Normal Final Trial Brief. SCSL-14-745. 27 November 2006. Freetown: Special Court for Sierra Leone.

2006g. Final Trial Brief of Third Accused Allieu Kondewa, re-filed. SCSL-14-756. 15 December 2006. Freetown: Special Court for Sierra Leone.

2006h. Fofana Final Trial Brief. SCSL-14-743. 24 November 2006. Freetown: Special Court for Sierra Leone.

2007a. Judgment. The Prosecutor Against Alex Tamba Brima, Brima Bazzy Kamara, Santigie Borbor Kanu. Trial Chamber II. SCSL-04-16-T. 20 June 2007. Freetown: Special Court for Sierra Leone.

2007b. Second Amended Indictment. The Prosecutor Against Charles Ghankay Taylor. Case No. SCSL-2003-01-PT. 29 May 2007. Freetown: Special Court for Sierra Leone.

2007c. Sentencing Judgment. The Prosecutor Against Alex Tamba Brima, Brima Bazzy Kamara, Santigie Borbor Kanu. Case No. SCSL-04-16-T. 19 July 2007. Freetown: Special Court for Sierra Leone.

2007d. Judgment. Prosecutor Against Moinina Fofana, Allieu Kondewa. SCSL-14-T. 2 August 2007. Freetown: Special Court for Sierra Leone.

2007e. Judgment on the Sentencing of Moinina Fofana and Allieu Kondewa. Trial Chamber 1. SCSL-04-14-T. 9 October 2007. Freetown: Special Court for Sierra Leone.

2008a. Judgment. In the Appeals Chamber. Prosecutor Against Alex Tamba Brima, Brima Bazzy Kamara, Santigie Borbor Kanu. Case No. SCSL-2004-16-A. 22 February 2008. Freetown: Special Court for Sierra Leone.

2008b. Judgment. In the Appeals Chamber. Prosecutor Against Moinina Fofana, Allieu Kondewa. Case No. SCSL-04-14-A. 28 May 2008. Freetown: Special Court for Sierra Leone.

n.d. The Special Court for Sierra Leone: Basic Facts. Freetown: Special Court for Sierra Leone.

Seidman, Robert B. 1965. Witch murder and mens rea: a problem of society under radical social change. *Modern Law Review* 28(1): 46–61.

1966. Mens rea and the reasonable African: the pre-scientific world-view and mistake of fact. *International and Comparative Law Quarterly* 15(4): 1135–64.

Shapiro, Martin. 1985. The deconstruction and reconstruction of intent. In *Criminal Justice: NOMOS XXVII*, edited by J. R. Pennock and J. W. Chapman. New York: New York University Press.

Shaw, Rosalind. 2000. 'Tok Af, Lef Af': a political economy of Temne techniques of secrecy and self. In *African Philosophy as Cultural Inquiry*, edited by I. Karp and D. A. Masolo. Bloomington: IA.

2001. Cannibal transformations: colonialism and commodification in the Sierra Leone hinterland. In *Magical Interpretations, Material Realities: Modernity, Witchcraft and the Occult in Postcolonial Africa*, edited by H. L. Moore and T. Sanders. London: Routledge.

2002. *Memories of the Slave Trade*. Chicago: University of Chicago Press.

2005. Rethinking Truth and Reconciliation Commissions: Lessons from Sierra Leone. *USIP Special Report 130*. Washington DC: United States Institute of Peace.

2006. History and the post-war work of memory: reintegration and the TRC in northern Sierra Leone. Paper presented to the Workshop Beyond the Toolkit: Rethinking the Paradigm of Transitional Justice. Bellagio: Rockefeller Foundation Bellagio Conference and Study Center.

Shklar, Judith N. 1964 and 1986. *Legalism: Law, Morals, and Political Trials*. Cambridge and London: Harvard University Press.

Simmel, Georg. 1906. The sociology of secrecy and of secret societies. *American Journal of Sociology* 11(4): 441–98.

Simpson, Gerry. 2007. *Law, War and Crime*. Cambridge: Polity Press.
Smith, Alison. 2004. Child recruitment and the Special Court for Sierra Leone. *Journal of International Criminal Justice* 2(4): 1141–53.
Snyder, Jack and Leslie Vinjamuri. 2003/4. Trials and errors: principle and pragmatism in strategies of international justice. *International Security* 28(3): 5–44.
Sriram, Chandra Lekha. 2006. Wrong-sizing international justice? The hybrid tribunal in Sierra Leone. *Fordham International Law Journal* 29(3): 472–506.
Sriram, Chandra Lekha and Amy Ross. 2007. Geographies of crime and justice: contemporary transitional justice and the creation of 'zones of impunity'. *International Journal of Transitional Justice* 1(1): 45–65.
Stovel, Laura. 2005. *Long Road Home: Building Reconciliation and Trust in Postwar Sierra Leone*. PhD thesis, Department of Sociology and Anthropology, Simon Fraser University.
Stover, Eric. 2004. Witnesses and the promise of justice at the Hague. In *My Neighbour, My Enemy: Justice and Community in the Aftermath of Mass Atrocity*, edited by E. Stover and H. M. Weinstein. Cambridge: Cambridge University Press.
Stover, Eric, and Harvey M. Weinstein. 2004a. Conclusion: a common objective, a universe of alternatives. In *My Neighbour, My Enemy: Justice and Community in the Aftermath of Mass Atrocity*, edited by E. Stover and H. M. Weinstein. Cambridge: Cambridge University Press.
2004b. Introduction: conflict, justice and reclamation. In *My Neighbour, My Enemy: Justice and Community in the Aftermath of Mass Atrocity*, edited by E. Stover and H. M. Weinstein. Cambridge: Cambridge University Press.
Stromseth, Jane, David Wippman, and Rosa Brooks. 2006. *Can Might Make Rights? Building the Rule of Law after Military Interventions*. Cambridge: Cambridge University Press.
Teitel, Ruti G. 2000. *Transitional Justice*. New York: Oxford University Press.
2003. Transitional justice genealogy. *Harvard Human Rights Journal* 16: 69–94.
Theroux, Louis. 2007. *The Call of the Weird: Travels in American Subcultures*. New York: De Capo Press.
TRC. 2004. *Witness to Truth: Report of the Sierra Leone Truth and Reconciliation Commission*. Accra: GPL Press and Truth and Reconciliation Commission – Sierra Leone.
Tylor, E. B. 1958 [1871]. *Primitive Culture: Researches into the Development of Mythology, Philosophy, Religion, Art, and Custom*. New York: Gordon Press.
Umphrey, Martha Merrill. 1999. The dialogics of legal meaning: spectacular trials, the unwritten law, and narratives of criminal responsibility. *Law and Society Review* 33(2): 393–423.

UNSC. 2004. *The Rule of Law and Transitional Justice in Conflict and Post-Conflict Societies – Report of the Secretary-General*. New York: United Nations Security Council, United Nations.

Utas, Mats. 2005. *Sweet Battlefields: Youth and the Liberian Civil War*. PhD thesis, Department of Cultural Anthropology and Ethnology, Uppsala University, Uppsala.

Van Tuyl, Penelope. 2008. Effective, Efficient, and Fair? An inquiry into the Investigative Practices of the Office of the Prosecutor at the Special Court for Sierra Leone. Berkeley: UC Berkeley War Crimes Studies Center.

Wallis, Braithwaite. 1905. The 'Poro' of the Mendi. *Journal of the Royal African Society* 4(14): 183–9.

Weber, Max. 1947. *The Theory of Social and Economic Organization, translated by A. R. Henderson and T. Parsons*. London: William Hodge and Co.

1968. *Economy and Society: An Outline of Interpretive Sociology. Edited by Guenther Roth and Claus Wittich*. New York: Bedminster Press.

Weinstein, Harvey M., Laurel E. Fletcher, Patrick Vinck and Phuong Pham. 2006. Stay the hand of justice: whose priorities take priority? A paper prepared for the conference, 'Beyond the Toolkit: rethinking the paradigm of transitional justice', Bellagio, Italy, November 2006.

Weinstein, Harvey, and Hugo van de Merwe. 2007. Editorial note. *International Journal of Transitional Justice* 1(1): 1–5.

Wild, Emma. 1998. 'Is it witchcraft? Is it Satan? It is a miracle.' Mai-Mai soldiers and Christian concepts of evil in North-East Congo. *Journal of Religion in Africa* 28(4): 450–67.

Wilson, Richard A. 2000. Reconciliation and revenge in post-Apartheid South Africa. *Current Anthropology* 41(1): 75–98.

2001. Children and war in Sierra Leone: a West African diary. *Anthropology Today* 17(5): 20–2.

2001. *The Politics of Truth and Reconciliation in South Africa: Legitimizing the Post-Apartheid State*. Cambridge: Cambridge University Press.

Woolard, Kathryn A. and Bambi Schieffelin. 1994. Language ideology. *Annual Review of Anthropology* 23: 55–82.

Zack-Williams, Tunde. 1999. Sierra Leone: the political economy of civil war, 1991–98. *Third World Quarterly* 20(1): 143–62.

INDEX